RECKONING

Also by Elliott Currie

DOPE AND TROUBLE

CONFRONTING CRIME: AN AMERICAN CHALLENGE

RECKONING

Drugs, the Cities, and the American Future

ELLIOTT CURRIE

HILL and WANG

A division of Farrar, Straus and Giroux

NEW YORK

Copyright © 1993 by Elliott Currie

ALL RIGHTS RESERVED

Printed in the United States of America

Published in Canada by HarperCollinsCanadaLtd

Designed by Tere LoPrete

Second printing, 1995

Preface to the paperback edition © 1994 by Elliott Currie

FIRST HILL AND WANG PAPERBACK EDITION, 1994

Library of Congress Cataloging-in-Publication Data

Currie, Elliott.

Reckoning : drugs, the cities, and the American future / Elliott
Currie. — 1st ed.

p.   cm.

Includes index.

1. Drug abuse—United States—Prevention.   2. Narcotics and crime—
United States.   3. Inner cities—United States.   4. Drug traffic—
Economic aspects—United States.   5. United States—Social
conditions—1980–   I. Title.

HV5825.C88   1992   362.29'0973—dc20   91-40276   CIP

Acknowledgments

Deep thanks, first of all, to those who toiled with skill and patience on this book at Hill and Wang, especially Sara Bershtel, Sally Singer, and David Frederickson. Their seriousness, commitment, and attention have been refreshing and gratefully received: they embody what publishing ought to be about but too rarely is. Thanks once again to John Brockman and Katinka Matson for helping to bring the book to life, and to Susannah Currie and Rachael Peltz for their patience—as the book steadily took over more of my time, and more of the house— and much else.

This book was written in response to what I took to be a crisis of social policy that confronts us here and now: but its roots go back much further. I've been very fortunate in having had an unusually stimulating group of teachers who, for more years than I care to think about, have shaped the way I look at these issues today, probably more than they realize; and I want especially to thank three of the best: David Matza, Sheldon Messinger, and Jerome Skolnick.

I've benefited greatly from the opportunity to try out some of the ideas in this book in a variety of earlier settings. Some overall thoughts on approaches to the drug problem first saw the light at a 1989 conference on the Future of Liberalism at the Roosevelt Institute in Hyde Park, New York: thanks especially to Arthur Schlesinger, Jr., for offering a forum and encouragement. A number of those ideas reappeared in modified form at a conference on Realist Criminology in Vancouver, British Columbia, the following year, the good work of John Lowman and Brian MacLean. Several of the arguments on drug policy also surfaced at a conference sponsored by the American Civil Liberties Union in San Francisco in 1989 (thanks to Gene Guerrero), and some of the views on treatment at a conference on drug policy later that year organized by the National Council on Crime and Delinquency (thanks to Barry Krisberg and James Austin). Some of the arguments on treatment also appeared, in abbreviated form, in remarks to a conference on International Developments in Crime and Social Policy at Edinburgh, Scotland, in 1991, and I'm particularly grateful to Vivien Stern of the National Association for the Care and Resettlement of Offenders (NACRO) for that opportunity. Part of the argument about legalization of drugs in Chapter 4 first saw the light, in different form, in *The American Prospect* magazine, under the title "The Limits of Legalization": thanks to Alice Chasan, Robert Kuttner, and Paul Starr for skillful and sensitive editing and for the opportunity to sound off. I hasten to add that not all of these good people will agree with everything I have to say here; but I deeply appreciate their help and the opportunity to fine-tune these ideas.

Much of the writing was done while I was a Visiting Scholar at the Institute for the Study of Social Change at the University of California, Berkeley: many thanks to all at the Institute, especially Troy Duster and Janice Tanigawa, for their support.

Special thanks as well to Jeffrey Fagan and Robert Gangi for providing helpful information on short notice, and to Lynn Curtis for several years of stimulating exchanges on these and related matters. The list of all those whose own work has inspired me and whose conversation and support have been crucial is much too long to fit here: but for now, let me single out a few without whom the last couple of years would have been far less lively: Robert Dunn, David Fogarty, Terry Kandal, Beth Paulson, Ian Taylor and David Wellman. Heartfelt thanks to all.

Preface to the Paperback Edition

Much has changed in the year since *Reckoning* first went to the printer. Not the drug problem itself, which remained unaffected by the sputtering drug war and indeed, if anything, got a little worse. Crack continued to savage the cities, medical emergencies from both heroin and cocaine abuse shot upward, and, for the first time in years, drug use among eighth-graders was increasing.

What *did* change was the public response to the drug problem. When I began writing this book, the drug war was in full swing, and opposition was mainly confined to a sprinkling of academics and reformers. By 1993, what had been a murmur of opposition had become a clamor. Judges, mayors, chiefs of police were openly declaring that the "war" wasn't working. The former police chief of San Jose, California, circulated a petition calling for an end to the drug war, signed by a distinguished roster of police executives and elected officials. Two federal judges in New York, disgusted over the rigid mandatory sentences they were forced to hand down for minor drug offenders, publicly refused to hear any more drug cases. One of them, Judge Jack B. Weinstein of the Eastern District of New York, called the war on drugs a "depressing failure" and predicted that "in the future we will look back on this horrendous period of overcharging and overpunishing as a temporary American aberration."

The Clinton administration, meanwhile, appointed an attorney general openly skeptical about the ability of the correctional system to solve the problems of crime and drug abuse, who had helped create an innovative "drug court" in Miami to divert minor drug offenders from prison. It appointed as its drug "czar" a respected pioneer in community policing. And it produced an official policy paper which—while short on specifics—did call for shifting anti-drug resources toward prevention and treatment. All this took us far beyond the posturing of the previous administration and signaled the beginnings of a new seriousness about drugs within the federal government.

Even more encouraging were the stirrings of a deeper change in American political culture. When *Reckoning* first went to press, we had been for more than a decade in the grip of a political philosophy that downplayed government's responsibility to do anything constructive about the social devastation at the root of the drug crisis. By the time the book appeared, the White House was occupied by a new president who had called in his campaign for a politics of "inclusion"—and, more specifically, for many of the things I said we needed in a real war on drugs: parental leave; a national apprenticeship program; accessible health care for all with an emphasis on prevention; the expansion of Head Start; investment in infrastructure to create jobs in the cities.

That these proposals are now part of the practical political agenda reflects a clear desire on the part of a majority of Americans to move beyond the cynicism and complacency that disfigured our social policy during the 1980s. Whether that desire will prevail, of course, is a tougher question. Like other critical social ills—violence, joblessness, the poverty of children—the drug crisis tests our collective seriousness, our capacity as a people to reckon honestly and openly with our shortcomings, to get on with the job of building a society that works. And on this score, so far, the signals have been mixed. We've seen a remarkably potent resistance in Congress, for example, to even the most modest proposals for public investment and job creation. But overcoming that kind of resistance is critical if we want, finally, to get serious about fighting drugs. If there is a solution to the drug problem that does *not* engage the issues of jobs, housing, and the support of families, that does *not* grapple with the shrinking future for America's youth and the continuing desperation of our cities, we have yet to hear it.

Contents

RECKONING

Introduction

The failure of American drug policy is depressingly apparent. Twenty years of the "war" on drugs have jammed our jails and prisons, immobilized the criminal justice system in many cities, swollen the ranks of the criminalized and unemployable minority poor, and diverted desperately needed resources from other social needs. Yet the drug crisis is still very much with us. This book is about why that crisis has proven so stubborn —and what we should do instead.

There are two drug problems in America. One is the drug problem of the affluent. It is by no means insignificant, and it has caused more than its share of personal tragedies. But it is a *manageable* problem, and it has been steadily decreasing for several years, for reasons unrelated to the war on drugs. The other one is the drug problem of America's have-nots. That problem has grown malignantly in the face of the drug war— and it is much farther from solution than it was when that war began. The crack cocaine epidemic of the 1980s was only the most recent manifestation of that second drug crisis; and though there were some indications that it had "peaked" by the 1990s, it has left us with staggering levels of crack abuse that continue to overwhelm the courts, hospitals, and child welfare systems. Meanwhile, the traditional scourge of the inner-city poor—heroin—has quietly spread. And alongside the rising problems of cocaine and heroin are other dismaying changes: the proliferation of drugs that were barely on the horizon a generation ago, including PCP, methamphetamine, and inhalants; the rising problem of multiple drug abuse; and the devastating link of drug use with AIDS.*

* Sorting out the variety of illegal drugs now routinely available in the United States can be confusing: I've included a brief discussion of their properties and effects in the Appendix.

In the field of public health there is a basic distinction between "epidemic" and "endemic" phases of a disease. Epidemics move swiftly and devastatingly through vulnerable populations and then subside, while an illness which has become deeply entrenched in a population and stubbornly resists eradication is said to be endemic. After two decades of the drug war, endemic hard-drug abuse among the poor and near-poor of the United States is higher than ever before. No coherent policies are now on our political agenda to remedy that tragic situation—or to build a strategy against drug abuse that could forestall the *next* epidemic.

In this book I want to suggest the elements of such a strategy. I don't simply wish to recount the failure of our current drug policies—that is important, but by itself not enough. The tougher job is to understand *why* we have failed so far, and what that tells us about the elements of a more success- ful approach. Before we can come up with a credible strat- egy against the drug crisis that continues to savage our cities, we need to answer the nagging, fundamental question about drug abuse in America: why—in the face of increasing risks of imprisonment, social marginality, impoverishment, life- threatening disease, and early death—do millions of Americans persist in abusing illegal and dangerous drugs?

Answering that question means exploring the ways in which drug abuse on the American scale reflects deeper structural problems in our economy and society. What is too often ignored in what now passes for our current "debate" about drug policy is that drug abuse is far worse in the United States than in any other country in the developed world. Just as we stand out from other industrial societies on levels of poverty, infant mortality, and violent crime, so it is with drugs. No country has been spared altogether, but what is a manageable problem in most advanced societies appears in the United States in grotesquely exaggerated form.

And within the United States, serious drug abuse is not evenly distributed; it runs "along the fault lines of our society."

It is concentrated among some groups and not others, and has been for at least half a century. Recognizing those realities is the first step in coming to grips with the drug crisis in America. It is sometimes said that drug use should be viewed as a medical problem, rather than a law-enforcement problem. In reality it is a little of both: but more than either, it is a *social* problem. And addressing it with appropriate seriousness means unflinchingly confronting its social roots.

This book is not, therefore, primarily about what's usually called "drug policy." Indeed, I will argue that a narrow focus on drugs themselves and on trying to control them through the criminal justice and medical "treatment" systems has been a main reason for our present impasse. Much does need changing in the way we approach both law enforcement and treatment, and I will have something to say about both. But no amount of tinkering with the courts or the treatment system will do the job that needs to be done.

The fundamental reason for the impasse is that up to now, most of our energy and resources have gone toward fighting the *symptoms* of the drug crisis, not its causes. Indeed, the Bush administration explicitly rejected an attack on the causes of drug abuse—warning that we should not succumb to what it curiously called the "easy temptation" to focus our energies on the "chronic problems of social environment" that "help to breed and spread the contagion of drug use." But by now it is painfully clear that the resulting search for quick-fix solutions has been ineffective, expensive, and self-defeating. Indeed, by the early 1990s the drug war itself had apparently peaked—a casualty of inflated expectations and shattered budgets. We were arresting fewer people on drug charges because there was no longer room for them in our swollen prisons, and no money to build new ones. But nothing resembling a compelling alternative strategy had replaced the floundering war on drugs. The result has been a sense of confusion and resignation. The response of the Bush administration (and much of Congress), as with many other urgent social problems, has been to call for more of the same. "The tools we need," George Bush told the nation after nearly two decades of the manifest failure of conventional antidrug strategies, "are the ones we have now." That view is no doubt comforting; it is also a prescription for futility. As I will demonstrate, there are clear and fundamental reasons why we will not police, treat, or imprison our way out of the drug crisis.

Nor, however, will we resolve the crisis by adopting a policy of laissez-faire. Given the appalling costs of the drug war in wasted resources, an overburdened justice system, and the erosion of democratic values, the appeal of deregulating drugs altogether and turning their production and distribution over to the "free market" is not hard to understand. But it is equally important to understand that the drug crisis would not disappear if we legalized hard drugs tomorrow. It is imperative that we adopt a much less punitive approach to drug users, and I will suggest some ways in which that can be accomplished. But understanding the urgent need to de-escalate the war on drugs is not the same as believing that ending drug "prohibition" would end the drug problem. The same deep social roots that make endemic drug abuse resistant to a strategy of punishment also guarantee that it will remain with us under whatever regulatory approach we devise—unless we address those roots head-on. Many advocates of drug legalization believe that the social costs of drug abuse have been greatly exaggerated, and that the real danger comes from the attempt to prohibit "free choice," not from the drugs themselves. But though the dangers of the drug war are very real, so are the costs of drug abuse —in violence, disease, family disintegration, and community demoralization; in blasted futures and wasted lives. And they are cruelly concentrated among the most vulnerable and disadvantaged people in America. Deregulating drug sales cannot much reduce those costs, and might increase them. The failure to offer more positive remedies has helped to marginalize many critics of the drug war and to minimize their influence on the course of social policy. Most Americans are appalled by what hard drugs have done to the fabric of social life, and they are right. Benign neglect will not suffice, either as policy or as politics. We do need a war on drugs. But the war we have been so haplessly fighting is the wrong war, fought with the wrong weapons, against the wrong enemies.

In this book I want to outline what it would take to launch a different kind of war, targeted at the real enemies: the deeper roots of endemic drug abuse. That war will necessarily be a much tougher proposition than the quick-fix forays of the past twenty years, because it forces us to tackle deep-seated social and economic deficits we have let fester much too long. The horrifying epidemic of crack abuse in the past decade did not spring up from nowhere, nor was it entirely unexpected. It is part of the reckoning we're paying for our failure to address those deficits with energy and vision when we first saw them. The task we're confronted with today is incalculably harder than it would have been had we moved swiftly to attack the roots of drug abuse when they first became apparent, forty years ago. That does not mean it is impossible; indeed, I'll argue in this book that though the remedies for the drug crisis are immensely difficult and challenging, they are not beyond our reach. It *does* mean that it's past time that we got on with the real job.

CHAPTER

I

The American Nightmare

To anyone observing the state of America's cities in the 1990s, it seems devastatingly obvious that we have failed to make much headway against the drug crisis. Americans living in the worst-hit neighborhoods still face the reality of dealers on their doorstep and shots in the night; many fear for their lives, or their children's lives, and sense that their communities have slid downward into a permanent state of terror and disintegration. Even those fortunate enough to live in better neighborhoods cannot pick up a newspaper or watch the news without confronting story after story about the toll of drugs and drug-related violence on communities and families. For most of us, the drug plague seems to have settled in, become a routine feature of an increasingly frightening and bewildering urban landscape.

Yet we also hear official reassurances that, despite appearances, we have made great progress in the war on drugs, or even that victory is just around the corner. The assertion that we are winning the war on drugs is designed to vindicate our present policies: to justify pouring ever-greater resources into what we have already tried, and, in a larger sense, to rationalize our current national priorities. But our visceral reactions are correct, and the cheerleading is premature. The American drug problem remains out of control. It vastly outstrips that of any other industrial nation. And it does so despite an orgy of punishment in the name of drug control that also has no counterpart in the rest of the developed world, or in our own history.

The news is not all bad. Middle-class drug use has declined, and the worst fury of the crack epidemic has abated in many cities. But the first happened in spite of the drug war, not because of it. And the second, while a welcome gain in the short term, pales beside the profoundly troubling long-term trend. Twenty years after the drug war began in earnest, we are far worse off than when we started. And the outlook for the future is not encouraging.

I

To appreciate the magnitude of the drug crisis in the United States, we need to compare it to the experience of other advanced industrial countries. Most Americans do not realize how atypical we are—in part because that most basic reality is curiously left out, or downplayed, in our national debate on drug policy. There is much discussion of the meaning of short-range fluctuations in drug use in the United States, but little about why we lead the world in drug abuse. Those who wish to minimize the implications of our unhappy leadership often point out that the drug problem has risen *everywhere*, not just in the United States; and there is an element of truth in that. Few countries have been spared some problem with illegal drugs during the last two decades; in some it is serious and increasing. But that should not blind us to the dramatic differences between the United States and otherwise comparable societies.

A revealing study by the Canadian scholars Reginald Smart

and Glenn Murray has shown that if the world's countries are divided into those with high, medium, and low drug problems, the United States is the *only* developed country that falls into the "high" category. The others—thirteen in all—are all developing countries: Afghanistan, Bolivia, Burma, Egypt, Iran, Lebanon, Malaysia, Pakistan, Peru, the Philippines, Singapore, Thailand, and Vietnam. It is sometimes argued that the reason for the peculiar severity of the American drug problem is that we are unusually affluent and excessively tolerant—or as one observer puts it, "richer and more liberal" than other countries with less severe drug problems. But the truth is precisely the opposite; *every* other country with a drug problem on the American scale or greater is a relatively poor country (though not always among the very poorest), and most are also authoritarian and intolerant, often dictatorial. Most are also "source" countries, which grow or manufacture much of the world's supply of heroin and cocaine; in many, the abuse of those drugs has become a crisis of unprecedented proportions, especially among the young. But in the developed world, no other country matches what one British observer has called the "American Nightmare"—or even comes close.

The British, as we will see, have a significant heroin problem which mushroomed in the early 1980s; the German drug problem, which had been relatively stable up through most of the eighties, began to rise again toward the end of the decade; Spain and Italy both have substantial problems with heroin and milder ones with cocaine. Yet none even *begins* to reach our overall levels of drug use; and in only a few developed countries has cocaine in any form, much less crack, made significant inroads.

This is hardly because suppliers are uninterested in the affluent European and Japanese markets; in the late 1980s the American market was so glutted with cocaine that many high-level suppliers began looking to Europe to absorb their surplus product. Yet by the end of the decade there were fewer known cocaine addicts in all of England, for example, than in many urban *neighborhoods* in the United States. There were 677 cocaine-related arrests in France in 1989, and 4,900 in the city of Boston. More people died in 1989 of the effects of cocaine abuse alone in Los Angeles than died of *all* drug-related causes in England. As many died from methamphetamine abuse in the city of San Diego as died of *all* drug-related causes in Holland, with fifteen times the population.

Even measured by surveys of high school students—which, as we shall see, *understate* the severity of the American drug problem because they miss our sprawling population of the socially and economically marginal—there are striking differences in the extent of drug abuse between the U.S. and Europe. Thus in 1989 something over 10 percent of American high school seniors admitted having tried cocaine—more than five times the proportion turned up by surveys in Germany, Italy, and England (three countries with relatively severe drug problems by European standards) and about *twenty* times the rate in Sweden, Holland, and Norway.

What is true of drug use also holds for its most deadly social and medical consequences. Drug-related violence is by no means absent in European countries, but on the American scale it is simply unknown. There are twice as many drug-related homicides annually in New York City as there are homicides of any kind in all of England, with seven times the population. There were more drug-related killings in the city of Washington, D.C. (population 600,000) in 1988 than there were murders of any type in all of Scandinavia (population eighteen million). No major European city lacks an illegal drug market, but in none of them are entire neighborhoods gripped by Uzi-wielding drug gangs or terrorized by routine drive-by shootings.

The magnitude of the link between drugs and AIDS in the United States is similarly unparalleled in the rest of the industrial world. Nearly 25 percent of the more than 200,000 diagnosed AIDS cases in the United States have intravenous drug use as the only risk factor; another 6 percent involve both

IV drug use and homosexuality. The proportion is far higher in some cities—40 percent in New York and 65 percent in Newark, the nation's drugs-AIDS capital. In Sweden, at the end of 1990, there were slightly more than five hundred known AIDS cases, of which only seventeen, or a little over 3 percent, involved IV drugs. In Holland, there were about seventy-five AIDS cases in 1989 in which IV drug use was the only risk factor, or about 7 percent of their total.

Moreover, the American drug crisis, by itself, is responsible for most of the rise in AIDS among *children* in the entire industrial world. In 83 percent of pediatric AIDS cases known by the end of 1990, the children had contracted the disease from their mothers—most of whom had been infected through contacts with IV drug users. Nationally, about 1.5 out of every 1,000 babies are now born to mothers with the AIDS virus (as of 1989); in one hospital in Newark, closer to 40 out of 1,000. Mother-child transmission of AIDS is a rare event in most other developed countries (though, again, common in parts of the Third World); in 1989, we had 55 times as many cases as West Germany, 65 times as many as the United Kingdom.

In pointing to these striking differences, I do not mean to idealize the European situation. In some European countries drug abuse is a problem of genuinely troubling dimensions, and in some the AIDS-drugs connection is worsening. But in none of those countries have drugs and drug-related crime rocked the foundations of the social order as they have in the United States, or turned the city streets into urban battle-grounds, or triggered a massive explosion of sexually trans-mitted disease.

I I

What makes the severity of the American nightmare especially frightening is that, like a fire that continues to rage after we have cut down half the forest to contain it, it has withstood the most ex*r*aordinary efforts at control. It is sometimes said that the war on drugs has never *really* been fought—that it has been more rhetoric than resources, more political posturing than serious commitment. When it comes to the "softer" approaches to drugs—treatment and prevention—that's generally true. But if we mean the conventional "war" waged with the weapons of law enforcement against drug dealers and users on America's streets, it is emphatically not true. We have been putting considerable resources into that war for twenty years —far more than any other nation—and it escalated enormously after the mid-1980s. The conventional drug war, in short, is an experiment that should have shown clear signs of success by now—if it was ever going to.

When the war on drugs began during the Nixon administration in the early 1970s, it absorbed about $200 million a year. By 1992 we were spending nearly $13 billion at the federal level alone—not counting the vast sums poured into the drug war by the states, cities, and counties—and the figure was still rising. Most of that money—roughly 70 percent during the Bush administration—has gone for police, courts, and prisons, and to a lesser extent for such related purposes as military aid to source countries and the "interdiction" of drugs at the borders.

That flood of spending has helped to transform the American justice system into the largest and most costly apparatus of surveillance and confinement in the world. Today the United States incarcerates a larger proportion of its citizens than any other country, having surpassed South Africa and the Soviet Union by the end of the 1980s. The drug war is not the only reason for the unprecedented explosion in incarceration; it has also been driven by rising street crime and an ever-harsher response to it by legislatures and courts. But it is the drug war that has most rapidly altered the character of the justice system.

Nationally, between 1980 and 1989 alone, drug arrests increased by 105 percent. But even that figure understates the escalation of the criminal-justice response to hard drugs, because it encompasses a slightly *declining* rate of arrests for marijuana offenses. When we look at the harder drugs—the drug war's main target—the increases in arrest rates are staggering. In 1980 about 11 out of every 100,000 Americans were arrested for the sale or manufacture of cocaine or heroin; by 1989, about 100 out of 100,000 were—an increase of over 800 percent. In California, the adult arrest rate for felony narcotics offenses increased threefold and the juvenile rate sixfold between 1983 and 1988. There is a common assumption that most drug arrests are for high-level drug trafficking. But more than twice as many people are arrested for *possessing* heroin or cocaine than for selling or manufacturing them; and the rate of those arrests, too, also shot up by over 800 percent from 1980 to 1989.

The rise in the sheer numbers of people arrested, coupled with increasingly harsh sentences, has flooded the courts, jails, and prisons with drug offenders—so much so that we now have a topsy-turvy system in which hardened violent criminals must be released to make room for people whose only crime is that they have been caught with small amounts of illegal drugs, or found "dirty" on a urine test.

The backlog of drug cases in the federal courts increased sixfold between 1989 and 1991 alone, despite a more than 80 percent increase in the courts' budget. The average sentence imposed for drug-related offenses of all kinds lengthened by a third from 1980 to 1986 (twice as much as for other crimes) and by about another third since. And that figure understates what has happened with specific drugs, particularly crack cocaine. Since 1988, federal law has mandated a five-year prison sentence for possession of 1.7 ounces of crack, and even life imprisonment is a possibility for larger amounts: A California ghetto twenty-two-year-old named Richard Winrow was sentenced to life without parole in federal court in 1989 for possessing 5.5 ounces of crack. Nor are these Draconian sentences reserved for repeat offenders or for the hardest drugs: In a 1991 federal case, a young California *first* offender faced twelve to fifteen years of "nonparolable" prison time for selling 1.56 grams of LSD.

Those long sentences, the sheer numbers of drug offenders, and a growing tendency to revoke probation or parole because of drug use have helped to cause a prison crisis that is unprecedented, in this country or any other, and created conditions that verge on the surreal. In Michigan, drug commitments more than tripled between 1986 and 1988 alone. Drug commitments are one of the main reasons for the quintupling of California's prison population from about 20,000 in 1979 to over 100,000 by early 1991—roughly the number behind bars in Great Britain and West Germany combined. More men are now in prison in California for drug offenses than were behind bars for *all* crimes in 1980; a fourth of the men and two-fifths of the women in the state's prisons are drug offenders. In New York State, where the prison budget was growing by $50 million a *month* at the end of the eighties, drug offenses grew from less than a fifth of new prison admissions in 1986 to nearly half by the end of the decade.

Again, it is important to be clear that the drive to imprison drug offenders has not been directed solely at the stereotypical high-flying gangland pusher. In Florida, about two out of five prison sentences for drug offenses are now for possession alone. And a rapidly growing number across the country are returned to prison for using drugs while on parole or probation. Drug testing of parolees and probationers was greatly expanded during the 1980s, on the theory that it would both deter drug-related crime and, by allowing offenders to be monitored outside prison walls, reduce prison populations as well. But the opposite has happened: drug testing has mainly served to increase the prison population dramatically. Drugs figure in almost two-thirds of parole revocations in California; nearly 19,000 people were sent back to prison for drug offenses in 1988—a number almost equal to the state's *entire* prison population ten years earlier.

Unsurprisingly, the huge flow of drug offenders has filled

many prison systems far past capacity. By 1991, most states were under court order to reduce overcrowding in their prisons—despite a record $18 billion spent nationally on prison construction and operation in 1990. California alone built nine new prisons between 1982 and 1990 and claimed to need another thirty-eight by the year 2000 simply to maintain an "acceptable" level of overcrowding—defined, in rather Orwellian fashion, as averaging no more than 125 inmates in space designed for 100. During 1989, the state of Michigan opened a new prison every eight to nine *weeks*, but the system remained desperately overcrowded. "We build prisons, we build prisons, we build prisons," lamented Michigan's prison director at a Senate hearing in 1990. "We thought we could build enough, [but] every week the shortage gets worse."

The most spectacular and counterproductive result has been that some prisons must periodically release large numbers of criminals—including the truly dangerous—to reduce the overcrowding caused by the influx of drug offenders. In Florida, where a conservative state government launched one of the harshest versions of the drug war during the eighties, drug offenders were being "herded into makeshift tent prisons" by 1987, despite the addition of 25,000 new prison beds. The resulting crush forced the state to establish an early-release program in which over 130,000 serious felons, including armed robbers and muggers, had been returned to the streets by 1991—one in three of whom went on to commit new crimes. Florida now presents the bizarre spectacle of a state so intent on incarcerating drug offenders—including low-level dealers and users—that it is willing to let armed robbers go free in their place. Moreover, the state had virtually no funds to provide follow-up supervision or services to released inmates. The result was what a report from the National Council on Crime and Delinquency described as "the worst of both worlds"—a "chaotic and ineffective prison system where very little treatment, supervision, or punishment" was administered. Indeed, a state legislative analysis in 1990 found that the

diversion of police and correctional resources to drug offenders
had "actually contributed significantly to an increase in the
property crime rate."

Florida is an extreme example, but in nearly every state the
costs of the conventional drug war have been both extreme
and often unanticipated. Letting dangerous criminals out onto
the streets to make room for drug addicts is only the most
visibly paradoxical of them. Other costs, over the long term,
may be more devastating.

First, the prison boom—heavily if not exclusively driven by
the drug war—has helped to impoverish some states to the
point where they have become unable to provide for even the
most basic public needs—including some with a direct bearing
on the prevention of drug abuse. The fivefold increase in
prison spending during the 1980s is one reason why, in 1991,
the state of California was reeling under a budget deficit of
more than $14 billion, a sum greater than the *total* budgets of
all but five states in the country. The resulting fiscal crisis has
undermined virtually every public institution in the state;
several school districts are on the verge of bankruptcy, and
already weakened public health, mental health, and child
protection agencies have been savaged beyond recognition,
along with aid to the homeless and income support for the
poorest of the poor. The prison boom is not the only source
of these troubles, but its ripple effects have helped to accelerate
everything from the closing of hospital emergency rooms and
fire stations to the gutting of student services, the restriction
of enrollments, and the partial closing of libraries in the state's
university system. In a stunningly self-defeating pattern, even
programs that could help prevent drug abuse or treat drug
users were cut in order to rescue state treasuries depleted in
part by efforts to jail drug offenders. Thus Oakland lost a third
of its methadone-treatment slots for heroin addicts; Los Angeles lost probation services for many "high-risk" youths. Across
the United States, in the tough fiscal climate of the early
nineties, the vast increases in prison space to accommodate

drug offenders have been bought at the expense of everything from prenatal care to police protection—and even drug treatment.

Second, the disproportionate focus of the drug war on the poor and near-poor has dramatically accelerated a massive "prisonization" of the disadvantaged young that began during the 1970s and whose long-range repercussions we're only beginning to feel. Studies by the Sentencing Project in Washington, D.C., and the New York State Coalition for Criminal Justice, among others, have detailed the extraordinary proportion of young minority men who are now "under correctional supervision," in the euphemistic language of the justice system. Nationally, nearly one in four black men and one in ten Hispanic men between the ages of twenty and twenty-nine are behind bars, on probation, or on parole; in California, the figure for black men is closer to one in three, and in Nevada and the District of Columbia it is *two in five*. In New York, two young black men are in prison for every one in college.

Under the impact of the drug war, indeed, the correctional system has become our principal public agency for disadvantaged young men—their chief source of publicly supported housing and one of their most important sources of employment, nutrition, and medical care. We now spend considerably more on institutional housing for the poor via the jail and prison systems than we do on ordinary public housing for low-income people: eight times as much is spent on corrections as on low-rent public housing, for example, and nearly twice as much as on public housing and rent subsidies for the poor combined.

The long-term social costs of this massive incarceration of minority youth are impossible to measure, but no serious observer doubts that they will be huge. And they involve much more than dollars and cents. In the name of reducing drug abuse, we have decimated entire communities and permanently

relegated great numbers of young Americans to the margins
of productive society. And the gutting of public funds in the
service of the prison boom means that we now have few
resources to do anything constructive with the newly criminalized when they return, as most of them will, to the streets of
the cities—a volatile and alienated army with little stake in
society and few realistic prospects for the future.

I I I

When it comes to the tools of criminal justice, in short, the
drug war has been fought, and fought hard—so hard that it
has transformed the justice system and caused considerable
social damage in its own right. What have we gotten in return?
Official reassurances notwithstanding, the most charitable answer is: not much.

Twenty years after the war on drugs began in earnest, the
American drug problem is vastly greater than it was before we
started. In 1967, the President's Commission on Law Enforcement and the Administration of Justice cited estimates that
there were fewer than sixty thousand heroin addicts in the
United States, and considered, but rejected, a higher estimate
of as many as two hundred thousand. Today, the low estimate
is roughly half a million and the high estimate is twice that.
The commission dismissed cocaine as a serious problem, on
the ground that it "does not create tolerance or physical
dependence" and was "not the major drug of abuse it once
was." Twenty-five years later, the low estimate of "hard-core"
cocaine abusers is 1.5 million, the high estimate 2.5 million.
Far more Americans today are seriously addicted to hard
drugs; they are addicted to a wider *range* of drugs; and the
consequences of their addiction have become increasingly
fearsome and costly in human as well as economic terms. Hard-
drug abuse has become embedded in the fabric of American
social life to a degree inconceivable a generation ago. "Take

my word for it," declared George Bush in his 1988 inaugural address, "this scourge will stop." But the "scourge" remains very much with us, and there are no signs that it will "stop" in the foreseeable future.

Two trends sometimes obscure this harsh reality. The first is that "casual" drug use has generally fallen, probably quite significantly, among the better-off—the "middle class." The other is that the specific epidemic of crack cocaine that struck with such ferocity at the inner-city poor has—at this writing— receded from its highest levels of the late eighties. The latter trend, especially, is good news, as far as it goes. If it continues, it will save lives and families, slow the spread of AIDS in the inner city, and ease the pressure on the justice and health-care systems. But it does not alter the long-term trend. Twenty— even ten—years ago, we had no crack at all. Today, crack has become increasingly normalized, as the drug joins heroin and powder cocaine as an established feature of the urban land-scape.

Unraveling the evidence behind any of these assertions is not easy. As with some other social ills—like crime or poverty —the question of whether drug abuse is better or worse now than at some point in the past is freighted with political significance. Those who stand to gain political ground by maximizing the success of the conventional drug war will brandish the statistics that put the war in its most favorable light; those who stand to lose will just as predictably trot out their own.

The difficulty in making sense of contested facts is com-pounded by the elusive nature of drug use itself. Since it is illegal, and increasingly subject to harsh penalties, drug abuse is mostly hidden—and consequently very difficult to measure. We need, then, to step back long enough to understand the uses and limits of the often conflicting indices used to measure the extent of the drug problem and its changes over time.

The most frequently cited data on patterns of drug use in the United States come from two questionnaire surveys done under the auspices of the National Institute on Drug Abuse (NIDA), an arm of the U.S. Department of Health and Human Services. Used carefully, these surveys, along with other sources of data, can help us piece together a provisional picture of the extent and trends of drug use. Used less carefully, they can be extremely misleading.

The first is an annual survey of 16,000 to 17,000 high-school seniors directed by social scientists at the University of Michigan's Survey Research Center. A confidential questionnaire administered to the students in their classrooms asks about the drugs they have taken during the past month, year, and in their lifetime, and also about their views on the risks of various drugs. Measured by what the survey calls "thirty-day prevalence"—that is, whether the respondent admitted using a drug at least once during the past month, generally considered a measure of more than casual use—the big change since the survey was inaugurated in 1975 is the large decline in reported use of marijuana, which dropped by nearly half from 1975 to 1990. If we start from the peak year of marijuana use by high-school seniors, 1979, the drop is more precipitous; reported use fell by over 60 percent.

For other drugs, the picture is more mixed. Cocaine use by seniors in the past month was roughly the same in 1990 as sixteen years earlier (just under 2 percent in both years). But the 1990 figure represented a sharp *drop* from the peak of more than 6 percent in 1985. The use of inhalants, on the other hand (substances such as glue, gasoline, and paint thinner), has *risen* over the years, to the point where inhalants now surpass cocaine as a drug of choice among high-school seniors.

The second survey produced by NIDA—a periodic survey of about nine thousand households across the United States—also shows generally declining use of many drugs from their earlier peaks. Among people aged twenty-six or older, for example, reported cocaine use in the past month more than doubled—from less than 1 percent to 2 percent—between 1979 and 1985, and then fell back to its 1979 level by the end of the 1980s (but rose significantly between 1990 and 1991).

What do we make of these figures? The declines in *reported* drug use since the mid-eighties (for cocaine) and late seventies (for marijuana) have been celebrated as reflecting a broad decline in the acceptability of drugs, especially among American teenagers, and, at least implicitly, a vindication of the conventional drug war. But two fundamental problems, inherent in the surveys, cast doubt on that view.

The first is the simplest: how do we know we can believe the answers? All such "self-report" surveys depend entirely on the willingness of the respondents to tell the truth. In the case of drug abuse, like any other illegal and disapproved activity, common sense would suggest that not all of them do, and careful research confirms that suspicion.

In the late 1980s the federal government, in what is called the Drug Use Forecasting Program (DUF), began administering similar questionnaires on drug use to people arrested in cities across the country. But they also administered urine tests, making it possible to check the self-report responses against harder physiological evidence. The results were striking; overall, only about half of the arrestees with positive urine tests admitted to using drugs. The proportion of honest responses, not surprisingly, was lowest for some of the hardest drugs— cocaine, PCP, and amphetamines—and higher for marijuana. In 1988, for instance, 24 percent of male arrestees reported that they had used cocaine in the past thirty days—but 49 percent "tested positive" for cocaine use within the last *two or three days*. Similarly, a recent study of juvenile delinquents in detention in Florida, using similar methods, found only about a *quarter* of those who tested positive for cocaine admitted recent use of the drug.

Since these studies focus on people involved in the criminal-justice system—people who may have had reason to be worried about what would happen to them if they admitted using drugs—it might be argued that the degree of underreporting of drug use may be higher than in other settings. But as it turns out, it is not only people who have been arrested or imprisoned who routinely lie about their drug use. Sally McNagny and Ruth Parker found the same split between self-reports and urinalysis in a study of men seeking help for various general medical problems in an inner-city public health clinic in Atlanta. Over 400 patients, most of them black, were asked to participate in what they were told was a study of sexually transmitted disease. They were questioned about drug use and were also asked to give urine samples—but were *not* told that the samples would be tested for drugs. A stunning 39 percent of these men tested positive for cocaine use, less than half of whom reported using the drug in the past week. The researchers conclude that "policymakers seeking information from surveys" must realize that self-reports "may provide severe underestimates of actual use."

Because the validity of the responses is so uncertain, we really do not know how accurately the figures found in the self-report surveys describe actual drug use; nor do we know to what extent the reported declines in use (or the rises, for that matter) are real ones, especially since drug use has become increasingly subject to criminal penalties and social disapproval since the mid-eighties.

And there is another, even more fundamental, limitation of both surveys. By definition, neither can tell us anything about drug use among people who are not found in conventional households or high-school classrooms. They tell us about only *part* of the population, and it is the part among whom serious drug use is *least* likely to be found. As a recent report from the National Institute of Justice puts it, "Self-report surveys tap mainstream Americans with stable living arrangements."

When we look at *other* kinds of Americans, the picture is much grimmer.

In 1986, the New York State Division of Substance Abuse Services surveyed drug use among New York's "transient" population—the homeless and those living in transient hotels and shelters—a high-risk group largely passed over by both the high school and household surveys. "The levels of drug abuse reported among these transients," the study concluded, "are among the highest encountered in epidemiologic surveys of drug abuse." Nearly half admitted using illicit drugs in the previous six months; over a quarter reported using cocaine, almost one in ten heroin. More than a fourth reported not only *using* illicit drugs, but feeling dependent on them. A 1991 study of homeless black men in Miami conducted by the U.S. Centers for Disease Control found an astonishing 57 percent had used crack in the month before they were interviewed.

Similarly, runaway and homeless teenagers interviewed in 1989 in eight Southeastern states reported "thirty-day" cocaine and crack use five times higher than adolescents in the NIDA household survey, and heroin use over eleven times higher. Among homeless adolescents surveyed in Hollywood in 1987, cocaine and crack use was *eighteen* times higher than that reported by youth of similar age in the household survey, the use of LSD and PCP thirty times higher.

These studies highlight a more general failure of the conventional surveys to detect patterns of drug use among more difficult populations of the young—who, even if they are not homeless, are much less likely to be in school and thus are routinely missed by the high-school surveys. In a study of multiple drug abuse among "seriously delinquent" youth in Miami, James Inciardi and Anne Pottieger found that *"all* of the juveniles interviewed had histories of multiple drug use," including a stunning 87 percent reporting regular current use of crack. Almost a fourth of this sample were out of school altogether, and the vast majority—87 percent—had been expelled or suspended from school at least once.

A recent survey of teenagers by Ernest Chavez and Randall Swaim further illustrates the significance of the exclusion of dropouts and other especially vulnerable groups. Chavez and Swaim administered questionnaires to several thousand eighth- and twelfth-graders, about half Mexican-American and half non-Hispanic whites. The survey uncovered a phenomenon that at first glance seems difficult to fathom: for many drugs, both recent (30-day) use and lifetime use were higher for the eighth-graders than the twelfth-graders. How could *lifetime* use be higher for the younger students? There are only two possibilities. Either these eighth-graders are much more prone to use drugs than their older counterparts, or a substantial proportion of the students who use drugs most heavily in the eighth grade drop out of school before reaching the twelfth— and therefore do not show up in the twelfth-grade statistics, which drop accordingly. Chavez and Swaim doubt the first interpretation, since it requires us to believe—contrary to all other surveys—that student drug use has dramatically *increased* in the last few years. The Mexican-American eighth-graders had a startling 5 percent rate of lifetime heroin use; the figure for twelfth-graders was 2 percent. Unless we believe that today's eighth-graders are more than twice as likely to use heroin as those of four years ago, these results mean that most of the heroin-using youth now old enough to be in the twelfth grade never made it to their senior year—and were therefore not available to answer the researchers' questionnaires.

Both of these limitations of the NIDA self-report surveys may help explain why *medical* data on drug-related deaths and emergencies paint a different, and considerably more troubling, picture of the trends in drug abuse in recent years. Much of that data comes from reports by hospitals and medical examiners in twenty-seven major metropolitan areas around the country affiliated with the Drug Abuse Warning Network, or DAWN, also sponsored by NIDA. The data are far from perfect; there is substantial variation in the definition of drug-related deaths, for example, between different jurisdictions.

But they do not depend on the dubious honesty of respondents, and they do not exclude the most vulnerable populations.

Between 1985 and 1989, while the national self-report surveys showed generally declining use of most drugs, deaths from cocaine abuse tripled in the United States as a whole. They increased more than four times in Los Angeles, seven times in Chicago, and almost nine times in Philadelphia. Cocaine-related medical emergencies quadrupled nationally in the same years, rising sixfold in Chicago and Washington, tenfold in Philadelphia, and thirteenfold in Atlanta.

Heroin deaths and emergencies also rose, if less spectacularly. Heroin barely appears at all in the conventional surveys; as NIDA points out, "a disproportionate number of heroin users are part of nonsampled populations"—including inmates and those without fixed addresses. And to the extent that it was measurable at all, heroin use showed if anything some declines during the late 1980s in the NIDA surveys. But the medical data tell a very different story. Just when the drug war was at its height, heroin-related deaths and medical emergencies both increased, by about 25 percent between 1985 and 1989. The pattern was uneven across the country; heroin deaths dropped in Detroit, for example, but skyrocketed in Philadelphia (where they rose 145 percent) and Chicago (400 percent). Deaths due to "speedballing"—combining cocaine and heroin—also tripled nationally in those years, and they quadrupled in Los Angeles, quintupled in Chicago, and increased thirteenfold in Philadelphia.

Thus the medical data cast further doubt on the capacity of the surveys to give an accurate picture of trends in drug abuse. And they also put the easing of the crack epidemic since the 1989 peak in troubling perspective. For they suggest that while cocaine abuse today may not be quite as bad as it was in 1989, the longer-term trend, like that for heroin, is upward.

There are many ways to die a "drug-related" death, and not all are counted in the DAWN reports. They leave out homicides in which drugs were involved, and also deaths involving AIDS, even where drugs were present. Because of that—and because only twenty-seven urban areas are represented—the total figures in DAWN considerably understate the numbers who die of drug-related causes each year. But they do point usefully to trends over time. And the trend since the middle of the 1980s looks very different through this lens. About 3,500 "accidental/ unintentional" deaths—mainly drug overdoses—were reported to DAWN in 1990, as against 2,230 in 1985, an increase of 57 percent.

When we focus on the specific illegal drugs most often implicated in drug-related deaths we see the same trend. DAWN counts what it calls drug "mentions" in addition to deaths—that is, all the drugs that may have contributed to the death in question. In 1985 heroin was the drug most frequently mentioned in drug-related deaths; there were 1,315 heroin mentions in that year. There were only 643 mentions of cocaine, less than half as many; indeed, more people in the DAWN areas died from the effects of antidepressant medications in that year than from cocaine. By 1990 things had changed considerably. There were 1,976 heroin mentions—an increase of 50 percent over 1985—and heroin had been surpassed by cocaine, at 2,483 mentions now the drug most often implicated in drug-related deaths. Thus, even after the "peak," cocaine was implicated in four times as many deaths as it had been five years earlier.

Moreover, as with the NIDA household survey, there was a disturbing resurgence in 1991 of both heroin- and cocaine-related medical emergencies in the DAWN reports. Confronted with this news, the Bush administration rushed to reassure us that the increases did not necessarily mean that drug abuse was rising. The numbers might mean, they said, that people who had been using drugs for a long time were suddenly having worse problems than they had had before. Concrete evidence for that wistful claim, however, was not forthcoming. In New York, meanwhile, after a modest decline during 1990, emergency-room admissions for both heroin and cocaine shot up dramatically the following year. Deaths from both drugs also rose, though less sharply.

The persistence of the drug plague among the most vulnerable shows up in other ways as well. One is the data on drug use among arrestees from the Drug Use Forecasting survey. At the height of the crack epidemic in Washington, D.C., in 1988, for example, 64 percent of male arrestees in that city tested positive for cocaine. By early 1991, the proportion had fallen—to precisely 50 percent. Summing up the evidence from various measures, a NIDA-sponsored working group reported in 1991 that although crack use in Washington "appears to be declining, it remains at high levels, and indications suggest that a crack-addict population has become entrenched in the area." A report from New York in the same year makes the point more vividly:

> One development that has emerged in the past year is the blatant use of crack in public places. Field researchers report observing more people smoking crack while waiting in movie lines, on trains and buses, in parks, playgrounds, and on the street. Many of these individuals make little effort to hide what they are doing.

There is yet another indicator of the continued spread of hard-drug abuse hidden from the conventional surveys: the frighteningly rapid rise in drug-related sexually transmitted diseases (STDs). In the case of AIDS, the long incubation period for the disease means that the current sharp increases in drug-related cases could reflect "high-risk" drug use and sexual behavior that took place before the drug war was at its height. But the same is not true for other STDs, which, like AIDS, have shot upward—propelled by IV drug use and frequent unprotected sex among infected drug users—in the face of the escalation of the drug war. Between 1985 and 1988, while drug use was falling in the self-report surveys, reported syphilis cases, heavily concentrated among drug-abusing heterosexuals,

leapt by 91 percent in Washington and 200 percent in Philadelphia. In Washington, during the same period, cases of
penicillin-resistant gonorrhea increased by 300 percent—also
most severely among drug-abusing heterosexuals. By the late
1980s, moreover, the plague of drug-driven sexually transmitted disease, which began in the inner cities, had spread well
beyond them to many rural areas. An epidemic of syphilis, for
example, "unprecedented since the introduction of penicillin,"
exploded in rural Georgia in the late 1980s "because of crack."
New syphilis cases increased in sixteen rural Georgia counties
by a stunning 800 percent between 1985 and 1988.

I V

To summarize this complicated evidence: While it is probably
true that the epidemic of cocaine has peaked, both cocaine and
heroin are now endemic in America at levels that far surpass
those before the start of the drug war. While there is credible
evidence that rising health consciousness and growing awareness of the adverse effects of drug abuse have altered the drug
habits of the more secure strata of American society, no such
evidence exists for the bottom quarter of the population.

Even many who support the thrust of our present drug
policies would acknowledge that the drug crisis among "hard-
core" users in the more marginal populations is understated
by the conventional statistics, and that it has proven remarkably
resistant to the conventional tools of the drug war. But they
would argue that the declines in *middle*-class drug use prove
that the drug war is "on the right track," and that if we only
redoubled our efforts we could make it work against the
admittedly tougher situation in the inner cities as well.

The trouble with that view is that the conventional drug war
had virtually nothing to do with the declines in drug use among
the better-off, for it was never *fought* against their drug use.
Despite occasional bursts of rhetoric about cracking down on

"recreational" drug use in the suburbs, so little did that crackdown actually take place even at the height of the drug war in the late eighties and early nineties that when several University of Virginia fraternities were raided in the spring of 1991—netting, to no one's great surprise, nothing more than small amounts of marijuana and LSD—the story was front-page news in the national press for days. In the Virginia case, law-enforcement officials were reported to have "expressed hope" that the raid would send the message that drug seizures and arrests would no longer "be limited mainly to poor neighborhoods." The drug war has been overwhelmingly targeted at the communities of the poor and near-poor, especially the minority poor. It's possible to argue over whether or not that emphasis is justified; it's not possible to deny that it exists.

Nationally, in 1989, about 40 percent of all arrests for all drug violations were of blacks, who are only 12 percent of the population. The proportion of jail inmates charged with a drug offense who were black or Hispanic rose from 55 percent in 1983 to 73 percent in 1989. The disproportion is even greater in areas where hard-drug use is heavily concentrated: In New York State, over 90 percent of those sent to state prison for drug felonies in 1988 were black or Hispanic, and the figure was even higher—about 95 percent—for the lower-level felonies that made up almost three-fifths of prison commitments for drug offenses. "Measured by jail and prison populations," notes a recent report of the New York State Coalition for Criminal Justice, "one can almost say that drug abuse has been legalized for middle-class whites."

In California, only 19 percent of adults and less than 9 percent of juveniles arrested for felony narcotic violations in 1989 were white and non-Hispanic. According to a report from the National Institute of Justice, the drug war was the main reason why the number of black and Hispanic youth held in short-term juvenile institutions nationwide increased by 30 percent between 1985 and 1987 alone—while detentions of non-Hispanic white youth rose by only 1 percent. Minority

youth were more likely to be detained once arrested than
whites, both for drug sales and possession. They were also
more likely than whites to be referred to courts for drug
offenses in the first place. The result was a 71 percent increase
in the number of nonwhite youth detained for drug offenses
in the space of just two years.

The drug war, in short, has been fought hardest—in some
places, almost exclusively—in precisely those communities
where drug use remains most severe and most stubborn, barely
at all in those where it has fallen. Likewise, it has been fought
most fiercely against the *drugs* that remain most stubbornly
persistent—heroin and especially cocaine—and barely at all
against marijuana, which has undergone the most significant
decline and indeed accounts for the bulk of the much trum-
peted fall in illicit drug use in the United States. In New York,
for example, research shows that the measures taken against
crack in the 1980s were far tougher than those for other
drugs—including "widespread arrests for sale and possession,
more stringent charging decisions, and harsher sentences."

Meanwhile, revealingly, marijuana use declined (according
to the self-report surveys) in spite of a very significant *let-up* in
the law-enforcement effort against it. Nationally, marijuana
possession arrests *dropped* by over 10 percent between 1980
and 1988, while arrests for possession of heroin and cocaine
exploded by 600 percent. In California, the pattern was even
more extreme: juvenile felony arrests for marijuana dropped
by well over half during the 1980s.

In short, whatever caused the decline in marijuana use among
American teenagers in the 1980s, it was certainly not the war
on drugs. In most places there *was* no war on marijuana use,
and in some, authorities had officially declared a truce.

What we know from careful analyses of the high-school drug
surveys, indeed, is that most of the decline in marijuana use
can be attributed to changing perceptions of its dangers to
health and well-being—changes which fit well with the long-
run trend toward increasing health-consciousness among

middle-class Americans, a trend that encompasses declines not only in drug use but in alcohol, smoking, and unhealthy diet, and increased exercise. These changes are all to the good, but they are *not* the result of the war on drugs. (Indeed, to the extent that they are related to specific antidrug strategies at all, they reflect efforts at education and prevention which the last two administrations have systematically slighted.)

Thus—astonishingly—it is not clear that the conventional drug war has had *any* positive effects in reducing drug abuse. Where there are credible long-term declines, they are unrelated to the drug war; where the drug war was most heavily fought, there are no credible long-term declines. On balance, I'm inclined to think that the war probably *has* had some short-term results, and that it may be *part* of the reason for the recent peak in the use of crack cocaine. After all, it's hard to imagine that the arrest and imprisonment of hundreds of thousands of drug users and dealers has had *no* impact whatsoever. But even that minimal assessment is based on little more than a hunch, without solid evidence to support it.

V

Reasonable people may legitimately debate the details. But there is no denying the fundamental realities: the American drug problem continues to tower above those of the rest of the industrial world, and it does so despite a truly extraordinary experiment in punitive control. We have unleashed the criminal-justice system against drug users and dealers with unprecedented ferocity, but drugs continue to destroy lives and shatter communities to a degree unmatched outside the Third World. And now the drug war itself contributes to that destruction—first in the incarceration of vast numbers of the young at what should be the start of their most productive years; and again in the depletion of resources that could otherwise be used to deal with the deeper problems of devastated communities.

It is time to change direction; and doing so requires us to look hard and unflinchingly at *why* the United States has the worst drug problem in the developed world, and why that problem has so stubbornly persisted despite the resources we continue to throw at it and the increasingly Draconian penalties we inflict on drug users. What is it about our society that leads a substantial segment of the American population—far larger than in any other industrial nation—to abuse hard drugs, in the face of the horrendous consequences they know full well may follow? That question, curiously, is rarely considered in our current drug "debate"; but it is the one that is most critical if we are ever to develop a serious response to the drug crisis.

Fortunately, there are some answers. In some quarters it has been fashionable to say that we don't know why some people rather than others abuse hard drugs, or why some who try drugs—even to the point of addiction—are able to stop abusing them while others are not. That view, with its implication that drug addiction is a sort of mysterious virus that strikes people almost at random because of some as yet undiscovered biological or psychological predisposition, supports a posture toward the drug problem that is simultaneously passive and repressive, and it fits well with the conservative tenor of the times.

But it is wrong. We know a great deal about who is most likely to abuse hard drugs and why, and our knowledge has been steadily accumulating for forty years. Part of the reason for our inability to get a grip on the drug crisis is that, hobbled by historical amnesia and a crippling addiction to short-term thinking, we ignore most of what we do know, and we are consequently forced to confront each successive drug crisis, every new "epidemic," as if it were brand new. But the outlines of a real antidrug strategy had been foreseen, and put on the national agenda, more than once by the late 1960s—along with sober warnings about what would happen if we did *not* address the roots of the drug problem. That we failed to do so is not because we lacked the knowledge, but because we were unwilling, as a nation, to take on the job. Instead, we moved in the opposite direction. We replaced an emerging consensus on the need to attack the *causes* of endemic drug abuse with the politically more palatable—but ultimately far more costly— strategy of declaring war on its symptoms while allowing those causes to fester.

The results are horrifyingly apparent. The first step, then, toward a real war on drug abuse is to reopen, without apology, the question of root causes.

CHAPTER

2

Roots of the Drug Crisis

The American drug crisis didn't suddenly spring up, full-blown, with the cocaine epidemic of the eighties. Most of its basic elements were in place shortly after World War II, when an epidemic of heroin abuse struck the inner cities.

In 1946, only 712 people were arrested for narcotics violations in New York; by 1956, almost 6,000. In Chicago, 424 were arrested in 1946, an unheard-of 9,000 ten years later. By today's standards the numbers were small; but as an urban phenomenon they were unprecedented—in the United States or elsewhere. As a federal report noted in the early 1950s, the rough contemporary estimate of as many as 60,000 narcotic addicts in America was "far more than the number reported by other Western nations." And the sudden increase in addiction was all the more alarming because those involved were disproportionately young. "The disease," worried a New York State attorney general's report in 1952, "has spread with alarming rapidity through the ranks of our adolescent society." Yet it was equally clear that the "disease" had not spread *evenly* among them. In 1955 in Detroit, 1,812 people were arrested for narcotics violations; 1,593 of these were classified as "Negro," 184 "white," 12 "yellow," and 23 "Mexican." As a joint report of the American Medical Association and the American Bar Association put it in the late 1950s, "the use of narcotic drugs appeared to have spread with epidemic force in the slum areas of our large cities, particularly among minority groups of the population."

I

The postwar surge of heroin use stimulated several important studies during the 1950s, of which one of the earliest and most influential was led by the New York University psychologist Isidor Chein. Chein's work—later published in a seminal book called *The Road to H*—offered an analysis of the urban drug crisis that remains remarkably compelling more than thirty years later.

Chein's study focused on heroin addiction among adolescent males in New York City—a group greatly overrepresented in the statistics on addiction. Each year between 1949 and 1955, an average of about 500 new cases of adolescent heroin addiction had come to the attention of the courts and hospitals in Manhattan, Brooklyn, and the Bronx. Chein and his co-workers collected the addresses of every known case and charted their distribution within the three boroughs.

The overall pattern was stark and unmistakable. Only 15 percent of the census tracts in the three boroughs accounted for over 80 percent of the new cases of adolescent narcotic addiction. The researchers were aware that this concentration might be interpreted as a reflection of the bias of police and courts, rather than the "true" distribution of heroin addiction: poorer addicts might be the ones who most often wound up in the hands of the police and courts, while those from other neighborhoods might be able to get private help for their addiction. But they discounted this interpretation. Surveying other social and medical agencies throughout the city, they did find cases not included in the records of the courts and public hospitals, but the *distribution* of those cases across the city was no different than the "official" ones. Nor was there any difference in the distribution of boys who had *voluntarily* committed themselves to hospitals for treatment versus those who had been sent by the courts. If there were significant numbers of uncounted juvenile addicts in New York, they would have had to have escaped the attention of *any* public or private social, legal, or medical agency in the city. Chein and his colleagues rejected that possibility; heroin addiction, they pointed out, was not something individuals could engage in all by themselves and escape detection for long. It required access to a supporting social network of suppliers and fellow users—unlike, say, auto theft. "Packets of heroin are not conveniently parked for use on the street," Chein wrote, "nor are they obtainable by the simple process of a few youngsters deciding to raise hell. Access to these drugs presupposes contact with a highly illegal traffic which is a target of vigorous police activity on federal, state, and local levels. . . . There simply cannot be a high degree of involvement among significant groups of youngsters without its drawing the attention of the police, school authorities, and others."

The overwhelming concentration of youthful heroin addiction in a few of the city's neighborhoods, then, was not just a statistical artifact but a new urban reality. The chief significance of this finding was that it undermined purely psychological models of addiction—dominant in the fifties, as now, in many quarters—which regarded addiction as simply a property of "maladjusted" individuals, and instead pointed clearly to the central role of social and economic forces in addiction. "If we find that some disease does not strike evenly over a city," Chein reasoned, "we have reason to suspect that clues to the full story of the spread of that disease are to be found in an examination of the differences between the areas where the disease strikes harder and where it strikes more lightly."

But what, specifically, characterized the neighborhoods with heavy concentrations of young addicts? The biggest concentration was in Harlem, with smaller but significant concentrations in south-central Bronx and along an arc in Brooklyn from Red Hook through Fort Greene and Bedford-Stuyvesant to Brownsville on the east. The NYU researchers labeled the fifteen tracts with the highest concentration of addicts "epidemic" areas and proceeded to compare them along several social, demographic, and economic dimensions with the other, "nonepidemic," tracts. Three connections stood out most sharply: the epidemic drug-use areas had high proportions of black or Puerto Rican residents, of people earning low incomes (under $2,000 in 1949), and of men working in low-status occupations. (On average, a third of the residents in epidemic areas were black, compared to less than 2 percent in the nonepidemic areas. The epidemic areas averaged six times the percentage of Puerto Ricans in the population as the nonepidemic tracts.)

"The epidemic areas," Chein concluded, "are, on average, areas of relatively concentrated settlement of underprivileged minority groups, of poverty and low economic status." They were also characterized by low educational attainment and large numbers of disrupted families. Importantly, the data made it clear that race itself was not the overriding factor: low incomes and poor jobs explained most of the link between drug use and race in these neighborhoods. It was not so much that the epidemic neighborhoods were *black* neighborhoods, but that black neighborhoods tended to have large concentrations of low-income people in low-status jobs.

But neither was material poverty alone the whole story. The social context of youthful addiction involved more than simply the lack of money. Chein and his colleagues found that, though the young addicts were overwhelmingly concentrated in the poorest neighborhoods of the city, they did not necessarily come from the poorest *families* within those neighborhoods. In the black neighborhoods, the expected correlation between heroin use and the most severe poverty among families held; but among Puerto Rican and white youth, addicts were likely to come from families that were slightly better off: they were poor, but not the poorest of the poor.

Why? Part of the explanation seemed to lie in another unexpected finding. The researchers had expected that adolescents from families who were newcomers to the city—migrants from Puerto Rico or the rural South—would have higher rates of addiction than those whose families had been in the city longer and had had more time to adapt to urban life. Narcotic addiction might be one response to the culture shock faced by new immigrants unprepared for the rigors of urban life; young men in Harlem or Bedford-Stuyvesant might be unable to "abide by conventional standards" because their immigrant parents lacked the "know-how" to teach them how to behave in a modern urban society. Instead, the opposite turned out to be true: "The families of addicts were residents of New York City for a significantly longer time" than the families of nonaddicted boys used as control cases. Boys who had themselves been born *outside* the country were rarely found among New York City addicts, and the sons of immigrants were also less likely to become addicted. Rather than inadequate preparation for urban culture, it was something about American urban society itself—specifically, "long residence in a deprived area"—that was most likely to lead to heroin addiction. The clear implication was that, if anything, there was something in the culture from which recent immigrants came that *protected* families against drug use and that shielded their children—for a time—from the stresses and deprivations of the city, even though they were often poorer. "The youngsters react to the values and practices they experience," wrote the researchers, "not simply to the material deprivations from which they suffer."

Chein and his colleagues emphasized the importance of the family as the key setting in which those "values and practices" were experienced. Most young men in these neighborhoods were exposed to the lures of heroin, especially in the black neighborhoods—in the areas of highest drug use, 45 percent of eighth-grade boys personally knew someone who used heroin—but those who grew up in supportive or "cohesive" families were less likely to become addicted. The families of the addicted youth were more often cold and conflictual, disrupted by divorce or separation, with unreasonably low (or sometimes unreasonably high) expectations for their sons' futures. The home, the researchers concluded, was "a more comfortable place" for the nonusers; they were less likely to have been "yelled at" or "punished by rejection—ordered out of the house, locked up, ignored."

Chein attributed the success of the cohesive family in protecting adolescents against heroin use to its "contribution to a sense of mutuality"—a "sense of human solidarity, a feeling of belonging, respect for the integrity and value of the individual human being, and the long-range motivation of things worth living for"—which was disturbingly rare in the areas of concentrated deprivation in American cities. In interviews, the addicts often expressed "profound pessimism and alienation," agreeing that there was "not much chance for a better world," that "most people were better off not born," and that everyone was "really out for himself: nobody cares." "A common theme" in the addicts' world-view, the NYU researchers noted, is that "people do not respect other people, that they are mean and arbitrary in pursuit of their private ends": that "the outlook for most people is indeed bleak," and that "the most sensible thing a person can do is to seek pleasure and gratification where he can find them."

Ideally, a strong, supportive family could shield adolescents against the "prevailing atmosphere of degenerated personal relationships" in these deprived neighborhoods. The catch, of course, was that it was precisely in neighborhoods like these that the family itself was especially vulnerable, as was clear from the high proportion of disrupted and pathological families in them.

As this suggests, Chein's picture of the addicts' backgrounds, personalities, and prospects was generally grim. Young heroin addicts were seen as the most extreme product of a chain of pathologies that began with the economic deprivation of the larger community and were exacerbated by the resulting disintegration or demoralization of many urban families. The boys who became addicted—at least in the white and Puerto Rican neighborhoods—were likely to be those who had suffered the most emotional damage from an inadequate and conflictual family life. But the study was equally emphatic that this was more than just a matter of individual psychopathology. The family's problems were rooted in the larger pathologies of the community—the general bleakness of life, the absence of opportunity, and the breakdown of more supportive cultural values in the American urban environment. In the *most* deprived areas, especially the black neighborhoods, individual pathology was even less helpful as an explanation for addiction: heroin was so prevalent that it could easily snare "normal" youth as well as the emotionally troubled. In interviews, black heroin users often emphasized conformity to the local peer culture as the main reason for using heroin—to "follow the fad," to "be down with the rest of the cats." In these extremely deprived black neighborhoods, in short, heroin had become part of the social landscape, a fact of life to which young men, of whatever psychological makeup, almost inevitably became exposed; and that helped explain why many young black heroin users showed no signs of psychological illness.

But what accounted for the disproportionate prevalence of heroin in the black neighborhoods, even compared to other deprived neighborhoods in the city? Chein and his coworkers suggested that it was the "*cumulative* impact of many unwholesome conditions," which produced what they called a "surplus of vulnerability" over and above the effects of the individual problems these neighborhoods faced. "Economic squalor" dominated the causal chain that led to drug use, but much more was involved.

Locked into neighborhoods where most people could expect only low-level jobs and moderate to severe poverty, stripped of the protective values and institutions that had sustained earlier generations in their rural origins, increasingly buffeted by family disruption, and demoralized by a world-view that emphasized the bleak and predatory character of social life, the youth of the Harlems and Fort Greenes were increasingly vulnerable to the lures of narcotics, the more so the longer they had been enmeshed in the culture and economy of New York City. Chein summed up the impact of these conditions on the urban young this way:

> There are segments of communities in which there is a relative breakdown in the fabric of human relationships. The individual has no roots in a permanent community. . . . He experiences himself as standing essentially alone against the rest of the world. The fellow human beings with whom he comes into contact are compelled by force of circumstances, if not by personal predilection, to scrabble around, each for his own needs—and he does not have the security of knowing that, should he need their support, he can rely upon them for this. He shares in the common dreams of a good life . . . but the bleak circumstances of his situation give him no realistic expectations of ever being able to achieve it, and he is confronted by an "endlessness of days." There does not appear to be any real point in working toward a brighter future, only in seizing upon the pleasures of the moment.

For urban youth living under those conditions, narcotics

> offer a quick and royal route to meeting the challenge of living. Heroin and its related subculture gives them a sense of well-being and of social acceptability and participation. If the price is a terrible one to pay . . . the pseudo-rewards, especially in the "honeymoon stage," are far more glittering than anything else their environment offers them.

These findings shaped the NYU researchers' views on what should be *done* about adolescent addiction. In particular, the fact that heroin addiction had clear, if complex, *social* roots led them to challenge the conventional view that addiction was a disease that could be cured through solely medical means, especially through what was at the time the most common practice—voluntary or forced hospitalization. "Is addiction a virulently contagious disease? All of the evidence . . . indicates that it is not. The spread of drug use is associated with human misery, not with any intrinsic contagiousness." They did believe that the punitive attitude toward the addict that emphasized arrest and imprisonment should be replaced by a more therapeutic and preventive one, but *not* one based on a simple medical model of addiction. Instead they proposed shifting the emphasis from large hospitals and compulsory treatment to clinics which would offer the young addict a "wide variety of services"—not only psychotherapy, where appropriate, but also family casework, vocational training, and a "sheltered workshop" for those who could not otherwise hold jobs.

Chein and his colleagues were especially critical of the tendency, gaining momentum in the 1950s, toward using the medical model of addiction to justify compulsory hospitalization, which they condemned as nothing more than "a device to get addicts out of the open society." "The simple fact of the matter" was that no successful treatment could be accomplished by force: "All that force can accomplish is to heighten the dependency and alienation of the patient." An addict while *in* the hospital might seem well-adjusted, but "he will shortly return to narcotics when he returns to his normal environment. He will in no sense have been cured."

Beyond the critique of forced therapy lay a deeper skepticism about the idea that the treatment of individual addicts could do much toward "meeting the manifold social and personal problems that make so many individuals vulnerable to drug use and addiction." What was needed was a "multipronged program" that went well beyond the "direct, manifest problems of addiction" to deal with those underlying problems. Chein and his coworkers provided no detailed blueprint of the program they had in mind, but they had a clear idea of its "most general objectives":

> to provide convincing evidence to the individual that he does not stand alone and that his fate does, in fact, matter to society and to provide him, in the fullest possible measure, with the competencies and aspirations most fitting to a human being.

Drug use, Chein wrote, was "one symptom among many" of the deeper economic deprivation and cultural and familial disintegration affecting urban youth. The overarching aim, therefore, was not so much the narrow one of preventing that symptom—drug use—itself, but the broader one of helping "personally damaged and environmentally deprived youths to grow up into healthy adults." Chein and his group acknowledged that their view might seem "visionary," but they argued that nothing less than visionary measures would address the roots of addiction. And if we were unable or unwilling to do anything about the "misery" that underlay urban drug addiction, we had no moral ground on which to justify taking away drugs from the poor who, in the absence of that effort, would be "entitled to their drug-induced nirvanas." "The price of moral indignation," they concluded, "is civic responsibility."

This study sketched out in remarkable detail a portrait of inner-city drug abuse that, as we shall see, in many respects holds true to this day. It firmly located the hard-drug problem in the complex deprivations of inner-city life—not only economic "squalor" but also cultural and familial disruption and the corrosive effects of American urban poverty on values and beliefs—the spread of a culture mandating a bitter scramble of all against all. And it also sketched out some of the elements of a strategy against addiction that flowed compellingly from the logic of their analysis of its causes. The fundamental point was starkly clear. If the deeper issue was not so much addiction itself but the "human misery" that bred it, then the practical problem was "not at all the problem of getting people to stay away from narcotic drugs. It is the problem of getting at the sources of such misery." And "unless and until we have got to work with a will" to deal with those sources of misery, "we will not have begun to touch on the real problem of narcotics addiction."

I I

Similar conclusions emerged from another influential study of youth drug abuse in the fifties, under the auspices of the Illinois Institute for Juvenile Research and the Chicago Area Project, a community-action program launched in the 1920s to mobilize local neighborhoods against juvenile delinquency.

As in New York, the Chicago researchers found the heaviest heroin use concentrated in a relative handful of the city's most economically deprived neighborhoods. Some of those communities had been studied for decades by researchers charting the roots of juvenile delinquency in Chicago, and it was not surprising that the neighborhoods with traditionally high rates of delinquency were also those with the highest concentration of heroin addiction—along with a host of other problems: "The highest concentrations of drug users," the researchers discovered, were found in "the communities displaying the highest rates of juvenile court delinquents, of Boys' Court cases, of tuberculosis, and of infant mortality"—which were also "the communities of lowest income in the city."

As in Chein's analysis, this hugely unbalanced distribution of heroin use suggested that there was something about the social environment of these neighborhoods that fostered addiction. The spread of heroin after World War II didn't strike these neighborhoods out of the blue: it "made its inroads within a distinctive and uniquely vulnerable social milieu"—among adolescents in the most disadvantaged areas of the city who were *already* prone to drug abuse. Heroin was only the latest and most spectacular example of the "frenetic search of the streetcorner boy for newer, stranger, and more status-giving intoxicants."

The lure of heroin in particular within this setting—especially its appeal to the young, black, and poor—was most thoughtfully explored in a classic analysis by the sociologist Harold Finestone. Seeking to explain why drug use "as a social problem" in Chicago "can be pinpointed with great accuracy as having its incidence preponderantly among the young male colored persons in a comparatively few local community areas," Finestone interviewed more than fifty heroin-using black men in their late teens and early twenties from the Chicago neighborhoods where heroin was most concentrated.

Finestone suggested that an important clue to the appeal of heroin to black youth in the cities was that the young black heroin user did not, in the real world, fit the conventional image of the drug addict as "a pitiful figure, a trapped unfortunate." Though there was a grain of truth in that image, that was not at all how the young addict—the "cat"—regarded himself or presented himself to others. On the contrary, Finestone discovered, "the cat experiences and manifests a certain zest in his mode of life which is far from self-pity." The heart of the cat's identity, his main purpose in life, was the search for "kicks"—especially, but not exclusively, the kick resulting from drug use. That search for kicks was a collective pursuit, not a solitary one; the cat was involved with others—a "society of cats"—which he regarded as an elite group, not a collection of losers. That sense of superiority accounted for a striking paradox in the persona of the addict: though the cat came from "the drabbest, most overcrowded, and physically deteriorated sections of the city," he nevertheless "discussed his pattern of living as though it were a consciously cultivated work of art." The cat took pride in not having to work for a living and instead developing a successful "hustle," a "nonviolent means of 'making some bread' which does not require work." For the cat, to be able to manipulate and outwit others, to "get what he wanted through persuasion and ingratiation," was to be "cool," and therefore vastly superior to the square who "toils for regular wages and who takes orders from his superiors without complaint." The "kick" of drug use—which Finestone noted could be supplied by marijuana or alcohol as well as heroin—and the ritual and intrigue connected with the drug culture, sharply distinguished the cat's existence from the "humdrum routine of daily life."

The use of heroin to achieve a sense of identity and superiority, Finestone pointed out, was not simply a response of individual black youth, but a genuine "social movement" among a substantial segment of the young black population. But why this kind of movement rather than something else, and why heroin in particular? What was it about the social situation of young black men in impoverished neighborhoods that led specifically to the collective rejection of conventional work and the celebration of a way of life based on the search for kicks?

Finestone's answer, like Chein's, was complex. At the root of youthful heroin addiction were poverty and racial discrimination, but they didn't, by themselves, explain the unique features of the cat culture. The roots of that culture were more specific. Segregation and discrimination, Finestone argued, had "withheld from individuals of the colored population the opportunity to achieve or to identify with status positions in the larger society." In a crucial sense, young black men in the postwar cities were caught half in and half out of the broader American culture and society around them. Following an analysis laid out earlier in Gunnar Myrdal's *American Dilemma*, Finestone argued that as blacks had moved into the cities in increasing numbers, they had gained an "increasing abstract knowledge of the world outside—of its opportunities, its rewards"—but were simultaneously blocked by still-powerful traditions of discrimination from fully obtaining them. The resulting bind placed great pressures on the sense of identity and self-esteem of the black adolescent:

> The emergence of the self-conception of the cat is an attempt to deal with the problems of status and identity in a situation where participation in the life of the broader community is denied, but where the colored adolescent is becoming increasingly sensitive to the values, the goals, and the notions of success which obtain in the dominant social order.

Caught in this dilemma—an "all too acute awareness of the values of the broader social order" coupled with powerful barriers to full participation in it—the black youth responded by turning the broader society's values upside down. His emphasis on the "kick"—on what was really a form of *play* deliberately opposed to work—was a way of challenging, and indeed reversing, the conventional value placed on work, and as such was tailor-made for young people who could not realistically expect to achieve status and identity through the normal labor market. The "status struggle," Finestone argued, consumed young black men as much as anyone else in America, but given their limited prospects it turned in on itself and assumed distorted, even inverted forms: "Exclusion from the 'serious' concerns of the broader community will result in such adaptations manifesting a strong element of play."

But this didn't wholly explain the sudden spread of heroin abuse, specifically, as the preferred solution to the dilemma of black youth poised partly in and partly out of the broader society. There were other possible responses; in particular, young men caught in this situation might try to *change* the system that blocked and frustrated them, rather than, in effect, accommodating themselves to that system by creating a sub-culture that celebrated the symptoms of their exclusion. Fine-stone suggested that the emergence of the "cat" response and

the simultaneous *absence* of "a social movement with the objective of changing the social order" was linked to both the
"tradition of accommodation to a subordinate status on the
part of the Negro" (he was writing before the full bloom of
the civil-rights movement) and the generally conservative social
climate in the years just after World War II. The long tradition
of living with racial subordination led disenfranchised and
frustrated black youth to make an "indirect" assault on the
larger society, rather than a direct one; the subculture of drug
use, with its deliberate inversion of the dominant values, offered
a sense of challenge and identity without running the risks that
would be entailed by directly confronting the class and racial
order of postwar America. (In that sense, the drug culture
could be regarded as an *alternative* to an authentic movement
for social change—an idea that, as we shall see, was to appear
more than once in the study of drug use in the ghetto.)

The deepest implication of Finestone's analysis was, like
Chein's, that heroin use was best understood as a *social* problem,
rather than a medical or psychiatric one. The drug epidemic
among urban adolescents had less to do with the effects of
heroin on the body—its pharmacological impact—than with
the social and social-psychological benefits of involvement in
an essentially oppositional drug culture. That culture had
emerged because it met certain basic needs—needs that were
themselves quite normal and common to all adolescents everywhere, but were difficult or impossible to fulfill normally, given
the social situation of urban black youth in postwar America.

Among other things, this view had important implications
for strategies to get black youth off heroin. One was that as
long as heroin helped black youth sustain a positive identity
and a sense of superiority in a world that denied them, they
would be unlikely to define its use as a *problem*—quite the
contrary—and they would accordingly feel little motivation to
seek help for it. Finestone recognized that the black adolescent's
experience with heroin was not all positive, especially after an
initial "honeymoon phase," as the legal, financial, and physical

consequences of heroin addiction began to outweigh the benefits. But even then, the cat was likely to be at best ambivalent about "seeking a cure for his addiction" because to do so would be to acknowledge, to himself and to the world, that he was not "cool" at all, but only a "junkie": to admit that the whole system of countervalues he had constructed against the realities of social exclusion was "largely a pose, a form of fantasy with little basis in fact." To acknowledge that he had a drug problem and needed help, in short, might bring down the cat's entire facade, forcing him to face the realization that he had adopted a life centered on kicks and play because he could never succeed at real work.

At the same time, the view of the "cat" as a social type rooted in very specific social dilemmas common to youth in very specific neighborhoods threw doubt on the dominant view of the addict as a sick person for whose illness some form of quasi-medical treatment was the most rational response. Where Isidor Chein had portrayed the young heroin addict as a mix of both psychological and environmental pathologies, Finestone took the social analysis a step further, pointing out that the concentration of addiction in a few disadvantaged neighborhoods wasn't matched by a corresponding concentration of individual personality defects. Instead, what shaped the distribution of heroin use was the "total social milieu" with which the young addict had to cope. Indeed, according to Finestone, both the "correctional" and the "medical" approaches to addiction—the attempt to eradicate it either by punishing or by treating the individual user—were fundamentally flawed because "they have both assumed a conception of addiction which attributes its etiology almost solely to factors either inherent within or expressive of the individual's makeup or problems." Only by recognizing that mass heroin use was "an aspect of a special type of community setting"—one with "a particularly destructive impact on its young persons"—would we make any headway against it.

I I I

But, beyond pointing to the need for a view of heroin addiction in the cities that would emphasize its social roots, Finestone had little to say about what, exactly, would be the strategic implications of that view. A strong sense of the limits of both criminal justice and individual "treatment" as responses to the youthful heroin problem suffused Finestone's work and the larger Chicago research of which it was a part, but what the focus on the "total social milieu" would mean more concretely for a strategy against heroin remained mostly unexplored. Those implications were developed further in the next several years, especially by a number of social scientists and activists whose work was influential in shaping the early stages of the War on Poverty in the 1960s. The broad view of heroin abuse as a reflection of human misery and racial exclusion was elaborated into a conception of drug abuse as one expression among many of the pathology of the urban slum, a symptom specifically of blocked opportunities for disadvantaged youth and one that called for a challenge to the larger forces that had made the slums what they were.

In a highly influential book, *Delinquency and Opportunity*, published in the late 1950s, the sociologists Richard Cloward and Lloyd Ohlin of the Columbia University School of Social Work built on Finestone's analysis of the roots of heroin addiction and took it several steps further. Their analysis of drug use among lower-class youth was only one facet of a more general theory of the roots of juvenile delinquency in the affluent society of postwar America. Drug use was one of several possible responses to the plight of the lower-class urban young in a generally wealthy country, which Cloward and Ohlin, like Finestone, located in the particular dilemma of being all too aware of the goals and standards of success dominant in the larger society but being blocked from achieving them—at least through "legitimate" means. In the face of that structural dilemma, they argued, lower-class adolescents had constructed three distinct kinds of responses—three distinct "subcultures"—which tended to emerge in distinct kinds of deprived urban communities. Not all slums were alike, and different kinds bred different reactions among lower-class youth. Adolescent drug abusers fell into what Cloward and Ohlin called a "retreatist" subculture, in which the dilemma of exclusion from the realistic possibility of achieving success as conventionally defined was solved by rejecting the value of success altogether and retreating into a world where striving and getting ahead were replaced by a "cool" emphasis on kicks and visceral experience. Finestone's depiction of the "cat" culture provided the basis for their view of the retreatist subculture, but Cloward and Ohlin also raised a further question: why were *some* adolescent subcultures in the slums organized around "kicks," while others were centered on very different pursuits? They singled out two other possible subcultural responses available to lower-class urban youth—one based on relatively organized criminal enterprises (the "criminal" subculture) and another on gang fighting (the "conflict" subculture), which emphasized the virtues of toughness and the capacity for violence.

Cloward and Ohlin argued that these differences in response to blocked aspirations reflected basic differences in the social organization of lower-class communities. The criminal subculture was likely to emerge in the traditional slum areas that had nurtured successive waves of white ethnic groups moving up the social ladder—the breeding grounds of Italian- and Irish-American organized crime. In those communities, an established criminal structure—what Cloward and Ohlin called an "illegitimate opportunity structure"—existed alongside the legitimate world of work, within which the enterprising slum youth, denied realistic chances to compete in the legitimate opportunity structure, could rise to a certain level of prestige and respect. But that kind of illegitimate opportunity depended, somewhat paradoxically, on the existence of a com-

munity stable enough to support an enduring criminal tradition
and pass it on across the generations. In the more disorganized
slum communities (often black or Hispanic) that had emerged
after the war in many cities, no such tradition existed. Lower-
class youth blocked from legitimate success therefore had no
established illegitimate ladder to climb, and were forced to
strive for status and esteem in other ways.

One way was through becoming skilled at physical violence,
and for Cloward and Ohlin this helped explain the emergence
of volatile fighting gangs in New York and other cities amid
the general affluence of postwar America. Even if a boy couldn't
make it in the schools and the legitimate labor market, *and* no
organized criminal subculture offered an alternative avenue of
success, he could still gain status and influence among his peers
within a hierarchy of prestige based on the skills of urban
combat—by having "heart," by establishing a "rep."

But not all lower-class slum boys had even that alternative;
physical bravado and the ability to fight were *also* skills, albeit
illicit ones. For those who couldn't make it in the hierarchy of
violence either, there had to be another kind of response to
the dilemma of sharply restricted opportunities in a society
that extolled success. That response, for Cloward and Ohlin,
was "retreatism," and particularly retreat into the world of
drug use. Young drug users in the subculture of retreatism
were, in this sense, "double failures"—failures in both the
legitimate world of schooling and work and the illegitimate
worlds of criminality and street-gang violence.

What this implied for action against inner-city drug addiction
(and other forms of subcultural delinquency) was more clearly
drawn out by Cloward and Ohlin than by Finestone; indeed,
their strategic argument was an important influence on the
federal social policy of the 1960s. The guiding theme was that
delinquency (including its retreatist, drug-abusing form) "is
not, in the final analysis, a property of individuals or even
subcultures; it is a property of the social systems in which these
individuals and groups are enmeshed." Cloward and Ohlin

were accordingly critical of conventional social-service approaches to the problems of lower-class youth, because they failed to address the underlying causes. Simply "extending services" to individual delinquents or groups of delinquent youth "cannot prevent the rise of delinquency among others"; the target for prevention had to be the "social setting" itself.

More specifically, dealing with delinquency in an enduring way called for nothing less than the "reorganization of slum communities." That task was now especially urgent, because lower-class neighborhoods in urban America were undergoing profound changes for the worse: several forces were simultaneously operating to erode what little social cohesion slum neighborhoods still possessed and to foster precisely the kind of deeper disorganization that, from their analysis, could be expected to generate more violence and more retreatist delinquency. The massive slum-clearance programs of the fifties, for example, had destroyed the cohesion of many traditional poor neighborhoods without creating new social bonds in its place; the new blocks of public-housing projects that were rapidly replacing older neighborhoods were typically nothing more than assemblages of strangers without common ties. The breakup of the traditional slums meant, among other things, that their older political organizations, which had provided some channels for legitimate achievement, would be likely to weaken in the future, as would the established criminal organizations. The young urban poor would thus be increasingly "deprived of both conventional and criminal opportunity." Such communities, moreover, increasingly fragmented and isolated, would be less able to sustain strong social controls over their young. The likely result would be an increase in both violence and the subculture of drug use—barring a serious effort to rebuild functioning institutions in lower-class urban communities. "Slum neighborhoods," Cloward and Ohlin warned at the start of the 1960s, "appear to us to be undergoing progressive disintegration. The old structures, which provided social control and avenues of social ascent, are breaking down."

The conclusion was clear and urgent: "Legitimate but functional substitutes for these traditional structures must be developed if we are to stem the trend toward violence and retreatism among adolescents in urban slums."

The fact that youthful drug addiction was a reflection not only of blocked opportunities for individual lower-class youth, but of the deterioration of the social structure of poor communities as a whole, then, led logically to a strategy that took the community as a whole as the problem, not the individual drug abuser or delinquent, and posited the comprehensive rebuilding of the community's basic institutions as the only enduring solution. A similar theme was developed in a study of the problems of youth in central Harlem in the mid-sixties, under the auspices of a community-based organization, Haryou-ACT, and directed by the noted social psychologist Kenneth B. Clark.

Writing several years farther down the road, these researchers painted a picture of the condition of ghetto youth that was even bleaker than those of Chein, Finestone, or Cloward and Ohlin. They described a "massive deterioration of the fabric of society and its institutions" in Harlem by the middle of the decade—a deterioration reflected in a wide range of pathologies, of which addiction was only one, but an increasingly pervasive one. Official statistics showed a rate of "habitual narcotics use" in central Harlem eight times that of New York City as a whole, heavily concentrated among youth and young adult men.

For the Haryou researchers, the heart of the pathology of the ghetto was the declining structure of what Cloward and Ohlin had called "legitimate opportunities"—especially the constricting opportunities for anything other than menial work. Clark stressed that the problem for Harlem's young men was not primarily the sheer lack of any jobs at all, but the prospect of nothing better than low-wage, low-status labor: "The roots of the multiple pathology of the dark ghetto," he wrote, "do not lie primarily in unemployment." Indeed, "if all of its residents were employed it would not materially alter the pathology of the community." More important than merely having some sort of job, Clark argued, "is the *kind* of job it is."

Almost two out of three workers in central Harlem, according to the Haryou report, were employed as semiskilled "operatives," service workers, or unskilled laborers, twice the city's overall proportion; a full quarter of central Harlem women in the labor force were private household servants. "The occupational roots of the pathology of the community lie mainly in the menial, low-paying, and unrewarding nature of the jobs held by most of the adults."

Interviews with Harlem street addicts graphically illustrated the direct connection between the lure of using—and selling —drugs and the entrapment of the majority of young blacks in the menial labor market through poor education and unyielding discrimination.

"I have nothing to shoot at. All I have to look forward to is a thrill, and they run me up on the roof to get that. . . . All I can look forward to is what I can get out of this bag, and that's nothing, really."

"You have to survive. . . . If you don't have the proper education that you should have, and you go downtown and work, they don't pay you any money worthwhile. You can work all your life and never have anything, and you will always be in debt. So you take to the streets, you understand? You take to the streets and try to make it in the street. . . . Being out in the street takes your mind off all these problems. You have no time to think about things, because you're trying to make some money. . . . I've been trying to make it so hard and trying to keep a piece of money. I'm trying not to work like a dog to get it, and being treated any sort of way to get it."

The Haryou researchers quoted a young dealer who expressed the same motives from the seller's point of view:

"I make $40 or $50 a day selling marijuana. You want me to go down to the garment district and push one of those trucks through the street and at the end of the week take home $40 or $50 if I'm lucky? Come off it. They don't have animals doing what you want me to do. There would be some society to protect animals if anybody had them pushing those damn trucks around."

For the Haryou researchers, as for Finestone or Cloward and Ohlin, drug use in the ghetto was not simply an *individual* response to blasted lives and restricted opportunities, but a collective one—a version of what Clark called a "strategy of despair," one strategy among many that young people in the ghetto might adopt to deal with the realities of ghetto life. As in Finestone's suggestion that the heroin culture might be a kind of *alternative* to a movement among urban blacks to change the conditions that shaped their lives, the implication in Clark's analysis was that drugs competed with other possible responses to the crisis of the ghetto—the "strategy of accommodation" practiced by the black middle class for generations, for example, or the "strategy of direct encounter" offered by the newer civil-rights groups.

One implication of this view of drug abuse as a collective strategy in response to demeaning and alienating conditions was that, as Clark wrote, "the possibility of an effective solution through the treatment of adolescent addicts seems remote." Clark quoted a Harlem minister closely involved with addicted youth: "The young boys and girls who use heroin love it, and they don't want, really, to give it up." Too narrow a focus on the drug problem itself would doom antidrug strategies to failure; eliminating drug abuse (or delinquency) in the ghetto had to involve the broader goal of "building a better life."

And that goal, for the Haryou researchers, was becoming

more and more urgent as the sixties wore on. Like Cloward and Ohlin, they believed that the social and economic forces undermining the possibility of a "better life" were intensifying. With what turned out to be considerable prescience, the Haryou report warned that Harlem's "multiple pathology" might well deepen because even the menial jobs then available to its youth were likely to be less available in the future. They cited estimates from the New York City Department of Labor that the city would lose as many as 80,000 unskilled and semiskilled jobs during the sixties; and without systematic, concerted efforts to train the men of the city's ghettos for the new jobs that would (hopefully) replace them, their future would be even more bleak.

I V

The devastating effect of the narrow—and by the mid-1960s, already shrinking—opportunities for rewarding or challenging work for the young men and women of the inner cities was revealed even more starkly in several late-1960s studies of urban drug abuse, which confirmed that in the face of rapidly diminishing opportunities and community disintegration, drugs and drug dealing were increasingly becoming an *alternative* to work—a source not only of income, but also of status, identity, and challenge.

To many of the postwar observers of the inner-city drug culture, addiction was a compound of social pathology and personal inadequacy. For Chein, it was the most psychologically vulnerable youth within a generally vulnerable community who were most at risk of becoming addicted; for Cloward and Ohlin, the "retreatist" drug user was categorized as a "double failure." The work of several urban ethnographers in the late 1960s, when heroin had become still more deeply entrenched in some parts of the cities, suggested a somewhat different, and in some ways even more disturbing, picture. Looking directly at the way addicts and dealers operated "on the street," in their natural habitat, these observers came to the troubling conclusion that where young people were denied legitimate channels for exercising their natural talents and energies, it was typically the *most* competent and energetic youth who (at least at first) became involved with heroin and other hard drugs, not the most inadequate or psychologically crippled. That discovery pushed the idea that the treatment of individual addicts was the most appropriate response to the inner-city drug problem even farther into the background. But the strategic implications were very similar to those of writers like Cloward and Ohlin. If the root of the problem was that young inner-city men were turning to heroin to satisfy deep needs for challenge, esteem, and a sense of purpose, then the appeal of narcotics could be reduced by providing broader opportunities to meet those quite ordinary needs in legitimate ways. If anything, these studies suggested a more optimistic view of the possibilities; if there was nothing wrong with drug users except the absence of normal opportunities, not much other than political inertia stood in the way of a real attack on the urban drug problem.

The most influential of these studies was the work of two anthropologists, Edward Preble and John Casey, who observed and interviewed heroin users—mainly black and Puerto Rican, but some Italian, Irish, and Jewish—in several poor New York City neighborhoods during the 1960s. Preble and Casey titled their resulting seminal article "Taking Care of Business: The Heroin User's Life on the Street." The title underscored their central argument: heroin addiction in poor neighborhoods was itself a kind of job—under the circumstances, the most challenging and exciting job available to inner-city youth.

Conventional descriptions of heroin addicts, Preble and Casey argued, stressed the "passive, dependent, withdrawn, generally inadequate features of their personality structure and social adjustment." But actual observation of addicts at "work" in the real world yielded strikingly different conclusions. The addicts' behavior was "anything but an escape from life":

They are actively engaged in meaningful activities and relationships seven days a week. The brief moments of euphoria after each administration of a small amount of heroin constitute a small fraction of their daily lives. The rest of the time they are aggressively pursuing a career that is exacting, challenging, adventurous, and rewarding.

The heroin user, indeed, had to be "alert, flexible, and resourceful" to succeed in the difficult business of being an addict. Preble and Casey even argued that you could tell the heroin users in a slum neighborhood by the way they walked: the user "walks with a fast, purposeful stride, as if he is late for an important appointment—indeed, he is." For the addict wasn't spending his time simply nodding out in a doorway; he had urgent tasks to attend to. He was "hustling"—stealing and robbing in order to support his illegal drug habit, selling stolen goods, looking for dealers to supply his drugs, ducking the police, dealing with people who had cheated him, and so on. In the addicts' own street language, the heroin user in his normal daily round was "taking care of business."

Preble and Casey insisted that heroin users were more like than unlike "legitimate" businessmen in pursuing their "careers":

> The heroin user is, in a way, like the compulsively hard-working business executive whose ostensible goal is the acquisition of money, but whose real satisfaction is in meeting the inordinate challenge he creates for himself.

As one of their addict informants put it, "When I'm home with the bag safely in my pocket, and I haven't been caught stealing all day, and I didn't get beat [cheated] and the cops didn't get me—I feel like a working man coming home: he's worked hard, but he knows he done something"—even though, he added, "I know it's not true."

Preble and Casey acknowledged that this description probably only applied to the lower-class heroin user; among the much smaller population of middle- and upper-class addicts, heroin use might have different motivations and meanings. But for the mass of lower-class addicts, "the quest for heroin is the quest for a meaningful life." They emphasized the key point already stressed by earlier observers like Finestone: the "meaning" sought by the addict was primarily social and cultural, not pharmacological—it "does not lie, primarily, in the effects of the drug on their minds and bodies; it lies in the gratification of accomplishing a series of challenging, exciting tasks, every day of the week." The heroin addict was addicted less to the drug itself than to the "entire career of a heroin user." They pointed out that the wave of heroin use among young people on the streets of New York in the early fifties was not initiated by the "weak, withdrawn, unadaptive street boy" but by the "tough, sophisticated, and respected" street-gang leaders. Heroin had indeed decimated the old fighting gangs in New York's slums, as the toughest gang leaders had shifted from fighting to heroin use, and the addict enjoying his "high" accordingly became the "new hero model" for lower-class youth. By the sixties, it was the addict who was resourceful and capable of "taking care of business"—successfully supporting himself and his habit through serious theft or robbery—who won high status in his community as a "real hustling dope fiend." Those less capable were denigrated as "non-hustling dope fiends," addicts who had to resort to begging or petty stealing to maintain even a minimal habit.

Preble and Casey graphically described the social conditions that drove so many young men to find meaning and challenge in the pseudo-work of heroin addiction. In the neighborhoods they studied, welfare dependency was four times the city's overall rate, and unemployment twice the city's rate; the average resident had not gone past the eighth grade. And beyond these bare statistics was the deeper and more general "desperation and hopelessness of life in the slums of New York."

In one short block where one of the authors worked, there was an average of one violent death a month over a period of three years—by fire, accident, homicide, and suicide. In Puerto Rican neighborhoods, sidewalk *recordatorios* (temporary shrines at the scenes of tragic deaths) are a regular feature.

But most crucial was the absence of alternative ways of achieving a sense of challenge and competence:

> Given the social conditions of the slums and their effects on family and individual development, the odds are strongly against the development of a legitimate, non-deviant career that is challenging and rewarding. The most common legitimate career is a menial job, with no future except in the periodic, statutory raises in the minimum wage level. If anyone can be called passive in the slums, it is not the heroin user, but the one who submits to and accepts these conditions.

Heroin was thus a way of beating the monotony of slum existence and the bleakness of a future constrained by menial work; it was also, as Preble and Casey put it, a way to get "revenge" on society for the "injustices and deprivations" the user had experienced. The sense of revenge, the thrill and challenge of "outslicking" the police and other conventional authorities, was part of the appeal of heroin use, and this had troubling implications for drug treatment. One of Preble and Casey's informants, for example, told them that programs to provide heroin to addicts legally would take the "fun" out of heroin use, because the thrill of the drug revolved precisely around the need to outsmart and outmaneuver the authorities. "Drugs," as one informant put it, "is a hell of a game."

———

The criminologist Alan Sutter drew a similar picture in a study
of street drug users on the West Coast. Sutter argued that it
was impossible to understand opiate use in the United States
without understanding the "romantic pull of the hustling world,
the colorful life of 'successful' hustlers, the sportlike challenge
of the hustling games." Even more than Preble and Casey,
Sutter argued against the view of the addict as retreatist, double
failure, or passive neurotic. Drugs were the center of a complex
and, in its own terms, rich existence centered on the hustle
and explicitly counterposed to the much-despised way of life
of ordinary poor people.

In street observations of hustlers in the San Francisco Bay
Area, Sutter described a hierarchical and invidious world in
which the highest status went to those with the most lucrative
hustles and the *least* visible sources of regular income. The
hustler considered that "any man who works laboriously for a
regular salary is a fool." In the inverted world of the inner-
city drug user, the *most* esteem went to the hustler who could
credibly claim the biggest dope habit—the "righteous dope
fiend"—because "since heroin is the most expensive drug on
the illegal market, the size of a person's habit indicates his
money-making power and his versatility as a hustler." By
contrast, "other types of drug users must be content with a less
expensive chemical and a lower-class existence." Echoing Preble
and Casey's view of the addict as businessman, Sutter argued
that moving, in the hustling world, from being only a low-level
"player" to the higher plane of the successful street hustler
meant shifting from a "preoccupation with the immediate
present" to "serious business," and developing one's budding
hustling skills into the "polished works of a craftsman."

The prestige conferred by using "harder" drugs helped
explain the otherwise perplexing fact that new volunteers were
constantly being recruited into the drug culture of the cities
despite the obvious adverse long-term consequences of drug
abuse. The sociologist Harvey Feldman, observing lower-class
(in this case, Italian-American) heroin users on New York's

Lower East Side, argued that it was precisely the capacity of heroin to bring down even the toughest street youth that led, paradoxically, to its persistent attraction for the inner-city young. They looked up to the kind of role model Feldman called the "stand-up cat," who was tough enough to take on the most dangerous situations and, more than other young men, willing to "challenge the bleak fate of being poor" through bravado and daring. It was the "stand-up cat" who had the nerve to experiment with new, hard drugs in the first place, Feldman argued, and it was the frantic desire of other adolescents to keep up with these leaders and demonstrate their *own* toughness that accounted for the amazing speed with which heroin spread through poor communities once it had developed a beachhead among the slum elite.

Once the first wave of users had been addicted for some months, other local youth could see in them at first hand most of the frightening consequences of addiction—sickness, arrest and jail, the pains of withdrawal, the possibility of death by overdose. "Still, in the face of evidence, new and eager recruits experiment." Why? Because by taking on a drug so dangerous that it had visibly undone the hardest and most esteemed "stand-up cats" in the neighborhood, new users would themselves acquire extraordinary status among their neighborhood peers. "Since he has seen previous stand-up cats buckle to the strength of heroin, the lure it holds as a route to prestige and status is enhanced." Taking up heroin, Feldman concluded, was "one route to becoming 'somebody' in the eyes of the important people who comprise the slum social network."

Heroin, in other words, was becoming entrenched not in *spite* of its risks but *because* of them. Young people faced with shrinking opportunities to feel capable, strong, or esteemed in other ways were carving out new value systems of their own which allowed them to construct an identity and to achieve a modicum of status around the use of hard drugs. This phenomenon also helped explain why the pattern of hard-drug use was typically very different among *less* deprived youth. By the mid-1950s, heroin could be found not only in the ghettos of Harlem or the South Side of Chicago, but in many white working-class neighborhoods as well. But in those neighbor- hoods, its use was neither as entrenched nor as widespread, and it often declined during the fifties and sixties just as it was spreading and deepening in the ghettos and barrios.

In a study of a working-class white neighborhood in Queens, for example, Julius Klein and Derek Phillips of New York University found that heroin use had been surprisingly prev- alent among its mostly Southern- and Central European street- gang youth in the fifties. They estimated that two-thirds of the members of one white ethnic street gang had been heroin users in the fifties and, as in Harlem, the "glamorous" image they presented had pulled many younger kids into drugs. But by the late fifties, as younger gang members began to see the adverse consequences of heroin use up close—jail, ostracism, hepatitis—they began to use heroin more sparingly, increas- ingly replacing it with softer drugs, especially marijuana, wine, and amphetamine pills. At the same time, the community as a whole began to look more and more unfavorably on hard-drug use and to put more resources into social agencies to deal with it. By the mid-1960s, only 7 percent of the street-gang youth were using heroin.

Why was this pattern so different from what happened in the ghettos? Klein and Phillips argued that the "Eastville" community, a "comparatively more stable and less disorganized working-class and lower-middle-class area," offered both more community resources and more realistic opportunities than the Harlem of, say, Clark's study; and that accounted for the relative ease with which most (though not all) white working- class youth moved voluntarily from harder to softer drugs. Hard drugs did not disappear altogether among Eastville's youth, and the softer drugs remained widespread. But few still used heroin, and its attractiveness compared to more benign drugs had plummeted.

V

By the late sixties, then, a rough consensus had emerged among serious observers on the social roots of the urban drug problem and their implications for social action to combat drug abuse. There were disagreements among them, most notably between observers like Preble and Casey or Sutter who emphasized the businesslike or even romantic character of the life of the addict, and those, like Finestone, Cloward and Ohlin, and Chein, who underscored the element of fantasy and failure in the user's culture and career. But there were far greater areas of agreement than disagreement.

The overarching one was the consistent view of addiction—in its mass, inner-city manifestation, if not necessarily its less common appearance in the suburbs or among the middle class—as a *social* issue first and foremost, and only secondarily as a problem that could be adequately explained by individual psychology or by the simple physical or pharmacological appeals of hard drugs. Drug use—especially though not exclusively heroin use—was a collective response of a broad segment of the disadvantaged urban young to specific social conditions in postwar America. Those conditions were multilayered and complex. It was not only poverty and unemployment that formed the social context of drug abuse, but a particularly devastating syndrome that included relative poverty in a surrounding society and culture of affluence and mass consumption and a single-minded emphasis on material success; the bleakness of confinement in menial and futureless occupations; and the resulting absence of legitimate avenues for gaining either an adequate income (as the larger society defined it), or the less tangible but equally fundamental requirements of a sense of challenge, place, and purpose, a stable and respected identity. Finally, there was the loosening of traditional controls and weakening of traditional values that seemed to result from systematic exposure to the urban culture of consumption and from the grinding effects of long-term poverty, restricted opportunities, and economic struggle on the supportive and socializing capacity of families and entire communities.

For young people, especially, growing up in these communities, drug use performed a variety of functions which, most observers agreed, reflected ordinary human—and specifically adolescent—needs, but ones which were difficult to fulfill in ordinary ways in these distinctly abnormal circumstances. There were differences of emphasis and specifics, but the serious observers of heroin addiction generally agreed that much more important than the physiological effects of the drug were its uses in helping to build an identity, buttress social status and the esteem of peers, and provide alternative and compelling sources of challenge and purposeful activity for people who were deprived of them through normal channels. In the topsy-turvy world of the shattered communities of the inner city, the very dangers and adversities associated with hard-drug use were transformed into appeals. It was precisely the illegality of heroin use, and the very real danger of arrest and jail, that helped provide the intrigue and "elite-group" identity that observers like Finestone found to be central to the "cat" culture: precisely the high risk of illness, pain, and abject enslavement to addiction that drew the "stand-up cat" to test his mettle against the toughest of drugs.

Finally, by the middle of the 1960s, there was widespread agreement that in the absence of concerted social action to address the roots of addiction, the problem, like the related ones of delinquency and street crime, would almost certainly worsen in the Harlems and Bronzevilles of the United States, because all of the forces that had brought it into being were likely to intensify in the coming years. Harold Finestone, in the mid-fifties, had expressed the hope that the culture of heroin addiction among black youth might wane as blacks, like other immigrant groups before them, became more and more assimilated into the larger society whose rewards had been both tantalizingly visible and realistically unattainable. But by the sixties it was already apparent that those on the bottom of the economic and social ladder in the cities wouldn't, without new kinds of help, move up in the traditional ways. The path upward was narrowing as the transformation of the urban economy took away many of the job opportunities that earlier groups had used to move up and out. At the same time, as Cloward and Ohlin most clearly argued, some of the bonds that held poor communities together in the past in the face of economic adversity, and that sustained values counter to the predatory and destructive ones of the emerging drug culture, were eroding—the casualties, among other things, of short-sighted urban policies that broke up natural communities and family networks.

The implications of these findings were far-reaching and fundamental, and strongly challenged the approaches to drug abuse that were then generally dominant in the United States. Within the stricken communities of the inner cities, drug use was not an *isolated* problem, but part of a syndrome that included family disintegration, delinquency, and alcohol abuse. Therefore trying to deal with addiction through policies narrowly directed at drugs alone was like punching a pillow; even if you achieved some success with one part of the problem it would surely pop up elsewhere in a different guise (as happened in the other direction, for example, when the fighting gangs of the slums of New York turned to heroin in the early sixties). Though several of the early students of heroin addiction did use the language of public health in describing it as an epidemic or a plague, they all emphasized that it was not really like a disease that struck suddenly in otherwise healthy individuals and populations; the agent responsible, the "virus," was of much less independent significance than the forces that made whole communities vulnerable to its attack.

That basic insight led logically to strong reservations about both law enforcement and conventional "treatment" as responses to the urban drug problem. Many observers already realized by the mid-fifties that stepped-up law enforcement against drug addicts during the postwar epidemic had been a failure; not only was there no clear deterrent effect of what Finestone called the "correctional" approach to drugs, but the implication in much of this research was that it might even be counterproductive, given that the drug subcultures of the cities *thrived* on illicit intrigue and the risks of arrest and even imprisonment. Young people used hard drugs, and became involved in drug-using peer groups, in part *because* doing so made them appear harder, "cooler," and more willing to take risks—and thus enabled them to distance themselves from the bleak, acquiescent lives most lower-class people faced. The threat of police and prison, then, would at best have an ambiguous effect. Realistically, drug users might fear the consequences of arrest and try to avoid them, but at the same time being arrested and put behind bars wouldn't diminish their reputation among their peers, their self-esteem, or their own sense of identity—in fact, would probably enhance them. Nor would the experience of arrest and jail do anything to change the conditions facing addicts when they were released. The social pressures and deficits that underlay addiction would accordingly be no less strong—and probably stronger, since the addict now carried the stigmas and disabilities of the ex-convict and would have an even slimmer chance of achieving a sufficiently respectable or rewarding place in the world of work to counter the powerful lures of drugs and the hustling life.

But if the research undermined the credibility of the idea that law enforcement alone could make much difference to the inner-city drug problem, it also cast doubt on the perspective that was most often offered as an alternative—what Finestone and others called the "medical" model of addiction. Since addiction was at bottom a *social* problem rooted in the harsh deprivations and cultural stresses that afflicted entire communities, it would not be solved by the medical or psychiatric treatment of the individual addict. To be sure, some addicts could benefit from individual treatment. But for others that approach made little sense, because they did not present any significant psychiatric problems. Even if they did, treating the isolated individual addict, even successfully, wouldn't stem the flow of *new* addicts generated by the same, unchanged social conditions. And since the problem of addiction lay less in the physiological effect of the drug than in its social and cultural appeals, the search for medical means of coping with mass addiction would necessarily be limited. This was perhaps the most crucial implication of all. Drug users were not people who had been suddenly struck by a disease which had invaded their bodies and which they desperately wanted cured. They were typically people who had sought out hard drugs to fill any of several important personal and social needs, they derived considerable fulfillment from using them, and they rarely regarded themselves as "ill"—or their use of drugs itself as their major problem.

None of this was to deny that many addicts desperately needed help. But it did shift the perspective on what help should *mean*, in two related ways. First, the research on addiction suggested that what many addicts most needed in the long run was changed lives—broader opportunities for good work and respectable incomes, full participation in the surrounding society. Second, while many addicts did need immediate assistance in the short run, they usually needed a wider range of help than traditional medical or psychiatric treatment offered —help that would enable them to cope with the multiple obstacles they faced in the increasingly inhospitable inner cities. Within this framework, some form of individual treatment could have an important place, but only if it shifted focus, away from the medical model of treating the individual in isolation and toward integration with broader efforts to provide better opportunities and better tools for taking advantage of them.

This view was made explicit in Preble and Casey's classic article. "The ultimate solution to the problem" of lower-class heroin addiction, they argued, "as with all the problems which result from social injustice, lies in the creation of legitimate opportunities for a meaningful life for those who want it." In the meantime, "reparative measures" were necessary. But given their emphasis on the lack of opportunities for good, challenging work as the root cause of the spread of addiction in the inner city, the measures Preble and Casey favored leaned heavily toward "educational and vocational training and placement," rather than chemical treatment with substitute drugs or antagonists, traditional psychotherapy, or group therapy. They proposed a model treatment program that would span a full three years: nine months of intensive vocational and educational training coupled with psychological counseling, and twenty-seven months devoted to "aftercare" in the community, which could involve further training and schooling as needed, along with social and psychological counseling—a "comprehensive social reparation" for those addicts not "too severely damaged by society."

The most elaborate and far-reaching proposals for a socially grounded approach to addiction were outlined by Haryou-ACT. A key theme in their report was that youthful drug addiction and dealing in Harlem were not rooted in material deprivation alone, but also in the profound alienation of Harlem's youth "from the world that made them." Countering that alienation required nothing less than a "new faith which could give them a sense of place and purpose in life." Accordingly, Haryou-ACT proposed an ambitious set of strategies that emphasized enlisting youth in efforts to transform their own communities. The "principal aspiration," they wrote, was "the creation of a youth movement intent upon changing the culture and face of Harlem." Large numbers of relatively unskilled Harlem youth would be hired to staff new community services—in education, health care, employment, and cultural activities. Through a Harlem Domestic Peace Corps and other new organizations, youth would be pressed into service—not as volunteers but at respectable wages—to provide crucial services that were systematically neglected by existing city agencies. Junior and senior academies for the more troubled youth would provide a degree of structure and serious schooling rarely found in most public schools, or in many of their families. Preschool and after-school programs would nurture and supervise Harlem's children throughout the day and provide support to hard-pressed families. Importantly, the plan called for youth themselves to be well represented as staff and aides in these programs. In addition, Haryou-ACT proposed to create a number of new community-based enterprises—in office equipment, industrial arts and design, and building renovation, for example—which would train and hire local youth while contributing to the economic development of the community. All of these efforts were designed to work together; young people trained in building renovation, for example, would rehabilitate storefronts to be used by the new preschool programs and community health centers. These enterprises would contribute to the development of Harlem's youth and the revitalization of the community as a whole in several simultaneous ways. They would generate income, help support the new community social-service programs, and expand job and training opportunities for many young people otherwise faced with only the bleakest of futures. Less tangibly, but no less importantly, they would ultimately help to "curtail the psychology of powerlessness which too often results from growing up in a community owned by outsiders."

The great virtue of proposals like Haryou-ACT's was that they flowed logically from the findings of the best research available on the roots of the inner-city drug problem: the link between analysis and strategy was clear and strong. If endemic drug abuse was a community *problem*, rooted in the grim and deteriorating prospects for the people of the inner cities, then it required a community *response* focused on expanding legitimate opportunities, enlisting the young in challenging and respected work, and restoring functioning local institutions to meet the developmental and social needs of the community's families and young people. Haryou's ambitious approach (like some others that emerged from the stirrings of the War on Poverty in the mid-sixties) was never fully realized in practice —though the community-action approach it championed did take hold among some community-based drug and youth programs from the sixties onward.

That we did not fulfill these agendas was not because the analyses they were based on were ever shown to be *wrong*. On the contrary—as we'll see, more recent research has overwhelmingly affirmed the broad themes raised by these observers in the fifties and sixties. But by the end of the sixties, the impulse behind these far-reaching proposals for community regeneration had been effectively derailed as a national movement, and the ideas themselves had been taken off the national agenda— casualties of the social retrenchment of the Nixon era and the voracious fiscal appetites of the Vietnam War. As a result, by the seventies what we were doing in response to drug abuse in the cities increasingly diverged from what we knew about its causes, leading to the schizophrenic divorce of analysis from strategy that has marked our urban drug policies ever since.

3

Lessons Ignored

Much has changed since the classic studies of the 1950s and 1960s. Most of those studies were about heroin: crack had not exploded in America's ghettos, cocaine was considered a minor problem, and drugs like methamphetamine and PCP had barely reared their heads. For that matter, heroin itself was a much smaller problem than it was to become. And the medical and social complications of drug abuse were nowhere near as threatening. AIDS was unknown, and its terrifying spread among drug users was yet in the future. The tragedies of infant addiction and family disintegration were far less shattering than they became in the age of crack. As the drug crisis has escalated, too, we have learned much more about its causes. An explosion of increasingly sophisticated research over the past twenty years has given us a wealth of knowledge unavailable a generation ago and allowed us to fill in and elaborate the portrait sketched by the pioneering researchers of the postwar era.

But the broad outlines of that portrait have stood the test of time remarkably well. An enormous body of accumulating evidence continues to link mass drug abuse with the intertwined social deficits described in the fifties and sixties: poverty amidst affluence, poor jobs and economic marginality, the disintegration of families and communities, the weakening of sustaining cultural values. Isidor Chein's argument that endemic drug use reflects a "surplus of vulnerability" has been repeatedly borne out—across a wide range of different drugs, different racial and ethnic groups, and different countries.

The good news is that we now know more than ever before about what it would take to attack the drug crisis at its roots. The bad news is that those roots have deepened and spread. The drug crisis has worsened along with the continuing exclusion of more and more Americans from the prospect of a fulfilling life in a sustaining and cohesive community. The economic and social trends of the past two decades have exacerbated the inequalities and stresses of American life: conditions once mainly confined to the urban ghettos have spread beyond them to engulf a much more diverse population of the economically insecure and socially disadvantaged.

These changes have not been confined to the United States, but they find their most extreme expression here. And they involve more than the (very real) growth of economic insecurity and deprivation. Material shifts in opportunities and living standards have been accompanied by less easily measured, but far-reaching, changes in community life and cultural values. And all of these changes hang together. None of the individual social ills—deepening poverty, declining labor markets, eroding families—taken alone accounts for the spread of the drug problem, but rather all of them together, within a context of widening inequality, government retrenchment, and a spreading culture of predatory consumerism. The formal research tends to focus on one part of the picture at a time, but it is the whole interlocking complex of changes in American society— our pervasive movement toward a more depriving, more stressful, more atomized and less supportive society—that accounts for the severity of the drug problem today. In this chapter, we'll look first at what the newer research tells us about the social conditions most likely to breed drug abuse, and about the related question, first raised by Finestone and others in the fifties: *Why* do people in those circumstances turn to drugs? What do drugs—and the surrounding drug cultures—*mean* for them? Finally, we'll return, in the light of these findings, to ask why the 1980s provided such fertile ground for the drug explosion.

I

The link between drug abuse and deprivation is one of the strongest in forty years of careful research. I am not suggesting that drug abuse is confined to the poor. But the evidence consistently tells us that endemic drug use is not randomly or evenly distributed, in the United States or elsewhere. The American drug problem is often portrayed as if it were classless; antidrug advertising, for example, is much given to images of fresh-faced suburban children or conservatively suited executives, with the explicit message that drugs afflict everyone—or, as an advertisement from the business-sponsored Partnership for a Drug-Free America puts it, "good families; families like *yours*." Superficially, of course, that is true: there are few middle-class communities in America without their closet heroin addicts or binge cocaine users, and in some affluent communities (and occupations) drug abuse is very high indeed. Many people emphasize this point in order to argue—justly— that a war on drugs fought almost entirely against the poor has been discriminatory as well as ineffective. Taken too far, however, the classless imagery distorts the reality of hard-drug abuse and hobbles our ability to come to grips with it. We will not begin to comprehend America's drug problem, much less resolve it, until we understand that drugs and inequality are closely and multiply linked. And our national willingness to tolerate unusually severe levels of social deprivation and marginality goes a long way toward explaining why we lead the world in drug abuse.

The complex, enduring connections between class, race, and drugs emerge from several different kinds of research. Consider first the difference between levels of hard-drug abuse found in surveys of the general population versus those of severely disadvantaged communities. In the annual NIDA household survey, slightly more than 1 percent of the U.S. population admits to having ever used heroin in any amount. But as far back as the 1960s, in one of the earliest surveys of drug use in a "high risk" community, the psychiatrist Lee Robins found that 10 percent of a sample of a "normal" population of low-income black men in St. Louis had been *addicted* to heroin at some point in their lives.

In a more recent, long-term study of young black men and women in Harlem, Ann Brunswick and her colleagues at the Columbia University School of Public Health found that 16 percent of men and 13 percent of women had engaged in "nonexperimental" heroin use—that is, they had used the drug more than once or twice. Twenty-one percent of their respondents reported using cocaine in the past *month*, versus about 3 percent of nonwhites in a national sample of young adults of similar age: and this was *before* the cocaine and crack epidemics of the late eighties. Fully 6 percent of the sample, by their late twenties and early thirties, had used illegal methadone on a "nonexperimental" basis. Among the Harlem heroin users, less than one in seven reported household incomes of more than $10,000 a year in the mid-1970s; on average, their mothers had not finished the twelfth grade.

Community studies have also shown sharp differences in levels of drug abuse between low-income neighborhoods and adjacent, more affluent ones. In the 1970s, a study of Brooklyn neighborhoods by Irving Lukoff and his colleagues found much higher rates of heroin use in the Bedford-Stuyvesant and Fort Greene areas—with large low-income black populations—than in Bay Ridge, at the time a nearly all-white area with half again

Bedford-Stuyvesant's median income. A surprising 21 percent of men aged twenty to twenty-four in Bedford-Stuyvesant had used heroin, versus 5 percent in Bay Ridge. A 5 percent rate of heroin use is by no means low—in fact, it is several times higher than the national rate—but it was nonetheless only a fourth the rate for young men in Bedford-Stuyvesant. Moreover, although heroin use tends to decline with age, other things being equal, men aged twenty-five to forty-four in the poorer minority communities were more likely to use heroin than men in their early twenties in Bay Ridge. In communities where rates of narcotics use were as high as in Bedford-Stuyvesant and Fort Greene, Lukoff concluded, drug abuse could not be adequately understood as a problem "confined to a collection of individuals who happen to choose a particular mode of adaptation"; instead, it had become a pervasive element of neighborhood life that "reverberates throughout the community and influences the community's ability to solve its problems of survival."

Similar heavy concentrations of hard-drug abuse have been repeatedly found in studies of low-income Hispanic communities in the United States. Among the most compelling is a study of East Los Angeles housing projects in the late 1970s by Robert Perez and Amado Padilla, then of UCLA's Spanish-Speaking Mental Health Center, and their colleagues. In these projects, about 85 percent of the residents were Hispanic, mostly Mexican-American; 60 percent of the families were headed by a single parent; and the median family income was less than $3,000 above the poverty level. Perez and Padilla found that the levels of drug use—especially of PCP and inhalants—among children and adolescents in this community were among the highest ever recorded anywhere. The use of PCP in particular had "reached epidemic proportions": 57 percent of young men and 41 percent of young women aged fifteen to seventeen had used PCP within the last six months —well over two-thirds of them within the last *week*. And though use of PCP was highest among older teenagers, almost a fourth of barrio boys aged *nine to eleven* had used PCP within the past six months. By contrast, in the 1979 NIDA household survey, 5 percent of twelve-to-seventeen-year-olds in the nation as a whole reported that they had used *any* hallucinogenic drug (including LSD as well as PCP) during the past *year*.

The suffusion of hard drugs throughout the fabric of community life has long been even more extreme in many low-income Puerto Rican neighborhoods, as studies by Joseph Fitzpatrick in New York in the seventies and Ron Glick in Chicago in the eighties have shown. Within the generally deprived neighborhoods in Fitzpatrick's study, the young people who became addicts were typically even *more* deprived than others in the community. Less than half were employed even part-time, versus two-thirds of the nonaddicted youth; only one-sixth, versus slightly over half of the nonaddicts, had graduated from high school. Less than a fourth had a parent whose occupation ranked "skilled or higher," versus three out of five of the nonaddicts. More important than the isolated effects of any of these factors, however, was the way the long-term conditions of mass poverty and limited opportunities had made drug abuse an integral, almost normal part of community life. Fitzpatrick's conclusion sums up what other researchers have found in similar communities:

> Drug use at the time of the study [1975 to 1978] was an all-pervasive aspect of this social environment, one dimension of the total mosaic of life with which everyone must deal in one way or another. . . . It was one aspect of a variegated culture of poor urban Puerto Ricans who deal with it as they deal with the manifold problems of human life.

The saturation of poor neighborhoods by drugs has become even more pronounced since the crack epidemic of the 1980s, and the evidence suggests that crack has struck hardest at the poorest of the poor. Crack's concentration in low-income areas appears even in the NIDA household survey. In the Washington, D.C., area, reported crack use during the past year was twice as high in 1990 in the neighborhoods with the lowest rents and housing values as in the rest of the city. And community studies offer an even more compelling picture. A study of the Bayview neighborhood in San Francisco, where much of the city's crack use has been concentrated, by Benjamin Bowser, Robert Fullilove, and Mindy Fullilove fits what we have learned about other neighborhoods hard hit by crack. Crack sales and use were not dispersed evenly throughout this largely working-class black neighborhood, but were concentrated almost exclusively in "isolated pockets of the community," especially the poorest public-housing projects, whose largely low-skilled residents "have been on the margins of the economy since the 1960s." Contrary to a common belief, the neighborhood as a *whole* was not "overrun with crack sales": few young people were seen selling crack except in the housing projects and along one particularly troubled street—"the specific areas of the community that were rapidly deteriorating as both physical and social units."

These community studies fill out what medical data on drug-related deaths and emergencies routinely show. In 1990, less than half of all deaths involving heroin abuse—and just a third of cocaine-related deaths—were of non-Hispanic whites. And the picture is very similar when we look at the link between drug use and AIDS—a tragedy disproportionately concentrated among the minority poor. Drug abuse is the principal reason why AIDS is now the leading cause of death of New York City Hispanics aged twenty-five to forty-four, and of Hispanic *children* aged one to four. Intravenous drug use is the key reason why AIDS has also become the leading killer of young black women in New York and New Jersey, having passed cancer and heart disease by the late 1980s. At the end of 1990, of children who had contracted AIDS from their mothers—most as a result of the mother's drug use—only 13 percent were white and non-Hispanic.

As these statistics suggest, though, endemic drug abuse is in
no sense a minority problem alone. The connection between
race and drug abuse, as Isidor Chein argued in the fifties, is
due less to any specific effect of race itself than to the fact that
the kind of multiple social deprivation that breeds drug abuse
is more often concentrated in minority communities. Since the
sixties, research has consistently shown that drug use in severely
deprived *white* populations is predictably higher than in better-
off minority communities. Lukoff's study of heroin use in and
around New York City ghettos in the seventies found the *highest*
rates of abuse of many drugs among the (admittedly atypical)
whites in the area. A national survey by John O'Donnell and
his colleagues in the mid-seventies found a 17 percent rate of
lifetime heroin use among the white unemployed—nearly as
high as that of unemployed blacks (20 percent) and much
higher than that of blacks employed full-time.

A 1970s study conducted by the National Center for Urban
Ethnic Affairs, similarly, found startlingly high levels of hard-
drug use among low-income, white ethnic youth in the cities.
The center surveyed over a thousand young people in inner-
city neighborhoods in Baltimore, Detroit, Cincinnati, and Prov-
idence. Most were children of blue-collar parents: more than
a third reported that their fathers had "no occupation." A
surprising 19 percent of Irish inner-city youth aged eighteen
to twenty-two reported "heavy" or "regular" heroin use, virtually identical with the proportion of blacks. Between 12 and
13 percent of Irish youth reported *heavy* use of amphetamines,
inhalants, or barbiturates as well. Among white non-Hispanic
high-school dropouts in the Southwest studied by Ernest
Chavez, Ruth Edwards, and E. R. Oetting in the 1980s, 33
percent of the boys and 40 percent of the girls had used
cocaine; 44 percent of the boys had used inhalants; 46 percent
of the boys and slightly more that 50 percent of the girls had
used amphetamines. Almost one in five male white dropouts
had used PCP.

A recent study of drug use among a multiracial group of

low-income delinquent youth in Miami drives the point home: 92 percent of the Hispanic delinquents, 88 percent of blacks, and 77 percent of whites reported having at some point been *regular* users of crack cocaine. More than a fourth of the white youth said they had used crack *daily* over the past ninety days.

Medical data, too, confirm that in areas where the low-income population is heavily made up of whites, so are the statistics on drug-related deaths and illness. In Seattle, for example, about three-fourths of heroin-related deaths are of whites. Methamphetamine—a significant part of the drug problem in the West and Southwest, and a major cause of drug-related violence, medical problems, and death—is a drug of choice primarily among the white poor and near-poor. The typical victim of a methamphetamine-related death is a thirty-two-year-old white male. Nine out of ten methamphetamine users in treatment in a NIDA study of San Diego, Portland, and Dallas were white; nearly half of the men had not graduated from high school.

The relationship between endemic drug abuse and social deprivation holds as well for other countries. No other industrial nation has a hard-drug problem that matches ours; but the problems they do have are, as here, predictably concentrated in areas of harsh social disadvantage and economic insecurity.

In Holland, for example—a country with a significant, if stable, heroin problem and a much smaller problem with cocaine (and as of this writing virtually no experience of crack)—hard-drug abuse is concentrated among "persons who have few possibilities of improving their social situation," including the poorly educated and members of disadvantaged immigrant groups, notably Surinamese, Moluccans, and second-generation youth from Moroccan and Turkish backgrounds. In Great Britain, where rising unemployment and poverty under the Thatcher regime provide a kind of natural experiment, studies of the epidemic of heroin abuse in the

1980s have given us some of the most compelling evidence we have of the links between drug abuse and social disadvantage.

An investigation of young heroin users in the economically stricken north of England, by Geoffrey Pearson of Middlesex Polytechnic and his coworkers, found that, because of the uneven availability of heroin, the epidemic had missed many northern cities entirely. But in cities where heroin did take hold, it was found primarily in poorer neighborhoods—and especially in specific enclaves within those neighborhoods characterized by a "gathering concentration of social deprivation." In the Closefields neighborhood in Greater Manchester, for example, the overall unemployment rate among men under twenty-five was 40 percent; in the smaller target area within the neighborhood where "a specific heroin network was at its highest density," the rate was a startling 66 percent. In the Docktown area of Liverpool, youth unemployment stood at 40 percent in 1981—and 60 percent in the section with the highest heroin use.

Another community hit hard by the British heroin epidemic of the eighties was Wirral, near Liverpool, studied by Howard Parker and his colleagues at Liverpool University. Here too, heroin use was concentrated among younger people in "socially deprived communities." Four small townships in Wirral, with only 12 percent of the population, accounted for 38 percent of the known opiate users (those who had come to the attention of police or treatment agencies). In one public-housing estate, one in ten young people were *known* users of heroin in the mid-1980s, a rate approaching that in inner-city American ghettos. There were strong correlations between heroin use and several related "indicators of social deprivation"—including unemployment, overcrowded housing, single-parent families, and lack of skills. Heroin, Parker and his colleagues concluded, was a "spectre which hangs over a predominantly deprived urban 'underclass' of unqualified, unskilled, and unemployed young adults."

A Glasgow study in the early 1980s, similarly, estimated that

10 to 15 percent of younger people aged fifteen to thirty-four in one "unemployment/deprivation blackspot" in the city were "using opiates on a regular basis"—mainly injecting heroin. And the same pattern of concentration holds even in British cities that have relatively low drug use overall. A Nottingham study in the mid-1980s, for example, found only 170 hard-drug users (mostly of heroin and methamphetamine) in a population of nearly half a million. But they were concentrated in areas of the city characterized by what the researchers called "multiple deprivation"—including low income, unemployment, low skills, poor housing, poor health, and family problems.

I I

Unemployment appears prominently in these studies, and a closer look at research on the specific links between employment and drug use clarifies and elaborates this crucial connection. Long-term unemployment is central to the syndrome of "surplus vulnerability" that breeds concentrated drug abuse—but so are *over*work and the proliferation of dead-end, low-paying jobs. As several of the pioneer drug researchers pointed out in the 1950s and 1960s, it is the overall quality of the labor market, not just the absence of work altogether, that is most crucial. The absence of opportunities for good work, moreover, affects not only those individuals who lose jobs or cannot find them: over the long term, it also affects family life and the social fabric of communities as a whole, in ways that encourage drug abuse and a culture of drugs and drug dealing.

Reported lifetime use of crack, inhalants, and PCP in the NIDA household survey is roughly twice as high among the unemployed as among those working full-time. And this survey, as we've seen, necessarily *understates* the connection between unemployment and drug abuse because it misses most of the people whose connection with a stable labor market is most tenuous: most of the homeless, those in and out of institutions, the disorganized poor. When we look at these more vulnerable populations, the connections become starker.

• Among arrestees in cities across the country, according to the Drug Use Forecasting survey—a population, again, heavily composed of hard-drug users—less than half were working full-time in 1988, and the figure was even lower for women and in some cities especially hard hit by drugs. In New York, nearly three out of five arrested men and almost *four* out of five women were unemployed.

• In a recent study of intravenous drug users in Dayton and Columbus, Ohio, only about a third reported that their main source of income was a job. Among "street" heroin users in central Harlem studied by Bruce Johnson and his colleagues in the late 1970s and early 1980s, things were even worse: 81 percent were unemployed. The majority of street users, these researchers conclude, "possess few or no life skills for legitimate work."

• Startlingly similar proportions turn up in research on the British heroin epidemic. Among known heroin users in Wirral, for example, 81 percent were unemployed and another 9 percent were working in low-wage manual jobs. An even higher proportion (91 percent) of "hidden" users—those who had *not* come to the attention of the treatment or justice systems—were unemployed, indicating that the overrepresentation of the jobless among known users was not simply a reflection of differences in the extent to which unemployed users were arrested or made use of drug treatment. The typical hidden heroin user had in fact been unemployed for three years, and indeed 62 percent of the unemployed users had *never* had a job since leaving school.

• The pattern is no different for crack: among clients admitted
in 1989 to treatment programs in Detroit for crack addiction,
for example, only 10 percent were employed full-time.

Few people seriously challenge these associations, especially
for those whose addiction is worst and who are most involved
in the street drug culture. But there has always been some
debate about the *direction* of this connection: Does unemployment *cause* drug abuse, or is it simply that people who abuse
drugs are likely to lose their jobs or to quit them? Confronted
with the data from the 1990 NIDA household survey revealing
rising numbers of unemployed drug users, for example, a
spokesman for the Bush administration opined that "I don't
believe that unemployment causes drug use. I do believe that
people who use drugs can't keep their jobs." No evidence was
offered to support that view, however; and the serious research
suggests that it is far too simplistic. As we might expect, the
connection between joblessness and drug use works in both
directions: unemployment does lead some people to use drugs,
and addicts do lose jobs—or avoid looking for them—because
of their drug use and the lure of the drug culture.

One reason why the loss of jobs due to drug use cannot
account for all of the drugs-unemployment connection is that
unemployment often *precedes* drug use. In a study of Scottish
youth by Martin Plant and his coworkers at the University of
Edinburgh, a thousand fifteen- and sixteen-year olds in five
secondary schools were asked about their drug use in 1979–
80 and again three years later, after they had been out of
school for two or three years. The use of LSD, opiates, and
marijuana was considerably higher among those who were
unemployed after leaving secondary school—even though it
had been the same as the rest of the sample while they were
still in school. Their unemployment, in short, came first, their
use of drugs afterwards. (In a later work, Plant and Peck also
found that the *duration* of unemployment after leaving school

—the length of time spent out of work—was associated with greater drug use.)

Other data corroborate the effect of unemployment from another angle. Plant and Peck show that as British unemployment rates rocketed upward, so did both the number of reported drug offenses and the number of addicts in treatment. From 1970 to 1984, average annual unemployment increased fivefold, cautions and convictions for drug offenses nearly tripled, and the number of addicts receiving methadone or other chemical treatment quadrupled. Obviously, the rises in drug addiction cannot have *caused* the (much broader) rises in joblessness; the strong implication is that the causal sequence works in the other direction.

That implication is supported by Howard Parker's study of heroin use in Wirral. The majority of Wirral addicts—about three in five—had never held a job since leaving school. Of those who *had* ever worked but were now unemployed, the most frequent reason was that they had been laid off, or had been employed on a short-term public employment project that had ended. To be sure, others *did* seem to have lost jobs *because* of their heroin use or its associated lifestyle: 23 percent had been fired, often for being late; another 14 percent had gone to prison. But most had lost jobs as the result of economic circumstances beyond their control.

The connection between unemployment and drug use also stands out in studies of the fate of addicts who have gone into treatment (which we will consider in more detail in Chapter 5). Since the early 1960s, for example, a number of studies have followed the "careers" of heroin addicts admitted to the two federal narcotic-treatment hospitals at Lexington, Kentucky, and Fort Worth, Texas. In one of the earlier studies, Lois DeFleur, John Ball, and Richard Snarr followed up fifty-three Puerto Rican men who had been addicted to heroin, treated at Lexington, and discharged between 1935 and 1963.

Of these men, only nine had been "steadily employed at legitimate occupations during most of their adult lives." Those nine had both very different backgrounds and very different outcomes than the rest of the group. Those who had been more steadily employed *before* they were addicted were more likely to work steadily after treatment and were far *less* likely to return to drug use or be arrested. The contrasts between these men and those who had never or almost never worked after their release were dramatic. Only 11 percent of the steadily employed men had been arrested in the three years prior to the study, versus 100 percent of the men who had been mainly unemployed. Not one of the latter, versus two-thirds of the steadily employed group, abstained from drug use for at least three years after treatment. For those who had come to drug use from a relatively stable work life in the first place, the researchers argued, the entire experience of addiction was probably different to begin with: they "occupied distinct positions in the social structure, implying involvement in different interactive environments and diverse processes of socialization." For them the outlook after treatment was encouraging. For the men who had been "only marginally participating in the labor force," on the other hand, "the prognosis appears to be unsatisfactory indeed."

A continuing follow-up of Lexington addicts, by the psychiatrist George Vaillant of Dartmouth Medical School, brings this picture up to the late eighties. Vaillant followed one hundred men, all from New York City, who were first admitted to Lexington in 1952. This important study—to which we will return in looking at treatment strategies—throws considerable light on the role of employment both in determining who will become addicted at all, and, equally importantly, in influencing their prospects for a stable and drug-free life *after* treatment.

Most of the addicts in Vaillant's sample came to Lexington with poor—or nonexistent—work histories. Though their average age was twenty-five when they were admitted to treatment, a third had never worked for as long as a year, and "few had regular work histories prior to addiction." And two-thirds of those who achieved "stable abstinence" after treatment—but *none* of those who suffered "sustained addiction"—had been employed for at least half of their adult lives.

The connections between unemployment and drug use, then, are complex, and they run in more than one direction. But they are strong and recurrent. Moreover, joblessness and entrapment in low-wage, unstable work also breed drug abuse indirectly—through their long-term impact on the stability and character of families and neighborhoods. Many people, after all, begin using—or dealing—hard drugs well before they are old enough to even have a job, much less lose one. In their study of drug use among Miami delinquents, for example, James Inciardi and Anne Pottieger found that the average age at which the youth first used heroin, crack, or methamphetamine was twelve—and eleven for powder cocaine. In a study of drug dealing among delinquents in the same city, Fernando Sorianno and Mario De La Rosa found that the white youth had begun *selling* hard drugs at an average age of thirteen and the Hispanic and black youth at twelve—too young, obviously, to have been driven to selling drugs by their own current lack of a job. On the other hand, many were growing up in families and neighborhoods where joblessness was rife: only *half* of the black dealers, for example, had any employed people in their households. For the very young, what is more important than their own work experience, or lack of it, is that they live in places where economic opportunities are so constricted that drug use and drug dealing have become an established alternative source of income and identity, which can attract young people well before they are eligible for regular jobs themselves.

Geoffrey Pearson's study of young heroin users in the north of England illustrates another way in which widespread unemployment can create a culture of drug use that influences the choices of the employed as well as the jobless. "In those areas where unemployment reaches such levels that it becomes the exception rather than the rule to be in work," Pearson writes, "even for those who are in work the value attached to employment status can become eroded." Pearson quotes one young man who had landed one of the few decent jobs in his neighborhood and was

> bringing in the money, 120 a week, when there weren't that many jobs around. . . . All the lads I knew were on the dole, like. . . . I mean nearly everyone around here's on the dole, you know what I mean . . . and they were just running around, just taking smack all week . . . and there I was, sweating my guts out at work. . . . No fun; no money cos I'd blown it all at the weekend. . . . Eventually I just jacked the job in, like. Just said, Fuck that, you know. Joined in with the rest of the lads, you know, just going for the smack. Taking it every day. I was soon knackered like the rest of 'em . . . but there you go.

III

Pervasive economic marginality, then, creates what some researchers call "neighborhood effects" that increase individuals' risks of drug abuse regardless of their personal fortunes in the labor market. And those effects are magnified because joblessness—and low-wage work—stress and weaken families in ways that erode their capacity to provide some protection against the lures of drugs and the culture of the street. Chein's research in the fifties suggested how the disintegration of family life in poor neighborhoods encouraged adolescent heroin addiction, and more recent studies affirm the continuing connection between economic decline, family problems, and the spread of drugs.

The basic findings on the kinds of families most at risk for drug use are remarkably consistent, and the picture has changed little since Chein's pioneering work. Studies both in the United States and in several foreign countries show that drug use (as well as the progression from occasional use to addiction) is more likely among young people whose families are cold or hostile, or physically and sexually abusive; where there is much conflict and unhappiness between the parents, and between them and the child; where the parents themselves abuse alcohol or drugs; and where discipline is inconsistent or harsh and punitive. And though those family problems can be found all across the social terrain, they are strongly linked with both unemployment and the effects of overwork in low-paying jobs.

The link is especially strong for the more serious forms of child abuse—itself increasingly found to be an important predictor of youthful drug abuse. Studies of delinquents in Florida institutions by Richard Dembo and his colleagues, for example, find that childhood experience of physical and sexual abuse is closely associated with levels of drug use; other studies have found that sexual abuse often appears in the backgrounds of women who abuse hard drugs. Thus the fact that the most typical child-abusing parent is "poorly educated, unskilled, unemployed, and most likely dependent on welfare allowances," as a recent Canadian study puts it, is part of the explanation for the high levels of drug abuse in communities suffering the long-term loss of stable jobs. The impact of joblessness and poor wages is compounded because the shrinking of economic opportunities forces families to move often in search of jobs or better income—isolating them from relatives, friends, and other sources of help and support. The resulting "social impoverishment," according to much research on the roots of child abuse, fuses with the economic and psychological stresses of unemployment or low-wage work to create a particularly fertile context for family violence.

But the absence of good jobs puts yet other pressures on the family that also foster drug abuse and the growth of drug cultures. Even if the stresses do not mount to the point of actual child abuse, long hours in low-wage jobs interfere with parents' ability to nurture and supervise their children—especially when the weak labor market is compounded by the lack of reliable child care. The connection is illustrated in a study of Cuban-American drug users in Miami by J. Bryan Page. Immigration to the United States placed great stresses on Cuban families torn from their traditional communities and faced with poverty and limited job opportunities in Miami. The resulting strains often broke families apart; but even if a family remained intact, it was often necessary for both parents to work long hours "to achieve a decent standard of living." Children left alone accordingly took most of their cues from their peers and from the already thriving street drug culture. "My mother worked from eight in the morning until nine at night," one of Page's informants reported. "I had all that time on my hands." For many, their peer groups had become the "principal social environment for learning to act like an adult." Churches, schools, and other community institutions that might have positively influenced the young were also weakened by migration and poverty, which helped to magnify the influence of the "street" on the values and behavior of Cuban-American youth.

I've seen the same pattern in my own interviews with teenaged drug users and dealers—as in these reflections of a fourteen-year-old female crack dealer from an inner-city California ghetto:

> My mother don't know nothing about it, 'cause she be at work, she don't know *what* happening! She don't even know when I get suspended from school. That's how long she be gone. It's like—it's weird for my mother, she pay the bills, go to work, come home, sleep, go to work, pay the bills. . . . She worked three jobs and she made pretty good money. . . . Now she's working two because it was too much for her . . . I mean like the only time I seen my mother was like seven o'clock in the morning when she

be gettin' ready to go to her other job. It was like I never
seen her. I could never see her until like seven o'clock,
she'll wake us up and say "I'm gonna go to work, I'm on
my way to work." At three o'clock when we come home
from school, "I'm on my way to work." It was like she
really never had time for us. And that's mainly why we
had to take care of ourselves a lot; we didn't have our
mother that much. She wasn't really there all the time to
help keep us through everything. In a way, some ways I
fault her, some ways I fault myself, for everything that's
happened to me. But it's like I didn't have too much
discipline behind me. So therefore I was really free to do
anything I wanted to do.

The problem, of course, is by no means confined to the
inner cities. Illicit drug use (and the use of alcohol and
cigarettes) is linked to low parental involvement and supervision across the income scale. A recent study from the school
of medicine at the University of Southern California finds that
children "who do not have adults to look after them for at
least one hour per school day—America's so-called latchkey
children—are at greater risk for substance abuse regardless of
their sex, race, family income, academic performance, involvement in sports or other extracurricular activities." But the
phenomenon of the two- or three-job parent is especially
widespread in low-income communities, and it helps explain
the speed with which drugs can spread among the young and
poor or near-poor. To recognize the adverse effects of parental
overwork isn't to blame the hardworking poor for their children's drug abuse. It *is* to say that having to work too long to
make ends meet can compromise parents' capacity to nurture
and socialize their children, and the resulting vacuum is fertile
ground for the spread of a culture of drugs among the disadvantaged young.

The significance of the impact of long-term economic decline
on families, children, and the community as a whole is illus-

trated in an important study of three Brooklyn neighborhoods by the anthropologist Mercer Sullivan, then of the Vera Institute of Justice in New York. Two of the neighborhoods—"Projectville" and "La Barriada"—were poor minority communities, mainly black and Hispanic respectively; the third, "Hamilton Park," mostly white and working-class. Sullivan found that the pattern of youth crime in general, and drug dealing in particular, was strongly influenced by the differing economic structure of the three communities. There was considerable youth crime in all three, but Projectville and La Barriada had more to begin with, and their youth were also much more likely to *continue* in crime—and in more serious kinds of crime—after their midteens. Projectville's youth were the most involved in drug dealing, and some of them "went on with age to participate in drug markets that extended far beyond their local neighborhood." Many of Hamilton Park's youth also sold drugs at some point, but they "generally did so as a sideline to legitimate employment and confined most of their selling to their own neighborhood." What accounted for these differences? The crucial factor, according to Sullivan, was that in Hamilton Park, a relatively stable working-class community, there were much greater and more varied opportunities for legitimate work—both for the young and for their parents. That in turn affected both the relative appeal of illicit work to the young and the capacity of the older generation to control their behavior. For youth in the two poorer minority communities,

> the primary causes for their greater willingness to engage in desperate, highly exposed crimes for uncertain and meager monetary returns were the greater poverty of their households, the specific and severe lack of employment opportunities . . . and the weakened local social control environment, itself a product of general poverty and joblessness among neighborhood residents.

In Hamilton Park, on the other hand, teenagers had considerable access to legitimate employment, though "usually part-time and off-the-books." At the same time, Hamilton Park's adults were sufficiently stable to be able to exert consistent supervision and authority over the young. They often had solid jobs, frequently union jobs, and their greater economic security and resources meant that they were able to "maintain more two-parent households and a more stable neighborhood environment." The youths from the minority neighborhoods, on the other hand,

> lived in much poorer households in which adults too suffered significant employment problems; severe youth unemployment was embedded in much higher levels of general poverty, unemployment, and underemployment. . . . The intensive criminal involvements during the middle teens of the youths from La Barriada and Projectville were the result not only of their severe individual employment problems but also of their greater and earlier need to procure income as well as the inability of their parents and neighbors to control their crimes.

Thus in Projectville, though some local residents tried to control the criminal behavior of youth on the streets, they were "largely unsuccessful, given the concentration of so many poor and jobless youths in such a heavily populated and anonymous environment."

Sullivan's study took place before the worst of the crack epidemic. More recent studies in the neighborhoods hit hardest by crack confirm the central point: that the underlying structure of employment—or the lack of it—shapes the character of a community in ways that profoudly influence its susceptibility to the spread of drugs and the drug culture. There seems to be a kind of tipping point beyond which neighborhoods wracked by widespread family poverty and economic marginality become incapable of controlling the behavior of their young or the activity in their streets. Bowser and Fullilove's research in San Francisco, for example, found a pervasive pattern of community disintegration in "the part of the African-American community that has been cut off from the city's economic life." Years of steadily shrinking employment opportunities not only blasted the prospects for individual young people in Bayview, but, over time, destroyed the cohesion of entire neighborhoods. "Without substantive jobs," they write, "it is only a matter of time before a community begins to disintegrate as a social unit." There are no longer enough stable people with a stake in the community to counter its general downward spiral. "Communities in rapid decline," they argue, "are not controlled by their residents. They are controlled by fragments of the underworld: the long-term underemployed, drug traffickers, addicts, and ex-offenders." In Bayview, this process varied from block to block: "On blocks where residents had control and a sense of ownership over public space, there was no crack trafficking or 'hanging out.' "

Children were able to play outside their homes; older residents kept a watchful eye during the day; and blinds and curtains were open to let sunlight in. In the declining and most depressed areas, children were kept inside their apartments. Despite relatively dense block populations, there were few people on the streets during the day or night. Curtains and blinds were closed 24 hours per day.

In a vicious cycle, the downward slide of these marginal communities is accelerated by the impact of drugs themselves —especially their impact on the stability and competence of adults in the community. That has been particularly true of crack cocaine, which spread more rapidly among adults— especially women—than most other hard drugs. The anthropologist Ansley Hamid has shown how the authority and

influence of parents in drug-ridden communities in New York
has often been undermined by their own crack use, which has
in turn boosted the influence of the youth street culture by
default. Parents who are themselves on drugs, and who are
dependent on the community's children for their supply,
quickly lose authority and credibility, which helps to create a
space in which the street culture's influence expands. More
generally, the collapse of parents who are heavily addicted to
drugs both forces children out on their own and often compels
them to deal drugs to make up for lost family income. "They
just want the fast money," a sixteen-year-old ghetto crack
dealer told me,

> so they can like, you know, help they *mother* out, or maybe
> buy they mother something. . . . Cause most of the mothers
> be on drugs! And if you got little brothers and sisters, you
> know, you don't want to see them all *dirty* and all that,
> you gonna make money any way you could, even if you
> *do* have to go to jail. At least they'll have some money or
> something. And they won't be starving or nothing.

What makes this process so insidious is that it is self-
reinforcing. Economic marginality encourages both adult drug
use and youthful drug dealing; the spread of drug abuse
weakens the economic viability of families and simultaneously
weakens their authority over the young; both of those in turn
increase the appeal of drug dealing and further reduce the
community's capacity to control it.

I V

The corrosive effect of long-term economic deprivation and
narrowing opportunities on family and community helps explain one of the most consistent and troubling findings in the
literature on drug abuse: as Chein and others argued forty

years ago, it predictably *increases* among groups who migrate to American cities the longer they are exposed to the conditions of life in urban America. The research continues to show that it is not the "backward" migrant from rural Tennessee or Puerto Rico who is most vulnerable to drug use and the "street" culture; instead, that vulnerability is acquired over time as part of socialization to lower-class urban life. There is something in the culture and community life from which many migrants come that shields them and their children from the lures of drugs, even if their communities of origin are very poor in material terms; and something about life at the bottom of modern American society that tends to strip away that protection.

As immigrants become more American, in short, they become more likely to abuse drugs. The long-discredited belief that the "rural culture" of poor minority immigrants lies behind most of the problems of the urban "underclass" has recently been resuscitated, but it is wrong. At least as regards drug abuse, it's clear that the immigrants' home cultures are usually considerably healthier and more sustaining than the one they come to.

In a study of Mexican-American heroin addicts in San Antonio, David Desmond and James Maddux found that 99 percent had been born in the United States, and only 1 percent in Mexico—despite the fact that at least 10 percent of the Mexican-Americans in San Antonio were Mexican-born. In Perez and Padilla's study of adolescent drug abuse in East Los Angeles, one of the most disturbing findings was that teenagers' abuse of PCP and inhalants was *positively* associated with the degree to which English was spoken in their homes. "As one moves into groups of more frequent users of drugs," they found, "one uniformly observes more English spoken." The implication—that the more these Mexican-American youngsters became acculturated into the Anglo society around them, the more they abused drugs—fits the evidence from studies of other migrant communities as well.

Studying low-income neighborhoods in Brooklyn in the late seventies, for example, Irving Lukoff and his coworkers found that blacks who had recently arrived from the West Indies had much lower rates of drug abuse than either native-born blacks or native-born whites. U.S.-born blacks were three times as likely to use heroin and two and a half times as likely to use cocaine as West Indian blacks. The key to the difference seemed to lie in what the researchers called "generational status"; among all three ethnic groups, second-generation residents, born in New York, were more likely to use drugs than migrants born elsewhere. West Indian blacks, more often recent migrants and closer to their traditional cultures, were apparently more able to maintain forms of group cohesion and shared values that made them less vulnerable to drug abuse—in part because they insulated young people from peer-group pressures to use drugs. As a community, the West Indians were more capable of sustaining values that discouraged the use of drugs as well as an "effective sanctioning network" to enforce them. The same was true of those (fewer) American-born blacks or whites who were also new migrants to the cities.

In short, as Chein had suggested twenty years earlier, the problem was not that new migrants were turning to drugs because they were bewildered by urban life and facing "culture shock." The migrants did *better*. It was something about the new conditions of urban life that encouraged drug abuse by eroding or breaking down the protective institutions of their traditional societies—stronger families with more consistent values, cohesive communities with networks of relatives and other adults capable of teaching and enforcing norms of conduct that discouraged the use of drugs.

That troubling finding has recently been affirmed in a study of drug use among Puerto Rican adolescents by Carmen Velez and Jane Ungemack. They studied patterns of drug use among four groups of Puerto Rican youth, two in New York City and two in Puerto Rico: the "New York Ricans," who were born in New York City and still lived there; the "New York migrants," who were born on the island and subsequently moved to the city; the "Puerto Rican islanders," who had been born in Puerto Rico and never left the island, and the "Puerto Rican immigrants"—adolescents who had been born in New York but had returned to live on the island. The four groups constituted a kind of natural experiment in the effects of different social and cultural settings on drug use.

The findings were unmistakable; the more enmeshed the teenagers were with the society and culture of New York City, the more likely they were to use drugs (including inhalants, marijuana and hashish, cocaine, amphetamines, heroin, psychedelics and barbiturates). On average, drug abuse among male "New York Ricans" was twice as high as among the islanders, and almost three times as high among females. And the relationship between generational status and drug abuse was linear: highest for both boys and girls among the New York Ricans, next for the migrants to New York, followed by those whose families had returned to the island, with those Puerto Rican youth who had never left the island at the bottom.

Moreover, the *longer* the New York migrants had been living in the city, the more likely they were to use illicit drugs. That was especially true for girls; with each year they spent in New York City, the Puerto Rican–born girls became significantly more likely to abuse drugs and closer to the boys in their level of drug use. Whatever forces operated in the city to encourage drug use apparently worked on them faster than on the boys.

But what, exactly, accounted for the higher drug use among youth more exposed to New York? This study (so far) offers only a few intriguing clues, but they are disturbing and consistent with earlier research. For one thing, higher drug use in New York seemed to be related to higher levels of stress and breakdown among Puerto Rican *families* in the city than on the island. Both on the island and in the city, youth from disrupted single-parent families were more likely to use drugs. But the rate of family disruption was much higher in the city; only about half of the New York Ricans versus three-quarters of the islanders lived in intact families. The city, in short, generated more youthful drug use in part through weakening the family.

That interpretation is backed by other studies that point to the changing character of families in migrant communities. Joseph Fitzpatrick reports that in New York the strength of families was crucial in deflecting drug use among Puerto Rican youth. But it was the presence of an *extended* family—not only blood relatives, but also ritual kin, "compadres and comadres"—that was "the most significant variable in assisting Puerto Rican youths to avoid drug use and addiction." And that broader "controlling and protecting network" has been increasingly weakened in many of these communities. Ronald Glick, for example, has shown how the breakdown of traditional families under the combined impact of urban poverty and the stresses of migration during the "Puerto Rican diaspora" was a key factor in the spread of heroin in Chicago's Puerto Rican community.

Thus one part of the explanation for the rise in drug abuse that accompanies long-time residence in the United States is that persistent economic marginality erodes migrants' families —especially the extended family networks that often characterized immigrant groups in their countries of origin. The disruption of family ties surely increases vulnerability to drugs in several ways. It diminishes the social and economic supports available to people at high risk of drug abuse; the effects of unemployment or low income, for example, are less easily cushioned by the resources of other family members. Children have fewer adult caretakers, supervisors, and mentors, and are therefore more vulnerable to the peer cultures of the street. More subtly—and less easily measured—the disintegration of families renders migrants much more vulnerable to the blandishments of a surrounding culture of exaggerated consumer values and a distorted emphasis on individual acquisition. It is through the family that alternative norms of cooperation and mutuality are transmitted and nurtured—norms about the importance of honoring family and community, of respecting elders and traditions, of valuing productive work for its own sake. As families weaken or splinter, so do the traditions they carry.

A similar process also helps explain why drugs are sometimes rampant in more affluent communities. Just as strong families and cultures can shield the materially deprived from drugs, so weakened families, the absence of available or concerned adults, and the pervasiveness of an insistent consumer culture can make the affluent more vulnerable. But the combination of economic and institutional breakdown in the communities of the poor is especially potent—and it helps to account for that decline of a "sense of human solidarity" that Chein saw as the hallmark of drug-ridden communities as far back as the fifties.

V

Forty years of accumulated research, then, confirms that endemic drug abuse is intimately related to conditions of mass social deprivation, economic marginality, and cultural and community breakdown—in Europe as in the United States, in the eighties and nineties as in the sixties, among poor whites and Hispanics as well as inner-city blacks. The effects of those conditions on individuals, families, and communities help explain why some kinds of people, in some kinds of places, are more vulnerable to drug abuse than others.

But although these connections help us predict which kinds of people are at greatest risk of drug abuse, they do not by themselves explain *why* people turn to drugs in response to those conditions, or why they find it so difficult to stop. Knowing that high levels of drug use are often found among the poor and marginal in otherwise affluent societies, for example, doesn't tell us what, exactly, drugs offer to people caught in those circumstances. Drug use, after all—like any other human behavior—isn't just an automatic response to structural conditions in the social environment; it involves a series of choices that are imbued with complex human meanings, and it persists because it provides specific satisfactions that may be difficult to obtain in other ways.

The newer research shows that drugs can provide more than one kind of satisfaction, and more than one kind of meaning —and affirms that these satisfactions are at least as much social and cultural as physiological. Drugs—and the subcultures of users and dealers in which they are embedded—can provide status, a sense of identity or of life structure, relief from tension, stress, and depression, solace in the face of adversity, peace of mind in the midst of chaos and difficulty. These functions aren't mutually exclusive, and they almost certainly vary according to different drugs of choice, as well as by gender, race, ethnicity, age, and stage of the drug-using career. But what is striking is that the same range of motives and meanings reappear over and over again, no matter what the specific drug, ethnic group, or even country.

At the risk of losing some of the complexity of these motives as they interact in the real world, let me suggest four models of drug use that may help sort out what the research tells us about the social and personal meanings of drug abuse where it is most stubborn and pervasive. I'll call them the status model, the coping model, the structure model, and the saturation model of drug abuse. These models, of course, are abstractions; they don't exhaust the alternatives, and in the real world they are likely to be found in some combination, rather than in pure form.

1. The status model harks back to the fundamental insight of researchers like Finestone or Cloward and Ohlin: one way in which economic deprivation and social exclusion generate drug abuse is by shutting off legitimate avenues of attaining esteem, a sense of respect—even a sense of community. The more recent research suggests that, if anything, this mechanism has become even more important in explaining the growth of the drug cultures of the 1980s and 1990s. Drug use is one response to a growing sense of exclusion from the kind of life others have—and one way of repudiating the constricted and often demeaning lives that increasingly face the young and poor. In the absence of more constructive ways of challenging those conditions, drugs and the drug culture offer an alternative set of values, different ways of testing one's worth, new means of achieving a sense of identity and social prestige. As in the 1950s and 1960s, the resulting culture is an oppositional one, in which toughness, risk-taking, outsmarting authorities, and having no visible licit source of income become cardinal virtues. In that upside-down world, the potential harmfulness of hard drugs becomes a main reason for their appeal; the threat of legal sanctions becomes an opportunity to demonstrate a kind of courage that has few legitimate channels of expression. And these patterns reappear with astonishing similarity—in this country and in others, and across the whole spectrum of illicit drugs.

In a study of Mexican-American heroin addicts in East Los Angeles, for example, Bruce Bullington describes the career of the addict as an exciting game—a "cops-and-robbers affair in which the addicts match their wits against those assigned to control their activities." Bullington finds an established hierarchy of heroin users in the barrio: Near the top of the scale, "the most revered" of addicts, is the "hope-to-die dope fiend," who typically begins heroin use at a very early age, develops a prolonged and heavy habit that he supports through illegal means ("generally those requiring the least effort, such as robberies or drug sales"), and spends extended periods in prison. Nearly equal in local esteem is the "regular" addict, who

> has used drugs for a lengthy period of time and who knows how to handle himself both in prison and on the streets. He is respected by his fellows, who perceive that he handles himself pridefully in all situations and thereby

demonstrates his machismo. . . . Most addicts in the barrio refer repeatedly to the "class" demonstrated by this user type.

Contrasted to these admired role models are the more marginal users, or "hope fiends," who

> aspire to be "regular" or "hope-to-die" users, but who often do not make it because they lack "class." "Hope fiends" usually make every attempt to associate with "hope-to-die" users both within and outside of prison. While institutionalized they too brag of their exploits, but invariably they are exposed as "blanks" by those who know them on the streets.

Even farther down the status hierarchy are the "pill-heads," who mainly use barbiturates and amphetamine pills and are not really part of the heroin scene.

The excitement and sense of belonging to an "elite" subculture standing out against an environment of poverty and resignation are also evident in recent research by Ron Glick on Puerto Rican addicts in Chicago. His subjects described the culture of heroin use as being "like a family"—and as a "cool, affluent, and supportive" alternative to the surrounding society of "lower-working-class Puerto Rican immigrants who avoided drugs and lacked their income, leisure, and sharp dress." Glick, too, found that addicts placed a strong *positive* value on the dangerous and illicit character of drug use; as one of his informants notes, being in the drug culture is "just like being a movie star. . . . So many people depend on you, want to stop you in the street, you know. The police is always on you. . . . You are a very important person." As in earlier descriptions of the drug culture—notably Harvey Feldman's depiction of the "stand-up cat"—Glick found that the "toughness" of the drug itself was a clear draw; Chicago heroin dealers would often attract new customers by telling macho street youth that they were "too young" to try heroin—"a challenge they would not let pass."

What Bullington and Glick find for Mexican-American and Puerto Rican heroin users resembles what Bryan Page found among Cuban cocaine and polydrug users in Miami. "Young newcomers to the street scene," Page discovered, "are already fascinated by its perceived romance and excitement when they arrive." Among his subjects, too, drugs perceived to be "harder"—which therefore can only be mastered by an elite few—were more likely to confer high status. As one put it, cocaine

> gives you a feeling of superiority. It gives you a feeling that you're higher than the others. You're above the crowd. . . . Everybody is your friend because they can see it in your eyes that you are coked up. They are not going to fuck around with this guy.

From another part of the country, and in respect to a different drug of choice, similar motives appear in the testimony of one seventeen-year-old methamphetamine user from a declining white working-class community in California:

> I like the stuff, actually. . . . Cause it gives you a high, you know, and . . . it makes you look *bigger*, you know? Makes you look big time, you know, when you got an 8-ball of crank in your pocket, and two hundred dollars in your other pocket, and you're walking around town and you've got nice clothes on and stuff like that, and you whip out the 8-ball, you snort a line and you're all—your eyes get all big, you're running around? [laughs] It's really fun, it's really cool. I like it.

[Interviewer]: Bigger?

To your friends, and to yourself. If you go up to some
dude and he's just totally nothing but *weed*, he can't even
find someone who sells crank, and you come up and you
say "Yeah, I got the connection, I just bought me an 8-
ball, and I got two hundred dollars for *another* two 8-
balls," and he says, "Whoa, dude!" you know? And you're
like [proudly] "All *right!*" Makes you look bigger, you
know? That you've got all these *drugs*, and stuff like that?

British research paints a very similar picture of the way
drugs can confer status and an aura of "toughness" on youths
otherwise shut out from avenues of esteem and prestige.
Among young heroin and inhalant users in London studied
by Lee O'Bryan in the mid-1980s, "there appeared to be a
strong emphasis on being 'hard' and 'able to take it'" among
the "opinion leaders" who were the first to try heroin or
inhalants. These "trendsetters," O'Bryan writes, "defined taking
the substances as a test of courage." A good part of the appeal
of inhalants to working-class London youth, indeed, "derived
from the negative connotations ascribed to the substances by
society at large."

Angela Burr, who studied white, mostly unemployed male
heroin users in London, similarly argues that heroin smoking
spread rapidly among deprived working-class youth in the
eighties because it fulfilled their needs for status and a sense
of community, by allowing them to invert the norms of conventional society. "The deviant image of the 'junkie' and related
criminality were particularly attractive."

Chasing the dragon [smoking heroin] together provided
a vehicle for expressing and articulating friendships and
for demonstrating leadership and daring. A high income
from thieving . . . a big habit, and connections with well-
known criminals became symbols of status and prestige.

Like the early American students of addiction, Burr concludes that most of these new heroin users do not fit the stereotype of the addict as mentally ill:

The widespread use of heroin now means that more "normal" youngsters are using heroin. . . . The majority of young heroin-misusers in this area were the sociable risktaking kind of youngster known locally as "Jack the Lad." It was their extensive peer relations which fostered their long-term use of heroin.

In the north of England, too, Geoffrey Pearson found that it was typically the *more* intelligent and adventurous youth who were most likely to experiment with heroin. Indeed, where heroin was a central feature of a community's youth culture, being a "smackhead" took on "something of a heroic status," and often involved a rejection of conventional authority: "Particularly if 'Maggie' is telling them it's no good," a youth worker told Pearson, "then it must be worth having a go."

Most of the research linking drug use to the quest for status—like most drug-abuse research in general—has focused on *male* drug users. But similar motives appear in studies of women's drug careers as well. Summarizing their research on female heroin addicts in California, Marsha Rosenbaum and Sheigla Murphy argue that

women enter the heroin world for a number of reasons, among them a perception that it provides an expansion of life options. They are attracted to heroin, because they want to be part of a social scene complete with the appearance (and sometimes the reality) of money, excitement, and the euphoric properties of drugs.

Heroin, moreover,

has a reputation as the "hardest drug," and, as such, its
users take on an outsider or outlaw status, which is
sometimes appealing to young women. These attractions
may add a new dimension to women's lives—lives that
they often describe as boring, alienated, and without
money.

A parallel finding emerges from recent studies of the street
crack culture. Studies of inner-city crack dealers, for example,
make clear that the risks and pitfalls of the "job" often outweigh
the typically unspectacular material benefits. Street-level crack
dealers can sometimes bring in hundreds of dollars for an
afternoon's or night's work, but as often the take is much less.
What drives legions of poorer adolescents into street crack
dealing is at least as much the opportunity for respect and
visibility as the less certain chance of making large sums of
money:

> Some are in it for money, and some are in it because they
> want to be *noticed*, or they want people to have respect for
> them, whatever. I mean, 'cause money . . . You know, it's
> just *throwaway* money. . . . It's just the simple fact that
> "Oh, you know such and such? Oh yeah, he's a big
> kingpin." Or "Yeah, such and such is my *cousin*, you know
> him? Yeah, *I* used to sell dope for him," you know, stuff
> like that. . . . That's all it is, you know, who's bigger than
> who.

As Inciardi and Pottieger point out in reflecting on their
own studies of Miami crack dealers, the fascination of the crack
lifestyle in the 1980s and 1990s has a familiar ring: it is
"reminiscent of descriptions applied some years ago to the
heroin-user subculture—the joys of hustling and 'taking care
of business,' the thrills of a 'cops and robbers' street life." But
one critical difference stands out when the "hustlers" of the
fifties and sixties are compared with those of the eighties and

nineties; violence has become a much more prominent part of the drug culture's appeal. And the status-enhancing function of violence is by no means confined to the crack culture alone—as is chillingly revealed in Carl Taylor's interviews with twelve- to fourteen-year-old members of a heroin-dealing gang in Detroit:

> Lot of jit niggahs trying to get with us. They want to hook up with us, 'cause they know the bitches want our crew. We're the shit at school and in our neighborhood. It's us the stars. . . . They be begging like little women, trying to get close to us. They be talkin' trash about what they done did . . . they done popped this niggah and they done did this [laughing]. Everybody at our school want to join the fellas.

As these descriptions suggest, the appeal of the new youth drug cultures involves much more than the instrumental rewards of drug dealing itself. Dealing is only *one* facet of a broader youth culture that combines an inner-city version of the American ethos of material success with an exaggerated emphasis on consumerism, a rejection of the values of "straight" working-class life, and a fierce and all-pervading emphasis on acceptance by one's youthful peers. Ansley Hamid, for example, describes the subculture of young crack dealers in New York City as revolving around the glorification of violence, the exploitation of women, and the valorization of the short, violent life—a "repudiation of the ordinary world (of low wages, low status, and ceaseless, petty frustrations)." That lifestyle, Hamid argues, is the soil out of which crack dealing grows in the inner city, but it is a far wider and more pervasive phenomenon than the drug itself: the culture "apparently absorbs whole neighborhoods faster than crack itself can addict." That aspect of "repudiation"—of opposition to the pervasive assaults to self-esteem and dignity inherent in the narrow legitimate options for poor youth—appears prominently in other studies as well.

The anthropologist Philippe Bourgois, for example, sees the inner-city youth drug culture as one part of a larger "culture of resistance" to an economically exclusive and often humiliating society. The street youth Bourgois observed in New York had often undergone several negative experiences in the low-wage labor market, regularly confronting "abusive, exploitative, and often racist bosses or supervisors." They were drawn to dealing and street crime not only because the money might be better but, as important, because self-employment in the illicit economy provided a "more dignified workplace"—one which offered at least the possibility of sustaining a "sense of autonomy and dignity."

These descriptions—which are supported by other studies of adolescent cocaine and heroin dealers—descend in a straight line from Finestone's portrait of the "cat" culture of the fifties. But they also show that the newer street cultures, with their more prominent themes of violence and materialism, have evolved in ways that make them disturbingly different from the earlier culture of heroin use. The implications of the spread of these cultures—which I've also seen in interviewing teenage crack and methamphetamine dealers in California—are complex and profound. Among other things, the fact that drug dealing is typically only *one* aspect of a much broader culture of violence, exploitation, and consumerism suggests that curtailing the drug trade itself—were that in fact possible—would not necessarily reduce the violence that now consumes inner-city youth as much as we might hope, a point to which we'll return. It also helps us understand why once such a culture is allowed to become entrenched, it is very resistant to change—even if the conditions that bring it into being were to change for the better. Once young people have been thoroughly immersed in a lifestyle centered on the excitement of violence, risk-taking, and illicit acquisition, it is much harder to interest them in accepting the constraints of steady work—even if we are able to offer it. That is one reason why our failure to attack the deprivation and marginality of the inner-city young a generation ago was a choice that will haunt us for many, many years to come.

2. *The "coping" model* emphasizes the role of drugs in moderating the stress and insecurity of life in unstable, disorganized, and deprived communities. It rests on the simple but too-often-neglected recognition that daily life is much tougher in those places than it is in better-endowed communities. It is harder to make ends meet, harder to cope day after day with family crises and abusive relationships, with lack of transportation, health care, and child care, with housing problems, stressful work, and the pervasive insecurity of lives lived at best on the edge of disaster. Being poor, as a recent review of the situation of homeless women puts it, "virtually insures a life of chronic hassles."

In this context of endemic stress, drugs become a way of getting away from daily problems, medicating emotional anguish, relieving stress, escaping pain—a strategy of "palliative coping." Drug use is in that sense a functional adaptation to the realities of difficult lives—a way of achieving "some mastery over specific life stresses," as Jeanne Marsh and Steven Shevell have put it.

Edward Preble employed this perspective in the sixties to help explain high drug use among Puerto Rican youth in New York City. For young Puerto Rican men who were living "a la canona," or "under the gun"—faced with an overabundance of problems at work and at home, and the low self-esteem associated with low income and poor prospects—narcotics provided at the very least a useful consolidation of problems. "Although the solution itself entails a formidable problem," Preble wrote, "—the daily acquisition of an illegal and expensive commodity—it is preferred by a significant number of Puerto Rican men and male adolescents. As one addict informant puts it: 'When you use drugs you substitute one big problem—

which you can concentrate on—for a whole lot of different little problems.' "

And more recent evidence backs up the insight. Surveys of adolescent drug use, for example, show that it is often preceded by depression, and that drugs are used in part as a medication to relieve depressive symptoms and psychological distress among the young. A study of drug use among Toronto street youth by Reginald Smart and Edward Adlaf found not only that many used drugs (and alcohol) in order to cope or escape from adverse conditions, but that those youth who used drugs for "coping" purposes used *more* drugs than those who used them for other reasons, including social or recreational ones. Most did not regard their use of drugs or alcohol itself as their most pressing problem, but as a response to much worse ones—including the lack of basic needs like food, shelter, and clothing. A third of these street youth showed high levels of depression; nearly half reported attempting suicide at least once. "Drug and alcohol use among street youth," the researchers concluded, "is partly a response to existence in a hazardous and dysfunctional environment."

Marsh and Shevell's study of heroin addicts in several cities in the mid-1970s found that the addicts' own descriptions of why they used heroin tended to fall along a continuum. On one end were "subcultural reasons" ("to be hip"); on the other, reasons related to the need to cope—"to help forget problems," "because of feeling down or depressed."

Some version of the "coping" model often appears in descriptions of the motivation for women's drug use in particular. Joan Moore's studies of women heroin addicts in the East Los Angeles barrio—where the drug has been endemic since the 1940s—show that while Mexican-American women often *started* heroin use because they wanted the sensation of getting high, over time their main motivation shifted: the same women came to enjoy heroin "for its tranquilizing rather than exhilarating effects." The appeal of heroin as tranquilizer, Moore suggests, reflects the "great turmoil" in the lives of these women. The connection is utterly direct in the remarks of a Mexican-American "tecata" (female addict) interviewed by the sociologist Jaime Jorquez: "I was all out of food stamps, and I didn't know where I was going to get food or money or medicine. I started to think about heroin."

A recent study of men and women hospitalized for cocaine addiction in Massachusetts found strong gender differences in cocaine abuse. The men more often used cocaine "as part of an overall pattern of antisocial behavior," while women used it for more specific reasons—"family and job pressures," depression, and health problems. The women also tended to have a harder time stopping cocaine use—partly, the researchers argue, because they were less often employed, or if they were working at all, were more often trapped in lower-paying, lower-status jobs.

But the use of drugs to cope with stress and everyday problems crosses gender lines—and national boundaries. One of the most poignant illustrations of the "coping" model comes from Geoffrey Pearson's study in the north of England.

> **Question:** So what is it about heroin, compared to blow or speed or . . .
> **Wendy:** Y'know, heroin, it teks everything away, don't it?
> **Cheryl:** Oh aye. No worries.
> **Wendy:** You feel reet at ease, like . . .
> **Wayne:** Teks all yer worries away and then becomes a bigger one itsen.
> **Mother:** Yeh, it does.

"On occasion," Pearson writes, "this feeling of release from external pressures was so all-pervasive in a person's recollections of their early heroin use that the positive drug effects (in the sense of a "buzz" or a "hit") hardly seemed to play an important part in their attachment to the drug." Pearson quotes one couple who started using heroin while living in dilapidated housing:

Question: How did you get into heroin, then?
Linda: Oh, it were terrible . . .
Brian: They knocked it down it were that bad . . . there were no gas, there were no watter, we had to go next door for us watter . . .
Linda: Chimney fell down . . .
Brian: Couldn't use upstairs cos all't rooves had fell in. . . . And we lost a young un through it, like . . . Linda were pregnant and she lost a young un through it. After that . . . that's what did it, weren't it? That's what started us.
Linda: Yes.
Brian: Too many problems and, like, we had some henry [heroin] one day like, and we went back to't house, and we forgot all about house, because we were . . . you know . . . just didn't see nowt. . . .
Linda: . . . It puts you, like, in Ethiopia at first . . . Ethiopia! [Laughs.] Utopia . . . Utopia!
Brian: It's just like . . . you're just not bothered about nowt then. It's . . . great.

3. *The "structure" model* best fits the kind of analysis pioneered a generation ago by Edward Preble and John Casey, emphasizing the ways drug use can give a sense of structure and purpose to lives otherwise denied them, especially in the absence of stable, meaningful work.

In his follow-up of addicts treated at the federal hospital in Lexington, George Vaillant found that the physical effects of the drug seemed less important in explaining the users' initial use of heroin than the fact that they had so few alternatives in their lives. They begin, Vaillant writes, more because they have "very little opportunity to engage in other competing forms of independent activity than because morphine or heroin per se is a powerful reinforcer or temptation."

Parker and his colleagues, similarly, show how the pull of heroin in relieving monotony and purposelessness among unemployed young people in Wirral overcomes any concern they may have about its adverse consequences—including addiction and the pains of withdrawal. The earliest group of heroin users in Wirral, they note, knew little about the adverse effects of the drug, and therefore had little to dissuade them from starting heroin. Those who came after them, however, could see the effects of addiction at first hand—but ignored them. "A significant proportion of these younger interviewees, both male and female," they write, "simply ignored the knowledge beginning to accumulate. When pressed on this point, a typical response was: 'Why not? There's nothing else to do anyway except spend all day watching the telly.'" "Why are young kids using?" responded a local heroin dealer in Burr's study of heroin use among working-class London youth. "They don't know how to occupy their minds. It gives them something to do, to go scoring and thieving. It's like a job."

The research suggests, then, that people abuse hard drugs in part because there are simply so few "legitimate" alternatives in some communities to compete for their allegiance, time, and energy. The sheer paucity of alternatives has a particularly crippling effect on the prospects for getting *off* of drugs once addicted; and it helps explain why there is such a strong and predictable connection between achieving long-term abstinence and having a stable job. One of Pearson's subjects makes the connection explicit:

It just seems like the hardest thing in the world to stay off smack. . . . Like I say, I've been off it a week, more than a week, but you just go back on it cos it's round here, you know. . . . I think, like, unemployment and that has got a lot to do with it. . . . With nothing to do, I'm sitting here,

like, doing nothing. . . . I'm not trying to blame anyone
else, like, but I'm bound to start thinking of smack again.

Vaillant's research found that the most important determinants
of whether addicts relapsed following treatment were "largely
nonpharmacological variables"—especially the degree of stability and structure in the addict's life before addiction and, as
important, "the discovery of competing sources of gratification"
afterward. One such source of gratification, in addition to
steady work, Vaillant found, was a stable family life, and—
more generally—the prospect of becoming not only more self-
sufficient but of being capable of caring for *others*.

Similar mechanisms help to explain why some users of hard
drugs remain at the recreational or occasional stage while
others slide deeper into heavy use or serious addiction. In a
study of Delaware heroin addicts, Charles Faupel and Carl
Klockars argue that it is precisely the presence or absence of a
"life structure" that determines the progress of a heroin user's
career. Like other researchers, they point out that, contrary to
the popular belief, heroin use "does not inevitably lead to a
deterioration of lifestyle": many users manage to maintain
family lives and work routines. But without the constraints of
work and family, addicts will expand their consumption "to
whatever level of use the availability of drugs or funds to buy
them makes possible." Thus at one extreme of the spectrum
of heroin users is what they call the "freewheeling junkie,"
whose essentially uncontrolled drug use is a result of an "almost
total absence of structures of restraint." The mother of a British
addict makes the point less formally:

> People what are working, if they've got good sense, they've
> got summat to look out for. They're not gonna take it,
> are they, through't week when they're going to work.
> Whereas you get somebody what's in't unemployed, they'll
> have it at weekend and they'll continue wi' it, cos they've
> got nowt else to do, have they?

It is the high levels of unemployment in the stricken British cities, according to Pearson, that help explain why patterns of occasional or "recreational" heroin use failed to emerge in working-class neighborhoods, and "why instead one finds runaway forms of daily use which can quickly assume an epidemic form." Like abstinence, occasional drug use is fostered where the imperatives of conventional life—work and family—enforce a concern with the consequences of uncontrolled use.

The lack of realistic prospects for rewarding work or stable family life is also deeply implicated in the high-risk sexual behavior that has increasingly tied drug abuse to AIDS and other sexually transmitted diseases. Unprotected sex with multiple partners was widespread among the youth in Bowser and Fullilove's study of crack-ridden neighborhoods in San Francisco, which helped explain their rapidly rising rates of gonorrhea and AIDS. The researchers argue that the pattern of heedless sexuality—like that of drug use itself—is deeply influenced by "long-term community economic conditions and opportunities." "What happens to adolescents," they ask, "in a community where parents and neighbors are cut off from—or at best marginal to—the economy?"

> If these young people see themselves through the eyes of their parents and neighbors, there is very little reason for them to see a different future for themselves. Very clearly there is less motivation to delay sexuality. . . . Early and more frequent sexual activity are predictable outcomes, as is teen pregnancy and the inability of these sexually active teens to form families.

"People who are not a part of the industrial world," they conclude, "have little reason to behave as if they are."

4. *The "saturation" model* is, in many ways, an extreme extension of the "structure" model of drug abuse. It suggests that communities that have been rendered hopeless and purposeless

for decades or generations by the restriction of social and economic opportunities may become so saturated with illicit drugs that drug use is often hardly planned or consciously chosen at all, but involves a kind of passive drift into a practice that "everybody" is doing.

I am borrowing this term from Joseph Fitzpatrick's studies of multiple drug use in Puerto Rican neighborhoods in New York in the 1970s—which, then as now, were among the most drug-ridden in the world: "saturated with drugs and people in drug traffic." In those communities, Fitzpatrick argues, the "macho subculture" model of drug use fit poorly: It was not only the more innovative "risk-takers" who used cocaine or heroin, but all types of young people of widely varying temperaments. "In many cases," Fitzpatrick argues, drug abuse among these youth "is almost a passive response to a surrounding situation rather than machismo."

Pearson's study of heroin users in the high-unemployment areas of several British cities suggests something similar. He describes addicts often "drifting" into heroin use without having made very clear conscious choices to do so, or, at least, not being able to clearly recollect them—"as if the person concerned had been not only unaware of what was happening, but also somehow uninvolved." Heroin users in cities where the drug is widespread, according to Pearson, often operate in a "gray area" where the consequences of what they're doing are not seriously considered, and where the nature and extent of their involvement with the drug is unclear both to them and to others around them.

The saturation of communities by drugs makes *quitting* drugs especially difficult, simply because the addict is surrounded by so many people who are still using. "I know if I go out," says one of Pearson's interviewees, "I'll either meet someone round the area, cos everyone I know is on heroin . . . anyone who'll bother with you. . . . So anyone I go and meet is on heroin, and before I know it I'm back smoking it again myself." In his study of the difficulties of "extricating" from heroin abuse among Mexican-American "tecatos," Jaime Jorquez similarly emphasizes the obstacles presented by the sheer fact that the addict's barrio is typically saturated with other heroin users. The urge to shoot heroin is exacerbated, Jorquez writes, in communities where the addict is "bombarded by stimuli associated with heroin use." Where heroin is pervasive and easily available, "even relatively insignificant stimuli can trigger powerful heroin craving in the ex-tecato." (As we'll see, the "saturation" model helps explain why reducing drug abuse on the community level is so difficult to accomplish through attempts to treat the *individual* user, however well-intended.)

Again, these "models" of the motives and meanings of drug abuse are by no means mutually exclusive. An impoverished eighteen-year-old in Detroit may use crack or heroin because doing so makes him seem "tough" in the eyes of his peers, because it soothes the stress of hassles at school or at home, *and* because he hasn't got much else to do in any case and is surrounded by others in the same situation. Moreover, the various motives for drug use may have different weight at different stages of the user's career. Most of the research I've described suggests that the status model probably best fits the early stages of drug use. Later, as the adverse effects of the drugs and the addict's encounters with the criminal-justice system become increasingly painful and distressing, the addict may continue using less for the inherent excitement or the thrill of belonging to a self-described elite than in an attempt to manage the habit itself and to cope with life's problems—which have by now become aggravated by addiction and the user's status as a criminal. Rosenbaum and Murphy put it this way:

> Initially, women addicts enjoy the beginnings of a heroin career. But the reality of life as a "junkie" quickly turns out to be different from life in the initial or honeymoon

phase. In the addicted stage, women become locked in, and the earlier illusion of a possible expansion of options transforms into a *funneling* or reduction of life options. . . . The heroin world is a chaotic one, nothing is predictable. Finding a consistent source of good street drugs occupies most of an addict's time. Holding down a legitimate job is nearly impossible. . . . Most women resort to illegitimate jobs with better pay and more flexible hours. Upon entering the world of illegal work, women addicts' lives become full of risk and chaos. . . . Encounters with or entry into the criminal-justice system escalate the funneling of life options out of the conventional world. . . . Because women addicts have no time for anything but heroin acquisition and use, children tend to be neglected, jobs get lost, and numerous health problems, including a gnawing, constant withdrawal, result.

Thus the meaning of drug use surely shifts over time for most addicts, and the specific conditions that breed it surely vary from individual to individual, and from one vulnerable group to another. But what the recent research most clearly reveals is that the similarities in the worlds of endemic drug abuse outweigh the differences. As Isidor Chein put it in the 1950s, "The balance of the structural materials may differ somewhat, but the final shape of the [drug user's] world is pretty much the same."

At bottom, what these studies tell us is that the central point emphasized again and again by the researchers of the 1950s and 1960s was correct. If we want to understand drug abuse on the mass or endemic level it reaches in many American (and some European) cities, we must begin by recognizing that it is a social phenomenon, not primarily an individual or biochemical one. It emerges, and endures, because in any of several ways it serves to meet human needs that are systematically thwarted by the social and economic structures of the world the users live in. And—as we will see in more detail in the second half of this book—the early researchers were right on another score as well. The fact that endemic drug abuse is a predictable response to social conditions that destroy self-esteem, hope, solidarity, stability, and a sense of purpose strongly limits most conventional antidrug strategies. It limits our ability to "deter" drug use, and drug dealing, through the courts and prisons; it limits the capacity of treatment programs to "cure"—or even enroll—addicts; and it limits our ability to reduce drug use and the associated risks of death and disease through education and prevention.

This does not mean that our hands are tied. It does mean that a more effective battle against the ravages of drugs will require measures that are very different from what we have done so far. And it also explains, as we'll now see, why the United States was so ripe for an explosion of drug abuse in the 1980s.

V I

To some observers it is as if the drug plague of the 1980s had come out of the blue. As one noted commentator puts it,

> The explosion of drug use—particularly use of crack—in the mid-1980s seemed to have nothing to do with any decline in opportunities, or indeed any change that should have increased the sense of despair and hopelessness that some claim is the reason for the resort to drugs.

The belief that the drug crisis was detached from any precipitating social context—a reflection of some mysterious failure of individual moral character, unrelated to systemic changes in the society as a whole—lends itself to the argument that the drug problem will be solved, if at all, by some combination of moral exhortation, force, and fear. But it does not square with the evidence. In fact, the drug crisis of the 1980s flourished in

the context of an unparalleled social and economic disaster
that swept low-income communities in America in ways that
virtually ensured that the drug problem would worsen. To be
sure, the sheer increase in the availability of drugs—especially
crack, which is not only powerfully appealing but also remarkably inexpensive and easy to distribute—was a crucial factor.
But crack was like a match thrown on dry tinder.

The most fundamental and far-reaching change, from which
much else has followed, has been the continuing decline of
what the researchers of the fifties and sixties called the "opportunity structure." We've seen that mass drug abuse is closely
associated both with long-term joblessness and with long-term
employment in jobs that offer no challenge and no future—
jobs that cannot support families or sustain communities. It
should not be surprising, therefore, that the drug crisis has
worsened simultaneously with one of the most radical shifts in
economic opportunities in American history. That shift was
predicted more than once in the 1950s and 1960s; but it has
gone much farther than anyone then imagined.

A crucial part of that change has been the accelerating
disappearance of the traditional blue-collar jobs that once
provided decent pay and a path into stable community and
family life for less-educated workers. As John Kasarda has
shown, the deindustrialization of the past fifteen to twenty
years has struck hardest at the central cities, where the loss of
blue-collar jobs was so great that it usually offset any gains in
other sectors of the urban economy—even in the years when
some areas of the country were enjoying considerable economic
growth. Between 1970 and 1980, New York City gained almost
275,000 managerial, professional, technical, and administrative
jobs, but lost over 360,000 in blue-collar manufacturing, clerical
work, and sales—a net loss of over 95,000 jobs in the central
city. Those losses were particularly devastating for people
without much formal schooling—not, however, only those who
had dropped out of school, but the entire "noncollege" half of
younger Americans. Thus Detroit lost well over 100,000 jobs

held by people without a high-school diploma and over 55,000 held by high-school graduates, and simultaneously gained 22,000 jobs for college graduates and 35,000 for people with some college.

By the 1980s, as a result, young people growing up in the cities could see less and less connection between completing high school and landing a decent job, unless they expected to go on to college; and that profound change has been especially crippling for minorities. As Kasarda points out, blacks in the cities are still "highly concentrated in the education category where city employment has rapidly declined . . . and greatly underrepresented in the educational-attainment categories where city employment is quickly expanding." This helps explain what seems at first to be a paradox; even the "boom" years of the eighties and the rapid growth of jobs in some urban areas generally failed to reverse the decline in oppor- tunities for less educated minority workers. To some observers, the coexistence of economic growth with lingering joblessness in the inner cities points to a cultural or "behavioral" expla- nation of the plight of the urban unemployed. But there is a more parsimonious explanation: by the 1970s, the fruits of economic growth were being distributed differently than in the past—increasingly divided by education, race, and residence.

Up through the late 1960s, economic growth pulled in the less educated and the better educated more equally. Between 1950 and 1970, Kasarda notes, "there was considerable growth in all cities in the number of blacks employed who had not completed twelve years of education." But "after 1970, the bottom fell out in urban industrial demand for poorly educated blacks." In Philadelphia, for example, the number of jobs lost in the seventies for blacks without a high-school diploma almost equaled the number added in the previous *two* decades.

What is critical about these declines is that they have not only affected the individuals who have lost jobs, but have essentially placed entire communities on the margins of the productive economy. In the Chicago ghetto neighborhoods of

Oakland and Grand Boulevard, according to William J. Wilson and his colleagues, fewer than one adult in four was gainfully employed by 1980, where well over half had been employed thirty years before.

The sharp decline in prospects for less-educated urban workers was partly—but only partly—matched by increased opportunities in the suburbs. Thus while New York City lost 95,000 jobs during the seventies, its suburbs gained almost 500,000; Chicago lost 88,000 jobs while its suburbs gained a whopping 630,000. But several formidable barriers kept most of those suburban jobs out of the hands of minorities from the inner cities. The economic boom in fast-growing Atlanta, for example, as Gary Orfield has shown, "did not produce strong outreach for black workers but drew many young, highly skilled, well-educated non-Southerners into the area, most of whom moved to the suburbs." Nor was this result entirely accidental. The maldistribution of job opportunities between suburbs and inner city was exacerbated by the deliberate restriction of housing opportunities for low-income people in the job-rich suburbs—and even deliberate resistance to extending public transportation from the inner city to suburban worksites, which meant that the new jobs were often as unreachable for poorer inner-city residents as if they had been on another planet. (Relatively few poor inner-city workers have access to a car: over three-quarters of the households in Chicago's West Side ghetto, for example, had no car in 1980.) Recent research by Mark Schneider and Thomas Phelan, moreover, shows that even when blacks moved to the suburbs, they were usually "found in highly segregated communities with comparatively slow job growth." Many newer, "clean" industries moved to some suburbs in the 1970s and early 1980s, but much more slowly, if at all, to those suburbs with "expanding black population concentrations."

Nor were inner-city blacks the only losers from these changes in the labor market. The sociologist Marta Tienda has shown how these shifts away from manufacturing and toward the suburbanization of new jobs have had an enormous impact on Puerto Rican Americans—among whom, as we've seen, hard-drug abuse has raged at crisis levels since the seventies. Because they are heavily concentrated in areas where good jobs for less educated workers have vanished, and are confined to the bottom of the "ethnic hiring queue," both unemployment and what Tienda calls "detachment from the labor force" have risen sharply among Puerto Ricans—more rapidly than among other Hispanic groups. In the early 1970s, about 13 percent of adult Puerto Rican men were "unstably active" in the labor force—that is, still connected to the job market but periodically unemployed. That was already exceptionally high, but ten years later, the proportion had risen to 19 percent, and to those had been added another 6 percent who were "stably inactive"—that is, they were out of the labor force and had not looked for work over a five-year period.

The rapid decline of industrial jobs, then—along with a mismatch between urban and suburban job growth—left many less educated workers stranded even in areas where the total number of jobs grew dramatically in the seventies and eighties. But equally crucial has been the downward trend in the quality of the *new* jobs available to most Americans—rural and small-town as well as urban. It is not just that the less prepared are being left behind in an economy increasingly dominated by high-tech postindustrial jobs requiring ever-higher skills and formal education. Though many new jobs do require more education than most poor people—black or white, urban or rural—possess, we have not created nearly enough of them to provide most Americans with good, stable work even if they *did* have the requisite education. The most conspicuous trend in the American labor market since the seventies, in fact, has been the growth of poorly paying, unstable jobs with little future.

In a 1988 study, for example, researchers from the Budget Committee of the U.S. Senate divided the jobs created in the American economy between 1979 and 1987 into three categories—those that paid poverty-level wages or below, those that paid more than four times the poverty level, and "middle-wage" jobs in between. The "dominant trend in American job creation in the 1980s," the committee reported, "has been for low-paying jobs to replace those which provided a middle-class standard of living." The growth of low-wage jobs was not, of course, the whole story: many high-wage jobs were created in those years. But the share of new jobs paying below-poverty wages grew twice as fast. More than four out of five net new jobs for men in the American economy in those years paid poverty-level wages or below. Though this shift varied region-ally (at least until the recession of the early 1990s), with some Northeastern and Midwestern states creating higher propor-tions of good jobs, the overall trend nationwide was toward "downward wage polarization."

What is especially relevant in understanding the social context of the drug crisis is that this decline in job quality struck hardest—indeed almost wholly—at *younger* workers. Between 1979 and 1987, the Senate committee calculates, there was a net loss of about 1.6 million middle-wage jobs for workers under thirty-five and a vast increase in low-wage ones, while for workers *over* thirty-five things actually improved slightly on the national level.

Increasingly, too, the jobs available to the young were more likely to be less than full-time. Overall, the proportion of American jobs that are part-time has grown by half since the late 1950s. Not all part-time jobs, of course, are poor ones. But as Chris Tilly has shown, most of the growth since the seventies has been in what he calls "secondary" part-time work, in jobs "characterized by low skill requirements, low pay and fringe benefits, low productivity, and high turnover" as well as little chance for advancement. Over a fourth of part-time workers, versus one in twenty full-time workers, earned no more than minimum wages in 1984. And the largest share of the growth in secondary part-time work was among youth aged sixteen to twenty-one and "prime age" men aged twenty-two to sixty-four—not among women, who were steadily shifting toward full-time work in those years. In short, not only were youth (and young adult men) facing the loss of traditional entry-level jobs, but their options were increasingly limited to jobs that were both poorly paid and part-time.

Once again, as Tilly makes clear, this shift was not accidental. It was one aspect of a quite deliberate strategy on the part of many employers to reduce their costs and become economically competitive by adopting a "low-wage, low-skill, high-turnover" policy rather than by increasing the skills and productivity of their work force. That choice, rather than the inevitable effects of neutral technological changes, is most responsible for the rapid downward shift in America's "opportunity structure." Besides the move toward part-time work, that strategy has involved the transfer of millions of jobs to low-wage havens both in poorer parts of the United States and overseas; aggressive resistance to unionization; the deliberate refusal to invest in serious training and retraining of workers (about which we shall hear more later); and fierce opposition to raises in the federal minimum wage, which consequently remained stagnant in the face of sharply rising costs of living throughout the 1980s. In 1974, full-time, year-round work at the minimum wage (then $2.00 an hour) brought an income fractionally more than that required to support a family of three at the poverty level, and about 80 percent of the poverty level for a family of four. By 1987, the same level of work at the minimum wage of $3.35 brought only 74 percent of what it took to support a family of three at the poverty level and merely 58 percent of the poverty level for a family of four.

When we add the trends in low-wage and part-time work to those in unemployment, we begin to see just how deeply the "opportunity structure" has been slashed for people in the bottom third of the income scale—especially the young. Robert Sheak and David Dabelko have compiled figures on the numbers of people who fall into one of four categories of what they call the "underemployed": the officially unemployed; those who are out of the labor force but would like a job now; those working part-time involuntarily, for economic reasons; and those working year-round, full-time, but earning less than the federal poverty level for a family of four. Together, they were about 23 percent of the total number of Americans employed in 1972, and 29 percent by 1987—in all, nearly 32 million people, up from only 19 million fifteen years before. Thirteen million people, in short, had joined the ranks of the poorly employed in the course of a decade and a half—a period that included several years of the Reagan economic "recovery."

The pervasive decline in job quality has reduced opportunities not only for minorities, but for younger and less educated whites as well—so much so that by the mid-1980s, young white men without much education were facing job prospects as bleak as those that blacks or Hispanics faced twenty years before. They were, in effect, falling into the same kinds of economic conditions that confronted urban blacks at the time of the ghetto riots of the sixties.

In one of the most revealing studies of this troubling pattern, the sociologist Daniel Lichter of Pennsylvania State University traced the growth of four types of "economic underemployment" between 1970 and 1982—the years immediately preceding the drug epidemic of the 1980s. In addition to looking at unemployment as officially defined—that is, being out of a job but actively looking for one within the past thirty days—Lichter also included what he called "subunemployment"—being without a job but not looking in the belief that none were available; underemployment resulting from low hours of work (working less than full-time and unable to find a full-time job); and underemployment resulting from low wages—which he defined as working full-time but earning less than 125 percent of the federal poverty level.

Measured in this way, Lichter shows, the 1970s and early 1980s were an economic catastrophe for younger and less educated American men of all races. Between 1970 and 1982, the overall level of underemployment roughly doubled among men in central cities; by 1982 more than one in three black men—but also nearly one in five white men—fell into one of those four categories of the "underemployed." 1982 was a recession year and 1970 was not, but that accounted for only part of the decline. By 1980, before the recession, underemployment had already risen by about 50 percent from its level in 1970. As many white men were underemployed in 1982 as black men had been in 1970—so that although black men remained twice as likely to be unemployed or in poor jobs as whites did, the situation was significantly and rapidly deteriorating for white men as well. (Black men were increasingly likely to be out of work altogether, but whites were closing the gap when it came to working in poor jobs with low pay and insufficient hours.)

Not surprisingly, Lichter found the problem of urban underemployment to be considerably worse for younger men, of both races. Already in 1970, 24 percent of young black men and 14 percent of young white men living in central cities were underemployed. By 1980 the figures had risen to 37 and 20 percent respectively, and in the recession of 1982 shot to 54 and 26 percent. In that year, in other words, over *half* of young black men and a quarter of young white men were either out of work or working at jobs with too few hours or too meager wages to provide a minimally decent living.

When we look at the connection between underemployment and education the portrait sharpens. Between 1970 and 1980 underemployment among *white* men with less than twelve years of schooling doubled; by 1982 it had tripled. In that recession year almost a third of white men with less than a high-school education were either jobless or working in poverty-level or near-poverty-level jobs—as were nearly half of blacks. Again, there was some racial convergence in the rates of underemployment in low-income work, but as Lichter tellingly comments, "this was largely because of increases in the white 'working poor' rather than declines in the fraction of less-educated blacks who were working at poverty wages." The narrowing of the difference between the races, in other words, was due to the declining economic conditions of young white men, rather than improving conditions for blacks.

Lichter concludes that in the seventies and early eighties there was a growing split by class and age in the "adequacy of employment among urban men." Men with low levels of education, in particular, were in *much* worse shape in the early eighties than their counterparts had been a decade earlier; the economic consequences of poor schooling had sharply increased. It was not that the skills or competence of younger urban men had fallen; rather, the kind of work available to them had changed markedly for the worse. More recent research shows that this trend has continued. Between 1973 and 1987, according to Sheldon Danziger and Gregory Acs, levels of schooling increased for working men of all races: the proportion of employed black men who had a high-school education or better, for example, more than doubled. But that increasing education did little for their chances of landing a good job. Indeed, men with a high-school education were more than twice as likely to be working in a low-wage job in 1987 as their counterparts in 1973. White men with a high-school diploma were as likely to be working in low-wage jobs in 1987 as blacks had been fifteen years before. What that has meant in human terms is that much greater numbers of younger people of all races, even if they successfully complete high school, now realistically have very little to look forward to in the world of work.

These adverse shifts in the "opportunity structure" were exacerbated by the simultaneous reduction in the public benefits that could have cushioned the economic impact of declining earnings from poorer jobs. To understand just how fateful the slashing of public income support has been since the early 1980s, we need to emphasize that even *before* the Reagan administration began a deliberate assault on the welfare state, the United States already ranked lowest among advanced industrial societies in the generosity of its safety net for the disadvantaged and in the degree to which income benefits kept people from sinking into poverty. The dimensions of this gap have been illuminated by the recent Luxemburg Income Study, which compares rates of poverty and the effectiveness of government benefits in the United States, Canada, Australia, West Germany, Sweden, and the United Kingdom at the start of the 1980s. With the exception of Australia, the American rate of what economists call "pretransfer" poverty—that is, the level of poverty before income benefits and taxes are counted —was already sharply higher than that of the other countries: more than half again as high as Sweden and nearly twice that of West Germany. But the gaps were even wider once the much more generous government benefits for the poor in other countries were added in. Families with children in the United States were three times as likely to be poor after transfers as families in Sweden, twice as likely as families in West Germany. Overall, according to the economist Timothy Smeeding, at the end of the 1970s it was already true that "government programs reduce poverty twice as much on average in the other countries as in the United States." One reason for these differences was that the benefit levels in our income support programs were far lower than those in the other countries. Another was that many American families, unlike those in other Western industrial democracies, did not participate in the meager programs available: they fell through the safety net altogether. In the United States, according to Smeeding, 27 percent of poor families with children "receive no public income support from the programs studied," while in every other country in this study, "at least 99 percent" of poor families with children received some form of income support.

And that was *before* the deliberate reductions in income support in the United States in the 1980s propelled hundreds of thousands more American families into poverty. (The effect of these cuts, too, was magnified because they came after several years of inflation that had already reduced the real value of income benefits for the poor.) Between 1979 and 1986, the average benefit under Aid to Families with Dependent Children (AFDC) fell by about 20 percent in real terms, while the proportion of poor children actually receiving benefits fell from 72 to 60 percent. By the late 1980s, thirty-five states and the District of Columbia paid average welfare benefits that were less than *half* the federal poverty level. And what was true for AFDC was also true for other kinds of income support, notably unemployment insurance. The proportion of jobless workers receiving benefits under the unemployment compensation system fell from a little more than half in the late 1970s (already extremely low by European standards) to less than a third by the late 1980s. All of this meant that, as the 1980s wore on, public benefits lifted fewer and fewer people out of poverty. In 1979, according to the Center on Budget and Policy Priorities, only about one poor family in five was pulled above the poverty line by some combination of AFDC, social security, and unemployment insurance: but by 1986, just one in *nine*. In absolute numbers, this meant that about half a million families remained in poverty who would have ceased to be poor had benefits been maintained at even their already minimal late-seventies levels.

The savage combination of a deteriorating job structure and reductions in income support benefits was responsible for sharply declining economic conditions for lower-income Americans in the seventies and eighties, both within the races and between them, and a deepening and hardening of poverty which, again, crossed racial and ethnic boundaries.

These adverse income shifts have struck hardest at the groups that are already most vulnerable to drug abuse—particularly disadvantaged young men and younger women raising children. By 1983, just before the crack epidemic leveled the inner cities, the median income of black families with a child under the age of six had fallen 23 percent since 1974, and for Hispanic families by 17 percent. Families headed by a single *woman* of *any* race with a child under six had seen their income drop by 25 percent since the mid-1970s.

The worst effects were at the bottom. More Americans became poor or nearly poor in the years just before the drug crisis, and the living conditions of those below the poverty line worsened by virtually every measure from the late 1970s onward—reversing what had been an erratic but generally upward twenty-year trend. Between 1979 and 1984, just when the drug epidemic of the eighties began to explode, 7 million white and 1.3 million black people joined the ranks of those living below 125 percent of the federal poverty level. The growth in poverty was especially dramatic in some cities, particularly those suffering sharp losses in relatively well-paying jobs—and it was already underway, in many cases, well before the eighties. The proportion of Hispanic families living in poverty, for example, more than doubled between 1969 and 1979 in several cities, including Cleveland and Bridgeport, and nearly doubled in Boston, Detroit, and Milwaukee.

Not only were there *more* of the poor, however; they were also poorer. The depth of poverty is sometimes measured by the "income deficit"—the amount of money it would take a poor family or individual to *reach* the poverty level. During the 1980s the average income deficit of poor families increased for all races and ethnic groups—but, again, it was worst of all for minorities. By the close of the decade the average poor black or Hispanic family was subsisting at more than $5,000 *below* the federal poverty level.

A recent Census Bureau study shows that this trend toward deepening deprivation among the poor occurred for both poor women and poor men, for both poor families and "unrelated individuals"—and that, in fact, it was *understated* by the conventional statistics. The average income deficit for all poor families rose by about 12 percent from 1973 to 1986; but since the average poor family was smaller over those years, the income deficit *per family member* rose more dramatically, by nearly 30 percent. Measured in terms of the real resources available to their families, indeed, the American poor were considerably poorer in 1986 than they had been in 1959, when the federal government first began collecting poverty data— and well before the "war on poverty" of the sixties.

It is sometimes argued that the decline in income among the poor simply reflects a rising proportion of poor people in families headed by women, who are more likely to be severely poor. But the deepening of the poverty gap was more general: the income deficit increased for families headed by men as well as by women, and for unrelated individuals of both sexes. Those hardest hit were poor men living outside of families, whose *average* income was less than half the poverty level in the eighties (less than $3,000) and who were considerably *worse* off than their counterparts had been in the early 1970s. Moreover, as the study points out, the growing ranks of the homeless are mostly not even included in these figures: the government's poverty statistics are based on a survey of *households*, which by definition—as we've seen in the case of surveys of drug use—excludes most people who live outside them. Were we to factor in the economic condition of men and women without stable homes who eluded the official surveys, the number of poor men and women who have sunk below half of the official poverty line would loom even larger. Ominously, too, the rising income deficit among the poor continued more or less steadily throughout the much-vaunted economic "recovery" of the 1980s; the state of the poorest, that is, was little affected by a growing economy, even when we had one.

Poverty, moreover, not only deepened but also became more concentrated geographically. More of the poor were trapped in communities mainly inhabited by other poor people. That was particularly true for blacks and Hispanics: persistent residential segregation and rising poverty rates worked together to cram growing numbers of people into neighborhoods that, as a result, were unusually lacking in collective economic and social resources. According to William J. Wilson and his colleagues, the proportion of blacks living in "extreme poverty areas"—where over 40 percent of the residents were poor—more than doubled between 1970 and 1980. Similarly, as Anne Santiago and Margaret Wilder have shown, by 1979 roughly 50 percent of the Hispanic poor in Boston, Cincinnati, Newark, and Philadelphia were living in areas of concentrated poverty, reflecting a "growing spatial isolation of impoverished Latinos from the larger population."

It is sometimes argued that the rises in poverty have been only among people who have chosen not to work, or whose inappropriate behavior has forced them out of the labor market—and that things have steadily improved for people who behave responsibly and work regularly. But that isn't true. Indeed, one of the most telling economic shifts during the 1970s and 1980s has been that the rewards of working regularly have fallen, not risen, for those at the lower end of the job scale. Marta Tienda, for example, shows that Mexican-American and Puerto Rican men who were "stably active" in the work force were more likely to be poor in 1985 than their counterparts fifteen years earlier. Hispanics, in particular, greatly increased their participation in the labor force in the 1970s and early 1980s, but their poverty rates rose faster than any other groups, mainly because of their increasing concentration in low-wage jobs. Among all races, the numbers of people who worked full-time and year-round but earned less than a poverty-level wage rose significantly from the early 1970s onward: they were about 8 percent of the total employed in 1972 and 12 percent by 1987. Moreover, their numbers steadily increased after the middle of the 1970s, growing—like the income deficit of the poor—even during the economic "recovery" after the early 1980s. Nor was the increase in the working poor confined to the inner cities; it was a national phenomenon that cut across the rural-urban divide as well as the racial one. In 1979, 32 percent of rural workers and 23 percent of urban workers earned less than enough from full-time, year-round work to support four people at the poverty level. By 1987 their numbers had risen sharply in *both* country and city, to 42 percent and 29 percent respectively. In many Southern and some Midwestern and Mountain states, nearly *half* of rural full-time workers, by the late 1980s, could not earn enough to bring a family of four above the poverty line.

What these bare statistics mean in real life is not only that growing numbers of working Americans face extremes of economic deprivation—but also that, more and more, working hard and hewing to middle-class norms of behavior may get you nothing more than long hours and continued poverty. That is obviously a recipe for frustration and alienation, and it has been psychologically aggravated by the simultaneous growth in conspicuous affluence at the other end of the income scale.

As poverty deepened and spread, many other American families of all races and ethnic groups were doing better and better, contributing to the stark splitting of life chances and material well-being that distinguishes the past fifteen years from any comparable period in our history. The proportion of white families making over $50,000 a year nearly doubled from the late sixties to the end of the eighties—and grew even more rapidly among blacks, by 168 percent from 1967 to 1989. Overall, measured by gains and losses at each fifth of the American income distribution, as reported by the House Ways and Means Committee, the bottom fifth of Americans lost about 12 percent in income between 1977 and 1990 while the top fifth gained over 30 percent—and the top 5 percent gained nearly 50 percent..

A recent Census Bureau study illustrates the growth of inequality from another vantage point. The study measures trends in "relative income"—defined as the proportion of the population with incomes either less than half or more than twice the national average. During the 1970s and 1980s, more and more Americans—white, black, and Latino—fell into one or the other of those extremes, with the numbers in the middle correspondingly shrinking. Given what we've seen about the impact of the changing job structure on younger and less educated people, it is not surprising that they suffered most from this growing economic bifurcation. In 1969 only 19 percent of people under eighteen had incomes below half the national average; by 1989, the figure was about 30 percent. Among people without a high-school diploma, the proportion with low relative incomes jumped from 23 percent in 1964 to 38 percent in 1989, and the rise was actually slightly *faster* for those who had finished high school but had not completed college. In short, a substantial part of the younger population, especially, saw its comparative fortunes plummeting—not only relative to the most affluent, but also to the middle; and they were therefore progressively less able to participate fully in the good life as it was lived by more fortunate Americans.

But the decline in living standards among poorer Americans has involved more than income alone. Shrinking opportunities and falling incomes have been exacerbated by the crisis in low-income housing and the effects of government retreat from the provision of public services. These have combined to increase the "surplus of vulnerability" that has laid many communities open to the ravages of hard drugs.

The housing crisis has contributed particularly heavily to that vulnerability. Without a stable place to live, people lose the community supports that could provide a buffer against the impact of economic decline. As Gary Orfield puts it,

Without being able to afford housing where the family can stay securely, there is no basic stability in a family's life and no consistent lasting relationship with institutions, friends, and community. Housing determines access to

schooling, safety, friends for the children, and the ability
to get to work in a reasonable time.

But stable housing became far more elusive for lower-income
people in the eighties, as the result of skyrocketing housing
costs, declining incomes, and the retreat of the federal government from housing support for the poor and near-poor. During
the years when the drug crisis struck with greatest force, the
federal government had virtually abandoned its already weak
commitment to the ideal of "a decent home and a suitable
living environment for every American family" embodied in
the Federal Housing Act passed just after World War II.
Indeed, low-income housing programs were "slashed more
deeply than any other federal activity" during the 1980s—by
roughly 75 percent from 1981 through 1989. Meanwhile, costs
in the private housing market were spinning out of control;
between 1974 and 1983, the number of rental units going for
less than $300 a month (in 1986 dollars) fell by almost a million.
Thus, just as the incomes of the poor fell steadily and the value
of housing benefits for poor families plummeted, housing costs
rose, in a perverse triple whammy. As a result, for families
with children in the bottom fifth of the income scale, the
"median rent burden"—rent as a proportion of total family
income—went up by fifty percent from 1974 to 1987. In
Atlanta, families below the poverty level were "forced to spend
more than two-thirds of their cash incomes for housing costs
by the early 1980s," according to Orfield, which meant that
many could not both meet those costs and "provide other basic
essentials for their children." The significance of this is illuminated if we look back at what the Kerner Commission on
the ghetto riots of the 1960s had to say about the state of
housing for the poor a quarter-century ago. "Grievances related
to housing," the commission found, "were important factors in
the structure of Negro discontent" that led to the disorders.
The commission singled out the rising rent burden as especially
troubling, and found it ominous that increasing numbers of

black families had to spend more than 25 *percent* of their income for rent, thereby "sacrificing other essential needs." They called, accordingly, for the provision of six million new units of low- and moderate-income housing to be built over the next five years. Instead, low-income housing construction dropped precipitously from roughly 50,000 units a year in the mid-sixties —which the commission regarded as desperately inadequate —to less than 25,000 in the 1980s. The results were entirely predictable. According to a survey by the U.S. Conference of Mayors, the wait for federal housing assistance had reached two years, on average, by 1989; so many people had signed up for federal help that two-thirds of the cities surveyed had closed their waiting lists to new applicants.

The whipsaw effect of rising housing costs, falling incomes, and the withdrawal of federal housing funds has aggravated the vulnerability to drugs in several ways. It not only drove some of the poor into homelessness but forced many more to move repeatedly in search of an affordable place to live— undermining the social cohesion of local communities and eroding traditional sources of social support for families hard-pressed by other social and economic adversities. Those trends have been much aggravated by the simultaneous collapse of other parts of the public sector in poor neighborhoods under the impact of budget cuts at the federal, state, and local levels. Especially significant was the withdrawal of many public services—from hospitals to recreation facilities to fire protection —in the 1970s and 1980s. In a startling analysis, Rodrick and Deborah Wallace have shown how cutbacks in fire protection in the South Bronx helped to create what they describe as a "general collapse of public health," including rises in tuberculosis, homicide, infant mortality—and drug abuse. From 1972 to 1976, they write, "some fifty New York firefighting units were either disbanded or removed, mainly from . . . overcrowded areas such as the South Bronx. . . . Fire department staffing fell from 14,700 to 10,200 between 1970 and 1976." The result was a massive "burnout" of local housing, which in turn "forced a vast transfer of population within the city, stressing not only disintegrating communities, but those overburdened by refugees." The consequent disintegration of social supports, they argue, was especially devastating for the minority poor.

VII

The policies of the seventies and eighties, then, did more than merely strip individuals of jobs and income. They created communities that lacked not only viable economic opportunities, but also hospitals, fire stations, movie theaters, stores, and neighborhood organizations—communities without strong ties of friendship or kinship, disproportionately populated by increasingly deprived and often disorganized people locked into the bottom of a rapidly deteriorating job market. In many cities these disruptive trends were accelerated by the physical destruction left by the ghetto riots of the 1960s or by urban-renewal projects and freeways that split or demolished older, more stable neighborhoods and dispersed their residents.

Some of the consequences of this community fragmentation are suggested in Carl Taylor's investigation of the youth drug-gang culture in Detroit. Taylor describes how certain neighborhoods were transformed, after the late 1960s, from "a close-knit, cooperative network of extended families and friends to a declining, less stable community with no vital organization and transient residents." The process was compounded by the virtual collapse of even the most basic institutions of the private and public economy. Recreational centers were closed down: "Institutions such as drugstores and movie houses were demolished. Neighborhood children were left idle." Neighborhoods were simultaneously depleted of both economic opportunities and anything resembling a sense of community or of mutual obligations. In the course of his research, Taylor asked gang members several questions about their relationship to their neighborhoods. When asked "Do you know your neighbors on your street?" only fourteen of eighty gang members said yes. Only twelve answered yes when asked if there were any businesses such as drugstores, grocery stores, or clothing stores in their neighborhood. Only five said they "cared about their neighborhood," or that it would matter to them if there was a dope house on their street. And only two of the eighty said that they helped their neighbors "with problems in the community."

The destruction of community institutions has also contributed to a more subtle and less easily measured demoralization of many low-income communities—a transformation of values and norms, especially among the young, that contributes to the spread of drug abuse. I do not intend to romanticize the way of life of the urban or rural slums in the past. But there is important, if scattered, evidence that the culture of many poor communities has altered hand in hand with the economic decline of the past twenty years. The weakening of their institutions by impoverishment, forced migration, and the retreat of public services has left a vacuum that has been filled by the norms and values of the increasingly strident consumer culture of post-1980s America.

We do not have hard, quantitative evidence to show the extent of the downward spread of that culture. But opinion surveys do tell us that through that decade more and more Americans, especially the young, came to define their life purpose in terms of acquiring large amounts of money and consumer goods. Research on the attitudes of high-school seniors, for example, shows a clear and sometimes startling national shift toward "consumption aspirations" between 1976 and 1986—including a sharp rise in the number of teenagers who considered "having lots of money" one of the most important goals in life, and who felt that it is very important to own "at least two cars," "clothes in the latest style," and other luxury goods. It is difficult not to see the connection between the broadcasting of those values at all levels of the economy and society and the growth of the mentality of predatory acquisition illuminated in street-level studies of the youth drug culture—as in these comments by female gang members Taylor interviewed in Detroit:

> If a guy ain't got no crew [gang], he probably ain't got no cash. Guys with no paper don't interest us. If you ain't got no paper, what do I need you for?

> This boy at my school wants to get with me. He's cute, plays on the basketball team at school. . . . This fool told me he had a job at the gas station. I said, "Look here, fella, how you going to get with me and you ain't got no paper?" . . . Fuck them. Got no cash, got no time.

> I want nice things. I likes BMWs, Volvos, and Benzos. Some niggah tried rapping to me, talking about going out on a date, taking the *bus*. . . . I said, "Niggah, please!"

It would be a mistake to imagine that these attitudes are confined to an urban underclass or that they reflect a distinct culture of the disadvantaged that stands apart from that of "mainstream" America. They are better understood as an only somewhat distorted version of the values that came to dominate all too much of mainstream economic life in the United States during the 1980s. The celebration of the consumer culture and its rewards—and the denigration of "ordinary" work and nonpecuniary values—hammered home through the media, has grown by default in the absence of countervailing values and norms rooted in viable communities and transmitted and enforced by effective families.

The transformation of poor communities has, in short, been cultural as well as structural—involving subtler changes in values and attitudes as well as massive shifts in economic opportunities and standards of living. Much discussion of the pathologies of the inner city—whether poverty, crime, or drugs—tends to fasten on one level of explanation or the other. But they are not mutually exclusive; they are intimately related, and indeed it is the simultaneous withering of economic opportunities and intensification of consumer values that has made the urban drug culture both so alluring and so difficult to dislodge through conventional policies. Rapidly constricting economic opportunities have severely weakened the indigenous institutions and traditions of poor communities, and the weakening of those institutions, in turn, has helped make possible the rise of a violent and materialistic street culture.

On closer examination, then, there is little mystery to why the 1980s drug crisis emerged when and where it did. Quite simply, life for many Americans had become bleaker, more stressful, less hopeful, and more atomized. These changes have been not only material, but cultural and familial. Black or white, men or women, urban or rural, the quality and character of life among less advantaged Americans, especially the young, have changed sharply for the worse, in ways that predictably increase their vulnerability to drug abuse.

It is not simply that many people have become poorer, but that they have become poorer in the context of declining opportunities for ever attaining a better life. It is not just that more young people, especially young men, are out of work, but that more and more are increasingly locked in to a future without anything much better. It is not just that material prospects have dimmed for the relatively young and poor, but that they have dimmed just when there has been an explosion of affluence and a growing celebration of material consumption at the other end. It is not just that families must contend with less, but that their sources of resilience and support have been sharply undermined. Never before in our recent history have so many been excluded from the realistic prospect of living the good life as their society defines it; never have so many been subjected to such severe and pervasive social and economic stress and such persistent insecurity; never have the public and private sources of help been so uncertain.

These changes were not the reflection of neutral forces over which we had no control. To be sure, there were profound technological and demographic changes rocking the foundations of American society just as they affected every other industrial country. But their specific impact on American life was decisively shaped by deliberate public policies. Indeed, had we set out consciously to prepare the ground for a fast-moving drug epidemic, we could hardly have done a better job. Over the course of the past twenty years, we have been busily "warring" on drugs with one hand while steadily exacerbating the social conditions that breed drug abuse with the other.

We know that social and economic deprivation and a sense of exclusion from the "good life" breed drug abuse; but we have consciously chosen policies that have spread and deepened poverty and widened the gap between the deprived and the affluent. We know that shrinking opportunities for stable and challenging work are central to the growth of drug abuse and the drug culture; but we have adopted policies toward economic development and the distribution of work and wages that have dramatically narrowed the chances for dignified and steady work, especially for the young and poorly educated. We know that the resulting stresses and deprivations place enormous pressures on the capacity of families and communities to resist the encroachment of drugs, but we have simultaneously gutted the public services and benefits that could help families and communities cope. We know that a culture of consumption married to a systematic denial of legitimate opportunities feeds the distorted values that animate the street drug culture; but we have steadily bombarded the young with the message that the most important sources of personal worth and identity are acquisition and display rather than contribution and creativity.

These are not separate trends; they are all strands of an ongoing attempt to reshape American society and culture which, following the British writer Alan Walker, we may call a "strategy of inequality." That strategy has been justified in the name of stimulating economic growth, of shrinking wasteful and costly government, and of spurring the poor to work harder and enter the mainstream of society. What it has given us is deepening poverty, widening inequality, fragmented communities, collapsing families—and a drug problem of unprecedented proportions. That is the situation we face as we try to come up with a workable strategy to reduce the dimensions of drug abuse in the United States.

CHAPTER

4

Rethinking Criminal Justice

One of the strongest implications of what we now know about the causes of endemic drug abuse is that the criminal-justice system's effect on the drug crisis will inevitably be limited. That shouldn't surprise us in the 1990s; it has, after all, been a central argument of drug research since the 1950s. Today, as the drug problem has worsened, the limits of the law are if anything even clearer. But that does not mean that the justice system has no role to play in a more effective strategy against drugs. Drugs will always be a "law-enforcement problem" in part, and the real job is to define what we want the police and the courts to accomplish.

We will never, for reasons that will shortly become clear, punish our way out of the drug crisis. We can, however, use the criminal-justice system, in small but significant ways, to improve the prospects of drug users who are now caught in an endless loop of court, jail, and street. And we can use law enforcement, in small but significant ways, to help strengthen the ability of drug-ridden communities to defend themselves against violence, fear, and demoralization. Today the criminal-justice system does very little of the first and not enough of the second. But doing these things well will require far-reaching changes in our priorities. Above all, we will have to shift from an approach in which discouraging drug use through punishment and fear takes central place to one that emphasizes three very different principles: the reintegration of drug abusers into productive life, the reduction of harm, and the promotion of community safety.

This is a tall order, but as we shall see, something similar is being practiced in many countries that suffer far less convulsing drug problems than we do. Their experience suggests that a different and more humane criminal-justice response to drugs is both possible and practical. Today, there is much debate about the role of the justice system in a rational drug policy— but for the most part, the debate is between those who would intensify the effort to control drugs through the courts and prisons and those who want to take drugs out of the orbit of the justice system altogether. I do not think that either approach takes sufficient account of the social realities of drug abuse; and both, consequently, exaggerate the role of regulatory policies in determining the shape and seriousness of the problem. But those are not the only alternatives. In between, there is a range of more promising strategies—what some Europeans call a "third way"—that are more attuned to those realities and more compatible with our democratic values.

I

One response to the failure of the drug war has been to call for more of what we've already done—even harsher sentences, still more money for jails and prisons—on the grounds that we have simply not provided enough resources to fight the war effectively. That position is shared by the Bush administration and many Democrats in Congress as well. But the strategy of upping the ante cannot work; and even to attempt it on a large scale would dramatically increase the social costs that an overreliance on punishment has already brought. We've seen that the effort to contain the drug problem through force and fear has already distorted our justice system in fundamental ways and caused a rippling of secondary costs throughout the society as a whole. Much more of this would alter the character of American society beyond recognition. And it would not solve the drug problem.

Why wouldn't more of the same do the job?

To understand why escalating the war on drugs would be unlikely to make much difference—short of efforts on a scale that would cause unprecedented social damage—we need to consider how the criminal-justice system is, in theory, *supposed* to work to reduce drug abuse and drug-related crime. Criminologists distinguish between two mechanisms by which punishment may decrease illegal behavior. One is "incapacitation," an unlovely term that simply means that locking people up will keep them—as long as they are behind bars—from engaging in the behavior we wish to suppress. The other is "deterrence," by which we mean either that people tempted to engage in the behavior will be persuaded otherwise by the threat of punishment ("general deterrence"), or that individuals, once punished, will be less likely to engage in the behavior again ("specific deterrence"). What makes the drug problem so resistant to even very heavy doses of criminalization is that neither mechanism works effectively for most drug offenders—particularly those most heavily involved in the drug subcultures of the street.

The main reason why incapacitation is unworkable as a strategy against drug offenders is that there are so many of them that a serious attempt to put them all—or even just the "hard core"—behind bars is unrealistic, even in the barest fiscal terms. This is obvious if we pause to recall the sheer number of people who use hard drugs in the United States. Consider the estimates of the number of people who have used drugs during the previous year provided annually by the NIDA

Household Survey—which, as we have seen, substantially *understate* the extent of hard-drug use. Even if we exclude the more than 20 million who used marijuana in the past year, the number of hard-drug users is enormous: the survey estimates over six million cocaine users in 1991 (including over a million who used crack), about 700,000 heroin users, and 5.7 million users of hallucinogens and inhalants. Even if we abandon the aim of imprisoning less serious hard-drug users, thus allowing the most conservative accounting of the costs of incapacitation, the problem remains staggering: by the lowest estimates, there are no fewer than 2 million hard-core abusers of cocaine and heroin alone.

If we take as a rough approximation that about 25 percent of America's prisoners are behind bars for drug offenses, that gives us roughly 300,000 drug offenders in prison at any given point—and this after several years of a hugely implemented war mainly directed at lower-level dealers and street drug users. We have seen what this flood of offenders has done to the nation's courts and prisons, but what is utterly sobering is that even this massive effort at repression has barely scratched the surface: according to the most optimistic estimate, we may at any point be incarcerating on drug-related charges about one-eighth of the country's hard-core cocaine and heroin abusers. And where drug addiction is truly endemic, the disparity is greater. By 1989 there were roughly 20,000 drug offenders on any given day in New York State's prisons, but there were an estimated 200,000 to 250,000 *heroin* addicts in New York City alone. To be sure, these figures obscure the fact that many prisoners behind bars for *non*drug offenses are also hard-core drug users; but the figures are skewed in the other direction by the large (if unknown) number of active drug dealers who are not themselves addicted.

Thus, though we cannot quantify these proportions with any precision, the basic point should be clear: the pool of *serious* addicts and active dealers is far, far larger than the numbers we now hold in prison—even in the midst of an unprecedented incarceration binge that has made us far and away the world's leader in imprisonment rates.

What would it mean to expand our prison capacity enough to put the *majority* of hard-core users and dealers behind bars for long terms? To triple the number of users and low-level dealers behind bars, even putting two drug offenders to a cell, would require about 300,000 new cells. At a conservative estimate of about $100,000 per cell, that means a $30 billion investment in construction alone. If we then assume an equally conservative estimate of about $25,000 in yearly operating costs per inmate, we add roughly $15 billion a year to our current costs. Yet this would leave the majority of drug dealers and hard-core addicts still on the streets, and, of course, would do nothing to prevent new ones from emerging in otherwise unchanged communities to take the place of those behind bars.

It is not entirely clear, moreover, what that huge expenditure would, in fact, accomplish. For if the goal is to prevent the drug dealing and other crimes that addicts commit, the remedy may literally cost more than the disease. Although drug addicts do commit a great many crimes, most of them are very minor ones, mainly petty theft and small-time drug dealing. This pattern has been best illuminated in the study of Harlem heroin addicts by Bruce Johnson and his coworkers. Most of the street addicts in this study were "primarily thieves and small-scale drug distributors who avoided serious crimes, like robbery, burglary, assault." The average income per nondrug crime among these addicts was $35. Even among the most criminally active group—what these researchers called "robber-dealers" —the annual income from crime amounted on average to only about $21,000, and for the great majority—about 70 percent —of less active addict-criminals, it ranged from $5,000 to $13,000. At the same time, the researchers estimated that the average cost per day of confining one addict in a New York City jail cell was roughly $100, or $37,000 a year. Putting these numbers together, Johnson and his coworkers came to the startling conclusion that it would cost considerably more to lock up all of Harlem's street addicts than to simply let them continue to "take care of business" on the street.

Nor, for that matter, would this tactic eliminate the drug abuse of the addicts we put behind bars. In the real world, incarceration does not reliably keep drug users from using drugs, or dealers from dealing them. As the New York *Times* reported at the end of the 1980s, "Drug use inside prisons across the United States has become a major problem." And as one corrections official pointed out, "What you have on the street is what you have inside." The *Times* reported that "often during their daytime rounds of noisy prison common rooms," guards detect "the familiar glazed look of a high addict. They tell of coming upon inmates shooting up in the private shadows of their cells."

Drugs are brought into the prisons both by guards and other staff members—sixty-six Illinois state-prison employees were arrested on contraband charges from 1986 through 1988— and by visitors. The strategies are ingenious and difficult to stop without extraordinarily drastic measures:

> One popular means of transmitting drugs is to exchange a balloon packed with drugs during a kiss. Some prisons videotape visiting rooms, and guards replay tapes of the initial embraces to spot suspicious kisses. Those prisoners will then undergo a particularly rigorous examination by guards after the visit before being returned to their cell. Some prisoners have been known to swallow the balloon before such searches and to recover the drugs later either by induced vomiting or retrieving the container from their own excrement in a day or two.

Some would object that this paints too gloomy a picture of what a tougher criminal-justice strategy could accomplish because it fails to consider the *deterrent* effect of high levels of arrest and incarceration on other addicts. In theory, if we arrest and punish enough users or dealers, we will frighten many others into giving up drugs or taking up a more legitimate line of work. This was the line of reasoning espoused by William Bennett, the Bush administration's first "drug czar," who declared that for the war on drugs to be successful, there had to be "more of a palpable fear of punishment"—an argument that served to justify the administration's one-sided investment in punitive responses to the drug crisis. But many of the same reasons that make an incapacitative strategy prohibitively costly also make the deterrent effect of formal punishment far less effective than its proponents assume.

When drug users are asked why they have stopped using drugs, either temporarily or permanently, the threat of punishment does not loom large in their decision. In an interesting study in the early seventies in Washington, D.C., Barry S. Brown and his colleagues asked addicts why they had begun using heroin and why they had tried to stop. Their answers were revealing. Not one of the adult men or women cited "concern about punishment for illegal acts" as the reason for their first attempt to withdraw from heroin, and just 13 percent of juvenile users did. Much higher proportions cited drug-related physical or family problems, the desire to change their "life pattern," or the expense of maintaining a habit. The reasons they offered for their *current* attempt to quit were not much different; only 7 percent of adult men, 10 percent of juveniles, and 16 percent of adult women cited concern about punishment as a reason for quitting.

Similar, if slightly less stark, findings emerged from a mid-1980s federal survey of drug abusers in treatment. Only about 33 percent of those who had quit using opiates daily, for example, reported that fear of going to jail was "very important" in their decision, and only 10 percent said it was "most important," a figure dwarfed by the 79 percent who cited either "being tired of the hassle" or "needing a life change."

What is true for use is also true for dealing: those studies that have directly asked dealers about their fear of punishment come up with sobering answers indeed. Thus among forty members of lower-level "scavenger" drug-dealing gangs in Detroit, none described themselves as "concerned" about prison as punishment; all forty declared themselves to be "unconcerned." Only six of another forty dealers—members of more highly organized "corporate" gangs—said they were "concerned" about prison.

Why do so few drug users and dealers seem concerned about punishment? Barry Brown and his coworkers speculated twenty years ago that "punishment is apparently either not seen as a real consequence of heroin use or is not a sufficient reason to stop use." The evidence suggests that *both* speculations are correct. Though addicts are frequently, often repeatedly, punished, the likelihood that they will be punished for any given offense—whether drug possession, dealing, or some related crime—is quite small. And addicts do not necessarily regard punishment as a sufficient reason to stop using drugs, nor dealers to stop dealing them. Indeed, they may often regard conventional punishment as hardly punishment at all.

Much of what we have learned about these issues comes from studies of the lifestyles of heroin addicts and, more recently, crack users and dealers. The picture these studies paint is sobering. Addicts commit an enormous amount of crime—not only drug offenses but also vast numbers of petty property crimes. A small but particularly troubling group engage in repeated higher-level felonies, mostly robberies and burglaries. Given the very high rate at which they commit crimes, most heavily involved street addicts are periodically arrested and frequently incarcerated. Yet most manage to avoid the criminal-justice system *most* of the time. Partly for that reason—and partly because arrest and imprisonment hold few terrors for most participants in the street-drug subculture—punishment has at best a modest effect on their drug use, or their high rates of drug dealing and other crimes. Overall, recent research confirms the long-standing finding from studies of the drug culture: most heavy addicts are deeply involved in a stubbornly entrenched lifestyle of drug use and crime that is extraordinarily compelling and hence very difficult to suppress.

In the early seventies, a Ford Foundation report, summarizing existing research, estimated that "almost all" heroin addicts were arrested at least once every two years and that they spent, on average, about 15 percent of their addiction "career" behind bars. More recent studies by John C. Ball and his colleagues confirm both the astonishing level of crimes among heroin addicts and their repeated experience with the justice system. Over the course of about fifteen years of addiction, the addicts in Ball's study had averaged about twelve arrests. But the repeated arrests obviously had not put an end to their drug careers, or appreciably diminished their extraordinary number of crimes, drug-related and otherwise. Over the course of eleven years of addiction, the addicts averaged 178 "crime days" per year. A more recent study of California addicts by Elizabeth Deschenes, Douglas Anglin, and George Speckart finds an even higher number of arrests—about twenty-two on average over a sixteen-year addiction period. But like the addicts in Ball's studies, the California addicts continued to chalk up enormous numbers of crimes despite those repeated arrests. Once arrested, moreover, the majority of heavy street addicts also undergo repeated stints behind bars, which have an equally minimal impact on the course of their drug careers. The active street addicts in Bruce Johnson's Harlem study who used heroin daily averaged almost ten arrests apiece and had spent an average of 5.6 years behind bars. According to one recent review, "the limited evidence available suggests that two-thirds or more of arrested heroin abusers return to heroin-cocaine use and their diverse criminal patterns within three months after release from detention."

The emergence of crack dealing as a widespread economic and status alternative in the face of the collapse of many inner-city economies has if anything exacerbated this pattern of high crime rates, frequent arrests, and incarceration—and little resulting change in drug use, crime, or drug dealing. The amount of crime committed by young participants in the crack culture is simply off the charts. The 254 young people in Inciardi and Pottieger's sample of Miami crack dealers and users had committed, by their own accounting, an astonishing 223,439 offenses in the single year before they were interviewed. The majority of those offenses—over 60 percent—were drug sales, and most of the rest, petty property crimes and vice offenses (especially prostitution). Unsurprisingly, because they committed crimes at such an extraordinary rate, few escaped arrest; about 87 percent were arrested at some point during the year. But at the same time, the likelihood of being arrested for any *particular* crime was minuscule: less than 1 percent of these youths' offenses resulted in an arrest.

Thus one reason why even relatively frequent punishment fails to affect the trajectory of the drug-using career is that the risk of being arrested, much less imprisoned, for any *specific* offense remains tiny. Johnson's Harlem research suggests another, related limitation on the deterrent effect of arrest and incarceration in the real world. When street addicts *were* caught and punished, it was likely to be for their less serious offenses. Even the "robber-dealers" who committed numerous serious felonies were typically arrested for petty crimes or small-scale drug offenses—not for their more serious ones. Thus the realistic risk of facing punishment that could counterbalance the potential rewards of their criminal lifestyle is considerably smaller than the routine risk of being "busted" for a minor offense and shuttled in and out of a justice system already so overburdened that it cannot spend much time or effort on petty offenses.

Indeed, some of the most serious drug-involved criminals are what Marcia Chaiken and Bruce Johnson call "winners"— young drug users who "commit hundreds of crimes each year but evade arrest for long periods." Were it possible to determine which of the vast numbers of drug-involved offenders who swarm into the courts on smaller charges are actually serious repeat offenders, we could in theory make a considerable dent in the overall crime rate by singling them out for special prosecution and long sentences. The problem is that the courts do not have sufficient information to sort out the serious from the less serious offenders, since most of the former's worst crimes remain hidden; and, despite considerable effort, no one has come up with other "predictors" that can reliably distinguish them.

But the uneven risk of arrest and imprisonment—especially for serious drug-related crimes—is only part of the reason for punishment's limited deterrent effect. Another is that even when addicts or dealers *are* put behind bars, the experience may hold few terrors for them—or for others who might be tempted to take up a "career" in the drug world.

Curiously, although the belief in a deterrent effect of incarceration is central to our present antidrug policies, there have been very few efforts to determine the magnitude of that effect—or whether, indeed, it exists at all. And what little research we have cannot be encouraging to advocates of increased punishment. In a recent study of drug offenders in New York City during the height of the crack epidemic, for example, Jeffrey Fagan found that whether those arrested were put behind bars or not had no significant effect on the likelihood of their being rearrested for drug offenses. This was not because the courts were inefficient or lenient. Eighty percent of arrested drug offenders were convicted, and forty percent of the convicted went behind bars. But whether they were jailed or put on probation did not seem to matter, nor was the *length* of the sentence for those who were jailed consistently related to the chances of rearrest. Overall, Fagan concludes, "the severity of criminal sanction" has little influence on the "likelihood of reoffending." Indeed, there were some counterintuitive results: those who got probation were *less* likely to commit violent felony offenses after release, or to be arrested for drug possession. Among those arrested for dealing, the chance of being rearrested for the same crime *increased* as the severity of their sentence rose.

Similar findings appear when we look specifically at the smaller group of addicts who are heavily involved in serious crime. A recent report from the National Institute of Justice summarizes research on the troubling group of "adult predatory drug-involved offenders" who are often arrested:

> The threat of incarceration does not appear to deter them from committing a variety of crimes, including robbery, assaults, burglary, theft, and drug sales. Being incarcerated—and committing different types of crimes almost every day they are free—is a way of life for them, their friends, and often their family members. . . . Although arrested for only a small percent of the crimes they commit, they are incarcerated frequently, often for relatively long periods; however, they are also likely to begin committing many crimes as soon as they are released. Parole is not likely to deter them; they simply fail to report.

That most addicts do in fact go through multiple spells of imprisonment over the course of their careers tells us that the deterrent effect of incarceration cannot be very large. But why isn't it? Why doesn't going to prison—often repeatedly—convince heavy users and dealers to stop? When we reflect on what we know about the social meanings of drug use and drug dealing, the failure of arrest and imprisonment to exert much deterrent effect is not hard to understand. Studies for forty years have shown that, if anything, the threat of arrest and jail is one reason for the *high* status accorded drug use in communities where it is endemic: the possibility of being caught and sent to prison is part of what makes drug-culture heroes stand out from the mass of the impoverished and defeated. More recent research suggests that as the inner cities have been even more thoroughly eviscerated by economic decline, and as the crack economy has become more pervasive, the status conferred by the risk of punishment has, if anything, become more pronounced. "When you sell it," notes a sixteen-year-old female California crack dealer, "then people respect you out there, 'cause you're taking the penitentiary chance out there selling it. It's like an adventure, because you're playing tag with the police. I mean it's like a risk—you want to see how far you can go without getting caught." Inciardi and Pottieger, similarly, found that among young Miami crack dealers the dangers of the crack lifestyle—including "street violence, arrest, overdose, and potential death"—were "perceived with particularly giddy enthusiasm as challenges to be outwitted and overcome." Young inmates in California Youth Authority institutions, according to Joan Petersilia, often steal state-issued prison clothing so they can display it proudly after their release: "Wearing it when they return to the community lets everyone know they have 'done hard time.' "

The conditions inside the prisons, moreover, may not appear terribly threatening to the kinds of people most often sent behind bars on drug charges. As Carl Taylor's interviews illustrate, young Detroit dealers are remarkably unfazed at the prospect of being sent to a youth home or even to "Jack town"—the Michigan state penitentiary at Jackson:

> The joint? Scared, worried about jail? No way, not the kid. . . . The youth home is really down. If you get sent to the youth home it ain't no big thing. . . . I ain't been to the big time, but when I do, it'll be cool. Everybody I know been to Jack house, three of my boys doing a bit now. . . . Going away is just part of being out here. . . . Most of the time you know everybody in the home, so it's like being with your crew inside.
>
> The big time is just there like the streets. . . . My brothers are inside Jack town and they say the joint just like the street . . . some dudes belong to the Muslims, some go

with their homeboys, and some just chill out. . . . You can get dope and anything else you want in the joint.

Pussy, money, food, you want it? You could get anything if you had the paper. . . . A lot of dudes like prison because it's where all their boys is.

But prison may not only fail to deter; it may make matters worse. The overuse of incarceration may strengthen the links between street and prison and help to cement users' and dealers' identity as members of an oppositional drug culture, while simultaneously shutting them off from the prospect of successfully participating in the economy outside the prison when they get out. For many marginal young people from collapsing communities with few stable families and bleak job prospects, the bonds forged with the "crew" both in and out of prison may be virtually the only stable or meaningful social relationships they have—as well as the chief source of prestige and a kind of upward mobility. Here too, the abstract idea of "palpable punishment" founders on the hard social realities of the meaning of drugs and the drug culture in a collapsing economy and an increasingly depriving and fragmented society.*

The concentrated flow of younger drug dealers and users, drawn mainly from a relatively narrow range of urban minority

* For that matter, some of those who are the intended targets of a strategy of "palpable punishment" may not even understand the stakes, as the following short news report makes clear:

Youth Tries to Pay with Vial of Crack

Elizabeth, N.J., March 26 (AP)—A teen-age boy offered his probation officer $6 in cash and a $10 vial of crack as his weekly restitution payment for damage he caused in a stolen-car chase, the police said today.

The 16-year-old boy, whose name was not released because he is a minor, had been paying $5 to $25 a week toward the $800 he owed for damages during a stolen-car chase, authorities said. The boy gave his probation officer the cash and the vial of crack, then asked for a receipt, the police said. "He was serious," Detective Rich Pushel of the Union County police said. "He couldn't understand why we wouldn't accept it."

The young man was charged with two counts of drug possession and one count of distribution.

neighborhoods, into the overcrowded prisons has made the link between prison and community formidable, enduring, and tenacious, an effective instrument for nurturing and transmitting the values and connections of the street drug cultures. On the basis of their interviews with imprisoned California drug dealers, Jerome Skolnick and his coworkers suggest that as the system snares more and more inner-city drug offenders, the prison itself "becomes a kind of neighborhood," conferring an "alternative kind of 'homeboy' status" on inmates and simultaneously providing the practical connections that help new recruits move up in the drug world:

> Today's California correctional institutions, overcrowded as they are with parole violators, have become in effect schools for advanced drug-dealing connections. Drug dealers who leave prison are rarely, if ever, reformed. On the contrary, imprisonment for drug dealers, both gang and individual, may well serve functions similar to those conventions perform for business people and scholars—as an opportunity for "networking."

These negative opportunities are made more attractive because there are so few constructive alternatives behind bars that could equip inmates for legitimate opportunities on the outside—an issue we'll return to shortly. In that vacuum the illicit identities and connections forged in the prison-street nexus often become the only real game in town—the only tangible structure of opportunity available.

Thus a key limitation on the deterrence of drug use and dealing through formal punishment is that the kinds of people most often arrested and imprisoned for drug offenses do not respond to these sanctions the way middle-class people probably would; and as the conditions of life in their communities continue to deteriorate, the gulf between those responses widens. What the proponents of boosting the "palpable fear" of punishment fail to understand is that, for most of the people who wind up in prison on drug charges, life is already very punishing indeed. It is harsh enough for the ordinary inner-city or rural poor, but still more so for the street-level legions of addicts and small-time dealers, many of whom survive from day to day and hand to mouth in environments that are almost unbelievably precarious, threatening, and violent. Some—increasing numbers—are homeless; many contend with routine threats of physical violence and illness, even death, every day.

For those at the very bottom, imprisonment may even represent an improvement; it can provide a roof, three relatively nutritious meals a day, and, in better institutions, a modicum of physical safety and medical attention—as well as a kind of "family" setting they may not experience outside. (Indeed, the family connection may be literal: two out of five youths incarcerated in state reformatories have at least one parent who has also been behind bars). In a recent study of drug offenders at New York's Rikers Island prison, almost one in five reported having at some point gotten arrested "to get a place to stay." At worst, prison is likely to be viewed as just one risk among many in a generally violent, chaotic social environment. For others less badly off, prison or jail still remains a place where street friendships and camaraderie can be maintained, important business connections made, neighborhood prestige enhanced, and drugs routinely enjoyed.

That does not mean that most addicts or street dealers enjoy going to jail, or that they would not, given the choice, prefer to be on the street. It does mean that the capacity of incarceration to deter their behavior is fundamentally compromised. That is a main reason why the drug war's incarceration binge has failed to stem the drug crisis, and why more of the same will not—cannot—make much difference.

I I

If we cannot expect much from intensified criminalization, would the legalization of hard drugs solve the drug crisis?

No: it would not. To understand why, we need to consider the claims for legalization's effects in the light of what we know about the roots and meanings of endemic drug abuse. First, however, we need to step back in order to sort out exactly what we *mean* by "legalization"—a frustratingly vague and often confused term which means very different things to different interpreters. Many, indeed, who argue most vehemently one way or the other about the merits of legalization are not really clear just what it is they are arguing *about*.

At one end of the spectrum are those who mean by legalization the total deregulation of the production, sale, and use of all drugs—hard and soft. Advocates of this position run the gamut from right-wing economists to some staunch liberals, united behind the principle that government has no business interfering in individuals' choice to ingest whatever substances they desire. Most who subscribe to that general view would add several qualifiers; for example, that drugs (like alcohol) should not be sold to minors, or that drug advertising should be regulated or prohibited, or (less often) that drugs should be sold only in government-run stores, as alcohol is in some states. But these are seen as necessary, if sometimes grudging, exceptions to the general rule that private drug transactions should not be the province of government intervention. For present purposes, I will call this the "free-market" approach to drug control, and describe its central aim as the "deregulation" of the drug market.

Another approach would not go so far as to deregulate the drug trade, but would opt for the controlled dispensation of drugs to addicts who have been certified by a physician, under strict guidelines as to amounts and conditions of use. Something like this "medical model," in varying forms, guided British policy toward heroin after the 1920s. Under the so-called British system, addicts could receive heroin from physicians or clinics—but the private production and distribution of heroin was always subject to strong penalties, as was the use of the drug except in its medical or "pharmaceutical" form. (A small-scale experiment in cocaine prescription is presently being tried in the city of Liverpool.) Since the seventies, the British have largely abandoned prescribing heroin in favor of methadone —a synthetic opiate that blocks the body's craving for heroin but, among other things, produces less of a pleasurable "high" and lasts considerably longer. The practice of dispensing methadone to heroin addicts came into wide use in the United States in the 1960s and remains a major form of treatment; we will hear more about it in the following chapter. Methadone prescription, of course, does not "legalize" heroin, and the possession or sale of methadone itself is highly illegal outside of the strictly controlled medical relationship.

Still another meaning sometimes given to legalization is what is more accurately called the "decriminalization" of drug *use*. We may continue to define the production and sale of certain drugs as crimes and subject them to heavy penalties, but not punish those who only *use* the drugs (or have small amounts in their possession), or punish them very lightly—with small fines, for example, rather than jail. Something close to this is the practice in Holland, which is often wrongly perceived as a country that has legalized drugs. Though drug use remains technically illegal, Dutch policy is to focus most law-enforcement resources on sales, especially on larger traffickers, while dealing with users mainly through treatment programs and other social services, rather than the police and courts.

Another aspect of Dutch policy illustrates a further possible meaning of legalization: we may selectively decriminalize *some* drugs, in some amounts, and not others. The Dutch, in practice—though not in law—have tolerated both sale and use of small amounts of marijuana and hashish, but not heroin or cocaine. A German court has recently ruled that possession of small amounts of hashish and marijuana is not a crime, and indeed, as we've seen, marijuana possession has largely been decriminalized in some American states, though usually as a matter of practical policy rather than legislation.

To add to the complexity, we may legalize some specific drugs for certain specific purposes only—for example, the medical use of marijuana to ease the pain of cancer or other illnesses. There have also been localized experiments in which specific parts of a city are defined as "free" zones where drugs may be used and sold with minimal interference, though they remain illegal under national law: the best-known example is the Swiss city of Zurich, which adopted such a policy in the 1980s and largely abandoned it in 1992.

Let me make my own view clear at the start. As I'll argue in more detail in the last section of this chapter, I think much would be gained if we followed the example of some European countries and moved toward decriminalization of the drug user. I also think there is a strong argument for treating marijuana differently from the harder drugs, and that there is room for careful experiment with strictly controlled medical prescription for some addicts. For reasons that will become clear, decriminalization is not a panacea; it will not end the drug crisis, but it could substantially decrease the irrationality and inhumanity of our present punitive war on drugs.

The free-market approach, on the other hand, is another matter entirely. Some variant of that approach is more prominent in drug-policy debates in the United States than in other developed societies, probably because it meshes with a strongly individualistic and antigovernment political culture. Indeed, the degree to which the debate over drug policy has been dominated by the clash between fervent drug "warriors" and equally ardent free-market advocates is a peculiarly American phenomenon. Much of that clash is about philosophical principles, and addressing those issues in detail would take us beyond the boundaries of this book. My aim here is simply to examine the empirical claims of the free-market perspective in the light of what we know about the social context of drug abuse. Here the free-market view fails to convince. It greatly exaggerates the benefits of deregulation while simultaneously underestimating the potential costs.

Philosophical views aside, the central point in the argument for full-scale legalization of the sale and use of hard drugs is that, as one recent advocate puts it, "most of the damage from drugs today results not from their use but from the ban on their use." Put another way, the empirical argument hinges on the assertion that most of the harmful effects of drugs are "secondary" ones, stemming from misguided regulatory policies, rather than "primary" ones resulting from the effects of the drugs and their associated lifestyle on bodies, minds, family relationships, and community morale. And there is an important element of truth in that assertion. There is no question that the criminalization of drugs produces negative secondary consequences—especially in the unusually punitive form that criminalization has taken in the United States. Nor is there much question that this argues for a root-and-branch rethinking of our current punitive strategy—to which we'll return later in this chapter—especially our approach to drug *users*.

But proponents of full-scale deregulation of hard drugs also tend to gloss over the very real primary costs of drug abuse— particularly on the American level—and to exaggerate the degree to which the multiple pathologies surrounding drug use in America are simply an unintended result of a "prohibitionist" regulatory policy. No country now legalizes the sale of hard drugs. Yet no other country has anything resembling the American drug problem. That alone should tell us that more than prohibition is involved in shaping the magnitude and severity of our drug crisis. But there is more technical evidence as well. It confirms that much (though, of course, not all) of the harm caused by endemic drug abuse is intrinsic to the impact of hard drugs themselves (and the street cultures in which drug abuse is embedded) within the context of a glaringly unequal, depriving, and deteriorating society. And it affirms that we will not substantially reduce that harm without attacking the social roots of the extraordinary demand for hard drugs in the United States. Just as we cannot punish our way out of the drug crisis, neither will we escape its grim toll by deregulating the drug market.

The most important argument for a free-market approach has traditionally been that it would reduce or eliminate the crime and violence now inextricably entwined with addiction to drugs and with the drug trade. In this view it is precisely the illegality of drug use that is responsible for drug-related crime—which, in turn, is seen as by far the largest part of the overall problem of urban violence. Criminal sanctions against drugs, as one observer insists, "cause the bulk of murders and property crime in major urban areas." Because criminalization makes drugs far more costly than they would otherwise be, addicts are forced to commit crimes in order to gain enough income to afford their habits. Moreover, they are forced to seek out actively criminal people in order to obtain their drugs, which exposes them to even more destructive criminal influences. At the same time, the fact that the drug trade is illegal means both that it is hugely profitable and that the inevitable conflicts and disputes over "turf" or between dealers and users cannot be resolved or moderated by legal mechanisms, and hence are usually resolved by violence.

For all of these reasons, it is argued, outlawing drugs has the unintended, but inevitable, effect of causing a flood of crime and urban violence that would not exist otherwise and sucking young people, especially, into a bloody drug trade. If we legalize the sale and use of hard drugs, the roots of drug-related violence would be severed, and much of the larger crisis of criminal violence in the cities would disappear.

But the evidence suggests that while this view contains an element of truth, it is far too simplistic—and that it relies on stereotypical assumptions about the relationship between drugs and crime that have been called into serious question since the classic drug research of the 1950s. In particular, the widely held notion that most of the crime committed by addicts can be explained by their need for money to buy illegal drugs does not fit well with the evidence.

In its popular form, the drugs-cause-crime argument is implicitly based on the assumption that addict crime is caused by pharmacological compulsion—as a recent British study puts it, on a kind of "enslavement" model in which the uncontrollable craving for drugs forces an otherwise law-abiding citizen to engage in crime for gain. As we've seen, however, a key finding of most of the research into the meaning of drug use and the growth of drug subcultures since the 1950s has been that the purely pharmacological craving for drugs is by no means the most important motive for drug use. Nor is it clear that those cravings are typically so uncontrollable that addicts are in any meaningful sense "driven" to crime to satisfy them.

On the surface, there is much to suggest a strong link between crime and the imperatives of addiction. The studies of addict crime by John Ball and Douglas Anglin and their colleagues show not only that the most heavily addicted commit huge numbers of crimes, but also that their crime rates seem to increase when their heroin use increases and to fall when it declines. Thus, for example, heroin addicts in Ball's study in Baltimore had an average of 255 "crime days" per year when they were actively addicted, versus about 65 when they were not. In general, the level of property crime appears in these studies to go up simultaneously with increasing intensity of drug use. One explanation, and perhaps the most common one, is that the increased need for money to buy drugs drives addicts into more crime.

But a closer look shows that things are considerably more complicated. To begin with, it is a recurrent finding that most people who both abuse drugs and commit crimes began committing the crimes *before* they began using drugs—meaning that their need for drugs cannot have caused their initial criminal involvement (though it may have accelerated it later). George Vaillant's follow-up study of addicts and alcoholics found, for example, that, unlike alcoholics, heroin addicts had typically been involved in delinquency and crime well before they began their career of substance abuse. While alcoholics seemed to become involved in crime as a *result* of their abuse of alcohol, more than half of the heroin addicts (versus just 5 percent of the alcoholics) "were known to have been delinquent *before* drug abuse." A federal survey of drug use among prison inmates in 1986, similarly, found that three-fifths of those who had ever used a "major drug" regularly—that is, heroin, cocaine, methadone, PCP, or LSD—had not done so until after their first arrest.

Other studies have found that for many addicts, drug use and crime seem to have begun more or less *independently* without one clearly causing the other. This was the finding, for example, in Faupel and Klockars' study of hard-core heroin addicts in Wilmington, Delaware. "All of our respondents," they note, "reported some criminal activity prior to their first use of heroin." Moreover, "perhaps most importantly, virtually all of our respondents reported that they believed that their criminal and drug careers began independently of one another, although both careers became intimately interconnected as each evolved."

More recent research shows that the drugs-crime relationship may be even more complex than this suggests. It is not only that crime may precede drug use, especially heavy or addictive use, or that both may emerge more or less independently; it is also likely that there are several *different* kinds of drugs-crime connections among different types of drug users. David Nurco of the University of Maryland and his colleagues, for example, studying heroin addicts in Baltimore and New York City, found that nine different kinds of addicts could be distinguished by the type and severity of their crimes. Like earlier researchers, they found that most addicts committed large numbers of crimes—mainly drug dealing and small-scale property crime, notably shoplifting, burglary, and fencing. Others were involved in illegal gambling and what the researchers called "deception crimes"—including forgery and con games—and a relatively small percentage had engaged in violent crime. On the whole, addicts heavily involved in one type of crime were not likely to be involved in others; as the researchers put it, they tended to be either "dealers or stealers," but rarely both. About 6 percent of the addicts, moreover, were "uninvolved" —they did not commit crimes either while addicted or before, or during periods of nonaddiction interspersed in the course of their longer addiction careers.

The most troubling group of addicts—what the researchers called "violent generalists"—were only about 7 percent of the total sample, but they were extremely active—and very dangerous; they accounted for over half of all the violent crimes committed by the entire sample. Moreover, revealingly, the violent generalists were very active in serious crime *before* they became addicted to narcotics as well as during periods of nonaddiction thereafter—again demonstrating that the violence was not dependent on their addiction itself. Nurco and his colleagues measured the addicts' criminal activity by what they called "crime days" per year. Addicts were asked how many days they had committed each of several types of crime; since on any given day they might have committed more than one type of crime, the resulting figure could add up to more than the number of days in the year. The violent generalists averaged an astonishing 900 crime days a year over the course of their careers. The rates were highest during periods when they were heavily addicted to drugs. But even *before* they were addicted, they averaged 573 crime days, and 491 after their addiction had ended. Indeed, the most active group of violent generalists engaged in more crime *prior* to addiction than any other group did *while* addicted. And they continued to commit crimes—often violent ones—long after they had ceased to be addicted to narcotics.

Other kinds of evidence support this more complex relationship between crime and drugs. Thus a recent survey by Bruce Johnson, Eric Wish, James Schmeidler, and David Huizinga of adolescents involved in drugs and crime found that, contrary to the "folk wisdom," "even among the heaviest drug users and delinquents, the majority did not report engaging in any illegal behavior to obtain drugs or alcohol." The youths who were most seriously involved with drugs did indeed commit many crimes, including both property crimes and assaults. But only 20 percent said they had committed nondrug crimes in order to get drugs (or alcohol). Higher proportions either stole drugs or sold them in order to get drugs for their own use, but still the majority neither engaged in property crimes nor dealt drugs in order to support their own drug use. The researchers speculate that either these highly delinquent and drug-using youth were not truly *dependent* on drugs or that they "may have sufficient [legal] income to purchase the drugs they use." In any case, most of the considerable crime they committed was not for the specific purpose of obtaining illegal drugs.

The more compelling view is that drugs and crime are—as Delbert Elliott and David Huizinga put it—"different manifestations of a common causal configuration." That view was argued as far back as the 1950s by Harold Finestone, in his observations of the "junkie" lifestyle in Chicago. Finestone pointed out that the postwar surge of narcotics occurred in communities where many young people already looked up to the local members of the addict subculture who were involved in both drug use and a variety of other criminal enterprises. Young people in deprived neighborhoods began to "simulate the mannerisms and philosophy of life of addicts before they themselves had become addicted." They were drawn not so much to either the drug lifestyle or the criminality of these older users, but to both at once:

> Thus, both the criminality and experimentation with narcotics stemmed, at least in part, from influences to which the youngsters were exposed, as represented by adult models within the local community. Both criminality and narcotics use came to be prestigeful forms of activity. In

this sense, it is irrelevant to ask whether the delinquency preceded the addiction or vice versa. Many of those who became addicted and were forced to engage in crime to support the high cost of their addiction would probably have gone on to engage in crime as adolescents regardless of whether or not they had become addicted.

As we saw in Chapter 3, the rougher culture of crack and heroin in the eighties and nineties has spawned a similar, but even harder-edged, valorization of criminality—and of violence—for its own sake, irrespective of its "instrumental" value in helping to get money to buy drugs or to promote the material goals of the drug business itself. The street-level research shows clearly that much of the violence that permeates the newer drug subcultures is eclectic and expressive.

A recent study of drugs and violence among cocaine users in New York City by Paul Goldstein and his coworkers is especially illuminating. Goldstein argues that there are not one but three ways in which drugs and violence may be related. One is what he calls "psychopharmacological" violence: that is, the chemical properties of the drug directly or indirectly lead to violent behavior on the part of the users, or to vulnerability to victimization by others. Thus some drugs can cause users to "become excitable and/or irrational," and to "act out in a violent fashion." Or violence may "result from the irritability associated with withdrawal syndromes." Or, for that matter, some may deliberately use drugs "in order to reduce nervousness or boost courage, and thereby facilitate the commission of previously intended violent crimes." A second possible connection is the one that most closely fits the popular assumption about the connection between addiction and crime—what Goldstein calls "economic-compulsive" violence, or violent crimes "to finance costly drug use." Finally, there is "systemic" violence, associated with the dynamics of the illicit drug trade.

Interviewing both male and female cocaine users in New York, Goldstein and his colleagues found that most of the violence—and there was a great deal of it among both sexes—among these users was not drug-related at all. They divided their subjects into "nonusers," "small users," and "big users" of cocaine. Among male "big users," and among women in all three categories, at least three-fifths of the violent events they'd been involved in were *not* related to their drug use. Moreover, among the men, violence among those who did *not* use cocaine, or used relatively little, was *more* likely than that of big users to be drug-related—confounding the expected connection between the volume of cocaine use and the volume of drug-related violence. For male big users of cocaine, the researchers concluded, violence was often "independent of drug use or distribution": the "universe of violence participated in by male users of large volumes of cocaine clearly contains much violence that is not related to cocaine distribution or use." Indeed, much of the violence among those heavy-using men consisted of robberies "which the perpetrators did not attribute to any need to obtain drugs." As the researchers concluded, this finding is "suggestive of a 'subculture of violence' in which cocaine use may be a correlate, but not a cause, of violence."

Moreover, the biggest part of the violence that *was* drug-related among these users turned out to fit neither the economic-compulsive model nor the systemic model, meaning that it was directly related not to the illegality of the drug but to its chemical effects on the users. Only 9 percent of the violent events among male users were classed as economic-compulsive—and the male users had the *highest* proportion of economic-compulsive violence. Among the women only 2 percent of big users' violence was related to the need to buy drugs—less than that among nonusers of cocaine. But 60 percent of the violence that female users of cocaine either perpetrated or suffered was psychopharmacological. And even male big users were four times as likely to engage in psychopharmacological as in economic-compulsive violence.

The lesson is *not* that there is no connection between the need for drugs, or the specific imperatives of the drug trade, and the violence that pervades the culture of street drug users. Indeed, an earlier New York study by Goldstein and his coworkers found very high proportions of drug-related *homicides*, specifically, to be systemic incidents associated with the drug trade itself. The lesson, rather, is that it is far too simplistic to assume that all or even most of the violence among drug abusers is simply secondary to the fact that drug use is illegal.

Nor, for that matter, is all of the violence committed even *within* the drug trade motivated by "business" considerations. Carl Taylor's interviews with young Detroit gang members offer startling backup for that conclusion. Some did subscribe to an ideology supporting the use of violence to keep business running smoothly: "If somebody messes with your property, then they need to be checked. I don't call that violence, that's just tightening your business up." But at the same time, they described much of the street-level violence as what in Detroit was known as "Zero action"—a "Zero" being "a person who does not care about anything; has nothing to lose; capable of anything at any time." Zeros, as another gang member complained,

> don't care about nothing. They ain't afraid to die over any stupid thing . . . they like to rape babes, beat up people, and kill somebody for fun. . . . They just like to beast on whoever's around. Our crew enforces when people ill on them. But I think some of them boys would beast on somebody for free.

As one Zero himself puts it,

> I likes to bust heads. . . . You got to dog everybody or they gonna dog you. Doggin' is my specialty. I'm the dog-master. I dogs men, boys, girls, bitches, my momma, teachers, policemen, policebitches, my momma's boy-friends, I'll just see somebody and start doggin' them in the street. Me and my boys like to crush mugs and kick

ass at school. . . . [Another gang] tried to dog us at a house party last month. I got so pissed that I got me a Uzi from my cousin and went to one of [their houses] and sprayed that sucker. . . . I got put out of school for beasting on this teacher. . . . It took four security guards to stop me from killing that bitch. They put me in the youth home; big fucking deal. They called my old man. He said they could keep me. FUCK him, he ain't shit, he's a crackhead just like my ho-assed mammy. . . . I love to jump on preppies, punk-ass dudes, or preppy ho's, it don't matter. . . . I likes seeing little scared preppies when we beast on their asses. My crew is the beasting crew— crushing asses is our way of having fun.

Similarly, members of a crack-dealing gang in Oakland, California, referred to their frequent violence against rivals as "gunning and funning"—more often related to personal vendettas involving real or imagined slights among gang members than to narrowly economic motives or clear struggles over "turf." Thus even the violence surrounding the youthful drug trade cannot be simply characterized as a function of the economic imperatives of the illegal market. Some of it, to be sure, does fit that model, but much of it has far deeper and more tangled social roots. It is about getting back at people who have shown disrespect in a generally disrespecting society, about the inverted self-esteem that derives from being good at inspiring fear in communities where opportunities to demonstrate that one is good at anything *else* are few and far between.

The complexity of the drugs-crime relationship emerges from British studies as well. One recent study of Scottish drug users, for example, found that moderate users of opiates "did not steal significantly more" or have greater income from crime than, for example, those who used nothing heavier than marijuana. Heavy opiate users did have higher levels of theft, but that seemed to be only one part of a larger lifestyle involving multiple drugs and criminality, and so "eliminating opioid use from this combination would have only a modest impact on theft." Echoing many American studies, the Scottish researchers confirm that "the association between opioids and crime is a matter of history not of pharmacology"—that is, a reflection of the heroin user's enmeshment in a broader lifestyle of "polydrug" use and petty crime. These findings, they conclude, "refute the legend that heroin or other drug addiction regularly compels otherwise honest people to become criminals."

In a more recent study, the same researchers tracked patterns of drug use and crime among new adolescent users in Glasgow. Again, the youths who used harder drugs, and more different kinds of drugs, were more likely to commit crimes as well, but not simply to pay for drugs: "Few, if any, of the present group were yet using drugs in such a dependent fashion that their routine drug habits were associated with routine crime to finance drug use." Instead, they were involved in a variety of crimes, and in drug use, more or less independently.

Research on how the "British system" of prescribing opiates affects crime also sheds light on this issue. As we have seen, British addicts could receive prescriptions for heroin from private doctors and, later, from carefully regulated medical clinics. But did addicts who could get heroin legally stop committing crimes? The evidence suggests that many did not —especially after the 1970s, when large numbers of poorer addicts emerged in Britain's cities. Thus a 1979 study of addicts who had been prescribed legal opiates at two London clinics concluded that "treatment for periods of up to 8.5 years had no effect on their overall crime rates." A more recent London study found that most addicts receiving either prescription heroin or methadone continued to commit crimes and to buy heroin in the illicit market.

If addicts could get heroin legally by going to a clinic, why did many continue both to commit crimes and to participate in the illegal market? The research on the British experience suggests that the reasons are not mysterious—and they fit closely with the theories of the meanings and motives of drug abuse we examined in previous chapters. People use heroin not simply to satisfy uncontrollable physical cravings, but as part of their participation in a broader subculture that typically includes several kinds of crime and the use of several other drugs; hence having a legal supply of heroin could not by itself be expected to eliminate either their overall drug use or their criminality. Moreover, it may not even end their search for illicit heroin—either because they want *more* of the drug than any clinic would legitimately prescribe, or because they prefer what they can get in the illicit market to what they can obtain in the clinic.

A study of heroin "scenes" in London by Angela Burr, indeed, argues that an illicit market for heroin and other drugs existed alongside the legal prescribing of "pharmaceutical" opiates as early as the late 1960s and early 1970s. Many heroin addicts used a wide variety of other drugs available on the black market; many wanted more or better heroin than they could get through prescription. Most crucially, Burr reminds us that the attraction of the drug scene is as much social as chemical; because "drugs have a role, status, and value in the drug subculture independent of the experience they induce in the individual drug user," it is mistaken to believe that simply providing opiates on prescription would suddenly turn members of that culture into conventional citizens leading "normal, conventional lives."

Philip Bean and Christine Wilkinson point out much the same in a study of the "illicit supply system" in Nottingham:

> There remains the interesting question, given that a number of users are in treatment and most could be so if they wished, why become involved in this illicit network at all? Twenty-one of thirty-seven users in treatment said they were not given sufficient drugs by the physicians and the remainder said they did not like what they were given. . . . Also central to the drug users' world was what they called a "treat." A "treat" is that luxury drug they endlessly

talked of. A "treat" could be justified when things were going badly, or when they were going well. It could be justified when nothing much was happening, when things were happening too quickly, when they feared going to prison, when they came out, when their friends went in or came out, and when they just felt like it. . . . It was the search for and the demand for the "treat" which among other things helped push users toward the illicit supply system.

None of this is to deny that serious addiction to heroin, or other illegal drugs, can accelerate the level of crime among participants in the drug culture, or stimulate crime even in some users who are otherwise not criminal. Higher levels of drug use *do* go hand in hand with increased crime, especially property crime. Certainly, many addicts mug, steal, or sell their bodies for drugs. The point is that—as the early drug researchers discovered in the 1950s—both crime and drug abuse tend to be spawned by the same set of unfavorable social circumstances, and they interact with one another in much more complex ways than the simple addiction-leads-to-crime view proposes. Simply providing drugs more easily to people enmeshed in the drug cultures of the cities is not likely to cut the deep social roots of addict crime.

We can illustrate the point from another angle. One way of expressing the fallacy in the free-market argument is that it confuses the effects of criminalization itself with those of social exclusion and deprivation. That helps explain why it attributes the growth of violent crime to prohibition and the consequent black market—even though no other "prohibitionist" country has anything resembling our levels of drug-related violence. Consider this example: Imagine a country that is quite "tough" on drugs—that, indeed, declares its official policy to be the attainment of a "drug-free" society. Yet despite its prohibitionist approach, the country does *not* exhibit the severe "secondary" consequences we see in the United States. There is, to be sure, an illicit drug market. But by our standards it is quite small; the cities are not besieged by hordes of addicted violent criminals or Uzi-toting drug gangsters, and the streets do not routinely resound with gunfire between rival drug gangs. Indeed, the crime rate as a whole is extremely modest by American standards; the homicide rate hovers at about a fifth of ours. Meanwhile, the drug problem has remained relatively small—despite the illicit profits to be made (in theory) in the drug trade. Drug use among adolescents is falling, heroin use has stabilized, and crack is virtually unknown. (Indeed, the biggest hard-drug problem is with methamphetamine.)

This country is not imaginary; it is called Sweden. And most European countries look more like Sweden in this respect than like the United States. What gives rise to the uniquely horrendous level of violence that accompanies our drug scene is not the fact of criminalization, which we share with other advanced industrial societies, but the extreme levels of deprivation and social disintegration which they do not share with us. Sweden, in short, does not have legions of poor youth sucked into the illicit and violent drug trade because Sweden does not have legions of poor youth. Again, that is not to argue that drug prohibition has no costs. It is to say that the magnitude of those costs depends on the magnitude of the social deficits in the surrounding environment—and that reducing those deficits ought to be our main concern.

The evidence, then, does not support the view that most crime committed in and around the drug cultures of the cities is simply a result of the imperatives of addiction or even of the iron economics of the drug trade. Much of it "co-varies" with drug use as part of a larger lifestyle, and some of it is psychopharmacological—deriving from the effects of the drugs themselves. That being the case, turning hard-drug sales over to the free market could not reduce crime to the extent that advocates assume. Indeed, how much, if at all, drug-related crime would fall under a free-market policy would depend on whether and to what extent the probable declines in systemic violence among dealers would be counterbalanced by increases in other forms of violence and property crime resulting from higher levels of drug consumption. Without a real-world experiment in deregulation, of course, no one knows what the precise impact would be, or how it might vary among different drugs. What is clear, however, is that the results would be more complex than the free-market model assumes.

Moreover, just as that model overstates the benefits of deregulation, it also underestimates the potential costs. Free-market advocates differ considerably in their recognition of the seriousness of the "primary" costs of drug abuse. At the extreme, there is a tendency among both liberal and conservative supporters to regard drug abuse as simply a benign lifestyle choice—or one that *would* be benign in the absence of the ill secondary effects of criminalization. But that view glosses over both the primary harms associated with hard-drug abuse—especially on the U.S. level—and their highly unequal concentration among the most vulnerable sectors of the population.

It is often argued that the harms are exaggerated because *most* drug users are not serious abusers; they can use drugs recreationally without being overwhelmed by them, and are capable of controlling their use within reasonable bounds. That is true, but the argument misses the point; the real concern is precisely with the more severe forms of drug abuse, which are widespread in the United States, and which have harmful and frequently tragic consequences that are disproportionately suffered by the most disadvantaged. The failure to take these realities seriously has been one of the most egregious mistakes of some of those who want to see a more humane drug policy in America, and it has helped to keep their influence on our drug policies minimal. Most Americans believe that *serious* drug abuse is harmful indeed, and they are right. That these harms are frequently exaggerated by fervent drug warriors does not make them any less real—or any less devastating to those who suffer them. The old myth that *any* drug use necessarily leads to dire consequences—quite properly discredited—has been replaced in some quarters by a newer myth of harmlessness. The truth is in between, and it is sobering.

I've already touched on the pattern of drug-related medical emergencies and deaths. Those numbers, already high enough, are understated because—as with alcohol or tobacco—they do not account for most of the less direct impacts of drug abuse on long-range health, which may appear on death certificates as deaths from cardiovascular or respiratory disease (or accidents). In the mid-eighties, the demographer R. T. Ravensholt, using (precrack) 1980 data, estimated that roughly 30,000 deaths per year in the United States could be attributed to "addictive substances" other than tobacco or alcohol. That number was far smaller, to be sure, than the 100,000 estimated by the same method for alcohol, and pales beside the half-million estimated for tobacco. But it is very large indeed—half again as high, for example, as deaths from homicide. And the crack epidemic's link with a range of health problems—from respiratory disease to heart problems to AIDS—will certainly increase those fatality figures considerably. Some of those deaths can be traced, in part, to the effects of forcing drug use into illicit channels—especially deaths from adulterated or contaminated drug supplies. But more reflect either the short-term effects of hard drugs themselves (especially overdoses) or their longer-term effects on health.

The secondary impacts of drug prohibition, moreover, explain little of the tragedies of fetal drug exposure or drug-related family disintegration and child abuse. Both issues leapt into public view with the crack epidemic, but neither is new. In New York, between 4 and 5 percent of mothers delivering babies at Harlem Hospital in the 1970s "either used illicit drugs (mainly heroin or phencyclidine) or were enrolled in methadone treatment." But by 1988 fully *17* percent of infants born at the same hospital had been exposed to cocaine alone. That experience is unfortunately not unusual in inner cities. One credible estimate suggests that 10 to 15 percent of women examined during pregnancy in inner-city hospitals use cocaine, with or without other drugs and alcohol, during their pregnancies; 21 percent of women in labor at one Bronx hospital had a positive urine test for cocaine. Estimates of the total number of drug-exposed infants nationwide each year range widely—from roughly 350,000, which is probably too high, to a much more credible, but still staggering, 100,000 who are "exposed to cocaine or other drugs during the critical period of fetal brain development." (These numbers may have declined slightly from their peak with the stabilization of the crack epidemic, but they remain high.)

It is too early to tell what the longer-term impact of crack use will be on exposed infants. But the gathering evidence on the short-term effects is troubling. One recent review offers this summary:

> Among the most compelling findings are consistent descriptions of increased rates of spontaneous abortions, abruptio placentae, and meconium-stained amniotic fluid. Intrauterine growth retardation has been found in all studies of reasonable size in which cocaine-exposed neonates were compared with non-drug-exposed neonates. Increased rates of prematurity and lowered gestational age in cocaine-exposed pregnancies have been found. . . . Furthermore, some, but not all, investigations of newborn infants have suggested a higher rate of congenital malformations in the form of cardiac, cranial, and genitourinary-tract anomalies. The central nervous system and cardiorespiratory systems may be especially vulnerable to in-utero exposure to cocaine.

Probably the most consistent and widespread finding is that of growth retardation, and corresponding low birth weight, among drug-exposed babies. At Harlem Hospital, cocaine-exposed infants average almost a pound lighter than nonex-posed babies, and they have "nearly twice the usual need for neonatal intensive care at birth." Low birth weight is especially troubling because it is one of the most important contributors to high levels of infant mortality; the death rate of babies born to substance-abusing mothers in New York City is two and one-half times the general citywide rate.

Fetal drug exposure is not solely a crack problem. Although cocaine-exposed infants have captured the public's attention, both heroin and other drugs, including PCP and methamphet-amine, have taken a sometimes hidden toll. Among Mexican-American gang women in Los Angeles studied by Joan Moore, 45 percent had used drugs during pregnancy; 14 percent had borne children addicted at birth. Phencyclidine has been found in up to 12 percent of women delivering at one inner-city hospital; in a recent study in Los Angeles, two-thirds of infants exposed to PCP in utero "manifested symptoms of neonatal narcotic withdrawal syndrome." Nor is in-utero drug exposure the only source of drug-related fetal damage. Another is sexually transmitted diseases (STDs), including AIDS and syphilis. At the start of the 1990s, between 3 and 4 percent of infants born at Harlem Hospital were HIV-positive, and 5 percent of those born in 1988 had congenital syphilis. Both resulted primarily from maternal behavior related to crack and cocaine abuse (and lack of prenatal care); syphilis was eight times as common among infants who had been exposed to cocaine in utero as among those who had not.

Beyond the clear evidence of physical damage to newborns through drug exposure and sexually transmitted disease are the sometimes confusing but deeply troubling indications of effects on infant behavior and development. Here the evidence must be treated with caution, because the samples are generally quite small, the methods not always the most rigorous, and the long-term effects impossible to determine until more time has passed. But on balance the best evidence suggests that at least in the first months of life, infants exposed to cocaine in utero are found to exhibit "inferior visual and auditory orienting skills, poorer motor abilities, decreased interactive behavior, decreased consolability, less adequate state regulation, and more abnormal reflexes." Disturbingly, these behavioral effects apparently become "more pronounced with increasing infant age."

It is important, as many critics have cautioned, not to take such findings as evidence that drug-exposed infants are doomed to a life of abnormality or failure. We know that many improve greatly if given adequate care in infancy and early childhood. Indeed, recent findings by Ira Chasnoff and his colleagues are especially encouraging: among an admittedly small sample, there were few significant developmental differences—other than smaller head size—at age two between low-income children who had been exposed to cocaine in utero and other low-income children who had not. The findings suggest that prenatal cocaine exposure may represent a "potential but not inevitable developmental insult." But no one denies that such exposure adds to the multiple disadvantages many poor children are saddled with at the beginning of life.

It is sometimes argued that much of the damage to infants from maternal drug use is really caused by other factors—poor nutrition, lack of prenatal care, or use of alcohol and tobacco—rather than by the illegal drugs themselves. Within limits, the point is important and valid: It is indeed difficult to single out the effects of drugs in general—much less of any single drug in particular—from the poverty, poor health care, and other adversities many drug-abusing women bring to pregnancy. But the point cannot be taken too far, for two reasons. First, the more recent and more careful research on the impact of drugs on fetal health and infant development does control, as far as possible, for these factors—and still comes up with independent effects of drug exposure on the fetus and the developing infant. For example, research by Barry Zuckerman and his colleagues at Boston University Medical School shows that even within a population of low-income mothers with a range of predictable social problems, those who used cocaine during pregnancy delivered significantly smaller and lighter babies with smaller head circumferences. When the effects of smoking and poor diet were added, the differences were aggravated considerably; women who were well-nourished and did not smoke or use cocaine had babies that weighed an average of a pound more than the others. And several still more recent studies show that, controlling for the impact of mothers' age, ethnicity, prematurity, and use of other drugs, cocaine-exposed infants showed "significantly reduced growth." Second, many of the confounding factors in such studies, particularly poor nutrition and prenatal care, may themselves be caused or aggravated by the mothers' drug use.

Both before birth and during childhood, as David Bateman of Harlem Hospital puts it, children of drug-abusing parents are victims of a "cruel interplay" of harmful medical and social forces. The childhood dangers include the risk of "passive" exposure to drugs, a problem that is particularly significant in the crack era. More than 2 percent of children seen in a Boston public hospital for fevers, coughs, and accidents had positive urine tests for cocaine—reflecting either the inhalation of cocaine fumes or the accidental ingestion of the drug. More devastatingly, the drug crisis—and especially the cocaine epidemic—has radically altered the picture of child abuse and neglect in the United States. Half of foster-care placements in New York City since 1986 were due to maternal cocaine abuse: drug abuse is the key reason why New York's foster-care population tripled in the 1980s. Here, too, the effect of drug abuse is difficult to extricate from those of poverty and social isolation. But to deny that drugs can powerfully aggravate those problems in ways that shatter families and injure children is naïve and misleading.

And the effects on infants, children, and families by no means exhaust the "primary" costs of endemic drug abuse. Others are sometimes more subtle and less often researched: the adverse long-range health consequences of adolescent drug use; the way early drug abuse forecloses opportunities in schooling and work to the disadvantaged young, cementing their economic and social marginality; and the long-term demoralization and paralysis of communities where drugs and the drug culture have displaced efforts to change social conditions and improve lives and opportunities—a demoralization that helps to perpetuate the worst inequalities in American society.

It is sometimes argued that these adverse effects would be lessened with drug legalization, because a less punitive approach to drug use would encourage people with severe drug problems to come forward for treatment, prenatal care, or other forms of help. That argument is half right. It is certainly true that the punitive response to drug users discourages many from seeking help and therefore—as we'll see in more detail later—needlessly aggravates the harms of drug use. But that is an argument for a more flexible, less punitive approach to drug *users*—not for the legalization of drug *sales*.

If we take these harms seriously, and I think we must, we cannot avoid being deeply concerned about anything that would significantly increase the availability of hard drugs within the American social context; and no one seriously doubts that legalization would indeed increase availability, and probably lower prices for many drugs. In turn, increased availability— as we know from the experience with alcohol—typically leads to increased consumption, and with it increased social and public-health costs. A growing body of research, for example, shows that most alcohol-related health problems, including deaths from cirrhosis and other diseases, were far lower during Prohibition than afterward, when per capita alcohol consumption rose dramatically (by about 75 percent, for example, between 1950 and 1980). It is difficult to imagine why a similar rise in consumption—and in the associated public-health problems—would not follow the full-scale legalization of cocaine, heroin, methamphetamine, and PCP (not to mention the array of as yet undiscovered "designer" drugs that a legalized corporate drug industry would be certain to develop).

If consumption increased, it would almost certainly increase most among the strata already most vulnerable to hard-drug use—thus exacerbating the social stratification of the drug crisis. It is among the poor and near-poor that offsetting measures like education and drug treatment are (as we'll see in the next chapter) least effective and where the countervailing social supports and opportunities are least strong. We would expect, therefore, that a free-market policy applied to hard drugs would produce the same result it has created with the *legal* killer drugs, tobacco and alcohol—namely, a widening disparity in use between the better-off and the disadvantaged. And that disparity is already stunning. According to a recent study by Colin McCord and Howard Freeman of Harlem Hospital, between 1979 and 1981—that is, *before* the crack epidemic of the eighties—Harlem blacks were 283 times as likely to die of drug dependency as whites in the general population. Drug deaths, combined with deaths from cirrhosis, alcoholism, cardiovascular disease, and homicide, helped to give black men in Harlem a shorter life expectancy than men in Bangladesh. That is the social reality that the rather abstract calls for the legalization of hard-drug sales tend to ignore.

It is sometimes argued, likewise, that the potential negative consequences of deregulation would be mitigated if we banned drug advertising. That is surely better than allowing crack advertisements on ghetto billboards, but it would probably make for less difference than some hope. Most studies of alcohol and tobacco, for example—in countries that have periodically adopted advertising bans of one kind or another —show that advertising only marginally affects levels of con-sumption. One recent study for the Organization for Economic Cooperation and Development, for example, estimates that a total ban on tobacco advertising would reduce consumption by a little less than 7 percent.

Others argue that one way to keep consumption of legalized drugs low would be to tax drug sales. But as critics have often pointed out, the problem remains: If we impose a tax onerous enough to discourage consumption, we generate a new black market in cheaper drugs that would perpetuate all of the problems that the free market is designed to eliminate. If we tax drug sales lightly, we are unlikely to discourage consumption significantly—especially for highly addictive substances like crack, which produce the urge to consume repeatedly without much regard for cost, dignity, or even life.

The case for the free market as a response to the hard-drug crisis founders for the same reason that the case for intensifying the conventional drug war does: both are divorced from the complex social realities of drug abuse in the United States.

But there is another issue as well. Evaluating the free-market model necessarily forces us to reflect on the kind of society we wish to strive toward. In the United States, drug abuse is endemic among the most vulnerable and disadvantaged people in the nation. Full-fledged deregulation of the production and sale of drugs could put the enormous economic and cultural power of some of America's largest corporations behind the task of making a profit by selling them demoralizing and disabling substances. Given the record of those corporations with alcohol and cigarettes, it is difficult to imagine that they would pursue those profits with anything less than full vigor or with any greater concern for the social, economic, and public-health consequences. Anyone who believes that this would not result in greater availability of hard drugs has the unenviable task of showing why not. Some who acknowledge this unhappy result go on to say that the money we could bring in by taxing formerly illegal substances could then be used to offset the damage increased consumption would bring—by funding more treatment programs, for example. But that is free-market reasoning at its most bizarre and socially perni-

cious: we first exacerbate social ills and then spend, after the fact, to try to mend what we have deliberately broken (with results that, as we'll see, are far from assured). What such a policy would mean in the real world is that we would officially encourage the devastation of poor communities by drugs, perpetuating the desperation and misery of whole strata of Americans whom we have quietly chosen to abandon. I do not think this is what we really want.

I I I

A more promising approach—a "third way"—would borrow heavily from those European countries whose drug policies have proven both more humane and more successful. The third way recognizes that the drug problem is frustratingly resistant to alteration through law enforcement, and that, accordingly, the most important battles in a real war on drugs must be fought outside the criminal-justice system. At the same time, it also recognizes that the justice system will always play a part in the social control of hard drugs, and that how it does so matters. Thus while we cannot expect too much from law enforcement, it is vitally important to think through what the system can contribute to a broader social strategy for dealing with drug abuse in ways that respect democratic values and reduce harm to individuals and communities. Four principles are fundamental:

1. Adopt more reasonable sentences for drug offenses. The most wasteful and irrational feature of our current drug war has been the extraordinary escalation of sentences for drug offenses—especially for low-level dealing and possession. It is now possible in a number of states, as well as under federal drug laws, to be sent to prison for life without possibility of parole for possession of a small quantity of hard drugs. We are now at a point where many judges are recoiling at the

harsh and counterproductive sentences they are forced to hand down for even small-scale offenses; and it is the extraordinary length of those sentences as much as the sheer number of offenders sentenced that is responsible for the overflowing of the courts and prisons. Yet there exists not a shred of empirical evidence that longer sentences deter serious drug offenses any better than shorter and more consistent ones. It is time to acknowledge that the escalation of penalties in the United States has done nothing to improve public safety or to diminish the drug crisis; and time to examine the alternatives. Other advanced industrial countries—even those that have adopted what they regard as a tough stance against drugs—generally impose far less severe sentences for drug offenses, and they are none the worse for it.

In Holland, where official attitudes toward drug use are among the most tolerant, the maximum penalty for illicit trafficking in hard drugs is twelve years. But that is also true in Sweden, with its self-consciously tough stance toward drugs. And Sweden's top penalty is reserved for multiple offenses of an especially grave kind. In general, even for trafficking offenses conducted "on a considerable scale," which involve "a particularly large quantity of drugs," or are "of an especially dangerous or ruthless nature"—what the Swedish law calls "aggravated" drug offenses—sentences range in theory from two to ten years. In practice, the longer penalties are very rarely invoked; according to one study of Swedish policy, the ten-year maximum was imposed only once during 1985, for example, and only eight sentences of more than five years' imprisonment for "pure" drug crimes were imposed in 1984. What the Swedish law calls "normal" drug offenses are punishable by up to three years' imprisonment, and "minor" offenses—small-scale dealing and possession—by fines or imprisonment for no more than six months. Again, this in a country whose official policy is "aimed at eliminating drug abuse."

That these sentences—quite modest by our standards—have

not resulted in the inundation of Swedish society by hard drugs is stunningly clear from the statistics. With a population of more than eight million, a bit larger than New York City, Sweden has an estimated 6,000 to 9,000 intravenous drug users (versus at least 200,000 heroin addicts alone in New York), and their numbers appear to be declining. IV drug use among young people "has diminished considerably," according to government estimates; and "new recruitment for IV drug abuse has been very limited in recent years." Youthful drug use of any kind is falling sharply: By 1990 only 3 percent of youth under sixteen had tried illegal drugs.

Reducing our currently outlandish sentences, and establishing alternatives to imprisonment for all but the most serious offenses, should be key elements of a more rational approach to drug policy in the United States. Saner sentences might indeed deter drug crimes more effectively, since by freeing up space and resources they would make it possible for us to more consistently impose meaningful sentences on the most serious offenders. What we now do is the opposite: we put some drug offenders, even relatively minor ones, behind bars for uselessly long periods, while cycling others through an overcrowded system that sometimes provides no serious consequences at all. Abandoning that rather bizarre strategy would be both more effective and more just. And it would save money.

It would also mesh with the views of the American public. It's often assumed that Americans, like most of their elected officials, are overwhelmingly punitive when it comes to drugs. But the reality is much more complicated, as a 1991 study by the Public Agenda Foundation shows. The foundation interviewed citizens in Delaware about their attitudes toward sentencing. The respondents were first given two choices—prison or probation—for offenders convicted of various crimes. Given *only* those two options, 56 percent would have sentenced a first offender convicted of selling "a small amount" of cocaine to prison. But when offered a range of alternative sanctions in between prison and ordinary probation—including "strict"

probation requiring several visits to a probation officer each week, strict probation coupled with community-service work, and a short-term "boot camp"—only 25 percent chose prison for the first offender. The vast majority—62 percent—supported some form of intermediate punishment. Even for a third conviction for selling a small amount of cocaine, 61 percent of Delawareans favored an alternative to prison if the offender was an addict who wished to enter a treatment program.

2. *Focus on traffickers, not users.* It is our punitive treatment of drug users, along with the severity of our sentences, that most distinguishes the U. S. approach from that of even some "tough" European countries. The Dutch have gone the farthest in decriminalizing, in practice, the use of drugs: but many other countries have also adopted a much less harsh approach toward users, combining a relatively sparing use of punishment with the provision of more accessible options for treatment and assistance.

As we've seen, the Dutch have not in fact legalized hard drugs—nor for that matter even marijuana. But they have adopted a pragmatic and flexible approach based on two specific strategies: treating hard drugs differently from soft drugs, and treating traffickers differently from users. The Dutch have adopted a de facto policy of tolerating small-scale sales and use of marijuana and hashish, while concentrating enforcement efforts against hard drugs—what they term drugs of "unacceptable risk." And they have deliberately adopted a reintegrative, rather than punitive, approach to drug users while taking a tough stance toward serious traffickers.

Both strategies are derived from the underlying principle that "efforts must be made to ensure that drug users are not caused more harm by criminal proceedings than by the use of the drug itself." The aim, in short, is to avoid the "secondary" consequences of drug control as much as possible. Specifically, the Dutch believe that adopting a tolerant attitude toward marijuana while remaining tough on hard drugs breaks the connection between the illicit supply networks for harder and softer drugs—and thus allows young people to experiment with soft drugs without being brought into the destructive world of hard-drug dealing and the hard-drug culture. They also believe that by largely removing the *use* of even the drugs of high risk from the threat of imprisonment, they allow hard-drug users to "surface"—making them accessible to a variety of government efforts at treatment and harm reduction (about which more below).

The Dutch explicitly counterpose this strategy of "normalization" of the drug user to the punitive and stigmatizing approach of the United States and, to a varying degree, of most other European countries—which, in their view, mainly serves to discourage drug users from seeking any kind of help, and exacerbates the social and personal *costs* of drug use. In the United States, it is now increasingly common to hear our unusually harsh approach to drug users justified on the grounds that addicts will not seek help unless they are forced to. Yet both Dutch and American experience would seem to belie that contention. As we will see in more detail in the following chapter, one of the most crucial limitations of drug treatment in the United States is that only a minority of drug abusers— especially younger ones—ever make use of it, in part because they are afraid that doing so will deliver them into the clutches of the law. In Holland, on the other hand, a surprising—by our standards—proportion of addicts are routinely in contact with treatment programs or other agencies of help; in the city of Amsterdam, for example, about 60 to 80 percent are being reached by one form of assistance or another at any given time, and the proportion is probably even higher outside the largest cities.

But a sharply different approach to users is also evident in other European countries with a less tolerant official stance than Holland. In Sweden, for example, drug possession is mainly punished by a fine—scaled according to income—rather than by a jail sentence. What a less punitive approach would accomplish in sheer fiscal terms in this country is worth pausing to consider, especially in a time of deepening budget constraints. At the end of the 1980s, for example, over 7 percent of inmates in California state prisons—more than 7,000 people—were behind bars for drug possession. At $25,000 per year per inmate, that amounts to $175 million a year for operating costs alone—in one state, and not counting local jails. To be sure, that figure includes some serious, large-scale traffickers. But at the same time, it does *not* include many thousands of inmates sent to custody on probation or parole violations involving drug use alone. In short, though we have no precise figures, there is no doubt that we are now spending very substantial amounts of money to imprison large numbers of people solely because of their use of drugs. And it is money that could be much more profitably used to help offenders deal with their drug problems outside prison walls.

Just as most Americans, when given alternatives, favor less Draconian approaches to sentencing, they also favor a policy that distinguishes between users and traffickers—almost as strongly as they reject free-market deregulation. In a 1990 survey in Washington, D.C., 70 percent of respondents said they were opposed to the "legalization of any illicit substances," while two-thirds agreed that drug users "should be treated medically rather than arrested or prosecuted." Three-fourths said that antidrug funds should be used for treatment and job training centers "instead of jails."

A precise blueprint of the best measures for different kinds of drug users is beyond the scope of this book—and probably premature: as Franklin Zimring and Gordon Hawkins put it, we should allow considerable room for specific measures to "trickle up" from careful experimentation. Ideally, we should explore a variety of approaches that fall somewhere between the tolerant Dutch strategy and the tough but compassionate

Swedish one—involving some discretionary use of legal coercion to nudge addicts into treatment in extreme cases, the use of fines in many others, and a general relaxation of the street law-enforcement effort against drug users. All of that would free up resources that would allow us to focus more effectively on serious traffickers. We could gain a great deal—both financially, by targeting our scarce criminal-justice resources more precisely, and socially, by avoiding the marginalization of drug users and making it more likely that they will come for help.

Would we also lose in public safety what we would gain in decreased social and fiscal costs? Not if the Dutch or Swedish experience is any guide. In its 1990 "National Drug Control Strategy," the Bush administration told the nation that the failure to adopt a national attitude of complete "intolerance" for *all* drug use had led to "social disaster" in those countries that had adopted a more pragmatic approach. In fact, there is no evidence that the Dutch strategy has caused social disaster —or even a more modest increase in drug use or drug-related social problems.* As we've seen, the Dutch hard-drug problem remains far less severe than our own; that is true despite the fact that the tolerant Dutch policy has traditionally lured many "junkie tourists" from other parts of Europe and around the world to Holland, where they are counted in the drug statistics. We've also seen that the Dutch cocaine problem remains small, and crack virtually nonexistent. Among Dutch heroin addicts, the average age has been rising for years, suggesting that there is decreasing recruitment of new users, despite the tolerant official policy. In general, as in Sweden, youthful drug use appears to be declining; the proportion of Dutch drug users under twenty-one fell sharply throughout the 1980s.

* The Zurich experiment in local deregulation *may* have been something of a disaster, but it represents a very different approach to drug regulation than the one suggested here. I have seen no careful evaluation of the experiment, but news accounts describe an unhappy mix of considerable drug-related crime and blatant public drug use in the Zurich park set aside as a "free" zone. If anything, what the Swiss experience most clearly suggests is the importance of the distinction between deregulation and decriminalization—between tolerance of drug trafficking and compassion for the drug user.

This is not to suggest that shifting most drug use out of the justice system is a cure-all. It would be wrong to believe that the more relaxed regulatory policy is the *cause* of the relatively lower rates of hard-drug use in Holland. As with other social problems—like violent crime or infant mortality—the positive Dutch performance mainly reflects the broader egalitarian social policies the Dutch have adopted for decades—policies which have strongly decreased social inequalities and provided comprehensive social services across the board. Rather, it is clear that what the Dutch regard as a "pragmatic"—not "lenient"—approach to users has not exacerbated their country's drug problem, and if anything may have mitigated it, while freeing most of their resources for prevention and treatment.

3. Provide serious help for drug abusers within the justice system. Even if we sharply reduce the number of small-scale drug offenders we jail, large numbers of drug abusers will still pass through the criminal-justice system in the foreseeable future —both for serious drug offenses and for nondrug crimes. Across the country, 35 percent of state-prison inmates in the late eighties used hard drugs *regularly* before prison.

The issue is what to do with these users once we have them. Despite increased awareness of the problem in the last few years, most drug-abusing inmates still receive no help of any kind for their drug problem, and for the minority who do, the help is often minimal or inappropriate. In 1987 only 11 percent of state-prison inmates were involved in some form of drug treatment. In California now the proportion is even smaller: less than 3 percent of adult prisoners (as of 1990) were in drug treatment; only about 4 percent were involved in *any* form of prerelease program. As a recent report from the state's Blue Ribbon Commission on Inmate Population Management notes, "aside from self-help groups such as Alcoholics Anonymous (AA) and other twelve-step programs, there is no mandate or resources for the corrections system to deal with drug-abusing offenders. Therefore, there are virtually no drug-treatment programs in our adult prisons."

Once again, what makes this absence of serious assistance so obviously self-defeating is that the system is being routinely flooded with offenders whose main crime *is* their drug use— or a property crime directly related to their addiction or their participation in the drug subculture. Thus it is possible in California to have your parole revoked and be sent back to state prison for the offense of living in a "drug-related area"; but once returned behind bars you will almost certainly receive no assistance in living anywhere else—nor in dealing with your drug problem or the lack of prospects that probably underlies it. The result is a merry-go-round in which everyone loses: inmates, the correctional system, and the community. A report from the nonprofit Center for Juvenile and Criminal Justice concludes that "most California parolees will leave prison with no marketable skills or job experience, no high school diploma, a sixth-grade reading level, and a drug problem." And though California is an extreme example, the revolving-door pattern exists across the country given the double failure to provide constructive programs for drug-using offenders either inside or outside the prison walls. As the California Blue Ribbon Commission puts it, "There are limited options, . . . other than return to prison, when drugs are detected. . . . Parole violators are returned to prison for very short terms and then returned to the same negative influences and antisocial lifestyles." The same is true for offenders on probation. As a result, both are "constantly recycling in our local and state corrections systems as arrests, probationers, prison and jail commitments, and parole violators."

A more responsible approach would rest on two general principles. First, it would seek to keep those minor drug offenders we do arrest out of institutions—whether as initial admissions or as probation and parole violators—and instead develop comprehensive programs for them outside prison walls. Second, it would provide the best possible services for those who must spend time inside, in order to prevent them from coming back once released.

We have no evidence that the long-term problems of drug abusers can be addressed any more effectively inside the prisons than outside them. It is probably true that, as recent research suggests, some drug abusers do *as* well when they are forced into treatment as when their participation is voluntary. But that does not mean that the supervision they need is best delivered inside an institution. What the research suggests, in fact, is that firm supervision and monitoring *outside* the prison is what counts. That conclusion, for example, emerged from George Vaillant's studies of what accounted for success among addicts who left the federal narcotic hospital at Lexington. Vaillant found that those addicts who had experienced a year of parole supervision were much more likely to remain off heroin than those who had not. But parole succeeded, Vaillant found, not because it punished but because it provided a consistent structure that helped the addict abstain from drugs.

More recent studies point to the same conclusion. For many drug offenders, and others who bring a severe drug problem to the justice system, it is surely true that firm supervision and guidance are necessary to help them make the changes in their lives that could move them away from drugs and the drug culture. But for all except the truly dangerous, the supervision and guidance are best accomplished in a community setting where they can receive several kinds of help—not just formal drug treatment, but also help with the problems that probably underlay their drug use in the first place: jobs, housing, family crises. Yet the resources to offer these services through probation or parole agencies have steadily dwindled in recent years, in direct proportion to the resources poured into the routine incarceration of people whose most immediate problem is their heavy drug use.

California's Blue Ribbon Commission proposes a comprehensive "continuum of care" for substance-abusing offenders, with an emphasis on help provided in the community—including links with parole officers who specialize in the problems of drug-using offenders and with community-based treatment programs. But the commission points out that "the financial and personnel resources for these additional controls and services at the community level have been steadily declining for years"—during the height of what we were calling a war on drugs. Reversing those upside-down priorities would go a long way toward providing tangible help for some of the drug users who need it the most, and it would simultaneously help to relieve the intolerable pressure on the prisons. And it, too, would save money. Serious help for drug users is not cheap. But it is cheaper than putting them in institutions over and over again.

Creating a "continuum of care" also means doing much more than we now do for those who must spend some time behind bars. That means providing drug treatment for a much greater proportion of those who need it, but more than ordinary treatment is required. As we'll see in detail in the following chapter, how well existing treatment programs work—in or out of prison—is a more complicated issue than is sometimes assumed. There is no magic bullet for addicted prisoners, no program that can be carbon-copied in every prison that will keep inmates from returning once released—especially given the often overwhelming problems they bring with them to prison and the daunting conditions most face when they leave. Still, the time inside the walls does offer a real opportunity to make a difference. Evaluations of the best-designed treatment programs for inmates, though mixed, are cautiously favorable, especially those that take the whole range of prisoners' needs into account. There is now some consensus that good treatment programs for prisoners should be seen as part of a larger and more inclusive plan for preparing them for release and reintegration into the community. The programs should firmly separate the addict from the in-prison drug culture. They should offer not just "treatment" but what Douglas Lipton and Harry Wexler call "habilitation"—teaching basic skills and helping prisoners develop the capacity to cope with their "survival needs" on the outside. Given the growing link between drug abuse and AIDS, they should provide preventive education on how to avoid high-risk behavior. And they should be consistently linked with a range of community services that can offer continuing help in the difficult period of adjustment after release. It's also increasingly recognized that not all prisoners who abuse drugs have the same needs; men and women, for example, may require very different kinds of settings to succeed. (An innovative Wisconsin program, called Passages, offers a nontraditional sixteen-week prerelease program for women drug abusers, addressing not only their drug habit but also many other problems they will confront on release—including employment and health problems, parenting issues, and abusive relationships.)

But though these principles are beginning to be understood in many correctional systems, putting them into practice on a level that meets the need is another matter. The U.S. General Accounting Office reported in 1991 that there was wide variation among states in the degree to which they had made serious prerelease help for addicted offenders a priority. Even in the more forward-looking states, most inmates were not getting the care they needed; in Wisconsin, where state officials estimated that 70 percent of inmates released in 1990 needed intensive help, less than 40 percent actually received it. Federal authorities, similarly, embarked on an innovative effort to provide comprehensive help to addicted inmates in the late 1980s, but as of 1991 there were still far too few programs to meet the need, and many that had been put in place were underfunded. In other jurisdictions, the situation is much worse; some still offer released drug abusers very little more than transportation back to communities rife with drugs and devoid of opportunity, which virtually guarantees that we will reimprison them over and over again, at great cost.

Realistically, however, providing serious assistance to those drug abusers we do put behind bars will depend on simultaneously reducing the numbers we put there. Again, the kind of help that shows some promise of working—teaching skills and basic competencies, following up released prisoners with strong community programs—is expensive. We will have to decide whether we wish to offer fewer prisoners better help— or offer skimpy services to large numbers of drug offenders, many of whom would be better, and more cheaply, helped in the community.

Recently, there has been considerable interest in establishing "boot camp" prisons for nonviolent drug offenders. The idea took off in the climate of fiscal austerity in the 1980s because it seemed to offer a way to impose "tough" sanctions on offenders and yet cost far less than ordinary prisons. By 1990, 16 states were operating some version of a correctional boot camp and another 17 were "planning" or "considering" them. Most camps enrolled younger offenders convicted of drug or property crimes, kept them for an average stay of three to four months, and subjected them to an often grueling (and sometimes humiliating) regimen of hard work, military-style discipline, and physical training. Boot camps are now politically quite popular; but are they useful?

Possibly. At worst, boot camps provide little more than a few months of fairly mindless and occasionally brutal "discipline," after which inmates are dumped, little helped, back into the same conditions from which they came. This is nothing more than another version of the revolving door, and it may not even save money, since the boot camp may get offenders who would otherwise have been put on probation—not those who would have gone into a regular prison. On the other hand, if a boot camp carefully selects offenders who would otherwise be sent to regular prison for longer sentences, provides skills training and education in addition to simple "discipline," and maintains services for its graduates when they return to their communities, it could be a solid investment.

Such concerns were built into legislation creating two boot camps for young drug-abusing offenders in California in 1992. The camps will take youths convicted of nonviolent offenses and enroll them for no more than four months in rigorous military-style physical training, but also provide education and counseling in avoiding substance abuse. During their final month, inmates will receive prerelease help in finding jobs and otherwise learning to cope with problems of reentry. After release, they will have six months of intensive supervision by officers with caseloads of no more than fifteen parolees. If the program actually accepts youths who would otherwise be prison-bound, it will save money: though the estimated cost per month will roughly equal that of regular youth prisons, the much shorter stay (by nine to twelve months) should substantially decrease the cost per inmate, meanwhile offering the inmates a powerful incentive to do well in the boot camp.

What is crucial is to link serious help inside the camp with real opportunities after release. As critics have pointed out, in the *real* military boot camp, the "tough" short-term regime is followed by acceptance into a supportive organization which, among other things, guarantees recruits a livelihood (as well as health care and housing) for as long as they remain in it. Simply marching "recruits" around for a few months, without anything to recruit them *into* afterwards, is not the same thing at all.

But there is no reason why we shouldn't aim higher in what we offer to motivated prisoners. We need not stop with the most basic forms of remedial education or skills training, for example. We might instead experiment with comprehensive programs to train qualified inmates for high-skill, high-demand work in expanding areas of the economy—such as health care —and to link them with real jobs in the community after release. There is much room for experiment here, since we do so little now. And creative experimentation is urgently needed. What we are now doing all too often represents the worst of all possibilities. We are punitive without purpose or reason. We overuse incarceration as a response to the drug problems of the young and poor, yet do nothing to help them deal with those problems once they're in prison. It would be hard to exaggerate the futility of this approach.

Whatever specific programs we devise, the basic principle is clear: We should regard the time when drug-using offenders are under correctional supervision, in or out of prison, as an opportunity, which we might not have otherwise, to intervene constructively. The Swedes make this principle integral to their approach to offenders with drug problems, defining their time in custody as "an opportunity of motivating drug abusers for care and rehabilitation." We should do no less.

*4. **Shift law-enforcement priorities toward community safety.*** We now use the police primarily to funnel drug users and dealers into the criminal-justice system for punishment. We've seen the crippling limitations of that strategy. But there is another way to think about the role of the police—in fact an older way—and that is as providers of community safety. What drug-ridden communities most need is help in protecting their residents from victimization by highly visible and volatile drug dealing and by the crime and violence that pervades the street drug culture. Making the reduction of violence and open drug dealing our first priority could both save lives and reduce the fear that now paralyzes many poor neighborhoods. And it could provide the breathing room that might enable a stricken community to regain enough sense of security to begin to work effectively on its larger problems.

By now we have a substantial body of research on the effects of different kinds of police strategies against street drug dealing and violence. Much of the emphasis thus far has been placed on staging police "crackdowns" on the heavy-drug-dealing areas of poor communities. And there is some evidence that crackdowns on open-air drug markets—at least relatively small ones—can, in the short run, both disrupt the drug trade and reduce the crime that tends to surround it. But the evidence is uneven and the positive results tend to be short-lived.

One of the best-known studies is by Mark Kleiman of Harvard, who examined the effects of a four-year police crackdown on a drug-dealing area in the small city of Lynn, Massachusetts. After heavy arrests over the first months of the crackdown, robberies and burglaries in the city dropped considerably for two years, and heroin use apparently declined as well—there was an 85 percent increase in the demand for drug treatment, suggesting that addicts' access to drug supplies had been substantially reduced. On the other hand, when Kleiman studied the crackdown on a larger drug market in Lawrence, Massachusetts, he found little positive impact—no evidence of a decline in drug use, and an *increase* in violent crime. Moreover, over time, even in Lynn the drop in crime began to be reversed; robbery rates, for example, slowly rose in the years after the crackdown to levels higher than before it began. There was, in short, evidence of what the criminologist Lawrence Sherman, in reviewing these studies, calls a "decay" of the apparent deterrent effect of the police crackdown over time.

The findings on other similar police efforts are even more mixed—especially for larger and more seriously drug-ridden areas. Operation Pressure Point, launched in 1984 by the New York police, flooded the Lower East Side of Manhattan with between 150 and 240 police officers, who at the start of the crackdown were making arrests at a rate of sixty-five per day. Initially, this massive police presence apparently reduced drug-related crime substantially within the target area. In the first eight months of 1986, after two years of Operation Pressure Point, robbery was 40 percent lower than during the same period in 1983, and homicide 69 percent lower. There was no

strong evidence, moreover, that street dealing and the associated violence had been simply displaced to other nearby
neighborhoods—though there was some evidence that it had
been displaced to markets in more distant parts of the city.

On the other hand, a massive citywide crackdown in Washington, D.C., Operation Clean Sweep, begun in 1986, brought
only "disappointing" results. Clean Sweep produced nearly
thirty thousand arrests in its first seventeen months. Those
arrested were, as a Rand Corporation analysis showed, quite
likely to be speedily tried and often put behind bars. The
crackdown, in short, was "well-executed and coordinated." But
it had little impact on Washington's drug problem. The number
of open drug markets in the city may have declined, but
apparently much of the dealing was simply displaced to other
neighborhoods—and the markets tended to reopen shortly
after the police turned off the pressure and moved on. Meanwhile, the city's drug crisis continued to deepen, as measured
by rising numbers of emergency-room incidents and drug-
related homicides, and rising proportions of arrestees testing
positive for cocaine and other drugs. The crackdown may have
been simply swamped by the flood of the crack epidemic, and
it is possible that things might have been even worse without
the intense police effort. But the results reveal the limits of the
"crackdown" approach in the face of epidemic levels of drug
use.

On balance, it is not that crackdowns make no difference,
but that, especially where drug dealing is heaviest and most
widespread, any effects they have are likely to be short-lived.
That may be considerably better than nothing, as Jerome
Skolnick argues in assessing a crackdown in Oakland, California. For Skolnick, the test of whether the program was successful is not whether it eliminated the city's drug problem,
but whether it improved the quality of community life. Skolnick
acknowledges that the strategy clearly "has not driven drug
dealers off the streets of Oakland," but he argues that it probably
kept drug dealing lower than it would have been otherwise

and reduced the blatant, wide-open marketplace atmosphere in the hardest-hit areas of the city. According to one police respondent, "you don't have the swarms of people all night long. They're still dealing, but not twenty-four hours a day. At least we've thinned it out so people can get in and out of their own driveways."

But no one really argues that the positive effects are anything more than short-range. The overriding problem is that, as Lawrence Sherman writes, "the market in some areas appears to be so strong that street dealing reappears almost as soon as police effort is reduced." The response in some cities has been to escalate the police "war" still further—to the point, for example, of cordoning off entire communities and restricting entry altogether, as the Los Angeles police did in several neighborhoods in the early 1990s.

But those massive police invasions suffer from the same basic problem that limits less spectacular crackdowns: where the street drug culture is very deeply entrenched, it tends to regroup quickly once the police presence is reduced. And the long-run damage from these escalated police efforts may outweigh any short-term gains—threatening basic civil liberties of ordinary residents and drug dealers alike, and driving a divisive wedge between police and community that makes cooperation in fighting the street drug trade less and less likely.

Even the more careful police crackdowns rarely involve any efforts at longer-term community security; nor do they make any attempt to provide alternatives for drug users who may be temporarily deterred from buying drugs in the illegal markets. But both responses are necessary, unless we are willing to resign ourselves to simply doing the same thing over and over again: sending in masses of police, arresting vast numbers of minor dealers and addicts—and then dumping them back on the street, where they will continue to "take care of business."

We will need to shift police priorities toward strategies

that are more preventive and more enduring—especially by developing more innovative and better-supported forms of "community-oriented" policing. That term now covers a wide range of practices—from simply putting more police on foot patrol in tough neighborhoods, to establishing "mini" police stations in the hardest-hit areas, to working with neighborhood organizations to develop specific strategies for coping with drug-related problems in public housing, parks, or residential areas.

In Albuquerque, for example, setting up a mini police station in one neighborhood wracked by heavy drug dealing substantially reduced the level of open-air dealing and gave residents a sense of having "taken back" their neighborhood. The mini station "not only provided police visibility, it also improved and strengthened once-strained relations between residents and the police. . . . Months will go by when the police don't receive calls about drug pushing in the neighborhood." In New Haven, police have partly reoriented their tactics from intensive street crackdowns to a more community-oriented approach—among other things, providing addicts with information about treatment programs and other sources of help in the city.

Research on the results of these strategies is mixed but generally encouraging. Most studies, both in the United States and abroad, suggest that local *crime* rates are stubbornly resistant to community policing. On the other hand, it seems clear that, where it is consistently implemented, community policing can help make residents less fearful and bolster a sense of cohesion in neighborhoods wracked by drugs and crime. A recent British study of community policing in London and Birmingham, for example, found no clear reductions in crime as a result of putting more police on the streets and having officers personally contact every household in the neighborhood at least once in the course of a year. But residents did report feeling more satisfaction with their neighborhoods and a greater sense of community after the program.

Obviously, those outcomes are not spectacular. But neither

are they insignificant, given the terrible demoralization that can overcome neighborhoods that are overrun by drugs and drug crime. And stronger effects may well be possible if we put more resources—and more consistent resources—into community policing. It is worth noting that New York City saw significant declines in street crime during 1991 from the previous year—just after the city raised the number of community-patrol officers from 786 to over 3,000. No one can say for certain that the declines in crime resulted from the expanded police presence—one year is far too short a time to judge—but it is noteworthy that New York's declines took place just as many otherwise similar cities were suffering significant increases in street crime.

But putting more resources into community policing would require a more-than-token shift in recent patterns of spending across the country. While we have been pouring vast sums into the "back end" of the system—into jails and prisons—we have cut back on money for the "front end": local police efforts that might prevent drug-related crime in the first place. To be sure, more than money is involved; many police departments have tended to spend in ineffective ways—on bloated administrative overhead or high-technology equipment of dubious effectiveness—while resisting the more labor-intensive strategies of community policing. But government spending priorities, especially at the federal level, have also played a conspicuous part in the distortion. One consequence of the massive decline in federal aid to the cities during the 1980s was that many cities were forced to cut back on police forces or delay increases in police personnel. The result was that the ratio of police to population fell in many cities just when the drug crisis hit the streets with strongest force—and just when the rhetorical war on drugs reached fever pitch. In some cities, additional police could be brought in to deal with the drug crisis only through heroic fiscal juggling and by making cutbacks in other critical urban services. That trend continues today, as we've seen, because of collapsing state and local budgets in the 1990s. It must be reversed, and it is best reversed by a consistent infusion of federal money specifically targeted for innovative community policing.

Along with the expansion of community policing, we need a serious commitment to helping communities provide their own mechanisms of public safety—especially civilian patrols. These have sprouted up in many drug-plagued neighborhoods across the country, sometimes under the wing of established community organizations, though usually without much funding or careful evaluation. But our neglect of civilian patrols is a mistake; they are a potentially significant part of an overall strategy for community safety. There is scattered, but interesting, evidence that civilian patrols can make a difference—at the very least, in improving a community's sense of security and perhaps in reducing blatant open drug trafficking and drug-related crime. And this is all the more remarkable because virtually all of the patrols have operated on a shoestring, with few resources and no continuity.

In a Bronx program supported by the Eisenhower Foundation, for example,

> The Mid-Bronx Desperadoes' successful civilian patrol was forced to plan its coverage of the neighborhood depending on whether it was able to borrow someone's car. The lack of a vehicle on a steady basis meant that the patrol was mainly on foot, which naturally limited its range. . . . Another member donated a car to the patrol, but it needed repairs and insurance, and the project director was still in the process of completing these arrangements at the end of the grant period.

Yet even with so minimal a level of resources, the patrol was well regarded in the neighborhood and seen as making a difference. "It's not a no-man's-land out there anymore," one member of the patrol said. "It's a no-nonsense place." What we might accomplish with fuller and longer-term funding, which could pay reasonable salaries for patrol work and provide continuity of staff (and adequate equipment), could be considerable; it is surely worth exploring.

Community antidrug and anticrime patrols offer several advantages at once. They can augment the efforts of community-oriented police—who cannot, after all, be everywhere. And they are cheaper than using the police to provide similar services, even if patrol workers are paid real stipends. They can be a significant source of meaningful employment for community residents, including many now poorly employed. Finally, they can provide one kind of enduring indigenous community institution that in its own small way helps to rebuild cohesive, well-functioning local neighborhoods. Given the impact of community fragmentation on the spread of drugs, that is an important plus.

This kind of local institution-building—helping to create what Paul Starr calls "civil society" in hard-hit communities— ought to be a main objective of the police in troubled neighborhoods. Mark Moore and Mark Kleiman make a similar point:

In confronting drug trafficking and use, then, the task of a police department is often to find a way to prime the community's own capacities for self-defense so that police efforts may be effectively leveraged through community self-help. . . . For example, it may be as important to organize community meetings as to make it easier for individuals to call the police over the phone. It may be more effective to organize and support citizen patrols than to chase the drug dealers from one block to another. It may be more effective to organize groups of parents, educators, and youth leaders to resist drug dealing in and around schools than to increase arrests of drug dealers by 20 percent.

Shifting our priorities in these four directions would transform the way our criminal-justice system now deals with the drug problem, and make it not only more effective but also less expensive and more in line with the values and aims of a democratic society. It is important to keep these benefits in perspective. There is no criminal-justice solution to the drug crisis, and we will be much better off if we accept that fact and steadily decrease the relative place of law enforcement in our overall approach to drugs. But at the same time, what the justice system *can* do is important. It can offer meaningful, but not Draconian, sanctions for serious drug offenders. It can provide tangible help for drug abusers inside and outside of correctional institutions. And it can make a more consistent commitment to protecting communities against inundation by drug dealing and drug-related violence.

There are common themes in all these proposals: using the justice system less to punish drug users and more to improve their capacity to lead productive lives; strengthening the ability of local communities to resist drugs and crime; providing crucial, if limited, support to other strategies to revitalize neighborhoods and expand opportunities. None of these actions will end the drug crisis, and without a simultaneous commitment to enhancing treatment and rebuilding shattered communities, these efforts will be easily undermined and overwhelmed. Alongside that commitment, they can take an honorable place in a real war on drugs.

CHAPTER

5

Redefining Treatment

The limits of the "correctional" approach, then—already apparent in the 1950s—have become more and more difficult to ignore as the drug war grinds fruitlessly on. In response, some argue that drugs should be seen as a medical problem rather than a law-enforcement problem, and that the remedy is not punishment but treatment "on demand." It is sometimes assumed that if there were enough treatment "slots" for all the addicted, the drug problem would be eliminated, or at least made manageable. That belief has led to calls for a massive expansion of our treatment capacity; at the height of the crack epidemic, there were proposals for vast treatment "campuses" for tens of thousands of cocaine addicts. But the assumption is false, and it rests on a misunderstanding of the nature and roots of endemic drug abuse in the United States. We do need more treatment. But treatment is not a panacea. Just as we will not punish our way out of the drug crisis, we will not treat our way out either.

It is true that many addicts are not getting the help they need—especially if they are among the poor and near-poor who make up the largest part of the addict population. There is plenty of *private* drug treatment available for those who can afford it; indeed, many private treatment programs are starved for clients. But poorer drug abusers are mainly dependent on the public system of drug treatment, which, like other public services in the United States, was inadequate to begin with and was then systematically scaled back during much of the 1980s —just when the national rhetoric about fighting drugs reached new heights. That those who most need help are least likely to get it is a real tragedy, and it virtually ensures that we will suffer needless levels of drug-related crime, illness, and family disintegration.

But more treatment, by itself, will not be enough. We also need *better* treatment, and different treatment. Indeed, we need to rethink what we mean by the concept of treatment altogether. If we simply throw money at existing programs, we are likely to be disappointed. The best evidence suggests that good treatment programs can be a helpful addition to other efforts to move drug abusers away from drugs and the culture of drug use. But much treatment is not good, and even good treatment is too often a revolving door. Treatment, moreover, works much more reliably for some kinds of people than others, and not necessarily for those who need help most. Many of the latter, in fact, find conventional treatment programs alienating or irrelevant, and either avoid entering treatment in the first place, or drop out at the first opportunity. And the evidence also suggests that some of those who do well after conventional treatment would have done as well without it.

Part of the problem is the pervasive stinginess which virtually guarantees that few programs can fulfill their potential. But there is a deeper conceptual problem as well.

Too much conventional drug treatment is disturbingly disconnected from what we know about the causes of drug abuse and about the factors that encourage addicts to get off drugs —and, more importantly, stay off. As we've seen, endemic drug abuse is primarily neither a law-enforcement problem *nor* a medical problem, but a *social* problem. Most addicts enter a career of drugs as one response to a variety of overlapping social deprivations. Those troubles may be aggravated by psychological problems, or they may not. Nor has drug abuse ever been persuasively linked to any specific predisposing genetic or biological condition. Yet very few drug-treatment programs are based on an understanding of the social roots of drug abuse or the social needs of drug abusers, and most operate, at least implicitly, on the principle that drug abuse is a psychological or biological disease to which some individuals are uniquely predisposed.

At the extreme, the "disease model" of addiction denies what forty years of research have shown us, and argues that the obvious social problems addicts present are solely the result, not the cause, of their "disease." "The disease concept," according to two enthusiasts,

> states that economic, family, individual, psychological, psychiatric, social and moral consequences ensue from addictive drug use. . . . The important link in the disease concept is that the consequences result from, and do not cause, the addiction. . . . The disease model begins with the basic assumption that the etiological agent, alcohol or drugs, interacts with the susceptible host, a person with the genetic predisposition to initiate a disease process. . . . Addictive people are sick as is evident in the hundreds of medical, psychiatric, and sociological complications from addiction.

In some versions of the "medical model," drug abuse is presented as if it were literally a disease, much like pneumonia or a kidney infection—and one for which a specific treatment exists, in the same way that antibiotics can cure bacterial infections. The problem then becomes simply one of delivering the appropriate cure to the infected. Something like this view is often invoked to support ever more vigorous criminalization

of drug use; if we can *force* enough addicts to take their
medicine by coercing them into treatment programs through
the criminal-justice system, we may bring the drug problem
under control. But the problem is that there is no such
treatment, in that strict sense, for drug addiction (the closest
is methadone maintenance for heroin addiction, about which
more later). There is no analogue to penicillin, no "shot" that
will wipe out the disease.

A more sophisticated variant of the disease model likens
drug addiction not to acute infections but to chronic disorders,
physical or psychological. As a recent (and generally very useful)
report from the U.S. Office of Technology Assessment puts it,
"Drug abuse is a chronic relapsing disorder; its pattern of
relapses and remissions resembles other chronic diseases, such
as arthritis and chronic depression." From that perspective,
the goal of treatment is not the elimination of the disease, but
the "amelioration of symptoms" and the "prolongation of
symptom-free intervals." But though this is a more realistic
description of what most often happens in drug treatment, the
imagery remains misleading. In fact, drug abuse is not at all
like arthritis, except in the superficial sense that both often
recur. Arthritics do not choose to have arthritis, and they
cannot choose to stop being arthritic; and no change in the
circumstances of their lives can end their disease, though it
may mitigate some of the symptoms. Drug abusers, on the
other hand, do choose to use drugs, and they do—more often
than many suppose—choose to stop using them or cut back
their use to manageable levels. And they frequently make that
choice as a direct or indirect result of other favorable changes
in their lives. Providing someone with a better job or a stable
family life will not cure their arthritis; it can, as we shall see,
"cure" their drug abuse.

None of this is to deny that many good treatment programs
exist, or that in some places the basic services drug users need

are in desperately short supply. But we need an approach to treatment that is both more attuned to what we know of the roots of the problem and more committed to addressing the full range of issues that underlie drug abuse and frustrate attempts to end it. Accordingly, we should first take a closer look at what research tells us about the uses and limits of the drug treatment we have now.

I

In contrast to the skepticism leveled against many other social programs—like those to reform juvenile delinquents or train the hard-core unemployed—there is a widespread and rather uncritical belief that drug treatment "works." But in fact, whether treatment works, how well it works, and for whom it works are complex, difficult, and unsettled questions.

On the surface, the problem of evaluating the effectiveness of drug treatment seems simple. People become addicted. They decide—or are forced—to enter a treatment program. They either succeed in that program—meaning that they use no drugs or fewer drugs, commit fewer crimes, find steady jobs, and otherwise adopt a more conventional life—or they do not.

But in the real world, things are vastly more complicated. Part of the problem is that the notion of drug treatment itself is both vague and unmanageably eclectic; it covers an enormous range of practices that share few principles in common. "Treatment" can mean drinking a dose of methadone—the synthetic opiate that reduces the craving for heroin—once a day; it can mean screaming at the top of one's lungs in a roomful of other "patients"; it can mean years of intensive individual psychotherapy; it can mean dropping in for a brief chat with a counselor about family problems. It can take place in locked hospital wards, outpatient clinics, storefront youth centers. It may follow a specific, often rigid psychological model, or it may have no underlying theoretical focus at all. All of these count as "treatment," which makes it hard to disentangle what is effective, and for whom, from what is not. We need, then, to look carefully at what we have learned from studies of this sprawling and poorly defined enterprise.

There has been an explosion of studies of the effects of treatment during the past twenty years. At first glance, these studies seem generally favorable to drug treatment. It wasn't always so. The early studies of the fate of treated addicts—mostly heroin addicts in this research—were quite pessimistic. One early follow-up of two hundred addicts treated at the federal hospital at Lexington, for example, found that 87 percent began using heroin again within six months of release, and two-thirds were actively readdicted. A national sample of young heroin users studied by John O'Donnell and his colleagues in the mid-seventies showed an 85 percent rate of relapse within four months after treatment. The high readdiction rates uncovered in most serious studies led a Ford Foundation report in the early 1970s to conclude that "existing treatment for drug abuse and drug dependence has not produced impressive results (except for some methadone programs)." The strategic implication was clear: "even if all drug abusers and drug-dependent persons had treatment available to them, the outcome would be uncertain."

More recent research has been, on the whole, far more positive. Consider first two major federal surveys that have sampled treatment programs across the United States, DARP (Drug Abuse Reporting Program) and TOPS (Treatment Outcome Prospective Study). These surveys break down the bewildering variety of treatment programs into three categories—methadone maintenance, residential "therapeutic communities," and "outpatient drug-free" programs—and examine each category (or "modality") separately.

Methadone maintenance has been the treatment most often studied, and the one with the most consistently favorable evaluations. It's important, however, to keep in mind that methadone treatment is designed for *heroin* addicts alone.

Many, indeed most, methadone clients use other drugs, and the research does suggest that some may also moderate their cocaine use while in treatment; but whatever the reason for that may be, it is not a result of the methadone itself—and no one argues that methadone can play much role in reducing the use of drugs other than heroin.

But on that narrower terrain, recent research is generally favorable. Many heroin addicts who enter methadone treatment do apparently improve considerably, by several measures, during and after treatment. According to TOPS, about 64 percent of methadone clients used heroin regularly in the year before treatment; one year *after* treatment, about 17 percent did (as measured, however, solely by their own reports of drug use) and about 18 percent three to five years after ending treatment. About 32 percent reported participating in "serious predatory crimes" in the year prior to treatment; a year later self-reported crime had fallen to 19 percent, and to 16 percent three to five years after entering the program. Though significant, in short, the decline in crime was less dramatic than in heroin use. And for employment, the picture was much less encouraging: about 25 percent of clients reported having been employed full-time in the year before treatment; but that proportion *fell* to 20 percent after one year and to 18 percent after three to five years. What TOPS reveals, then, is a sharp reduction in heroin use for those who stay in methadone programs, a significant drop in crime, and a continued inability to find productive work.

The survey data on methadone are generally backed by other kinds of studies. Patients who were forced back onto the street when some methadone clinics closed in California in the 1970s, for example, returned to heroin use much more often than those who were able to enroll in another methadone program. A careful study of six methadone programs published by John Ball and his colleagues in the late 1980s found strong declines in intravenous heroin use among addicts who remained in treatment for several years. About 81 percent of addicts entering the six programs were IV heroin users at admission; within a month of admission only 63 percent were. By three years in treatment the number acknowledging IV use had dropped to 42 percent, and in their fourth year, to 29 percent. And many of those who did continue to shoot heroin did so less frequently.

The consensus is less solid for other kinds of drug treatment —though here too, the recent research is more often positive than not. Indeed, at first glance the record of residential "therapeutic community" (TC) programs appears even better than methadone. (These programs are typically based on some form of encounter-group therapy, usually with very strict rules of behavior for clients and rigid internal hierarchies.) In TOPS, for example, 31 percent of TC clients were "regular" heroin users in the year before treatment; three to five years afterward, only 12 percent were. Unlike methadone, these programs can in theory work equally for all drugs of abuse; TC clients' regular cocaine use, for example, dropped from 28 percent before treatment to 10 percent three to five years after. Serious "predatory crime" fell from 61 percent to 20 percent. Employment improved significantly, with 15 percent of clients working full-time before treatment and 39 percent three to five years later—though that figure, among the highest found for ex-addicts in any national study, still means that 61 percent were *not* working full-time, even after sustained drug treatment.

For the third category, "outpatient drug-free treatment"— which includes most nonresidential programs that do not dispense methadone—the apparent improvements are generally somewhat less, but still significant. In TOPS, only about 9 percent of entrants to these diverse programs were regular heroin users in the first place, but three to five years after treatment only about 5 percent were. The 13 percent who reported being regular cocaine users before admission were reduced to 6 percent. Serious crime fell more sharply than in other modes of treatment—from 34 percent to 8 percent of clients, according to their own reports.

What do we make of these findings? Some use them to argue that drug treatment has been proven to be effective and that indeed "any treatment is better than none." But as most serious students of treatment evaluation acknowledge, matters are actually far more complicated. For a variety of reasons, the conventional outcome figures considerably overstate the effectiveness of treatment itself in reducing drug use and crime and in reintegrating former addicts into the world of work. The issues are often highly technical, but they are crucial in understanding what drug treatment can and cannot accomplish.

One problem is that most of the studies showing large improvements as a result of treatment stack the deck by comparing addicts' lives after treatment with their *most extreme* period of pretreatment addiction and crime—not with their *typical* pattern before treatment. Addicts often begin a treatment program when they have hit rock bottom, often when they have been arrested or have been on a severe binge of drug use. As George Vaillant writes, "In any chronic illness with a fluctuating course, hospitalization is usually sought during clinical nadirs; thus, seeming post-hospital improvement may be attributed either to treatment or to the natural history of any fluctuating disorder." The problem was well stated by the Canadian scholar Reginald Smart in assessing the findings of the federal DARP survey in the 1970s:

It is notable that most changes, especially in drug use, occurred early, often in the first few months after treatment. . . . This, of course, raises the possibility that when patients come into treatment they are at the bottom of a cycle and "ready to improve." . . . It appears as if addicts enter treatment at a time when their resources are depleted. That is, they tend to be unemployed, harassed by the law, separated or divorced, and tired of chasing drugs. Often their social stability is lowest at the point of entering treatment, or lower than it has been for some time. This suggests that posttreatment changes in criminality and employment need not be very great to create a statistically significant difference.

That issue may be even more significant for assessing addicts' crime than their drug use, since addicts so often enter treatment *because* they have been arrested. The phenomenon is illuminated in a 1977 evaluation of a methadone program in New York City by Paula Kleinman, Irving Lukoff, and Barbara Lynn Kail. Clients' overall rates of crime two years after entering the program were modestly but significantly lower (by about 18 percent) than in the year before entry. But compared with their average crime rates during the *entire* period from the "onset" of drug use to the point at which they entered the program, the rates after two years of treatment were in fact 28 percent *higher*.

A second problem is that most studies considerably inflate the successes of treatment by failing to include the large numbers of clients who have *dropped out* of treatment altogether—which means that the positive conclusions are based only on those addicts who were doing well enough to stay with the program for some time. But that makes the conclusions suspiciously circular; it is tantamount to proving that treatment works well for those addicts for whom it works well. The TOPS survey, for example, considers only those clients who remain in treatment three months or more; but the dropout rate is highest precisely in the first months of treatment. The problem is least severe for methadone maintenance, which tends to have a better record of retaining its clients than other forms of treatment. But in John Ball's study of six relatively stable and well-funded methadone programs, for example, fully a third of the clients dropped out in the first year. And the dropout problem is even more significant in assessing TC programs, where dropout rates are staggeringly high. Indeed, the *majority* of addicts entering TCs drop out early, most within weeks of entering; 56 percent of TC clients in the TOPS survey were no longer in treatment after three months—and therefore were not included in the assessment. The positive findings, in other words, are based solely on the 44 percent of clients who actually stayed with the program. The "overall impact" of TCs, as the review by the U.S. Office of Technology Assessment notes, is therefore "severely impaired by their limited ability to keep clients in treatment." By the end of the first year, only some 15 to 25 percent of TC clients remain in treatment, and still fewer—10 to 15 percent —complete the treatment they started. If we were to count all the dropouts as failures, rather than excluding them from the assessment altogether, the figures would look dramatically different.

The dropout problem is especially critical because the evidence suggests that those who drop out are disproportionately the tougher cases. Again, what that means is that conventional outcome statistics tend to be circular and self-confirming; they tell us, in effect, that the programs are likely to be successful for those who are most likely to succeed. Addicts with more severe problems or fewer resources often simply fall out of the picture altogether. Reginald Smart noted in the late 1970s that the typical treatment dropout was "male, younger, single, living alone, poorly educated, previously unemployed," with "a history of juvenile delinquency and many arrests." By excluding dropouts from the analysis, he noted, the surveys wound up including "too many socially stable, well motivated, and easy-to-treat cases"—thus biasing the results upward. In John Ball's more recent study of methadone treatment, the one-third of clients who had dropped out of treatment were somewhat younger and only half as likely to have been employed before treatment as those who stayed for a year or more. Dropout rates among *adolescent* drug abusers are even higher than among adults, which means that treatment statistics end up being disproportionately based on older addicts and cannot be easily generalized to the young. Even *middle-class* youth are difficult to retain in treatment; for example, a recent study of a day treatment program for adolescents on Long Island found that only 14 percent of a sample of its largely white and middle-to-working-class clients had graduated from the program.

In general, drug treatment of whatever type is repeatedly shown to be more effective for those who enter it with better prospects and resources in the first place. Thus the positive results often seen in treatment studies must be tempered by the recognition that they mainly reflect the performance of those drug users who are already in relatively good shape, not those who arguably need help the most.

Some of the most striking results in treatment evaluations come from programs that enroll relatively well-situated clients in the first place. That is illustrated in a recent assessment by the psychologist Charles Winick of a therapeutic community program in New York called ACI. Interviewed after treatment, most of the first hundred former clients reported favorable changes; 75 percent said they had abstained from *all* drug use, including alcohol; 79 percent reported that they were working or at school full-time. As Winick points out, these outcomes were much more impressive than those reported for any other treatment program. But the results were made far more predictable by the highly atypical character of the clients admitted to the program—who were drawn from an unusually advantaged population to begin with, and then rigidly screened to admit only those deemed most likely to do well—a strategy often called "creaming." All the clients were white, and came from middle- to upper-middle-class backgrounds. They appeared to be better educated, and to have somewhat higher-status occupations than clients at other TCs in the New York area. In short, they were "fairly homogeneous and [had] relative access to society's opportunity structure." The program charged its clients $150 a day, carefully screened applicants for factors that might cause them to fail in treatment, and indeed required them to sit through a group interview lasting several hours in which the staff determined whether they had sufficient motivation to succeed and were relatively free of such impediments as participation in the subcultures of street drugs and crime.

ACI is only an extreme example of the skewing of successful treatment results toward the better prepared and more favorably situated. In general, those with better resources and greater opportunities—who are of course less likely to abuse hard drugs to begin with—are consistently more likely to end up as statistics on treatment success. As one recent review of the evidence puts it,

> Abusers who have a more stable family background, an intact marriage, a job, a history of minimal criminality, less evidence of alcohol and polydrug use, and less severe psychiatric disorders are more likely to achieve a better outcome in most programs.

In practice, this means that success in most conventional treatment is less likely for minority addicts. Data from the federal DARP survey in the 1970s, for example, showed that both Mexican-Americans and Puerto Ricans were less likely than average to stay in treatment—more likely to be expelled or to drop out. Mexican-Americans, moreover, had the smallest reduction in heroin use from pretreatment levels, and the highest rates of arrest and incarceration after treatment. In a more recent study of California methadone programs, Chicano clients were found to have more relapses to drug use, more crime, and more drug dealing after treatment than Anglos. "This may be due," the researchers conclude, "to the fact that Chicanos in general come from lower socioeconomic status families and had lower educational achievement. The lack of developed vocational skills results in fewer economic alternatives for them that are legal."

The conventional data on treatment success also obscure the fact that some of the purported victories over drug abuse may be more apparent than real—requiring a definition of success which, while technically accurate, is less than inspiring. Some treated addicts who stop using illegal drugs compensate by abusing alcohol instead: In Maddux and Desmond's study of Chicano heroin addicts in Texas, for example, alcohol substitution "was a prominent factor in prolonged abstinence from opioids":

> By 1982, when the mean age of the sample had reached forty-four, 38 of the 248 subjects (15 percent) had been identified as chronic alcoholics. One hundred and six others (43 percent) were classifiable as dysfunctional drinkers at some point in their lives. . . . Methadone maintenance, alcoholism, and death appear to account for much of the marked decrease in the percentage using illicit opioids after age forty.

The raw figures on treatment outcome, in short, suggest that it is indeed possible to get some addicts to stop using illegal drugs, especially heroin; they do not necessarily tell us that much else has changed for the better in their lives, including the overall severity of their abuse of destructive chemicals. Shifting an addict from one drug to another may be statistically impressive, but it is not much cause for celebration. The issue of just what we want the treatment of abusers to accomplish is a complex one, to which we will return shortly. But surely it is no great victory to change someone from being unemployed, socially impoverished, and addicted to heroin, to being unemployed, socially impoverished, and addicted to methadone and alcohol.

But there is an even more basic issue, which is both the most important and the least discussed in conventional assessments of drug treatment: most drug abusers do not go into treatment at all, at least for many years into their addiction, and so are not affected by treatment programs one way or another during most of their addiction career. Obviously, studies that make large claims for treatment effectiveness on the basis of only the minority of addicts who are formally treated may greatly overstate the potential contribution of treatment to the solution of the drug problem as a whole. If we want a more realistic appraisal of the place of expanded treatment in an antidrug strategy, we need to confront the fact that many addicts are so uninterested in treatment, or repelled by it, that they do not make use of the treatment programs that are already available.

In the early seventies, the Ford Foundation report estimated that only 15 percent of heroin addicts in Washington and 10 percent in New York were in treatment, and newer studies confirm that the pattern still holds. A recent study of IV cocaine and heroin users in Houston, for example, found that nearly three-fourths of a sample of street drug users not currently enrolled in a treatment program had *never* been in treatment —this despite the fact that those over forty had been injecting drugs for over *nineteen years* on average, and those under twenty-five for almost six years. In a New York City sample of over five hundred crack, cocaine, heroin, and polydrug users studied by Jeffrey Fagan and Ko-Lin Chin, about 9 percent were in treatment. Almost nine out of ten women IV drug users interviewed in a recent study by Abt Associates were not in treatment, "despite high levels of drug use and criminal activity." In a recent Department of Justice survey of jail inmates, less than half of those who used hard drugs *every day* in the month before their recent offense had *ever* been in a treatment program.

It is sometimes assumed that addicts who do not come to formal treatment probably have less severe problems to begin with, but that assumption is problematic at best. In the Houston study, for example, 55 percent of older cocaine users who had never been in treatment *injected* the drug at least daily. In their study of street heroin addicts in New York, Bruce Johnson and his colleagues found that most of these very serious addicts were "quite successful at avoiding or limiting their contacts" with the formal treatment system—as with the criminal-justice system. Indeed, disturbingly, their analysis "suggests that subjects who are the most criminal and the heaviest heroin users are the least likely to be in treatment." Overall, three-fourths of the Harlem heroin addicts had no methadone treatment during the course of the study; methadone treatment was even less likely for those seriously involved in robbery, burglary, and theft, 92 percent of whom were not in treatment.

Why are so few addicts—even those with the most severe problems—in treatment? One explanation is that the problem is simply one of supply—not enough treatment is available to come even close to meeting the demand. And indeed, in some places, and for some kinds of treatment, there are clear shortages, and part of the explanation for the low percentage of addicts enrolled is that there is nowhere for them to go. But that is only *part* of the explanation—even for methadone maintenance, the treatment with the most clearly demonstrated effectiveness and the one most in demand by addicts. As a recent study by the U.S. General Accounting Office shows, there are long waiting lists for some methadone programs in some cities—but not others. Fourteen of twenty-four programs studied—all in states with relatively large numbers of addicts —had no waiting lists. Even within New York, which has more heroin addicts than any other city and an unusually high demand for methadone treatment, some programs are perennially underenrolled while others have addicts backed up on waiting lists. A recent New York survey found that ten of twenty-three programs it contacted in the city were full and had waiting lists; the others had anywhere up to eighty vacant treatment "slots."

National statistics put this into perspective. In 1989, at the height of the cocaine epidemic, programs providing drug treatment were operating at a national average of 79 percent of capacity. Public treatment facilities under the auspices of state and local government were the fullest, at 86 percent of

capacity; private, for-profit programs—which now compete
feverishly for a dwindling clientele of middle-class drug users
—were operating at just 60 percent of capacity.

It's true that these national figures mask the very real pressure
on some big-city programs in areas hard hit by the drug crisis.
But the magnitude of that backed-up demand for treatment
must be put in perspective. In 1989, about 350,000 drug
users were in treatment at any given point, according to the
federal National Drug and Alcohol Treatment Unit Survey
(NDATUS); other surveys suggest that there were in the
neighborhood of 67,000 substance abusers—including both
alcohol and drug abusers—on waiting lists for treatment. That
is a significant number, and it should be reduced, but it looks
a great deal smaller compared with the highly conservative
estimate of over 2 million "hard-core" heroin and cocaine users
alone in the United States.

Most cocaine and heroin addicts, in short (not to mention
methamphetamine, PCP, or solvent abusers), are neither in
formal treatment programs nor on waiting lists for them. That
could be interpreted to mean that many are discouraged even
from applying for treatment because they know there isn't
room for them; and that is surely the case in some high-
drug-use areas. But it is not the whole story. The reality is that
many addicts deliberately avoid treatment: They do not seek
it even when it *is* available. Indeed, the Harlem research by
Johnson and his coworkers found that many do not go to
treatment even if they are given special help in doing so. The
researchers decided early on to help the addicts they were
studying get treatment if they wanted it:

> If a subject was ready to go into treatment, a staff member
> would refer him to the program of his choice and help
> him gain admission. With one exception . . . expressions
> of interest were not followed by a decision to seek ad-
> mission.

Those studies that have tried to determine why addicts avoid
formal treatment do not, on the whole, find that it's primarily
because they believe treatment is unavailable. On the contrary,
it seems clear that—as the researchers of the 1950s and 1960s
foresaw—many do not seek treatment, especially early in their
drug careers, because they do not regard the drug itself as the
problem that needs fixing in their lives: many, indeed, regard
it as the solution. If and when they do begin to define their
drug use as a problem, addicts often reject treatment either
because they believe they can deal with their problem on their
own, or because they regard conventional treatment programs
as unhelpful, punitive, overly regimented, or likely to draw
them into the orbit of the criminal-justice system. Studies by
Patrick Biernacki, Dan Waldorf, and their colleagues of addicts
who had chosen to resolve their problem on their own found
that more than 90 percent had rejected formal treatment as
an option:

> Most rejected treatment because they thought they could
> manage the situation themselves. Others did not believe
> treatment would help them. Still others reported that they
> feared further stigmatization or that they did not wish to
> be humiliated or degraded. These reports are not unusual.
> Surveys of addicts in San Francisco show that even if
> treatment slots were available, many would not volunteer
> to take them, because they are not interested in treatment
> or because they view treatment programs as too intrusive,
> controlling, and regimented.

The problem is by no means confined to the United States;
the British research, for example, finds a similar tendency for
addicts to avoid formal treatment and to be "ambivalent about
the helping regimes," as Howard Parker and his colleagues
describe their Wirral subjects. Geoffrey Pearson writes that

it is a disturbing feature of the accounts which heroin users and ex-users give of their experiences in trying to secure assistance that they often felt that they were met with what they perceived as a mixture of indifference, incompetence, and sometimes even a malevolently punitive attitude. . . . the outcome of these unhappy exchanges was that heroin users and their families were often thrust back onto their own resources in trying to combat the problems in their lives.

One implication of this—to which we'll return—is that making help more attractive to those who need it is crucial if we want treatment to make more of an impact than it now does. But the fact that many serious drug abusers never seek formal treatment at all also tells us that by themselves, the usual statistics on the effects of treatment give a very misleading picture of the potential impact of the treatment system on the addict population as a whole.

A still more vexing question about the effectiveness of treatment is whether, for those who do get better after entering treatment, it is the treatment itself that actually makes the difference. The tendency in many studies is simply to *assume* that if addicts come out of treatment better than when they went in, it was the treatment that caused the improvement. But that ignores the possibility that the addict might have improved in any case, even without formal treatment. And it is clear from what is by now a thirty-year body of research that many addicts do indeed get better without any drug treatment at all.

That finding goes against the widespread belief that drug addiction is a permanent condition, or at least a deeply resistant illness that cannot get better without professional help. "Addiction gets worse," runs an advertisement for a private treatment program in a Western state, "never better." But the folk belief that addicts invariably remain addicted, or get worse, until they enter treatment, die, or go behind bars was challenged as far back as the early 1960s. In a classic study, Charles Winick described a phenomenon he called "maturing out" of drug addiction. Looking at federal records of contact between addicts and the criminal-justice or medical systems, Winick discovered that a significant proportion of those reported to official agencies at one point no longer appeared several years later. Thus of over 45,000 addicts officially recorded in the late 1950s, more than 7,000 had no contact with any official agency over the next five years and had apparently dropped out of addiction. Winick considered, but rejected, the possibility that many of them might still be seriously addicted but had escaped notice: "Experience has shown that it is almost impossible for a regular user of narcotics to avoid coming to the attention of the authorities within a period of about two years." (Recall that Isidor Chein had made the same argument in studying New York addicts in the same period.) The strong implication was that a substantial proportion of the 7,000 had stopped using narcotics—and that stopping was somehow related to their getting older. Few quit when they were very young—less than one in five disappeared from the records before age twenty-seven. But about half of those addicts who no longer appeared in the official records had "dropped out" by their early thirties, about three-fourths by their late thirties. Overall, Winick speculated that as many as two-thirds of narcotic addicts probably "matured out" in time—either because of something about the process of aging itself or as a function of the length of an addict's drug-use career. Winick favored the view that age was the crucial factor; the addict matured out of addiction as "the problems for which he originally began taking drugs become less salient and less urgent." By their thirties, addicts often reached a point where the "stresses and strains of life" had become sufficiently bearable for the addict to "face them without the support provided by narcotics."

Later research affirmed that many addicts "terminated" their addiction—and that many did so without benefit of formal treatment, perhaps more of them without formal help than with it. The psychiatrist Lee Robins, as we've seen, found that a startling one in ten men in her sample of St. Louis blacks had been addicted to heroin at some point—but only 14 percent of those who had ever been addicted reported having used the drug in the previous year. Heroin addiction, Robins concluded, was not a permanent condition but a "remitting illness." More-over, current heroin use was *higher* among those who had been treated at a Public Health Service hospital than among those who hadn't: 22 percent as against 14 percent. The conclusion was not necessarily that treatment was harmful, or even un-helpful, since "the most seriously addicted members of the addict population" might be the ones who went to treatment hospitals in the first place. But what the figures did make clear was that not only occasional users, but serious heroin addicts as well, often stopped without treatment; and it was at the very least unproven that treatment improved their chances of "re-covery" at all.

Similarly, in a late 1960s study of over four hundred male addicts in New York State by the sociologist Dan Waldorf, two out of five addicts had voluntarily quit using heroin for at least three months at a stretch *outside* of a treatment program or jail; one in five had "abstained" voluntarily for at least eight months at a time. Like Winick, Waldorf found that abstaining was more likely as the addicts aged and as the length of their addiction career increased. Almost three out of five addicts over age twenty-six who had been using for ten years or more had abstained, at some point, for at least eight months. Unlike Winick, Waldorf concluded that the length of addiction was more important in determining when "de-addiction" took place than age itself:

It may be that persons "burn out" of heroin use and addiction after an extended period of use rather than mature out with age. Rather than being the result of some life-cycle process, a social and physical maturing out of

heroin, de-addiction may occur when the addict reaches
some saturation level where his heroin use and the addict
life become too much for him; and he makes an all-out
effort to stay off opiates.

But whether de-addiction resulted from "maturation" or
"burnout," it was increasingly apparent that it did take place,
often without either formal treatment or imprisonment. The
Vietnam War provided a natural experiment that even more
dramatically challenged the conventional once-an-addict,
always-an-addict view. High-quality, potent heroin was widely
available to American servicemen in Vietnam—and large numbers, not surprisingly, became addicted. But a seminal study
by Lee Robins found that the vast majority of those who were
addicted in Vietnam ended their addiction on coming back to
the United States, and that they were no more likely to have
done so if they had been treated for their addiction than if
they had not.

When Robins examined the "natural history" of Vietnam
servicemen's drug use in 1971, it had "reached epidemic
proportions." Among a random sample of over four hundred
returning servicemen, an astonishing 43 percent had used
narcotics in Vietnam; of those, nearly half reported having
been addicted. Indeed, almost a fourth of the users had tested
positive when the military screened their urine for heroin just
before they left Vietnam, even though they knew they would
be tested and that positive results would hold up their return
to the United States. But eight to twelve months after their
return, only 10 percent of the Vietnam users reported they
were still using heroin, and only 7 percent of those—or less
than 1 percent of the entire sample—said they had been
addicted since their return. In other words, the proportion
addicted to heroin had dropped from something over 20
percent in Vietnam to about 1 percent in the United States—
an unprecedented 95 percent "remission rate." Even among a
smaller group of those men who reported having been *most*

seriously addicted in Vietnam—who had suffered serious withdrawal symptoms and were still using heroin right up until
their departure—almost three out of five said they hadn't used
drugs since they came back, and less than one in ten reported
that they were currently "readdicted."

These results strongly reinforced the growing doubt that
getting off drugs necessarily required formal treatment. And
since the early seventies, as a recent review by Robb Stall and
Patrick Biernacki has shown, a considerable body of evidence
has demonstrated that this process of "natural recovery" happens regularly, not only among abusers of hard drugs, but
with food, tobacco, and alcohol as well.

That many addicts "recover" without formal treatment has
important, and complex, implications. On one level, it is a
generally encouraging finding in that it demonstrates that
addicts are not permanently doomed to their "disease," and it
encourages the search for the factors that make recovery,
natural or otherwise, most likely. But it also forces us to rethink
the figures on how well treatment itself works. Obviously, if
some proportion of drug abusers will "get well" by themselves,
whether or not they ever go into a program, then the statistics
on treatment success must be viewed against that backdrop. If
a program claims a success rate of 40 percent, but we know
that 30 percent of a typical group of addicts would succeed in
abstaining from drugs even if they hadn't enrolled in the
program, the claim for some special effect of the treatment
itself shrinks accordingly—especially if those most likely to
succeed in treatment are precisely those somewhat older and
longer-using addicts who are most likely to mature out or burn
out of addiction in any case.

Ideally, to understand how much effect, if any, the experience
of treatment has on drug use, we would need to track what
happens to a population of addicts among whom some enter
treatment and some do not. And a few studies have attempted

just that. The most illuminating findings come from the study of young black men and women in Harlem by Ann Brunswick and her colleagues at the Columbia University School of Public Health. Since the focus of the study was a group of randomly selected youth whose drug use was followed in the community over time—rather than a population of addicts already in treatment—Brunswick was able to contrast what happened to otherwise generally similar young drug users who did and did not enter some form of treatment.

Recall that hard-drug use was widespread among the Harlem youth: 16 percent of young men and 10 percent of young women, for example, had been "nonexperimental" users of heroin. Like earlier researchers, Brunswick found that significant periods of abstinence were common among these heroin users; indeed, the *majority* of those who had ever used the drug had not used it during the year before their interview. In this sample, unlike some others, more heroin users than not had encountered some form of treatment program, however minimal. Were they more likely to abstain than those who had never been in treatment? Carefully controlling for a number of other characteristics of the youth, Brunswick and Peter Messeri found that the effectiveness of treatment apparently varied according to gender. For young women, treatment clearly helped; their rates of abstinence from heroin "increased dramatically following first-time treatment entry." For young men, on the other hand, the experience of treatment made virtually no difference: "the rates of abstinence which young black males achieved through treatment were but marginally greater than those arrived at naturally without treatment." Why the striking gender difference? Brunswick and Messeri speculated that the young women may have had fewer resources available to enable "spontaneous" abstention from drugs— fewer social supports, for example, and fewer "social role alternatives," including stable jobs. Accordingly, formal treatment provided them with supports for ending drug use they were unable to find otherwise—while the young men were more likely to have alternative sources of support, including better job opportunities.

As Brunswick and others are quick to note, these findings do not tell us that formal drug treatment doesn't work. For one thing, this study stacks the deck against treatment by including *any* kind of treatment experience, however minimal and of whatever kind, in comparing the drug use of treated versus untreated heroin users. Presumably, the results would be different if no treatment were compared with *good* treatment, sustained over time. And it remains possible—though nowhere proven—that those who entered formal treatment may have started with worse problems than those who did not, thus making the two groups less than strictly comparable.

What the research on recovery from drug abuse—in or out of treatment—*does* tell us is that something other than treatment itself is most important in determining whether or not addicts are able to stop using drugs or to control their use. Successful recovery has less to do with the chemistry of the drug itself or the particular modality of treatment than with the realistic possibilities for an alternative way of life. And this has crucial implications for our vision of what drug treatment should be about.

Again, this is by no means a new insight. In the early 1960s, the sociologist Marsh Ray described what he called a "cycle of abstinence and relapse" among heroin addicts in Chicago. That cycle was determined, Ray found, less by the properties of heroin itself than by the way the surrounding society responded to the addict's attempts to form a new identity as an ordinary citizen. "Addiction to narcotic drugs in our society," Ray argued, "commits the participant in this activity to a status and identity that has complex secondary characteristics." That identity had to be abandoned if the addict was to move successfully away from drugs. Often, that process began when the addict for one reason or another developed "some feeling of alienation from

. . . his present identity and [called] it into question." The addict might, for example, become sick of the deception and "hassle" of the addict culture and decide to break off relations with his fellow users. But successfully doing so required being able to take on a *new* identity in the conventional, nonaddicted world. Acquiring that new "nonaddict" identity involved an interaction between the addicts' own behavior (getting a job, staying clean, looking presentable) and the attitudes of other, nonaddicted people in response. As nonaddicts began to accept him as one of their own, the ex-addict began to solidify an identity that distanced him from the addict culture. Too often, however, the addict's effort at forging a new identity was not "ratified" by the straight world: and, unable to fully make it into that world, he experienced a sense of social isolation and a longing for the status and sense of identity that the addict world provided. The relapse to heroin, as one addict put it, "was like coming home."

Ray's finding of the crucial importance of the social setting in either encouraging or hindering abstention has been repeatedly confirmed in more recent research, both on natural recovery and on the outcome of formal treatment. Dan Waldorf's study of voluntary abstinence among New York heroin users found, for example, that education and the support of family and friends considerably helped addicts to maintain periods of long abstinence. Those who had finished high school were twice as likely as those who had dropped out of school to stay off heroin for more than eight months. But the support of others was even more crucial: "The real battleground for adjustment is with people—one's family and peers." Revealingly, Waldorf found that heroin users who said that others had "treated them like an addict" when they tried to abstain were far less able to maintain long periods off drugs.

Later work by Waldorf, Pat Biernacki, Robb Stall, and Jaime Jorquez has considerably expanded our understanding of what enables some addicts, and not others, to stay off drugs. Like earlier researchers, they argue that successful recovery requires much more than simply managing physical cravings. Addicts (at least those enmeshed in the drug culture) must resolve to develop an entirely new identity for themselves, and they must be able to translate that resolve into permanent changes in their lives. That, in turn, depends on their ability to "become ordinary," as Biernacki puts it—to construct a new way of life, a new self-concept, and a set of new relationships. Those shifts will be harder in proportion to the "degree to which, as addicts, they were involved in the world of addiction to the exclusion of activities in other, more ordinary social worlds." Getting successfully out of their old networks and relationships requires forming new ones, and that depends on support from nonusers and what Stall and Biernacki describe as the "integration into new, nonusing social networks."

The research on what helps addicts succeed *in* treatment, similarly, points over and over again to the crucial importance of what we could call a social "stake." Addicts do better after treatment if they have social support and encouragement from families or spouses; if they have stable jobs; if they have others to care for; and if someone cares enough about what happens to them to consistently supervise their behavior and otherwise take on a caring and firm role in their lives.

Among the most illuminating studies we have of these issues is George Vaillant's follow-up of 100 male addicts first admitted to the Lexington hospital in 1952 and interviewed at several intervals thereafter, the latest at twenty years after discharge. By that time, about 35 percent of the men had achieved what Vaillant called "stable abstinence," 25 percent were still actively addicted, 23 percent had died, and 17 percent were of "uncertain status." What accounted for the absence of relapse among the successful 35 percent? It was not, Vaillant showed, their experience in the narcotic hospital. Only 3 percent of episodes of hospital treatment were followed by as much as a year of abstinence. Nor was it the experience of going to prison; only 3 percent of prison stints had resulted in a year of abstinence. On the other hand, 65 percent of experiences with methadone maintenance were followed by a year of abstinence, and even higher proportions—71 percent—of periods of incarceration followed by a year of parole. We've noted this finding in the last chapter: but why, exactly, did being supervised on parole make a difference? Vaillant argued that parole "was not successful because it punished":

> Rather, parole was successful because it altered an addict's schedule of reinforcement. Parole required weekly proof of employment in individuals previously convinced they could not hold a job. It altered friendship networks. . . . Parole . . . provided an external superego and external source of vigilance against relapse. It was probably no accident that several addicts with no other history of regular employment successfully completed tours of duty in the highly supervised setting of the armed forces. Work provides structure to the addict's life and structure interferes with addiction.

The achievement of a new kind of structure, then—whether it was provided by a job or by firm supervision or both—was crucial in preventing relapse (a finding which meshes closely with what I've called the "structure model" of drug abuse). Overall, significant proportions of abstinent heroin addicts had experienced some form of "compulsory supervision," a "substitute dependence," or the "formation of new relationships" —particularly ones in which "another person was openly dependent on the addict or conversely trusted him to be independent." Interestingly, Vaillant noted that three of the successfully abstinent heroin addicts (as well as several of a parallel sample of treated alcoholics) had themselves become "formally involved in the addiction treatment field"; the opportunity of serving others, he argued, helped them move beyond their own preoccupations and considerably boosted their sense of competence.

Staying off drugs over the long term, Vaillant wrote in the

sixties, "depends more upon the addict's discovering gratifying alternatives than upon treatment per se"—precisely the conclusion that emerges from the research on recovery *without* treatment. What is most important in trying to move away from drugs and the drug world, with or without treatment, is the ability to create alternatives—in work, friendships, family relations. And therein lies the problem at the root of the depressing statistics on the frequency of relapse. Staying off is difficult enough in the face of the multiple attractions of drug use and the drug culture; it is made much more so by the lack of materials for building those alternatives in the communities from which most hard-drug abusers come. And this helps explain why treatment so often fails—why so many addicts are simply cycled from treatment program to street and back again. It also tells us that treatment—by itself—will inevitably be frustrated more often than not if we cannot provide better opportunities for addicts in the community outside. And it reminds us, once again, of the devastating consequences of the social policies toward work and family we've adopted for the past twenty years. As we have steadily chipped away at the structure of opportunity in both urban and rural areas, and correspondingly stressed, isolated, and weakened families and community networks, we have created "thin" communities in which drug abuse is not only far more likely in the first place, but where successful recovery from addiction is much harder. But by the same token, these findings also point to the basic elements of a different, and more effective, approach to treatment.

I I

How can we improve drug treatment?

We should start by shifting the emphasis from curing disease to building capacities and increasing opportunities. As the Dutch specialist Govert van de Wijngaart puts it, "Treatment must be directed towards building up a new life." At the same time, even the best efforts to rebuild lives won't have much impact on the drug problem if only a minority of drug users ever make use of them. Accordingly, it's urgent that we make treatment both more attractive and more accessible, and simultaneously develop more creative ways of reaching drug abusers—and those at high risk of becoming abusers—in their natural surroundings, outside of formal treatment settings. The evidence points to several directions we should take if we wish to provide addicts with "the competencies and aspirations most fitting to a human being."

1. Taking treatment seriously. It should be obvious that whatever variety of treatment we put in place will only work well if it is adequately funded and delivered by staff with sufficient skills and commitment. Yet it is only recently that we've paid much attention to the *quality* of treatment. If we are to put more money into treatment—and we should—we must insist that the programs we support meet far more rigorous standards than we have so far applied.

Some of what passes for drug treatment is unworthy of the name and of the funds we now spend on it. At the other pole, there are programs staffed by competent, caring, and dedicated people, doing the best job anyone knows how to do. In between, the range and quality of services is enormous.

Even relatively good programs rarely provide much beyond individual or group counseling, and often not much of that. In the six programs in John Ball's study of methadone maintenance, the average amount of time spent in "individual counseling" was about one hour per month. Only six out of twenty-four methadone-maintenance programs surveyed by the General Accounting Office in 1989 had any on-site educational services. And even these figures may exaggerate what is actually provided: when programs say that they offer "family therapy," for example, they may mean that spouses are sometimes included in the infrequent individual chats that make up much "counseling" in those programs; a "vocational development component" may mean that a client was told of a possible job opening on the other side of town.

Not surprisingly, there is a close connection between quality and success. In the six methadone programs in Ball's study, the proportion of addicts still using IV heroin after treatment ranged from less than 10 percent to a staggering 57 percent. (And this *understates* the enormous variation in effectiveness of methadone programs, because the researchers only chose programs that were relatively well-managed.) Lower staff turnover was unsurprisingly a key factor in improving the clients' outcomes, as was a close and caring relationship between counselors and clients.

Certainly we can improve treatment by providing more, and more consistent, funding and better staff training. But that must be accompanied by greater accountability and more serious criteria of evaluation. Outside of methadone treatment—which does at least have certain defined federal and state guidelines—the range of what actually goes on in "drug programs" is even wider. We know too little about the day-to-day character of services in most of those programs, and we have paid too little attention to finding out which of the things they do are actually worthwhile—and to developing mechanisms to ensure that they are done well.

2. ***Making treatment "user-friendly."*** Perhaps the most basic lesson to be learned from a generation of research on drug use is that *most* drug users are best understood as people with reasonably normal needs and motivations living in quite abnormal circumstances. That recognition is now a central theme in Dutch drug policy. As one of the architects of that policy, E. L. Engelsman, puts it, "Drug takers or even addicts should neither be seen as criminals, nor as dependent patients, but as 'normal' citizens of whom we make 'normal' demands and to whom we offer 'normal' opportunities."

But too many treatment programs *do* regard addicts as

criminals or dependent patients—or worse. The attitudes of
the director of a methadone maintenance clinic in California
(from my own field notes) are unfortunately not uncommon:
"What you have to understand is that the clients are fuckups.
They will always *be* fuckups. They don't even have it together
enough to know they have to get their act together." No one
who has worked with serious drug abusers would deny that
they are on the whole a difficult and often deeply troubled
population. But in the culture of many treatment programs,
there is a tendency to view addicts as incapable of change, even
unworthy of support and assistance. In some programs, indeed,
it is taken for granted that to help addicts cope with the urgent
problems in their lives would be "bad for them"—that it would
only make them more dependent and less willing to "take
responsibility for their lives." (Ironically, that view became
steadily more entrenched in the 1980s, the very years in which
the realistic possibilities for addicts to stand on their own feet
radically diminished.)

Those negative and sometimes punitive attitudes help account, as we've seen, for the reluctance of many of those who
most need help to seek treatment at all, and hinder their
chances of success once they do. Stronger outreach programs
are often called for as one way to increase addicts' participation
in treatment; and that's all to the good. But no amount of
outreach will overcome the alienating effects of a treatment
culture that makes drug users feel so badly about themselves
that they are too demoralized to seek help, and then humiliates
them if and when they do. The work of Biernacki and others
on natural recovery makes it clear that stigmatization is one of
the most pervasive obstacles addicts face in moving toward an
alternative life; and it is imperative that treatment programs
neither contribute to that stigmatization nor exacerbate the
already abysmally low self-esteem of most addicts.

More positively, we should work toward what some European
experts call "user-friendly" or "low-threshold" assistance to
drug users. Since the greatest single problem with the current

treatment system is its failure to attract the majority of abusers, we need to make it more accessible, more credible, and more attuned to the problems that drug users themselves regard as most important. Once stated, that seems obvious enough, but in fact the concerns of abusers and those of treatment programs are often poles apart. Addicts are likely to be most concerned over health problems, housing crises, the lack of jobs and skills, family and legal hassles. But those are only rarely treated as serious issues in most treatment programs, much less addressed with sufficient resources. Instead, with some notable exceptions, even well-run programs tend to define addicts' problems as mainly psychological ones, and to allocate their resources accordingly. In Ball's study of methadone treatment, virtually all of the clients were assigned an individual counselor; but only 2 percent received any educational services, less than 3 percent any vocational services, and 2 percent family therapy. "Staff qualified to provide these services," the researchers note, "were not available in most programs." These priorities help explain why many addicts prefer to deal with their problem on their own, and why others—especially as they get older or deeper into drug use—say both that they *want* help and that they do not like what help is currently available.

User-friendly does not mean permissive. The evidence is clear that consistent supervision is a crucial element in helping people stay off of hard drugs, and programs need to convey the unmistakable message that they care enough about addicts to make firm demands on them. But firmness and punitiveness are very different things. Perhaps most crucially, treatment must be more effectively "delinked" from the criminal-justice system. Drug abusers need to be assured that by coming to treatment they are not placing themselves in danger of arrest or of losing a job or their children. Our recent thrust, however, has been in the opposite direction—toward making the connections between treatment and the justice system even stronger than they are already. It is argued that for most addicts nothing short of legal coercion will compel them to enter treatment or to stay in it long enough to be helped. Stated so baldly, that is surely wrong; we've seen not only that many addicts seek treatment voluntarily but that many more would do so if they were less fearful of the consequences. There is nothing wrong with using compulsory treatment as an *alternative* to incarceration, if the treatment is serious—and the evidence does suggest that addicts compelled to enter treatment may do just as well as those who enter voluntarily. But we need to make certain that addicts are not deterred from volunteering for treatment by the threat of prosecution. Treatment may be useful as a bridge *out* of the justice system, but should not be seen as a tunnel into it.

"User-friendly" treatment also means that programs must fit the culture of the people needing help. That many treatment programs are experienced as alienating by minority drug users has been understood for a long time—but too rarely acted upon. For example, Desmond and Maddux note that Mexican-American addicts are "especially unlikely to participate in traditional therapeutic communities and group psychotherapy," where the treatment strategy of confrontation and incessant self-revelation is heavily based on middle-class and Protestant models of the process of individual change. In most parts of the country, too, the lack of Hispanic treatment staff is a barrier. Mexican-Americans are "grossly underrepresented" on the staffs of treatment programs in the Southwest, despite their relatively high proportion in the addict population. Small changes can make a big difference: When a Hispanic interviewer was assigned to the screening unit of a treatment program in New Haven, the number of Puerto Rican addicts admitted increased fivefold.

In general, the poor, who most need serious assistance, are least likely to seek out formal treatment. Changing that means developing much better and more sensitive outreach in poor communities, and, even more importantly, creating a better balance between traditional "counseling" approaches and the provision of tangible help with problems of family, work, housing, and daily survival.

3. *Linking treatment with harm reduction.* The AIDS epidemic has forced a shift in immediate priorities away from promoting abstention from drugs and toward reducing the kinds of behavior that put drug users at high risk of HIV infection. The scope of the need for what are called "harm reduction" or "harm minimization" measures is apparent from recent studies of the sexual behavior and injecting practices of hard-drug abusers in the inner city. In a NIDA-funded study of IV drug users in Denver, El Paso, and Baltimore, over 70 percent admitted sharing needles with other users. More than half of the men had sex with multiple partners. Women averaged an astonishing nineteen sex partners in the six months before being interviewed. Only 6 percent of the sample always used a condom during sex, and fully 66 percent *never* did. "Regardless of the sexual act, type of sexual partner, or gender of the subject," the researchers found, unprotected sex was the norm. All told, just 4 percent of the respondents practiced both safe needle use and safe sex. "These data," the researchers conclude, "appear to forecast a grim future for the subjects included in this study." Twenty-five percent of black teenaged crack users in California interviewed by Robert Fullilove and his colleagues reported that they had either given or received sexual favors in exchange for drugs or money for drugs; 27 percent of the boys reported having more than ten sexual partners during the last year (about five times the proportion in the young adult male population); and only 23 percent reported using a condom in their most recent sexual encounter. Indeed, those who had *already* suffered at least one bout of a sexually transmitted disease were no more likely to use condoms than those who had not.

Thus it isn't surprising that strategies to wean addicts away from risky needle use and unsafe sex have received urgent attention. The most common have been aggressive outreach programs to educate drug users about AIDS, to give out free condoms, to provide bleach to clean drug equipment, and, most controversially, programs offering addicts fresh needles and syringes in exchange for used ones. Especially for needle-exchange programs, the United States has been slower to embrace harm-reduction strategies than some other countries, including Britain, Holland, and Australia, primarily because of the belief that such programs encourage drug use, or at least send a wrong signal of tolerance to drug users. In many states, it is illegal to possess needles, and in only a few cities (including Tacoma and Los Angeles) are there firmly established—and legal—exchange programs. In other cities needle exchanges operate in the face of pressure from law enforcement and hostility from community groups, especially in minority communities, where there is understandable distaste for anything that appears to perpetuate drug abuse and its surrounding culture.

That is changing, however, in part because of the dawning recognition of the full scope of the AIDS threat among drug abusers, and in part because of reassurances from careful research that needle exchanges do *not* increase the use of hard drugs. Studies of an early needle-exchange program in Amsterdam, for example, found that it reduced needle-sharing and the use of dirty equipment among addicts, without increasing self-reported use of heroin. An Australian study of a needle-exchange program connected to a methadone-treatment center found, using urinalysis rather than self-reports, that addicts participating in the needle exchange did not increase their use of injectable drugs compared to a control group of methadone patients without special access to clean needles.

But if the experiments so far show that harm-reduction strategies haven't led to increased drug use, as some feared, there is also a more sobering finding: They have been only moderately successful at reducing high-risk behavior, and especially high-risk sex. Indeed, drug abusers seem astonishingly committed not only to using drugs in the face of the AIDS threat, but to using them in ways that maximize the danger of infection, meanwhile refusing to alter their similarly risky sexual practices. And they do so, to a disturbing degree, despite the best efforts to reach them with programs designed to minimize that behavior. This points once again to the tenacious effect of the social forces that underlie drug abuse—and the limits of measures that set out to change the behavior of drug abusers without changing the conditions of their lives. And it accordingly suggests the need to link harm-reduction strategies with longer-range efforts to build capacities and expand opportunities.

There is evidence that *some* addicts do change their ways in response to programs designed to educate them about the risks of unsafe needle use, and that provide either clean needles or kits to help them clean their "works." Addicts exposed to harm-reduction programs are more likely to report that they have adopted safer use of equipment than those not exposed; and the spread of HIV infection appears to have been slowed somewhat in places where needle-exchange programs have been widely implemented, as in Holland. There is also general consensus that needle exchanges and other harm-reduction programs can provide a "low-threshold" point of contact through which many previously elusive users may be brought into reach of longer-term help. But the studies also make clear that such long-term help is critical, for though the best-designed harm-reduction efforts have had some effect on high-risk behavior, that effect is both limited and uneven.

In Baltimore, where broad education and outreach programs for IV drug users were begun in 1983 and 1984, a study six years later found that while addicts were somewhat less likely to use contaminated or shared needles than before the programs, the improvement was not great. Despite the overwhelming visibility of the AIDS epidemic and the availability of a well-implemented education program, new IV users continued to be recruited; and among the new users, roughly half admitted sharing a needle and two-thirds to using unclean equipment.

A study in Portland, Oregon, where it has long been *legal* to buy needles and syringes, illustrates still more dramatically the resistance to safe needle use. Even though fresh needles could be bought at the nearest drugstore, over half the IV drug users in Portland shared needles anyway. Moreover, the addicts displayed a stunningly high rate of unsafe needle use despite having been exposed to considerable information on the connection between shared needles and AIDS. Why did they fail to heed those warnings, even though the means to do so were readily available and the risks widely understood? The Portland researchers conclude that for most addicts, "the desire for drugs overrides all other considerations." They are so desperately concerned with getting high that they often cannot be bothered with taking precautions: "The risk of HIV infection is not seen as sufficient to outweigh the perceived need to 'get high,' and many IVDUs will shoot up unsafely," regardless of the dangers they fully understand. The implication, for these authors, is that it may be vain to hope that addicts will use drugs *safely* as long as their lives are so dominated by the need to use drugs in the first place.

And what is true of needle use is even more true of risky sex, which has proven still more difficult to change through education and even through aggressive outreach to provide users with both information and free condoms. In San Francisco, for example, "street" outreach programs were begun in 1986 to distribute free condoms to IV drug abusers. Yet one year later, 80 percent of a sample of male IV drug users reported having multiple sex partners, and 73 percent said they *never* used condoms. The same tenacity of risky sex in the face of the AIDS threat, despite concerted efforts to reduce it, appears in virtually every recent study of the sexual practices of IV or crack users. The reasons are complex, but like the resistance to safe needle use, they lie in the social realities of endemic drug use. The entire way of life of heavy drug abusers discourages sexual caution in several mutually reinforcing ways. The drugs themselves (especially crack) are strongly disinhibiting; pressures for sex in exchange for drugs are often immediate and compelling, overriding other concerns; and the unequal power of women in relationships, especially if they have little capacity for economic independence, makes it difficult for them to demand that their partners practice safe sex. Moreover, as we've seen, the general absence of structure and of opportunity in the lives of most addicts tends to discourage concern for the social and medical consequences of unsafe sex; for many addicts, it is difficult to find consistent reasons to care very much about the future.

None of this tells us that harm-reduction programs aren't critically important. What it tells us is that changing the risky behavior of many addicts will require changing their lives in ways that foster more reliable concern for their own well-being. That is a long-term job, but we can begin by bringing high-risk addicts into comprehensive treatment programs that improve their chances for the future and thus give them a stake in prudence. Harm-reduction programs have reached many users who otherwise elude help, providing an encouraging opportunity to work with them. But that opportunity will be realized only if other barriers between treatment and the drug user are broken down. We desperately need to bring high-risk drug users into longer-term care, because without that care they are unlikely to do even the most rudimentary things to protect themselves, or others, from deadly disease. But they will not come unless what they are being offered is more appealing, less alienating, and more oriented toward addressing the whole range of social needs they bring with them.

4. ***Making aftercare a priority.*** Given that most addicts "relapse"—often repeatedly—after they leave treatment, it is widely agreed that some means of working with clients after they formally leave a course of treatment is critical. But

systematic aftercare remains rare. In the mid-eighties, David Hawkins and Richard Catalano of the University of Washington concluded that

> The crisis model of providing emergency services for people when they are most dysfunctional continues to drive drug treatment resource allocation. Given the almost universal lack of attention to treatment maintenance in the form of aftercare services, it is not surprising that primary treatment is often a revolving door through which many drug abusers periodically recycle. . . . In the long run, an investment in maintaining the gains made in treatment is likely to be more cost-effective than repeatedly re-treating addicts who are unable to avoid readdiction in the larger community.

The criticism still holds; only one of twenty-four methadone-maintenance programs surveyed by the General Accounting Office in 1989, for example, had separate aftercare services. That is unfortunate, because there is some encouraging evidence that well-designed aftercare can make a difference in preventing relapse. In one of the most careful recent studies, William McAuliffe and his coworkers at the School of Public Health at Harvard randomly assigned recovering addicts in Massachusetts, Rhode Island, and Hong Kong to a voluntary aftercare program that ran for up to a year. Addicts met in outpatient groups for three hours a day—half of that time devoted to a "recovery training" session led by a professional counselor, the other half to a "self-help" session run by a recovering addict. Group members also met informally outside the meetings, and took part in recreational activities together.

Despite what seem to be modest interventions, the program clearly made a difference. Compared to control groups, the program participants were significantly less likely to relapse into serious drug use: those who had been unemployed were more likely to find and hold a job. To be sure, the clients were untypical; more than 90 percent of the American participants were white and their average level of education was beyond high school. Moreover, as McAuliffe points out, it is not clear exactly which aspects of the program made the difference. We need to know more about what specific aftercare strategies work best, and also how to make them work for the tougher populations more typical of the mass of disadvantaged addicts in America.

Not surprisingly, the evidence we do have suggests that improving the community supports available to ex-addicts is especially important. In a review of research on what works in aftercare, Hawkins and Catalano note that "social support services which seek to strengthen or create informal/nonprofessional community support for treated drug abusers" are likely to hold greater promise than "approaches which simply extend contact with therapists or counselors."

Like treatment itself, aftercare can mean a great many things, only some of which are effective. Moreover, as with initial treatment, many ex-addicts who could most benefit from extended support do not make use of what now exists—suggesting that the content of many aftercare programs is also failing to draw them. Thus we need not only to expand aftercare but to enhance it. In particular, aftercare ought to mean more than simply offering support groups for ex-addicts. It should also include a strong component of advocacy in order to help vulnerable ex-addicts negotiate the increasingly inhospitable housing and labor markets, as well as the criminal-justice system.

5. *Linking treatment to work.* The connection between addiction and poor employment is unequivocal; so, too, is the link between treatment success and a stable job. The treatment system itself, of course, cannot provide steady job work for most addicts. But treatment programs can help by making preparation for stable work, as van de Wijngaart puts it, "an inseparable part of the treatment."

Preparing hard-drug addicts for steady jobs is no easy task. Some are so far removed from the world of legitimate work that the process is necessarily long and frustrating. But it can be done: Indeed, it has been done.

In 1972, the Vera Institute of Justice in New York City created a work program for addicts called the Wildcat Service Corporation. Wildcat was a "supported-work" program: that is, it operated on the theory that even very troubled long-term addicts could be put to productive work, with resulting reductions in welfare dependency, crime, and drug use, if they were given a work setting that at least initially was less stressful, offered supportive counseling and other assistance, and allowed greater latitude for mistakes. Over the next four years, Wildcat put more than four thousand ex-addicts and ex-offenders to work, many in city agencies. The program was extraordinarily innovative in matching workers to city needs. Wildcat clients did office work and printing for the Board of Education, and clerical work in the public libraries; they booked tickets for hospital performances, worked as counselors in programs for high-risk youth, and made hot lunches for senior citizens. Since a substantial number of Wildcat workers were Spanish-speaking, Wildcat took advantage of their bilingualism and put them to work translating for the Bronx District Attorney, neighborhood legal services, and the emergency room at Mount Sinai Hospital. They painted public schools and Head Start centers, renovated buildings in the South Bronx, delivered messages and packages for the mayor's office, and, in considerable numbers, did maintenance work for the police department. Note that these jobs were not make-work; Wildcat workers were taken on (enthusiastically) by the agencies they worked for and produced tangible and useful results.

The stereotype is that the kind of people who abuse drugs do not want to work, but of one group of over three hundred addicts offered jobs in Wildcat, "all but thirty showed up for work." Moreover, more than half of those who started work stayed on the job for at least a year. The typical supported work participant was absent one day in ten. About one-third of Wildcat workers graduated to nonsubsidized jobs and most held on to those jobs for at least six months. The longer an employee stayed at Wildcat, the more likely the employee was to find subsequent employment.

Indeed, disadvantaged addicts flocked to the program, and, from its first day of operation, Wildcat attracted more applicants than it could accommodate. Once enrolled, participants stuck with the program, and did not want to leave. Wildcat employees seemed particularly drawn to jobs that provided visible service to the community and allowed them to help others.

What were the results? Vera followed up 401 applicants, about half of whom were offered jobs with Wildcat; the others served as a control group. Both groups comprised essentially similar and extremely difficult populations. They applied at an average age of thirty-one, after eleven years of heroin addiction, eight recorded arrests, and four criminal convictions. Sixty percent were black and thirty percent Hispanic. Most were on welfare and all had "spotty or nonexistent work records."

Over the next three years, the Wildcat workers did significantly better than the others on a variety of measures. They worked more than twice as many weeks and earned two and one-half times what the control group did. Almost half (46 percent) of them received no welfare at all while in the project, versus only 6 percent of the controls. Less strikingly but still significantly, a smaller proportion were arrested during the three years. Moreover, among *both* the Wildcat participants and the control group, more employment was closely associated with fewer arrests. The control subjects, after all, were not necessarily jobless during the course of the study; and those who worked during more than half of the three-year study period were arrested less than half as often as those who worked less.

Something similar happened with their drug use. Overall, the differences between Wildcat participants and the others were not large—about half of both groups used some drug during the three years. But among both groups, those who *worked* more than half of the time were much more likely to cut back their drug use.

The program also seemed to "encourage family stability." Participants more often married or entered common-law relationships; they were more likely to be supporting dependents and living with their children. "In sum," the Vera researchers concluded,

> Wildcat appears to have helped a significant proportion of its employees lead productive lives. Although the control-group data indicates that many Wildcat employees would have restored their lives without supported work, Wildcat appears to have provided a headstart for some and been the critical vehicle of rehabilitation for others.

The program was also cost-effective; the researchers calculated that taxpayers got back $1.12 for every dollar put into it.

Wildcat's success led to a much larger experiment in supported work under the auspices of the nonprofit Manpower Demonstration Research Corporation (MDRC). The supported-work concept was extended to four groups: ex-addicts, high-risk youth, welfare mothers, and ex-offenders. Elaborate evaluations found that the program worked best for the welfare mothers—and for the addicts. As in Wildcat, what was especially encouraging was that the groups selected to participate were much more difficult than the typical clientele of job programs. About 40 percent had not worked in the past two years; 5 percent had *never* worked. Two in five were on welfare, and nine in ten had been arrested, spending an average of almost two and a half years behind bars.

The program put them to work for twelve to eighteen months in supported environments at jobs paying about the minimum wage, which, like the Wildcat jobs, were mainly in the public and nonprofit sectors. The program considerably improved the participants' employment and earnings—both while they were in the supported jobs and afterwards—as compared to controls. Even more critically, participants were significantly less likely to be arrested and convicted—both during the program and after it. Over the course of the full thirty-six months of the study period, only 0.2 percent of the experimentals were arrested for robbery—versus over 13 percent of the controls. Less than a fifth of experimentals, but a third of controls, were convicted of any crime. The controls were twice as likely to be arrested on drug charges.

The program was less successful in reducing drug use, which declined for some groups of addicts but not others. Nevertheless, like Wildcat, the success in making addicts more productive and less criminal meant that the program was extremely cost-effective overall. (The reduction in crime was particularly important in this respect.) The evaluators calculated that the program saved taxpayers several thousand dollars per client.

When the MDRC researchers probed more deeply into what caused the beneficial effects on the addicts' patterns of crime and work, it seemed clear that what made the most difference was not the money they earned (as in most such subsidized work programs, the pay was set deliberately lower than prevailing private wages)—but something about the experience of participation in useful work and the related changes in self-concept. Given what we know about the meaning of the subculture of drugs and drug-related crime, for young addicts in particular, that outcome shouldn't surprise us. We've seen that a big part of the appeal of those cultures is that they offer a sense of challenge and of participation in a common activity that is extremely compelling in the absence of legitimate alternatives. Supported work, on a small scale, seems to have offered a modicum of that sense of involvement and participation—at least enough to draw many more applicants to the program than could be admitted, and to make some very difficult clients stop committing crimes.

In both Wildcat and the MDRC program, however, the positive effects tended to wane as the time away from the program increased. What that tells us is not that the programs didn't work or that employment is unimportant, but that the absence of strong opportunities after the program ended was a serious obstacle to continued success. There were simply not enough good jobs in the regular labor market to maintain the same level of involvement and challenge achieved in the program. That pattern of diminishing effect reaffirms the need for broader, national-level employment policies that can make long-term stable jobs a reality for addicts who succeed in treatment—and we will return to that issue in the next chapter. It also means that programs with higher expectations and tighter connections with permanent, skilled job opportunities may promise even better and more enduring results.

One example is Binding Together Incorporated (BTI) in New York, which trains ex-addicts in printing and bookbinding skills. The program provides residential housing for the (frequently homeless) participants while they train and helps them to set aside money for rental deposits when they graduate and find a job. And most of them *do* find jobs. Of 125 clients enrolled in BTI since 1988, as of 1991 there were still 30 in training, 13 had dropped out, and 82 had graduated from the training program—of whom 76 got jobs. And more than four out of five of those who did find jobs were still working six months later. That rate of "nonsubsidized" employment is rare indeed—not only for programs involving addicts but for employment programs of any kind. Part of the explanation is that, like many treatment programs, BTI "creams" its clients by means of fairly strict criteria for admission. But it also reflects the high skill level of the printing jobs themselves— the participants are trained to operate and maintain state-of-the-art high-tech printing and copying equipment—and the strong linkage of training to real job opportunities in private companies, several of which are represented on the board of the program. Unfortunately, such programs are few and far between—and not only for drug abusers.

III

Thus the gap between what drug abusers need and what conventional treatment typically offers is wide—and the problem is not just a matter of quantity. The treatment programs we now have are too often disconnected from the realities of addicts' lives, and sometimes so alienating that many who most need help avoid what help is available. Tragically, that is especially true for two of the groups that need effective help the most: teenagers and women. There is much rhetoric about the need for "treatment and prevention" for adolescents and, especially since the onset of the crack epidemic, for women—particularly pregnant women. But though the needs are both clear and urgent, the response has been weak and halting.

It is universally understood that most illicit drug use starts in the teen years, and universally agreed that it is better to intervene early than to wait for young people to become seriously addicted adults, and then try to treat them. Yet for the most part that is what we do. Most of the youth at greatest risk are not reached by conventional treatment and prevention programs at all; for those who are, the help they get is often minimal and inappropriate.

They are only sporadically engaged by the existing treatment system, for several reasons. Teenagers are frequently turned off by the punitive character of much formal drug treatment, or threatened by its often close connections with the criminal-justice system. They are particularly underrepresented in therapeutic-community programs, partly because they do not like the rigidly psychological and confrontational approach, and also because TCs typically emphasize the evils of all drug use at a time when most young drug users neither share that view nor trust those who promote it. TCs, moreover, like residential treatment programs generally, also typically sever the teenager's connection with school. As the TOPS researchers note, most TCs do not "allow a youth to attend school outside the program during the early phases of residence;" but few provide alternative schooling of their own. Relatively few adolescents have a heroin habit sufficiently large to call for methadone treatment, and with some exceptions, they are barred from methadone programs in any case.

Teenagers are much less likely than adults to be heavily addicted to drugs; and they are often still caught up in the exciting aspects of the drug culture. They rarely regard drugs as their most pressing problem: indeed, as one review notes, most "feel that they are helped by the drugs they take." As Harvey Feldman and his colleagues put it, teenage drug use is

> enmeshed in a complex of other and often more impor-
> tant issues and problems. Those range from personal
> problems (boredom, restrictions at home or school, etc.)
> to a range of interlocking crises (arrest, impending court
> hearing, incarceration, loss of job, attorney costs, home-
> lessness . . .).

This is especially true for youths in communities where drug abuse is endemic, for whom the struggle for the basics of life —shelter, income, a respite from violent or dysfunctional families—can be all-consuming. For them, as Richard Dembo and his colleagues conclude, "efforts utilizing individual, family, or group counseling and/or psychotherapeutic drugs are mis-placed." Instead, "stress should be given to addressing the issues of housing, vocational training, remedial education, job development, and peer relationships." Yet few existing treat-ment programs really address these broader needs—even though there is some evidence that programs that do so have better luck in keeping adolescents from serious abuse. In one national study, the most important factor in reducing teenagers' drug use during treatment was "the provision of special services, specifically school, recreational, vocational, and contraceptive counseling." Yet the failure to link treatment with work or training, especially, is even more glaring for adolescents than for adults. In Ann Brunswick's study of Harlem youth, 44 percent of young men who had been in drug treatment had undergone "personal" therapy and 19 percent "encounter" therapy—but only 3 percent had received any "job help." In the TOPS national sample, less than 11 percent of young men aged eighteen to nineteen who had been in residential treatment, and only 6 percent of young women, received any kind of vocational assistance.

For all of these reasons, teenagers, especially those with the more severe problems, are even less likely than adults to seek out formal help, and more likely to drop out when they do. That is true even for middle-class youth, and much more so for the poorer and more isolated participants in the street drug cultures of the cities. Dembo and his associates, for example, found that minority youth in a South Bronx junior high school were less likely to look to conventional sources— drug programs, teachers, doctors, police—for help as their level of drug involvement and their sense of the "toughness" of their neighborhood increased. The rise of crack in the 1980s, as Benjamin Bowser points out, has widened this social and cultural gap: the crack epidemic created a distinct and hard-to-penetrate adolescent culture whose extreme social isolation and alienation "closes the avenues of prevention and intervention." Fewer than 4 percent of the heavily drug-involved delinquents in Inciardi and Pottieger's Miami study had *ever* been in treatment. The reluctance of inner-city youth to make use of what treatment is available helps account for the odd skewing of the adolescent treatment population away from minority youth—despite the well-documented levels of endemic drug use in many minority communities. The TOPS national study, for example, found that only two out of ten youths in residential treatment and only one out of ten in "outpatient drug-free" programs were nonwhite.

That so few teenagers seek treatment at all—and so many drop out if they do—means that positive results from adolescent treatment programs are even more questionable than similar statistics for adults. And it also means that the majority of young drug abusers in fact get little real help at all. Consequently, most formal help for drug abusers is reactive rather than preventive, mainly provided to those who have already been caught in a drug-oriented lifestyle for some years, and who may be nearing the age at which they might "mature out" of drug abuse in any case. By that time, however, much damage may have already been done. Some will have been involved in a violent drug subculture and will be fortunate to survive intact. Others will have contracted STDs or suffered other drug-related health problems. Even if they escape those dangers, many will have opted out of school and the job market just when they should be acquiring better skills and the beginnings of a career. Even if they are belatedly helped by treatment at thirty or thirty-five, their futures will have been dramatically and often irrevocably narrowed.

There is, therefore, an urgent need to reach young drug abusers early. And since few at-risk adolescents really fit the medical model of addiction, what they most need is not formal treatment but something closer to what is usually called "prevention." Yet though it is widely agreed that prevention should be a central goal in our approach to teenage drug problems, much of what has gone on under that rubric has barely touched the growing needs of high-risk youth. Indeed, the notion of prevention itself—like "treatment"—is frustratingly vague, and it covers a great variety of programs, most of which have been disappointing.

It's noteworthy that in the United States the idea of prevention of adolescent drug abuse has traditionally been identified almost entirely with what are essentially *educational* efforts of one kind or another—programs designed to increase young people's understanding of drugs and their effects, boost their self-esteem, or strengthen their ability to resist peer pressures to use drugs. Indeed, "treatment and education" are often touted in one breath as the answer to youthful drug problems. That is in contrast to some European countries, where prevention—though it includes educational approaches—is understood more broadly to encompass more "structural" strategies as well, emphasizing ways of increasing opportunities for youth to participate more fully in social life. A brochure on drug-abuse prevention from the Swedish Ministry of Health and Social Affairs, for example, prominently stresses the preventive effect of "measures against youth unemployment" and programs to "improve the conditions for children and youth."

In the United States, the tendency to equate prevention with antidrug education means that most adolescent drug-prevention programs have been based in the schools. For that matter, most research on the effectiveness of these programs has focused mainly on middle-class, and typically white, students, and on marijuana, alcohol, and cigarettes rather than harder drugs.

Even within those limits, moreover, the findings for many years were not encouraging. Programs that simply tried to prevent drug use by teaching students about drugs fared the worst, for though it wasn't difficult to increase students' knowledge about drugs, that knowledge didn't necessarily translate into decreased use—and sometimes seemed to *increase* it. That was especially, and notoriously, the case for programs that used scare tactics to warn young people away from drugs; such efforts often backfired, in part apparently because their exaggeration of the harmful impact of all drug use destroyed their credibility among savvier youth. There were better results for "peer" or "social-skills" programs, which are based on the idea that since young people are often pressed to use drugs by their peer groups, prevention must involve teaching ways of resisting that pressure. A major review by Nancy Tobler in 1986 found peer programs far and away the most effective; but overall, the results from school-based programs were discouragingly slim, even for middle-class youth. As another review concluded in 1988, "substance-abuse education has, for the most part, failed to achieve its primary goal, the prevention of drug and alcohol abuse."

Two recent experiments, both quite sophisticated, have claimed more encouraging results. One is a program called Project Alert, launched in thirty schools in Oregon and California, and evaluated by the Rand Corporation. Unlike most earlier school-based prevention programs, Project Alert was specifically designed to include a broader range of schools and more minority students. It was based on what the Rand researchers call a "social-influence" model, in which seventh-graders received eight classroom lessons designed to help them "develop reasons not to use drugs, identify pressures to use them, counter prodrug messages, [and] learn how to say no to internal and external pressures." The original eight were followed a year later by three "booster" lessons during eighth grade. The Rand researchers conclude that the program "works," but that stretches the evidence somewhat. There were some reductions in cigarette and marijuana use, but little for alcohol; moreover, students who had already begun using any of the substances before the program were least affected by it. Among those who had already tried marijuana, for example, any positive effects of the program wore off after a year.

The second, more encouraging, recent experiment is the Midwestern Prevention Project (MPP), launched in the mid-1980s in junior high schools in Kansas City and Indianapolis and evaluated by a team from the University of Southern California. The MPP expanded the scope of prevention to include not only classroom instruction, but efforts to involve parents, the media, and other community institutions in a comprehensive program to "bombard the adolescents with antidrug messages." The program sought to teach parents how to "establish family rules concerning substance use, discuss the consequences of use, and share their reasons for not wanting their child to become involved with alcohol or other drugs." It developed materials for the mass media to raise community awareness of drug issues, and pushed enforcement of laws against public smoking and selling of alcohol to minors. Five years into the program, results were generally positive. Students participating in the program were somewhat less likely to drink or smoke than otherwise similar "controls"; for example, about 14 percent admitted using marijuana in the past month, versus 20 percent of nonparticipating youth. Most encouragingly, preliminary data from some of the program schools showed that, according to self-reports, the program students were significantly less likely to use cocaine (and crack)—1.6 percent of program students versus 3.7 percent of the others admitted cocaine use in the past month.

If that finding holds up for all the schools and for a longer time period, it is genuinely encouraging—and it indicates the advantages of a program that moves beyond classroom instruction to involve families in drug prevention. The central point —that outside pressures to use drugs can "undo the effects of even the most thorough school programs if prevention messages and support are not consistently provided throughout a community"—is surely a sound one, and it fits with what we know of the social causes of adolescent drug use.

Yet the limits are equally apparent. A program like MPP assumes that the social influences most affecting youthful drug use operate in the school and family, and to a lesser extent the media and other community institutions. But for the youth at *highest* risk, as we've seen, these connections are usually weak or nonexistent. They are likely to be out of school, or enrolled only sporadically; they often come from inadequate families or have no family at all; and, increasingly, given the deterioration of social institutions in deprived neighborhoods, they may be cut off from stable community influences of any kind and deeply enmeshed in an isolated and, to them, extraordinarily attractive street culture.

For them, something more is needed, and its basic principles are suggested by what we know of the roots of drug abuse, violence, and unsafe sex among these youth. To begin with, a prevention strategy for adolescent drug users should not focus on drugs alone, but address drug problems as part of a larger, more holistic approach to improving health and welfare. Since adolescents typically do not regard their drugs as the main problem in their lives, but as a means of coping with more pressing problems, our offers of help will not be compelling unless they address the range of issues that adolescents themselves consider most important. Given the elusiveness and insularity of much of the hard-core youth drug culture, the strategy needs to be both active and sensitive in reaching out to youth in their natural settings: Given their mistrust of conventional authorities, it should be emphatically distanced from anything that smacks of law enforcement or the juvenile-justice system. At the same time, it should be stable enough to become an established, and trusted, presence in the community.

One way to accomplish these goals would be through a network of public, community-based health clinics—available to all adolescents as a matter of right. The clinics would offer comprehensive health care, along with fully confidential advice on everything from the properties and effects of drugs to family problems and safe sex. They would earn the allegiance of youth by adopting the role of advocates for young people's health and welfare needs in an increasingly neglectful and punitive society, and by visibly offering an oasis of reliable care and concern in fragmented and struggling communities. They would also include indigenous youth leaders in advisory capacities. Making such clinics part of a universally accessible system of public health care would give them a distinct advantage over short-term prevention programs dependent on on-again, off-again funding. And it would clearly distinguish them from the usual authorities. It would also avoid some of the disadvantages of clinics based in public schools, which have been established in several cities. There may be a fiscal advantage to using existing school facilities, but—again—many of the youth who most need help are not in school at all, and some of those who *are* mistrust school authorities as much as they mistrust the police and juvenile courts. Offering help with drug problems in the context of a broader preventive-health-care program may make it possible to draw in young people who may be more willing to talk about contraception or STDs than about drug use. Once they come to trust the program because of its sensitivity in dealing with those issues, they are far more likely to voluntarily seek help for a drug problem.

Doing this cannot be cheap, but—as we'll see over and over again for many promising antidrug strategies—the initial investments are likely to bring substantial savings over the long run. To the extent that we can keep teenagers *out* of drug treatment, AIDS wards, and trauma centers through preventive intervention, we will save money as well as lives.

Consistent, accessible, broad-based preventive health care is one way to reach and help the youth at highest risk. Another is through community-based programs that offer structure, challenge, even something resembling a home to adolescents for whom these essentials are routinely lacking. We now have some encouraging examples, but most are struggling, and there are far too few of them.

One example is the Dorchester Youth Collaborative, a Boston program begun in the late 1970s in a low-income, racially mixed neighborhood with high levels of drug use, school dropouts, and delinquency. DYC set up "prevention clubs" explicitly designed to offer challenging alternatives to the lure of the street culture. The clubs provided several kinds of structured activities for kids whose lives outside DYC were often chaotic and insecure. Two formed teams that played in a basketball league. Another, all female, began a performing dance troupe. A mixed-sex club formed a breakdance group that performed widely throughout the Boston area and beyond. Unlike many prevention programs, DYC enrolled very high-risk, difficult-to-reach youngsters, many of whom had a history of school failure, troubled families, and heavy drug use, and few of whom had previously been involved in structured activities of any kind. Some came from such deprived conditions that the first meal they had in the day was often a snack provided by the program. As it turned out, bringing them into the prevention clubs did not require an elaborate outreach effort; so many neighborhood youth flocked into the program on their own that it could not accommodate them all. Despite irregular funding, evaluations show that DYC had a strongly positive impact. Drug and alcohol abuse fell substantially, and half of those who had dropped out of school returned. The program was not successful with all of its youth, but overall, as the evaluation by a team from Rutgers University concludes,

> It appears that the program provided a structured yet supportive environment, during a turbulent time of life in a difficult neighborhood. Many of those interviewed talked about DYC being a family, sometimes more of a family than the people they lived with.

Programs along these lines—what we might call "structural prevention"—hold considerable promise in reaching kids who usually elude more conventional approaches to prevention. I'm not suggesting that offering meals and a breakdance group amounts to a solution for inner-city drug abuse—particularly without a simultaneous expansion of tangible opportunities for the young in the labor market, which we'll consider in the next chapter. But they can help. Indeed, such "alternative" programs for youth outside the normal schools were ranked as among the most effective in Tobler's 1986 study, even though they usually enrolled tougher populations.

Up to now, however, most community-based youth prevention programs have operated on a shoestring. They have been among the most consistent victims of the fiscal starvation of the cities that has perversely accompanied the overblown rhetoric of the war on drugs. Cuts in federal funding have decimated all but the hardiest programs, and those that have survived face constant problems of meager resources, high staff turnover, and pervasive burnout. Coupled with the simultaneous erosion of more traditional sources of adult care and supervision, this leaves many of the urban (and more and more rural) young without consistent sources of help at all, outside their peer groups.

Building local community institutions they can trust, and that address their needs for advice and support, is an essential step in reducing their isolation and keeping them from being engulfed by the culture of drugs and violence that surrounds them. We need more of these institutions, and we need to fund them far more consistently. The Eisenhower Foundation has called for the creation of a Youth Investment Corporation to seek out the best examples of effective community programs for high-risk youth and to fund replications of them across the country. That could be a crucial first step.

IV

For women, a group equally underserved in traditional drug treatment, the issues are different. The lack of fit between their needs and the existing treatment system has been noted repeatedly over the past twenty years. We have known for a long time what we most need in treatment programs for women. What's missing are the resources to put our best knowledge into practice. Across the country, there are scattered examples of well-conceived, comprehensive treatment programs for addicted women, many spurred by the unusually devastating impact of crack on adult women. But so far they barely touch the need.

Women tend to use drugs for somewhat different reasons than men do, and to bring different, and in some respects more difficult, problems to treatment. Addicted women are more likely than men to come from families where drug or alcohol use was common, and where physical and sexual abuse were the norm. (A recent study by Teresa Hagan of women in treatment in Philadelphia found that 67 percent had been sexually abused and 60 percent physically abused in childhood; 83 percent came from families where at least one parent abused drugs, alcohol, or both.) Addicted women are more likely to be in a relationship with someone who is also a drug user, and the relationship is often abusive and violent as well. They are more likely to be dependent on those destructive relationships for economic support, or on the welfare system. They are correspondingly less likely to support themselves through legitimate work, and have even fewer resources for doing so than male addicts; they tend to have few job skills and little schooling. Some research suggests that women addicts are even disadvantaged in the world of *illegal* work: one study describes low-income black women addicts as lacking "opportunities in both the drug-abusing and non-drug-abusing world," since they have not only higher unemployment but less access to the better "jobs" in drug dealing and nondrug crime. Like male addicts, they suffer increasingly from homelessness or recurrent housing crises; among women seen in a comprehensive treatment program in Philadelphia, 10 percent were homeless and over 50 percent experienced "periodic problems with housing," and a recent NIDA survey of pregnant substance abusers found 20 percent homeless. Women who abuse drugs are more likely than their male counterparts to suffer a variety of health problems and to seek drug treatment in order to deal with them. They are also more likely to be socially isolated—cut off from both formal and informal sources of support, especially outside the drug culture: one study describes many white drug-abusing women as suffering a "virtual absence of ties with the non-drug-using world." These issues are by no means universal among women; in particular, the specific problems women bring to treatment vary considerably by race and class. But it is abundantly clear that for the majority of low-income women who abuse drugs, the drug itself is only one aspect of a much wider set of interrelated problems—and often a means, if a self-defeating one, of trying to deal with them.

Again, there is some evidence that women may be more helped by serious treatment than men—perhaps in part because they have fewer resources to tackle their drug problems on their own. But they are strongly disadvantaged in the treatment system as well. This is partly because of the insufficiency of treatment slots for women—in California in the early 1990s only 67 of 366 publicly funded treatment programs accepted women at all. But even many programs that do in theory accept women create formidable obstacles to their participation.

The biggest single problem is the lack of provision for child care. Women who abuse drugs are more likely than men to be caring for children; about 70 percent of heroin-addicted women in Marsha Rosenbaum's research, for example, were mothers. Indeed, because women—like men—tend to enter treatment when they are somewhat older and well into their drug-using careers, they often have *several* children. But few treatment programs offer child care, and few women addicts can afford private care. The problem is worse in residential programs; few accept children, and not many women addicts can afford high-quality outside care for their children while they undertake residential treatment even if they were willing to leave their children for that long. To compound the problem, the social isolation of many addicted women means that they are rarely able to call on relatives or friends to help care for their children. Understandably, few are willing to give up children to foster care in order to enter residential treatment. But this helps to ensure that many addicted women simply do not go, or go only sporadically, to get help.

For treatment to be either attractive or effective, then, programs will need to provide care for children on-site or arrange outside care. The research suggests that when programs do provide services for children, women's participation increases dramatically. Moreover, involving children in women's treatment services can accomplish much more than just baby-sitting. Including child care in treatment programs "provides a natural forum for working with parents on parenting skills and child-development issues"—often crucial matters for addicted women. A study of mothers on methadone in New York, for example, found that women who were able to find day care for their children did better in treatment, and their children performed considerably better on a variety of tests of development.

More generally, as with adolescents, the evidence on the needs of addicted women points to the importance of providing a broad range of help with other practical issues in their lives —not just narrow pharmacological or psychological "treatment." That means linking treatment to health care, housing, and—above all—employment.

Linking treatment to training and opportunities for good work, as I've argued, is critical for all addicts; but it is arguably even more so for women—many of whom are trapped in a spiral of drug abuse primarily because they have so few options for legitimate self-support. (In one study of admissions to an inner-city methadone program, Barbara Lynn Kail and Irving Lukoff found that nearly half the men, versus just a fourth of the women, had worked during the year before treatment.) The lack of options not only exacerbates the problems that led to their drug use in the first place; it also locks them into relationships with abusive and drug-using men and cuts off the possibility of forming new relationships outside the drug culture. Yet serious efforts to build the capacity for stable, self-supporting work are even more rare for women in treatment than for men—despite the fact that many addicted women clearly *want* them. As Rebecca Moise, Beth Reed, and Virginia Ryan put it in a review of these issues, "traditional drug programs have a poor record in finding employment for their female clients, in part because clients have virtually no job experience or job-related identity, and in part because the importance of this is sometimes not recognized for women." Some treatment programs follow traditional stereotypes about women's economic role: for men, the goal is to prepare them for steady work; for women, to prepare them for marriage to men who are working. Many treatment programs have not absorbed the reality of the changing economic position of women, and accordingly do even less to prepare women for challenging work outside the home than they do for men. Yet given their abysmal economic condition, many women addicts "will never remain in recovery without some hope of economic improvement."

Not surprisingly, the lack of job training that could make self-support possible is a recurrent lament of women in treatment. Interviews with women in a prison-based treatment program in New York State, for example, found many complaining that "they are trying their best to stay off drugs and straighten their lives out; but with lack of vocational training they will have no economic opportunities once they leave prison . . . they will have to depend on the welfare system or go back to selling drugs to earn a living."

How and where services are provided can also be important. Because so few treatment programs are "user-friendly" to women, many women—even those who both need and want help—do not seek it from conventional treatment programs, and sometimes not even from conventional health-care providers. Women may fear going to jail or losing their children; often, too, they are frightened by the male street subculture that surrounds many treatment programs, and alienated by the rigidity of therapeutic-community programs. Reaching addicted women, then, means both developing treatment settings that are more attractive and more appropriate, and finding new and more flexible ways of reaching them outside of formal treatment.

One way to make treatment more attractive to women is to exclude men. A recent study of treatment programs for addicted women by the New York State Coalition for Criminal Justice found that for many women the chance to participate in groups for women only was all-important in shaping their feelings about the usefulness of treatment:

> Most of the women thought that an all-women's program was beneficial to them. They learned how to make friendships with other women, learned how to be supportive, and felt free to talk about any problems, including domestic relationships. They did not have to compete for male attention or to form relationships. . . . They did not think they would have gained as much from a program that was co-ed. They did not think they could talk about problems they have had with men in a mixed group.

A program in Detroit to offer help to addicted women first seen in hospital emergency rooms illustrates the potential of strategies to reach addicted women outside of treatment. Given the general state of American public health care for the poor, the emergency room is often the treatment provider of first resort for women with drug-related medical problems. But though emergency rooms can deal with immediate crises, for long-term help they must refer addicted women to outside treatment programs. Yet most do not go. According to Marcia Anderson, the majority of the women in the Detroit study had experienced treatment at least once before, and "chose not to repeat those experiences." Most did want *someone* to help them with their drug problems, but "the traditional treatment modalities were not desired." In response, the hospital sent public-health nurses into the community to work with the women in their own homes. Over eight weeks, they met once a week to work out a strategy tailored to the specific needs each woman defined as most important. Among other things, they dealt with persistent health problems, referred many women to high-school completion courses, and counseled them on family issues. Despite the program's short duration and modest ambitions, it made a difference; women randomly assigned to the "personalized nursing" spent less money on drugs and reported less stress and anxiety than a control group. Overall, the program was both inexpensive and quite successful in reaching and motivating women who had, in effect, seceded from the formal drug-treatment system.

The crack epidemic has forced long-overdue attention to the need for better and more accessible care for pregant drug users specifically. There is not much disagreement that comprehensive programs combining drug treatment and prenatal care are urgently needed, and there is an emerging consensus on what they should offer. But the follow-through has been less than impressive. What Wendy Chavkin of Columbia University describes for New York City is even more true in many other parts of the United States:

> there are waiting lists in most programs, and few are geared to address the growing percentage of drug abusers using cocaine. In addition, many drug treatment programs do not accept pregnant women or those with small children. Those few that do accept pregnant women have traditionally not integrated the necessary health care services into their programs, either through on-site provision of prenatal care or through firm linkages with medical providers.

A 1990 report from the U.S. General Accounting Office (GAO) noted that there were only 15 places in residential programs for pregnant women in the entire state of Massachusetts. In 1991, there were 10 residential slots in San Francisco for an estimated 750 pregnant drug abusers. That, along with the fear of legal punishment or the loss of children, has deterred many pregnant drug users from seeking care. Indeed, the combination has kept addicted women from obtaining prenatal care of *any* kind. The GAO found that some had begun "delivering their babies at home in order to prevent the state from discovering their drug use." As one San Francisco report puts it, "The drug culture has created an underground of pregnant women who avoid any prenatal medical care and drug treatment whatsoever."

That is doubly tragic, because the consequences of avoiding care can be catastrophic, and because those consequences are largely preventable if adequate care is available. At Harlem Hospital in New York, as we saw in the last chapter, congenital syphilis was eight times as prevalent among cocaine-exposed infants: 70 percent of their mothers had poor prenatal care, and 30 percent had no prenatal care at all. Poor prenatal care (like drug use) is also a strong correlate of low birth weight— itself the most important cause of infant mortality. One Philadelphia study estimates that the rate of low birth weight among the infants of opiate-using women who do not receive prenatal care is close to 50 percent. Yet *with* adequate prenatal care, these ills are eminently preventable. Syphilis in pregnancy is easily detected through screening and effectively treated with antibiotics; prenatal care and good nutrition can greatly decrease the likelihood of low birth weight. As the GAO notes, in one comprehensive prenatal program, the incidence of low birth weight among infants of drug-abusing mothers dropped from 50 to 18 percent.

The general outlines of appropriate treatment programs for pregnant addicts aren't much different from those for other women. What pregnant addicts most need is less any specific modality of drug treatment than a shift in priorities—away from concentration on the narrow issue of the drug itself toward the whole complex of conditions women usually bring to treatment. As Wendy Chavkin puts it,

Whatever specific drug treatment modality is employed, it should be integrated with a comprehensive system of care. Drug-treatment, obstetric, and pediatric care should be coordinated, and services such as day care, job preparation, and training to resist domestic violence must be incorporated if the women are to stand a meaningful chance at long-term recovery.

Separating care from the criminal-justice system is especially crucial for pregnant women, who may face losing their children to child-protective services; in some states addicted women are now liable for prosecution for child abuse if they bear drug-exposed children. We have no evidence that the threat of prosecution deters women from using drugs during pregnancy, but considerable evidence that it keeps them from seeking treatment or prenatal care.

One program that exemplifies the comprehensive approach we most need is the Family Center at Thomas Jefferson University Hospital in Philadelphia—an outpatient methadone-treatment program for heroin-addicted women. It serves a largely low-income population, about half white, half black and Hispanic, who bring an "enormous" range of physical problems and are simultaneously "weakened by unemployment, illiteracy, homelessness, and legal issues." To attract wary women to the program, the center uses indigenous outreach workers familiar with the women's neighborhoods and cultures; if necessary, they provide transportation to the clinic. Once there, pregnant addicts receive comprehensive prenatal care, nutritional advice, and HIV counseling and testing, in addition to obstetrical services by staff "specifically trained in the field of addiction and high-risk pregnancy." The 60 percent of infants born in a state of drug withdrawal are treated in intensive-care nurseries.

But beyond trying to ensure a healthy pregnancy and birth, the center works to deal with the whole range of women's social and psychological issues—the social ones first: The assumption is that if issues of housing, clothing, and food are not attended to, "women rarely respond to drug treatment. When provisions for consistent shelter, clothing, and food are secured, dramatic increases in initial recovery occur." Accordingly, the center puts considerable emphasis on finding adequate housing for its clients, and it operates a clothing bank and a small food bank, since "it is not unusual for pregnant addicts to appear at Family Center without having eaten for several days." For this extremely disadvantaged population, "the combination of a nourishing meal and a way to return to the Family Center" encourages women to participate who otherwise would remain beyond reach.

The center operates women-only discussion groups, in part because of the high proportion of clients who have experienced physical and sexual abuse from men. It offers classes in prenatal care and child-development skills, in order to forestall the pattern of "intergenerational substance abuse" that typifies the histories of many of these women. It offers instruction on newborn care and home visits to assist women who've recently delivered. A Children's Center under the same roof offers a safe place for the children of women in treatment, and provides a setting where parenting skills can be improved.

This is only one possible model, of course; and it is specifically aimed at pregnant heroin users, not cocaine or polydrug abusers. But aside from the methadone component, the rest of the center's strategy seems eminently applicable to other pregnant drug users—especially the fusing of medical care with real-world help in finding housing, food, and child care.

And that returns us to the crucial point: whether we are dealing with pregnant addicts or adolescents or jobless and homeless men, the most compelling needs of drug abusers are ones all too few treatment programs now address. Moving our treatment system toward more serious and more consistent provision for those needs will cost money, but it is well worth it. When we fail to deal with the underlying *social* issues of inadequate work, poor housing, abusive families, and poor health care that shape most addicts' lives, we virtually ensure that drug treatment will become a revolving door. And what is truly expensive is cycling drug abusers from treatment to shattered and dismal lives and back again.

Across the country, there are encouraging attempts to break that depressing cycle. But the collapse of state and local budgets in the 1990s and the continued skewing of federal antidrug spending toward punishment have meant that we have barely begun to meet the need. Moreover, even the best, most comprehensive programs to help addicts transform their lives will inevitably be compromised if we do not simultaneously address the powerful social forces that are destroying the communities to which they must return.

C H A P T E R

6

Reconstructing Communities

In the long run, dealing with America's drug crisis means attacking the conditions that breed it—a principle we have come to accept in most other realms of life. We no longer believe that the best way to ward off disease is to build more hospitals. We no longer think that the best way to cope with environmental problems is to wait for disasters to happen and clean up the damage afterward. But our approach to drugs is still mainly reactive, not preventive.

Just as unbreathable air and an endless flood of toxic wastes tell us that something is fundamentally awry in the way we organize our technologies of production, endemic drug abuse tells us that something is fundamentally amiss in our *social* organization. Healthy societies are not overwhelmed by hard drugs. Those that *are* overwhelmed, around the world, are invariably riddled with other preventable social problems—mass poverty, glaring inequalities, widespread waste of human resources, endemic violence, high levels of infant mortality and preventable disease. It is not accidental that the United States has both the developed world's worst drug problem *and* its worst violence, poverty, and social exclusion, together with its least adequate provision of health care, income support, and social services. Taking on the drug problem in an enduring way means tackling those social deficits head-on.

To say that it is time to seriously address causes is not to say we should do nothing else. We've seen that there is much to be done by way of more comprehensive and accessible treatment, better-targeted prevention programs, harm-reduction measures, and a more rational use of criminal-justice resources. But by now it should be apparent that none of these, singly or in combination, is an answer to the drug crisis; and even our best efforts along those lines will be undermined if we allow the social forces that promote drug abuse to remain unchanged. We may develop sensitive treatment programs, but our efforts will be routinely frustrated if clients go back to the same social conditions that encouraged their drug use in the first place. We may even provide help with education and family problems, but abusers will not escape the brutal cycle of addiction and crime unless genuine work opportunities enable them to turn their lives around permanently. We may educate addicts about the risks of AIDS and other diseases, but we will make only a moderate difference in their behavior if we cannot alter the sense of futurelessness that encourages heedless attitudes toward sex and disease. We may launch "user-friendly" programs that successfully reach high-risk young people, but we will not crack the very real appeals of drug dealing and the drug culture if we cannot offer much in their place. We may strike a better balance between prison and community alternatives for drug offenders—but our justice system will remain swollen, costly, and volatile unless we address the social conditions that cause the heavy flow of new offenders in the first place. All of these efforts are worthwhile, and we should support them. They will make a difference, and some will save lives. But they are not about causes.

We are reluctant to come to grips with the causes in part because the task is both long-term and enormously challenging.

It entails nothing less than altering an entire process of social development—one that has excluded millions of Americans from a productive and respected role in our common life, eroded the strengths of families and communities, and blighted the prospects of an entire generation. But we are well past the point where muddling through will suffice. It is difficult to exaggerate the social devastation we have encouraged in the past generation and how deeply it constrains all other efforts to do something about the drug problem. Put simply, we have let the destruction of basic social institutions in the cities go on for much too long. Now we are paying the price. In much of our debate about drugs, there is massive denial on this score; like addicts, we have trouble looking reality in the face, and our first task on the road to recovery is to acknowledge that we have a much more serious problem than we have been willing to recognize.

To mount a comprehensive attack on the roots of drug abuse we must be tough-minded enough to acknowledge the need for fundamental change and pragmatic enough to plan for the long term. We must acknowledge that the drug crisis reflects a deeper crisis of culture and spirit, of family and community, as well as of material well-being. We must accordingly strive to re-create a sense of purpose and participation, of contribution to a common enterprise, of membership in a sustaining society. We must provide greatly expanded opportunities for stable and respected work. We must restore and enhance critical public institutions in communities savaged by economic decline and fiscal retreat. And we must provide a new array of supports for families, children, and youth. We must, in short, replace the "strategy of inequality" with what I will call a "strategy of inclusion," designed to bring as many Americans as possible into productive roles within what the late Robert Kennedy called "communities of security, achievement, and dignity."

A strategy of inclusion is not the same thing as simply redistributing income to the disadvantaged or providing after-the-fact social services to those who have been damaged by their exclusion—or their parents' exclusion—from a sustaining place in the society around them. It is an effort to forestall social pathologies by guaranteeing a fundamental level of economic and social participation. To be sure, that is a tall order. But it is not beyond our reach. Many of the measures we need, in fact, are already in place in other countries that, not coincidentally, have far less severe drug problems than we do. It is not, after all, that those countries have discovered some wildly successful form of drug treatment, or some marvelously effective prevention program, of which we are ignorant; if they had, we would have found it out by now. The difference lies at a more basic level of social policy and national priorities: other industrial nations have adopted policies deliberately designed to provide a higher level of citizenship for all, to narrow inequalities in economic opportunities and social benefits, and to include their citizens in productive roles in a less savagely bifurcated economy. And we can learn much from those countries' example. These international differences are not immutable. They reflect quite deliberate social decisions. And they show that things in this country need not be as they are.

I

Given the extent of the devastation inflicted on the cities and the poor by the unleashing of the strategy of inequality, there is a sense in which almost anything we do to improve the conditions of life for those most at risk could help to reduce drug abuse. But we need to make more specific choices. Some measures are likely to be more important than others, and our knowledge of the root causes of drug abuse and the obstacles to successful recovery allows us to be more focused—to sort out the crucial from the merely worthy. Here, then, are five crucial elements of a long-term strategy against endemic drug abuse, all of which are also both economically sustainable and congruent with a larger vision of the society we wish to achieve. They are not intended as a complete blueprint, but as a foundation. All of them are related, and all are designed to directly attack the economic exclusion, family disintegration, and community decline that underlie our drug crisis.

EXPANDING THE OPPORTUNITY STRUCTURE

We saw in Chapter 3 that it is the long-term decline of opportunities for stable and rewarding work that most powerfully drives the syndrome of multiple deprivation that breeds endemic drug abuse. The problem goes far beyond unemployment itself—and far beyond the immediate effects of the current recession. There has been a twenty-year downward shift in economic prospects, especially for the less educated young, whose situation, even in the era of postwar economic expansion before that, was already dismal. It is not, in short, a problem that will go away when (or if) the economy pulls out of its present doldrums.

Moreover, the decline in opportunities has now spread well beyond the inner cities, and its effects are no longer confined to minority youth or a small "hard core" of the dropouts and the disorganized poor. It represents a structural change in the level of economic citizenship available to all younger Americans—a social tragedy that will frustrate our best efforts at drug prevention and treatment (and much else) if we do not reverse it.

As we've seen, the radical loss of opportunities breeds drug abuse in multiple ways—not just by raising the jobless rate, but, more insidiously, by denying a sense of purpose and usefulness, whipsawing workers between low wages and high costs of living, weakening families, and eroding the ability of communities to offer support, guidance, or exemplary values. Over time, at the extreme, it creates a vacuum of socialization and supervision in which drug cultures easily proliferate. It creates "thin" communities with few legitimate avenues of advance or escape, and breeds a culture of defeat and predation that is very difficult to counter through the conventional means of social intervention. It is, in short, a deep fault in our social organization, and its effects reverberate throughout American society.

This is not a process that can somehow correct itself, or be reversed simply by the operation of the free market. No one, officially, is *against* creating better economic opportunities. But between being vaguely in favor of better prospects for the young and actually having a commitment to public action to create them lies a world of difference. In the United States, we have been hobbled in this respect by our insistence that the shape of the opportunity structure ought to be left up to the private decisions of private employers. Our explicit reliance on the "market" to produce adequate jobs and income is unmatched in any other advanced industrial society, and it goes a long way toward explaining the scope and speed of the decline of good work—and the growth of poverty—in the United States. Reversing that decline requires what in some European countries is called an "active labor-market policy," which consciously uses the power of government to create opportunities beyond those the market can provide on its own.

The current decline of the American labor market has two related causes—both of them direct expressions of what I have called the strategy of inequality. One is the failure of *private* employers to provide the kind of training and investment in human resources that their counterparts in many other industrial societies do. The other is our national refusal to make a strong *public* investment in employment and training—a refusal that likewise sets us apart.

To the degree that we can be said to have a national employment policy, it is predicated on the assumption that the best way to create jobs and income is to redistribute resources upward—by slashing business taxes, keeping wages low, eliminating public-sector jobs, and reducing social benefits. By now, however, we have followed that approach for over twenty years, and it has brought us economic conditions that increasingly resemble those of a middle-income developing country. It should now be obvious that simply promoting *any* kind of economic "growth," by whatever means, does not guarantee inclusion for all; expansion at the top no longer reliably "trickles down" to the excluded in the form of stable work and solid wages. Even in those parts of the country that saw rapid economic growth during the 1980s, job prospects for most of the poor—especially inner-city minorities—failed, as we've seen, to improve. It is time to follow the example of more successful industrial nations and commit ourselves to investing in the skills and capacities of the American workforce in ways we have so far resisted.

A key first step is to raise the quality and skill levels of the jobs available in private industry—and to do a much better job of training Americans to fill them. There has been much talk of a growing "skills shortage" in the United States—a lack of workers with enough education and training to staff an increasingly complex and demanding economy. The implication is that the economy has produced an abundance of good jobs, but that a poorly educated and generally incompetent workforce is unprepared to fill them. But while that surely holds for some parts of the economy, the overall reality is quite different. The Commission on the Skills of the American Workforce, composed of experts from business, labor, and the universities, concluded in 1989 that in only a few specific occupations—including nursing and some skilled crafts—is there now a shortage of skills; indeed, our workforce is generally *overeducated* for most of the increasingly poor jobs available in the economy.

The commission found that very few American companies —around 5 percent—are concerned about a lack of skills among their workers and potential workers. The majority of American employers, instead, have adopted what some call a "dumbing-down" strategy toward their workforce, with calamitous effects for America's cities. Faced with the need to remain profitable in an increasingly competitive international arena, there are two ways employers can respond. They can seek profits and competitiveness by increasing the skills and productivity of their workers, or they can opt for a low-wage, high-turnover strategy. As Ira Magaziner of the Workforce Commission puts it, American companies, with few exceptions—in sharp contrast to many firms in Europe and Japan—have not moved toward "high-performance, high-productive work organizations," but have chosen to "go for low wages" instead. That may mean either moving to low-wage countries, or, if they cannot move, using "more and more temporary workers, part-time workers, workers that they cycle through simple jobs." As Magaziner sums up the commission's message, "America is now opting for a choice, very silently and very gradually, for low wages. . . . Five percent—and that may grow to 10 percent—of our companies are moving in the other direction; they are opting for high skills. But they are a small minority."

That choice, as Magaziner notes, has its most adverse effect on the "75 percent of the people who don't get four-year college educations" and who are "basically being de-skilled compared to the rest of the world." All of this helps explain why the majority of new jobs available to younger Americans have been poorly paying and often unstable ones—and why the much-vaunted job growth of the eighties actually *worsened* the living conditions of the less educated half of Americans. We have "grown" in recent years largely by "throwing people at the economy" rather than by training them for higher-productivity jobs. And this has profound implications for any credible strategy for reviving the economic prospects in the inner cities and rural America, especially for the young. If growth is to translate into better lives for those caught in the lower reaches of the economy, private employers must begin to "see their employees as opportunities for investment rather than as costs to be minimized."

One way employers in other countries make that investment

is by serious efforts to set the young in school firmly on course toward skilled work when they graduate—the "school-to-work transition." Some countries—most notably Germany, Austria, and Switzerland—have developed elaborate apprenticeship programs that may hold important lessons for the United States. In Germany, for example, 70 percent of young people entering the job market do so through an apprenticeship. Students are taught about specific jobs in seventh through ninth grade; by ages sixteen to eighteen, most have signed contracts with future employers detailing the type of training they will receive and what they will be paid. As Robert Lerman and Hillard Pouncy describe the German system,

> The students receive on-the-job training and stipends from their employers, but they must also attend school part-time. Apprentices demonstrate their abilities by taking interim and final examinations offered by boards of examiners established by employer and worker organizations. After receiving their certification, more than half of the apprentices remain with the firms that trained them; many of the rest stay in the same occupation.

The system is controlled by a quasi-public agency whose members are drawn from business, government, and the unions. The agency sets competency standards for hundreds of different occupations, but individual employers determine the number of apprenticeships that will be offered. The system provides very tangible benefits both to the trainees and to the businesses that hire them. For the apprentices, it nearly guarantees them, early on, a good job after their schooling ends, as long as they fulfill the training requirements. Employers, meanwhile, reap the benefits of a skilled and loyal workforce. "German executives," Lerman and Pouncy argue, "attribute much of their business success to their sophisticated workforce trained largely under the apprenticeship program."

Lerman and Pouncy point to several ways a similar approach

would usefully address the current crisis of the disadvantaged young in the United States. Most obviously, by connecting education to real jobs and potential careers, it would dramatically increase the value of education in their eyes and thus help keep them in school and off the street. "The bleak career outlook for workers without college education," they argue, "discourages young people, particularly inner-city minority youth, to whom the gains from studying look trivial in comparison to the lures of the street." Indeed, as it now stands, young people's often correct perception that what they do in school is largely irrelevant to their job future "contributes to peer pressure that discourages many from working hard in school."

A formal mechanism to link inner-city students with good jobs would also counter one of the main problems that now keeps them unemployed or out of the labor force altogether —the absence of helpful informal contacts with the world of good work. "The increasing isolation of inner-city minorities," Lerman and Pouncy write, "means that minority young people, often raised in single-parent households, have less and less access to a network of jobholders. The loss of informal contacts increases the importance of formal mechanisms that can reach the vast bulk of minority youth." And this is equally true for disadvantaged white and rural young people. Not only has opportunity narrowed for them in the labor market, but gaining access to the dwindling number of good jobs that still exist depends increasingly on precisely the kinds of informal networks of "connected" jobholders that are usually absent in their deprived and fragmented communities. If they were able to count on the formal mechanism of an apprenticeship system, they would be much less dependent on those elusive and shrinking informal connections.

Similarly, a serious apprenticeship system would link youth with new peer groups and role models. There has been much discussion about the need for "mentors" for young people in the cities—but most mentoring programs now connect youth artificially, and often briefly, with adults who may be sympathetic but who have no real influence on their prospects for a rewarding career. In an established apprenticeship system, though, as Lerman and Pouncy point out, youth would be automatically "drawn into an adult work environment" and "exposed to expert workers who could be their mentors"— spending correspondingly less time surrounded only by other adolescents with limited futures and few links to a stable and successful adult world. Over time, that link could alter the entire atmosphere of the schools, turning them into places where hard work would be "respected rather than denigrated."

Several other strategies on the national level would help to encourage employers to upgrade jobs and invest in their workers—and counter the "throwaway" approach to our human resources. One is steady increases in the federal minimum wage, designed to bring our wage floor closer to that in many European countries. We've seen that the real value of the minimum wage fell sharply through the 1980s; recent legislation has increased it, but not even to its inflation-adjusted level of a decade ago. Today full-time work at the federal minimum wage of $4.25 provides an annual income more than $4,000 below the poverty level for a family of four and $1,000 below poverty for a family of three. And the promise of poverty as the reward for steady work is one of the most reliable ways to ensure a sense of alienation and social exclusion. Rock-bottom minimum wages are accordingly a marvelous recruiting device for illegal occupations, including drug dealing and predatory street crime. They also guarantee that many who do continue to abide by the "middle-class" values of hard work and self-sufficiency will be forced to work so long and so hard that they will have little time to raise their children or participate in their community's life. The claim that a higher wage floor would hurt the performance of the economy is simply false: minimum wages are closer to the average earnings of workers in many European countries whose economies now routinely outperform ours. It is sometimes objected that higher minimum wages would price many young people out of the labor market. But an extensive body of research on the effects of changes in the minimum wage in the United States consistently finds that minor losses of employment among teenagers—if any—are more than offset by substantial gains in earnings for adult workers: and it is the promise of a good job as an adult, not the reality of a low-paid job as a teenager, that is most important in deterring drug abuse.

But more is needed than a higher minimum wage. In Scandinavia, labor relations have long been premised on what is called a "solidaristic" wage policy, in which systematic efforts are made to narrow the inequalities in wages within occupations and between them. That approach helps to reduce glaring and alienating divisions between haves and have-nots, and to foster a broader sense of common participation in economic and social life. In the United States, Gary Loveman and Chris Tilly have argued for a somewhat similar creation of "binding wage floors that are uniform across industries or occupations."

Such a "solidaristic" approach to jobs and earnings in the private economy would be particularly beneficial for women. Up to now I've been discussing the problem of a low-wage, "dumbing-down" employment policy as if it were neutral with respect to gender. But in fact it is women who hold most of the poorest-paying jobs in America. And their entrapment in the lowest reaches of the "throwaway" economy has many profound repercussions on the drug problem. It creates enormous levels of stress and routine "hassle" which make poor working women highly vulnerable to drug use. It is a major reason for growing homelessness among young women and their children—another spur to drug abuse. It heightens the risks of child abuse, which (as we've seen) predisposes children to drug use, and it traps women into relationships with men that are abusive, or drug-ridden, or both. For all these reasons, sustained efforts to raise wages in heavily "female" jobs and to narrow the wage gap between women and men are crucial to a long-run strategy against drugs.

We also urgently need measures (in addition to apprentice-ship programs) to ensure that private employers undertake to train and retrain workers for higher productivity. Despite much lip service, such efforts are all too rare today: in the fast-growing Atlanta area during the 1980s, "employers were training less than 1 percent of those in need." Several labor and business organizations have proposed that companies should either commit a certain proportion of their income to internal training programs or pay equivalent taxes into a national training fund—1 percent of payroll costs, for example, in a version suggested by the Coalition for Democratic Values. Something like this system prevails today in most European industrial societies. As David Crawford points out, "Most of our major international trading partners require employers to provide or subsidize worker training." The exact form of that policy, he notes, "is not so important as the basic idea that we must increase private investment in workers' skills."

The two kinds of measures—improving wages and increasing skills—obviously go hand in hand. If we do not raise the productivity of workers through better training and job up-grading to match, we will not be able to afford to pay them a decent wage, and we will continue to condemn many of them —particularly women and the young of both sexes—to the stresses and privations of working poverty. If we do train them, and continually invest in redesigning production to absorb a smarter and better-skilled workforce, we can also successfully accommodate a more civilized floor of wages that would do more than virtually any other measure to provide the basic elements of full citizenship for those now excluded. (Bringing the federal minimum wage from $3.85 to $4.25, according to one recent estimate, brought close to 200,000 working families above the poverty line; larger increases would do much more.)

Finally, we will need to provide disincentives for employers to replace good jobs in the United States with low-wage ones in other countries. Much damage has already been done through our failure to impose any costs on this routine dismantling of America's opportunity structure. But we can limit similar damage in the future by requiring employers to "internalize" the costs of job displacement—perhaps by paying into an adjustment fund that would be used to create new jobs in the United States to replace those lost.

The United States has long boasted, if that is the word, the smallest public effort at employment and training in the advanced industrial world—a failure of public policy that is particularly crippling precisely because it has gone hand in hand with a throwaway mentality and downward wage strategy in the *private* sector.

Data from the Organization for Cooperation and Development (OECD) on national government spending for employment and training are especially revealing. Overall, in the late 1980s, our public spending on labor market programs amounted to about 0.6 percent of our gross domestic product (GDP). That was about half of what Austria spent, two-fifths of what Britain spent, slightly more than one-fourth what the Germans or Swedes spent, and a sixth of what the Dutch spent on labor market programs. But those differences actually *understate* America's relative failure to develop active strategies to train and employ its citizens. Well over half of American public spending on job programs is devoted to the passive support of people *out* of jobs—mainly unemployment insurance. When we focus on more active programs to train them or put them to work, the national discrepancies widen. Thus Germany spent 3.7 times what the U.S. did on labor market programs generally—but spent 21 times as much on what the OECD calls "work schemes outside the ordinary labor market," including direct job creation and sheltered work. Sweden spent proportionately about 3.8 times what the United States did on all labor market programs, but a stunning 47 times what we spent on work programs outside the ordinary labor market.

That we find it more acceptable to maintain people in idleness than to create jobs or serious training for them seems quite irrational, but is not accidental. It is a major feature of the strategy of inequality. At least since the Depression of the thirties, American employers have fought tooth and nail against public job creation, on the ground that the jobs would be so attractive to workers that they would be drawn away from the private sector. Maintaining a pool of workers subsisting—poorly—on meager jobless benefits (or public welfare), on the other hand, has the supreme virtue of making even the poorest private jobs look attractive by comparison. Like rock-bottom minimum wages and the refusal to invest in training, the resistance to putting people to work at public tasks has been one prop to a larger strategy of maintaining high profit margins without investing in human resources or enhancing productivity.

But the consequences for society as a whole have been disastrous—especially because *private* employers in the United States also do so little to train workers. Thus Germany boasts *both* elaborate private-sector apprenticeship programs and high levels of public spending for job training; countries like Japan and Switzerland, which have relatively low levels of public spending on jobs and job training, need it less because they put considerable effort into private-sector efforts that help ensure full employment—like Japan's well-known system of "lifetime employment" and continual retraining at work for many private employees.

The history of our failure to invest in job creation and job training, by contrast, is dismaying. It is not simply that we have "lacked the will" to make that investment, but that we have actively *opposed* it—even when, or especially when, we have evidence that the programs work. In the 1930s, business interests fought to dismantle national programs like the Civil Works Administration and the National Youth Administration, which put millions of disadvantaged Americans to useful work when no other work was to be had. The complaint of business was not that the programs didn't work but that they *did*—and therefore provided excessive competition to private enterprise. Much the same happened after World War II, when a strong movement to establish what would have been a European-style federal commitment to jobs and training was drastically watered down in Congress on the initiative of private business. Since then, with the partial exception of a brief period during the recession of the 1970s, our employment and training system has been deliberately kept small, in line with the low-wage, high-turnover strategy increasingly adopted by private business. In the seventies, under the Carter administration, we did put several hundred thousand Americans, most of them poor, to work at public jobs under the Comprehensive Employment and Training Act (CETA). But the effort remained meager as compared both with that of many European countries and with our own Depression-era past (at its peak, CETA employed less than 12 percent of the country's unemployed workers), and was in any event virtually abolished by the Reagan administration in the 1980s. (Federal spending on employment programs of all kinds dropped from $10.3 billion in 1980 to $5.4 billion in 1990.)

The federal job-creation-and-training system we have today —the Job Training Partnership Act (JTPA)—enrolls only about 5 percent of those eligible for assistance, and as David Crawford notes, it is the wrong 5 percent. A 1991 assessment by the U.S. General Accounting Office concluded that much JTPA training actually involves placing "trainees" in low-skill work rather than investing in improving skills. Indeed, studies of how JTPA works in practice reveal that its main function has been to provide a stream of low-wage workers—most of them already comparatively "job-ready"—to private employers who would probably have hired similar people anyway without the program. (One JTPA program to train workers in word processing required trainees to be high-school graduates who could already type 40 words per minute.)

These distorted priorities have been especially destructive for the young and for low-income women. What Gary Orfield

and Carole Ashkinaze found for Atlanta has been true nationally of youth employment efforts under the JTPA. The program, they write,

> placed many in what turned out to be marginal, short-
> term, part-time jobs with high turnover rates. What ap-
> peared to be high placements at low cost often actually
> involved spending many hundreds of dollars per young
> person to get a part-time job that would have been available
> without training and which lasted less than three months.

For women, similarly, the thrust of the current federal training
system has been less to provide skill training than to channel
already relatively well-prepared women into traditionally "female" and low-paying jobs in private industry. Thus in Atlanta
the local JTPA "concentrated its resources on training black
women with high-school degrees for traditional low-wage, dead-
end, entry-level jobs, a substantial number of them as hotel
maids."

We can do much better than this. What is so frustrating about
the drift of national employment policy is that better models
already exist—not only overseas, but at home. We have growing
evidence, for example, that programs that train the unskilled
for *better* jobs, and that simultaneously provide a range of
supportive services along the way, can be remarkably effective
—principally because they offer the promise of genuinely
marketable skills and a more rewarding future. Thus a recent
Rockefeller Foundation–funded study points to the potential
of training programs for women that emphasize developing
skills in higher-paying occupations—including "nontraditional"
ones—as opposed to simply channeling women into low-wage
jobs or concentrating on basic remedial education, as many
training programs have done in the past. The foundation
sponsored programs for unskilled women in four cities: three

stressed "the popular back-to-basics regimen of remedial English and mathematics," while the fourth, in San Jose, California, trained women immediately in sheet-metal work, a well-paying (and traditionally "male") skill. The program also provided child care and other supportive services. In the three remedial programs, low-income single mothers were no more likely to land better jobs or earn better wages than a control group; in the San Jose program, participants were considerably more likely to find jobs after training than were controls and earned half again as much. Simple classroom-style education, in short—where many of these women had failed before—was not the answer; what worked was the tangible possibility of a good job.

That is only common sense, and the experience is backed by what we know about the ingredients of success in training programs for youth. The federal Job Corps program, for example, first launched in the 1960s, is among the most solidly successful and carefully evaluated social programs of any kind in the United States. The Job Corps is an intensive and comprehensive program for high-risk young people of both sexes that offers remedial education and health care in addition to training in specific skills. In 1991 it trained roughly seventy thousand young people aged sixteen to twenty-two, most of them at serious risk of drug abuse, delinquency, and welfare dependency. The average family income of Job Corps participants was less than $6,000; two out of five came from families on public assistance; more than four out of five were high-school dropouts.

The Job Corps is not perfect, but its results have been consistently positive and its performance highly cost-effective. A 1991 analysis by the Congressional Budget Office calculated that for each $10,000 invested in the average participant in the mid-1980s, society received roughly $15,000 in returns—including about $8,000 in "increased output of participants" and another $6,000 in the "reductions in the cost of crime-related activities." Yet, curiously, expanding the Job Corps—

or something like it—to serve a substantially larger number of high-risk youth has never been given priority by recent administrations: indeed the program has been forced, throughout the Reagan and Bush era, to struggle to maintain its current level of funding. To be sure, the program is not cheap; a year in the Job Corps cost about $19,000 in 1991 (though the usual stay was somewhat shorter, and hence the cost per trainee somewhat less). But no one seriously challenges that the cost remains lower than the $30,000 average for a year in a juvenile prison—or that the money provides a much more impressive return than the similar $19,000 average cost for long-term residential drug treatment, which rarely provides anything resembling serious preparation for the world of work.

The failure to mount a national effort to train and employ the young that aims higher than the minimal and inappropriate system we have now, therefore, reflects ideological constraints more than economic ones. Even at best, we have usually operated our youth-employment schemes on the assumption that where young people really belong is in the private labor market. But that assumption needs to be altered in the light of the unprecedented recent changes in the private economy. We've seen that the quality of private jobs available to younger people has fallen radically in the past twenty years. And though upgrading work in the private sector is one part of the answer, the hard reality is that there simply will not be enough good jobs for all of the young unless we expand *public* job opportunities at the same time. Even during better economic times, the private economy has been decreasingly capable of providing steady employment for high-school graduates, let alone dropouts; in tougher times, job prospects have withered for college graduates as well. We must acknowledge that the need for public employment opportunities for the young is now a *permanent* one, and redesign our employment and training systems accordingly.

The basic principles are easily derived from the nature of the crisis that confronts us. A redesigned employment and training system would emphasize placing young people in challenging jobs that directly address pressing national and community needs now systematically neglected by the private economy. Rather than channeling young people into private-sector low-wage jobs of uncertain future and dubious social benefit, it would take the growing crisis of the cities and rural areas as an opportunity to harness youthful energies to rebuild a vital public and nonprofit sector savaged by years of economic decline and official neglect. It would be available to all youth, not just the most disadvantaged—thereby avoiding the stigma and stinginess that usually accompany programs targeted only on the hardest cases. It would provide a continuum of work and training environments for youth with different capacities and different needs. And it would encourage their participation—and reduce their sense of powerlessness, alienation, and lack of respect—by enlisting them in every phase of program design and operation, including the highest levels of decision-making. Some of those opportunities might be in public agencies, others in nonprofit organizations, still others—as the Haryou activists suggested in the 1960s—in a network of new, community-based enterprises. The specific auspices are less important than the general principle: the direct creation of useful jobs in areas that visibly serve community needs.

The potential benefits are many, and obvious. Adolescents who now see little in their futures beyond Burger King or a T-shirt shop could look forward, if they fulfilled their part of the schooling-and-training bargain, to a guaranteed job performing useful work that helped to revitalize their community—and to having a voice in determining what that work would be. The effect on their attitudes toward schooling, drug and alcohol use, risky sex, and the culture of the street would be immediate and profound. The community would benefit equally by harnessing now underused youthful capacities to accomplish critical social tasks that are now increasingly left undone because they are not profitable for private industry.

There is no shortage of work to be done, and a comprehensive youth-employment system would devise innovative ways of linking youths' specific needs for schooling, training, and housing with different levels of involvement in community-building work. For youth with stable families and those in school, it would develop a wide variety of opportunities for part-time work enhancing the "social infrastructure" of their communities—providing transportation and home health care for the elderly, offering counseling and recreation for younger children, and working to improve public safety. For those who cannot perform well in conventional schools, it would offer programs that combine alternative education and public-service work. As it now stands, those who do poorly in the conventional classroom are virtually condemned to the margins of productive life. That is a recipe for social disaster, and a more creative youth-employment system would devote itself to finding out what those who do not do well in school *can* do well, and helping them to do it.

At the far end of the continuum, for youth without homes and stable families, a comprehensive system would provide programs that combine housing, schooling, and work. There are useful models for this, both overseas and, as importantly, in our own past. One of the most compelling comes from the Depression of the 1930s—the National Youth Administration (NYA). The NYA is a relatively hidden part of our national experience, but it carries important lessons for the present. Until its funding was cut off shortly before World War II, the NYA housed, fed, schooled, and employed hundreds of thousands of young people—most of whom would now be considered at risk for drug abuse and delinquency, many of whom were homeless, illiterate, or badly nourished. Most were assigned to "resident centers" where "young people, both boys and girls, live together, work and study, learn useful skills, and experience group life on a civilized plane." They were not confined to marginal make-work: in just one year in the late 1930s, they built 324 schools and refurbished almost 4,000 others; built or improved 23,000 public parks; made over 8 million items of medical supplies in their own workshops; planted 7 million trees; and produced 3 million pounds of food, most of it distributed to poor households. Their work cushioned the effect of the Depression on many communities, and left enduring public monuments that are visible to this day. They accomplished important public tasks that would not otherwise have been done, and they learned important skills in the process. Something similar to the NYA could transform the lives of many of the youth at highest risk in America's shattered communities, both urban and rural. Only by enlisting them in a comprehensive project to "change the face of their communities," as Haryou proposed in the 1960s, can we break the hold of the culture of drugs, violence, and risk that now surrounds them.

It is sometimes objected that even the chance at a good, rewarding job is unlikely to draw the young away from the huge profits to be gained in the illicit drug trade. The problem is real, but the prognosis is overly pessimistic. For one thing, it greatly exaggerates the financial rewards of the typical dealing career. Except at the top, drug dealing is typically a much less rewarding enterprise than is often supposed. At the lower levels, whether the trade is in crack, heroin, or methamphetamine, the drug business more closely resembles an illegal extension of the "secondary" youth-labor market in general than the lucrative and enthralling enterprise sometimes described. The research of Ansley Hamid, Terry Williams, and others into the lives of crack dealers, for example, makes it clear that (as Gina Kolata of the New York *Times* sums up the findings) "most of the people in the business work round the clock, six to seven days a week, for low real wages in an atmosphere of physical threat and control."

And the uncertainty, danger, and shifting rewards are not restricted to crack dealing, or to the lowest levels of the drug business, as is revealed in Thomas Mieczkowski's study of a major Detroit heroin-selling gang, Young Boys Incorporated. YBI was a highly structured and relatively sophisticated operation, with a quasi-bureaucratic organization and high profits. Unlike the less organized "hustlers" described in much research on drug dealing, most of the dealers in YBI were not themselves addicted to heroin, and maintained a strict, businesslike approach to their work. Mieczkowski estimates that the average peak earnings for skilled "runners" in the Detroit heroin trade—the young men who actually did the selling on the street—ranged widely but averaged $160 a day for ten and one-half hours of work, or about $14 an hour. Fourteen dollars an hour is a good wage for a young man, but it is less than spectacular: assuming fifty weeks of steady work, it translates into $28,000 a year, and that certainly exaggerates the annual income most runners make in practice, since the job is extremely unstable and business may be off for days at a time. Meanwhile, the runner faces a host of frightening and sometimes deadly risks: rip-offs by both customers and fellow workers, arrests by undercover police agents, betrayal by customers who may turn him in for money. Even for workers at the next level up, the "crew bosses," the risks are enormous and multiple. They are "tempting targets for predatory criminals," and they may also "be 'fingered' or deliberately targeted" by other crew members aiming to set them up "for a 'hit' or armed robbery." Heroin-selling "work groups" are ripe with manipulative intrigues, ruthless scams, and mutual mistrust. As a result, the average working life of a crew was short: "they considered themselves an 'old' organization if they operated continuously for a month."

Even in what was clearly a far more organized and lucrative enterprise than the run-of-the-mill street-selling operation, then, the money was not so great as to negate the appeals of a *good* "straight" job, and it came with risks that far outweighed those of most legitimate work. Moreover, although a few dealers move up in the dealing business, the career ladder is an unusually tough one. Moving up generally means displacing those already at the top—a risky business indeed. Meanwhile, racking up years of experience in the illicit market does nothing for young dealers' résumés; it does not help them get a legitimate job if they decide that the risks and hassles are beginning to outweigh the benefits. Even if dealers do not fall prey to their own drug use or to the machinations of others in the trade, in other words, they have often positioned themselves so far outside the normal labor market that they may well find future options even more closed than they are for other disadvantaged youth.

In sum, it is not that dealing is so overwhelmingly attractive, but that the alternatives are so utterly dreary. And as we've seen, the appeal lies at least as much in the sense of challenge and the respect that dealing often confers, in the absence of other means of attaining them, as in the financial returns. If we can create sufficient alternative avenues of respect and challenge, we will have built the strongest counterweight to the appeal of drug dealing (as of drug abuse itself).

But it is equally clear that we cannot expect to create that alternative if we try to do it piecemeal. We will need much more than a few scattered experimental job programs for the worst-off among the urban young. We will need to commit ourselves to offering a serious job and adequate training to *every* young person willing to take on the responsibilities.* If we do that, we can begin to foster that "sense of place and purpose" that Kenneth Clark recognized in the 1960s as the

---

* Legislation introduced in the United States Senate in 1992 to create a "National Youth Community Corps" is a step in this direction. The proposal, sponsored by Senators David Boren and Paul Simon, would "create camps, or dormitory units in urban areas, for young people age 17 to 22 to work on projects ranging from reforestation to auxiliary police work to town beautification." Among other things, it would use former military bases to house Corps workers, and former military personnel to train and supervise them. Corps workers would earn $10,000 in educational benefits, or $5,000 in cash, for every year spent in the program. The Corps would give preference to young people from families on welfare or below the poverty line, but would be open to others if sufficient funding was available.

key to ending the profound alienation of inner-city youth. No one should underestimate how difficult it will be, even with that kind of commitment, to revive the struggling communities where drug abuse is now endemic. But over time, we can shift the social and cultural balance—turning blasted wastelands where the dominant youth occupations are idleness, drug dealing, and sporadic work in poor jobs into vital neighborhoods where most of the young are either in school or working at respected jobs with a visible impact on their community. We can gradually establish a neighborhood culture of competence and contribution that will overshadow the subculture of predation and desperation.

That transformation will not be sudden, and it will not be cheap. But recall how stunningly little we now spend on employment and training in comparison with many other countries. If we were simply to raise our spending on public jobs and training to 1 percent of our GDP—from 0.6 percent today—we would have roughly $20 billion each year to fund an ambitious and creative strategy to put the young to useful work. That investment would in turn create many more jobs through its stimulation of the private economy. And we would still be spending less than half the proportion spent by many European nations on employment and training.

A national, active employment and training policy, then, would accomplish several things at once that are crucial to any effective strategy against endemic drug abuse. It would provide meaningful work and legitimate income for many people at high risk of using (and selling) drugs, and would deliver vital services to communities where basic needs are now routinely unmet. It would reduce the gaping inequality that produces the thwarted prospects and bleak living conditions in which drug abuse thrives. And in the process it would help to stimulate an upward spiral of economic and social development in areas now suffering from decades of decline. It would do these things best if linked to four other critical national strategies for social reconstruction: revitalizing public health care, supporting families, assuring decent shelter for all, and rebuilding the nation's physical infrastructure. Combined with an active labor market policy, these strategies would address the roots of drug abuse in several ways—some by providing direct support to those most vulnerable to drug abuse, some by contributing to a more general expansion of opportunities and rebuilding of community institutions, and some in both ways at once.

REVITALIZING PUBLIC HEALTH CARE

With the uninspiring exception of South Africa, the United States is alone among advanced industrial nations in lacking a national health system which makes care available to everyone. The public health system in the United States, always minimal by international standards, is now tottering, and in some places on the verge of collapse, after more than a decade of abandonment by the federal government. Federal funding for public health has fallen each year for the past decade—in the face of explosive rises in sexually transmitted diseases, drug abuse, and violence. Health care for the affluent continues, meanwhile, to be very good indeed, leading to a growing disparity in health and access to care which, as one critic notes, "resembles the situation found in developing countries."

As with so many other social services in the United States, what remains of the public system of care has shifted by default toward reactive intervention, sacrificing preventive measures —which are less costly but also less urgent, and are therefore the first to feel the budget axe. The resulting fragmentary system comes close to being the worst of all possible worlds; it is both expensive and ineffective, and it perpetuates a cycle in which the failure to forestall preventable illnesses makes for costly and sometimes hopeless efforts to treat them later on.

The resulting crisis is both tragedy and opportunity. A national commitment to extend public, preventive care to areas now desperately underserved would address the drug crisis in several mutually reinforcing ways. It would provide the funds for services critical to drug abusers that are now shortchanged: better and more accessible treatment, "user-friendly" adolescent health clinics, comprehensive prenatal care for addicted women. It would enormously enhance the general health conditions among the bottom third of the population, thereby helping to prepare them for productive roles in a vital community. And it would generate hundreds of thousands of useful and challenging jobs in what are now shattered communities with weak labor markets and few prospects for dignified work, helping to stimulate an upward cycle of social development and economic revitalization. Consider just a few of the most critical needs:

• In the face of sharp rises in the diseases of the poor—including AIDS, syphilis, and a "tide of violence"—"over half of the full-time positions for registered nurses at Harlem Hospital are currently unfilled," according to David Bateman. "To provide the bulk of its care, the hospital depends heavily on per diem nurses who, when they are obtainable, may have little loyalty either to the patients or to the institution. In the neo-natal intensive care unit (NICU), nurse-to-patient ratios have declined by 50 percent since 1984; at least 15 percent of the NICU's nursing shifts are filled by nurses working their second consecutive tour (i.e., a 16-hour day). . . . These nursing shortages have occurred during the 1986–89 epidemic of births of cocaine-exposed low-birthweight babies, a period when the average daily census of the unit rose by more than 60 percent."

Across the country, inner-city public clinics face similar crippling shortages of nurses, public health workers, and the most rudimentary equipment. In Washington, D.C., "there have been shortages of gloves, tubes for drawing blood, disinfectants, towels, sheets, and Band-Aids. Clinics that had full-time specialists now share them with other clinics. Social workers, once a standard clinic resource, are now a luxury. The city once had some 200 field nurses for outreach activities.

By 1990, fewer than a dozen remained. One has to look no farther to know why visits to the city's clinics have dropped nearly 25 percent since 1984."

• Since the 1980s, as a poverty-driven epidemic of sexually transmitted diseases raged in the inner cities, public STD services have been "overwhelmed and inadequately supported." As Sevgai Aral and King K. Holmes of the U.S. Public Health Service describe the current situation: "STD clinics are closing earlier in the day, patients are waiting longer hours to receive care, and greater numbers of people are being turned away without receiving care." The results are both frightening and self-defeating: "The close association of STD with drug use and with sex for drugs ensures that many potential patients will continue to spread infection after being turned away." Nineteen of twenty-three STD clinics across the country surveyed by Aral and Holmes shared at least some features of this "pattern of delayed treatment." The researchers conclude that if we hope to turn the tide of the STD epidemic, clinical services to diagnose and treat STDs must be greatly expanded so that "all patients can be examined and treated on the same day that they present themselves." Beyond those basics, long-term control of STDs in the inner city calls for more innovative approaches—including satellite clinics in poor neighborhoods, mobile clinics and vans to reach the homeless, and aggressive outreach to adolescents at risk.

The shortage of staff and services to cope with STDs will become even more critical in the coming years as many among the large pool of people now infected with the HIV virus develop full-blown AIDS. The U.S. Conference of Mayors estimates that the cities "have yet to face at least 80 percent of AIDS cases, at a time when recession and federal cutbacks constrict city budgets." Half of the cities surveyed by the conference in 1991 reported that they could not meet the *current* demand for AIDS care, much less the expected increases. To fill what Aral and Holmes describe as a "desperate need for services" means training and deploying large numbers of new health workers, from physicians to medical technicians and outreach workers.

• The shrinkage of public health care for some groups, even outside the central cities, has reached such crisis proportions that, in an odd reversal, some who need care are crossing the borders to get it. According to a recent analysis of health care needs among Hispanic Americans, in the entire U.S.–Mexico border area running from southern California to eastern Texas there is "only one fully supported public hospital (located in El Paso) that serves as a facility of last resort for the poor." One result is that "many Mexican-Americans cross back into Mexico when they have to buy pharmaceuticals or obtain health or dental care." Meanwhile, Hispanics are greatly underrepresented in health care occupations; among RNs, dentists, therapists, and pharmacists Hispanics are between 2 and 3 percent.

• A survey released in 1991 by the National Association of Public Hospitals found that the average wait for a bed in public-hospital emergency rooms was more than five and a half hours and that "waits of three to four days were not uncommon." Saddled with "long waiting times, overcrowding, staff shortages, and lack of adequate equipment" in the face of rising numbers of people using emergency rooms as their primary source of care, hospitals have often responded by turning away incoming ambulances, refusing to accept new emergency patients, and transferring some patients to other hospitals—a process that can take hours. In California, there was one public hospital bed for every 1,300 people in 1980, one for every 2,000 a decade later. At Harbor-UCLA Medical Center in Los Angeles, many seriously ill or injured patients "were so discouraged by long waits that they simply left without being treated."

• A recent analysis of the maternal- and infant-care system in New York City reveals "a crisis in both capacity and access— a system on a collision course with the growing reproductive health needs of the country." Infant-mortality rates are rising in many cities and the United States ranks dismally high among industrial societies in those rates—yet perinatal services throughout the country have been crippled by "cutbacks in services and funds, reductions in numbers of beds, and staff shortages." The number of obstetric services fell by 17 percent in New York City during 1987 alone. Women wanting a first prenatal or gynecological appointment now wait for up to sixty days on average in some public clinics. "Without an increase in the supply of health-care workers," Wendy Chavkin and her colleagues write, "expansion of inpatient and outpatient services will be very difficult. Unfortunately, the shortage of health-care workers is likely to worsen in the face of rising need."

In contrast to virtually every other advanced industrial nation, we have no comprehensive, accessible system of prenatal care available to women as a matter of right. What makes this so tragic—and needlessly costly—is that most of the worst prenatal and infant problems are easily preventable, given adequate resources. By now we know a great deal about what good prenatal care for poor women requires: active outreach, home visits to expecting and new mothers, advice on nutrition and family planning, and, if necessary, transportation to and from clinics. But the few existing comprehensive programs are piecemeal and "financially hamstrung," as a recent Washington *Post* report reveals. In Washington, "just one clinic has evening hours, and it has them only once a week. Tight budgets forced all the other clinics to abandon the program—even though it had hiked attendance at one facility by 30 percent. One of two outreach vans, a 1969 camper used for prenatal exams, broke down within months of the program's inception. It remains unrepaired and unreplaced. . . . The clinic turns away ten needy women every day

[and] lacks the funding, space and manpower to expand beyond eighteen deliveries a month."

A list of only the most critical public health needs could be much longer. We need health workers to screen poor women for breast cancer: in New York City, for example, without adequate screening, the breast-cancer death rate for poor women is three times the national average. We need workers to screen children for lead exposure and to remove lead-based paint from the homes of the estimated three to four million children who, according to the Secretary of Health and Human Services, "may have blood lead levels high enough to cause mental and behavioral problems." We need to restore tuberculosis control programs gutted by budget cuts during the 1980s—cuts that have resulted in a surge of new tuberculosis cases in many cities across the United States. There are, in short, enormous unmet needs in public health. There are great numbers of vulnerable people needing useful work. Putting the two together addresses both problems at once, while providing considerable economic stimulation in the bargain.

Supporting Families

As with health care, so with family policy: the United States stands out among developed countries in its failure to ensure the well-being of families. On a host of measures—legislation to ease the conflicts between family and work, provision of child care, and adequate income support—we lag behind not only most of Europe, but also some parts of the developing world. And the gap has generally widened in the last ten years with the single-minded pursuit of the strategy of inequality. Bringing the United States closer to the practice of other countries would boost the living conditions of American families in ways that would directly counter some of the most important causes of endemic drug abuse. And a generous family support policy could be another important stimulus for community regeneration and a source of hundreds of thousands of good, stable jobs in the public and nonprofit sectors of the economy.

In the 1990s no one needs to be reminded that the combined demands of family life and paid work can be overwhelming, especially for low-income families; and we have seen how the resulting overload contributes, in several ways, to the drug problem. Parents forced to combine child-rearing responsibilities and long work hours may be stressed to the point where drugs offer an appealing time-out, or a way to get through the day. Children may be undersupervised, bored, and potentially vulnerable to the surrounding street culture—or abused. Two measures, common in other countries, are especially crucial in reducing these stresses.

Paid family leaves to enable parents to spend time with their children—at birth, when they are ill, or for other family emergencies—are available in most of Europe, and in a number of Third World countries as well. In Sweden, parents are now entitled to 15 months of leave, the first 12 at 90 percent of earnings, the last three at a flat (but generous) rate. Either parent can also opt for a six-hour workday until the child is eight. Austria offers 16 weeks of leave, and Germany 14, at full earnings. Even poorer European countries provide substantial paid leaves—three months at full earnings in Portugal, for example—as do Costa Rica, Cuba, Panama, Brazil, and numerous others.

In the United States, on the other hand, our halting attempts to pass national legislation requiring *unpaid* family leaves— twelve weeks' worth, in its most recent incarnation—have been repeatedly stymied by business lobbyists in Congress or by Presidential veto. Employers have objected to mandated family leave on the ground that it infringes on the unfettered operation of the free market. Yet here, as in so many other realms, there is nothing "free" about the market. The absence of legislation to reduce the strains of family and work amounts to a massive public subsidy to private employers, since it forces the public to pay for the consequences of the resulting family stress and disintegration—from delinquency to drug abuse to mental illness. The resistance to family leave is one more expression of the tendency of American business to regard its workforce as disposable. Whatever short-term advantages this "throwaway" attitude brings to employers must in the long run be paid for many times over by society as a whole.

The United States also trails most industrialized countries in the provision of child care—a default that again presents us with both a crisis and an opportunity. The psychologist Edward Zigler has pointed out that the child-care crisis is nothing new: the 1970 White House Conference on Children singled it out as the most serious problem facing families in the United States. In the more than twenty years since, "our nation has not come a single step closer to providing a solution." That is mainly because, as with other basic social needs, we have largely left the provision of child care up to the private market. In Europe, by contrast, accessible child care for all families has long been regarded as a fundamental *public* responsibility. Most European children aged three to five, for example, are now enrolled in public or publicly supported care, either in the form of near-universal preschool programs (as in France or Denmark) or free-standing child-care centers (as in Sweden). Those programs are "all heavily subsidized, operate largely within the public sector, are free or charge modest, income-related fees, and cover, at least, the normal school day." In the United States, on the other hand, and to some degree in Britain, reliance on the market has led to the growth of an odd dual system of child care: grudging and often hard-to-find public care for the most deprived and expensive private care for those who can afford it.

For low-income American families, the resulting crisis involves quality as well as availability. As a recent report from the National Research Council emphasizes, the benefits of child care hold only for good programs with adequate staff and resources: "poor-quality care, more than any single type of program or arrangement, threatens children's development." But in quality of care no less than in accessibility, we have fallen well behind most European countries. Much of the child care in the United States is offered by proprietary providers with few· resources, up to 90 percent of whom are "neither licensed nor monitored." The turnover rate for day-care workers has been enormous, in part because 60 percent of them earned less than $5 an hour in the late 1980s, and fully 90 percent of them earned less than the federal poverty level. "We are paying to the caregivers of our next generation," Zigler writes, "about what we pay to zoo keepers, and less than we pay to janitors." In France, on the other hand, child-care and preschool workers are paid on the same level as elementary-school teachers, with the result that turnover is low and continuity of care much improved.

Again, a sustained expansion of high-quality child care would address the drug crisis in several ways at once. It would enable many more women with drug problems to enter treatment, or to undertake serious job training. More generally, it would provide a crucial social support for their efforts to move away from the drug culture and from abusive and destructive relationships. As it stands, the absence of adequate child care cripples the ability of low-income women to support themselves: it keeps many out of the labor force altogether and consumes too much of their earnings if they *do* work. A recent Department of Labor study shows that over a million young mothers were out of the labor force because of child-care problems in 1986 —almost 25 percent of all mothers aged twenty-one to twenty-nine, and 40 percent of Hispanic and 30 percent of black mothers that age. For poor women *in* the labor force, child-care costs consumed more than a fourth of their entire weekly income. A national commitment to expand child care would go a long way toward eliminating some of the steepest barriers to self-support and economic independence. It would help to guarantee nurturing and competent care for children now vulnerable because they are too often left on their own or in disruptive and unstable child-care arrangements. And—coupled with a push for better wages and working conditions for

child-care workers—it could significantly expand the opportunity structure and contribute to the economic and social
development of poor communities.

Both family leaves and better child care would help reduce
drug abuse by preventing one of its important precursors—
child abuse and neglect. So too would programs specifically
designed to provide help with child rearing to families at high
risk of mistreating children. But our never-generous family
support system has been badly undermined by the federal
government's retreat from social provision since the early
1980s. By 1990, as a major review concludes, the social-service
system for children and families had become "so constricted
that children can gain access to help only if they have been
abused or severely neglected, are found delinquent, or run
away."

As with public health care, child and family services have
been savaged by budget cuts just when "there are more cases
(and more difficult cases) coming to them for help." What
money is available is largely devoted to dealing with family
emergencies after the fact; it goes mainly to child protection
and out-of-home placement and rarely to preventive services,
and then usually only to the worst cases and not to "troubled
children and families whose problems are serious but who are
not necessarily in crisis." This means that we have few chances
to intervene in high-risk families until they have collapsed, at
which point the children are likely to be carted off to foster
care or the juvenile-justice system. That is one reason why, as
we've seen, the foster-care caseload in many cities has skyrocketed under the impact of the drug epidemic of the eighties.

Fortunately, we are beginning to learn a good deal about
what kinds of programs for families can prevent this trajectory.
The Prenatal-Early Infancy Program (PEIP) in Elmira, New
York, for example, sent trained public health nurses to offer
guidance and support to "high risk" parents just before the
birth of their child and for up to two years thereafter—
covering everything from nutrition to child-rearing skills to

problems of daily economic survival. Careful evaluations showed that PEIP was extremely successful in reducing child abuse; women visited by the nurses had roughly one-fifth as many cases of child abuse as a control group without their help. PEIP, however, was significantly weakened by budget cuts during the 1980s, as were many other promising prevention efforts. As an unusually forthright report commissioned by the Bush administration commented in 1990, "Investment in prevention of child maltreatment remains inadequate, fragmentary, and inefficient."

But the failure to make that investment is shortsighted and self-defeating, for these programs are both effective and relatively inexpensive. More comprehensive family support programs, capable of addressing the entire range of problems that afflict families at high risk of child maltreatment and drug abuse, may be even more promising, and there are now several encouraging examples.

One is the Center for Family Life in Brooklyn, New York, which offers a broad range of services to a largely poor and working-class population, including

• A play group for children aged six months to three years, and a simultaneous support group for parents.

• A weekly group to help mothers of children aged three and four improve their parenting skills.

• Extensive help for parents in dealing with schools and other community agencies to ensure that they get the educational, income support, housing, child-care, vocational, and home-making help they need.

• Comprehensive after-school, five-day-a-week child care.

• A two-night-a-week program of recreation, dramatic arts, and tutoring for teenagers.

• Community-wide forums and workshops on various parenting
issues and concerns.

   This program is still too new to have been formally evaluated.
But similar family support programs across the country have,
and the results are strongly encouraging. We know that well-
designed, well-staffed, and comprehensive family support programs improve the quality of family life and child-rearing skills
and can reduce the risks of child abuse and neglect. They can
consequently play an important role, along with broader national family support policies, in mitigating the family problems
that contribute to drug abuse. As with community-based health
clinics, whether we develop these programs under public or
nonprofit auspices is not the crucial issue. What matters is
whether we provide sufficient resources for them to succeed.
And again, as with health clinics, family support services are
labor-intensive. There are critical roles for child-development
workers, counselors, community advocates, teachers—all opportunities for rewarding and useful work.
   The same potential to create jobs while simultaneously delivering much-needed services holds for another important component of an antidrug family policy—the expansion and
enhancement of the Head Start program for preschool children. Enough has now been written about the benefits of Head
Start—in reducing school failure, delinquency, welfare dependency, and drug use—that we needn't recapitulate it here.
If anything, the program's benefits are now sometimes
exaggerated—as if Head Start were a magic bullet for the
problems of inner-city children and youth. It is not. The
benefits of Head Start are significant but limited, and most
tend to wear off once children enter regular schools and
confront otherwise unchanged conditions in their communities
and families. But within well-charted limits, Head Start is an
effective program, and is now widely recognized as such across
most of the political spectrum. Yet despite increases in federal

support in the early 1990s, it remains underfunded, and consequently forced to choose between providing poor services for all eligible children and providing better-quality services for a few. Extending Head Start to all eligible children and upgrading the quality of teaching and supportive services will require more funding—especially for better training, pay, and benefits (in the late 1980s, half of all Head Start workers earned less than $10,000 a year). As it stands, the low pay leads to rapid and disruptive staff turnover, which diminishes the quality of care; and not enough staff have sufficient training to cope with the increasingly complex problems (including parental drug abuse) children are bringing with them to the program.

ASSURING SHELTER

The housing emergency for low-income Americans figures prominently in our drug crisis. Levels of drug abuse in homeless populations are among the highest anywhere; more generally, the shortage of affordable housing contributes to the rootlessness, family stress, and community fragmentation that help to encourage endemic drug abuse. According to one recent estimate, there are less than five million low-rent housing units, public or private, to house over eleven million poor families in the United States. Without addressing that gap, we will make little headway against either the homeless drug problem or the larger community erosion that the housing crisis fosters.

To be sure, part of what homeless drug abusers need is the same as what other drug abusers need—better and more accessible treatment, health care, and harm-reduction programs. But it's increasingly clear that those services, even if carefully designed, won't suffice if the recipients have no housing more stable than temporary shelters or short-term "transitional" accommodation. A few innovative community-based programs that have linked drug (and alcohol) treatment with affordable housing have had promising results, but they have been small and nowhere near sufficient to meet the need. Nothing short of a national commitment to affordable housing for the poor will do that.

Here too, as with family policy or employment strategies, there are valuable foreign lessons we can draw upon. Like drug abuse itself, the problems of homelessness and inadequate housing are conspicuously greater in the United States than in most other advanced industrial societies. One reason is that their more generous income-support policies mitigate the extreme poverty that usually precedes homelessness; another is that most other advanced countries make the public provision of secure housing a national priority.

To witness the dramatic impact of those more generous housing policies, we need look no farther than Canada—where federal, local, and provincial governments have long taken responsibility for helping "those not served by the private housing marketplace." To be sure, there are homeless and poorly housed people in Canada; but, as Peter Dreier and J. David Hulchanski point out, Canada does not have slums that match the level of physical and social deterioration in the inner cities of the United States, "nor are Canada's cities overwhelmed with citizens sleeping in shelters, streets, and subways." Even after cutbacks by a conservative federal government in the mid-1980s, Canada—with roughly one-ninth the United States' population—was providing about the *same* number of units of publicly supported housing for low-income people. Bringing our dwindling public-housing effort up to the level of Canada (or France or Scandinavia) would amount to a giant step against the roots of drug abuse—by stabilizing housing (and cushioning severe poverty) for those most at risk, enhancing community cohesion, and generating substantial numbers of new, community-sustaining jobs.

As a beginning, we should steadily restore the roughly $25 billion in annual housing assistance chopped from the federal budget during the 1980s, and use it to fund a program to build, restore, and rehabilitate the low-income housing stock.

This does not require vast new fortresslike housing projects that jam the disorganized poor together in impoverished isolation; nor does it require a massive federal bureaucracy to oversee it. In the United States—as in Canada—the most innovative new low-income housing has been small-scale, and developed primarily by nonprofit groups—notably churches and local community-development corporations. Those groups have by now acquired an impressive record of creating successful housing projects, in many of which significant tenant involvement and management ensure a considerable sense of ownership and social cohesion. We know, in short, both from American and foreign experience, how to build and run affordable housing; what's missing are the resources to match the need.

With those resources in hand, we could put a great many now marginalized people to work. The House Committee on Banking, Finance, and Urban Affairs estimates that a $15.7 billion investment in assistance to state and local governments under already existing federal housing and community-development programs would generate over $29 billion in private construction contracts and create almost 600,000 jobs. Spending $2 billion to restore now-vacant public-housing units to livable condition would make 80,000 such units available for occupancy while creating almost 40,000 jobs. Similarly, $2.65 billion for low-income loans for rural housing, just to cope with the current backlog of applications for assistance, would underwrite 50,000 new homes in hard-hit rural communities and simultaneously provide 46,000 new jobs. All of this could be achieved within existing federal programs, and the dollar amounts would still leave us significantly below the levels we maintained in our federal housing effort during the 1970s—even then minimal by international standards.

Other eminently feasible housing policies promise similar gains in employment. Weatherization of low-income housing, for example, is highly labor-intensive, employing three times as many people per dollar of investment as highway construction. But, as Michael Renner of the Worldwatch Institute points out in a recent review, only about one-fifth of eligible households have been assisted under federal and state weatherization programs. Serving the remaining 18 million households would generate up to 1.8 million "job years" of useful work.

REBUILDING THE INFRASTRUCTURE

After more than a decade of particularly egregious neglect, America's physical infrastructure—its roads, bridges, streets, waterways, transportation systems—has become so decrepit that observers across the political spectrum, and even corporate executives, have begun to fear that its collapse will further cripple an already lurching economy. As Robert Heilbroner has written, the infrastructure is the "public underpinnings without which a society cannot be healthy or an economy prosperous": it is fundamental to both the quality of life and the nation's "collective efficiency." Yet federal spending on building and maintaining the infrastructure was cut almost in half during the 1980s—from a high of close to 5 percent of all federal outlays in 1977 to just 2.5 percent in 1990. As with public health care or family policy, this distinguishes us— unfavorably—from most of our industrial competitors: we are, Heilbroner notes, "the only major industrial society that is not renewing and expanding its infrastructure," and the consequences are painfully apparent in the cities. In New York, "more than half of the city's 842 bridges are considered structurally deficient." Fifty have "large holes through their decks." Another 60 are supported by wooden pillars "that must often be replaced because homeless people are stealing them and using them for firewood."

The Congressional Budget Office estimates that rebuilding the decayed infrastructure would cost roughly $60 billion a year over ten years, and other estimates range much higher. If even the low estimates are correct, a sustained investment in the infrastructure would generate massive numbers of new jobs—which would in turn help firm up the *social* infrastructure. Ten billion dollars per year dedicated to a comprehensive public-works program would supply close to a quarter of a million new jobs.

Some investments would be especially fruitful. During the 1980s, for example, while we spent substantial sums on airports and highways, we also slashed funds for rail transportation, which is one reason why rail transport remains so rudimentary in this country compared to many others. In 1980 we spent $1.6 billion of federal funds on railroads; by 1990, less than $50 million. A serious program to rebuild and modernize the railroads would stimulate the economy, reduce traffic congestion and air pollution, and simultaneously expand the opportunity structure.

Linking a national program to build and maintain the infrastructure with a national youth-employment policy, in particular, makes sense from every point of view. With both in place, we could employ tens of thousands of young people now condemned to the margins of the economy and train them in work that helps rebuild their communities and enhance the indispensable physical foundation of the country. The work would be challenging, often physically demanding, and visibly useful; it could help transform bleak and depressed communities into places residents could be proud of—all at considerable benefit to the larger economy.

This list of critical needs is by no means exhaustive. There is more to be said about the schools, for example, and about the importance of tough enforcement of antidiscrimination laws. But let me sum up the powerful advantages these five strategies share. They would dramatically expand the structure of opportunities for those now denied the chance to contribute to their society. They would achieve what is sometimes called "primary prevention" by reducing the enormous social deficits that lead to endemic drug use. They would deliver critical health and social services to those most at risk. And they would do so in ways that mesh with our most fundamental social values. They would make people more productive and less dependent. They would strengthen families and stabilize local communities. And they would improve the functioning of the economy by making better use of our human resources.

Would putting these strategies into place eliminate drug abuse in America? Of course not. But they are a beginning, and without them we will forever be swimming upstream. It may be objected that the intricacies of the economics of housing rehabilitation or prenatal care take us very far from the topic of drug policy. But it is precisely because we have ignored these broader needs that we have failed to make much headway against drugs. And we will continue to fail unless we make a sustained commitment to public investment in our social and physical infrastructure.

That a healthier, less volatile, and less drug-ridden America would require what the Kerner Commission called a "massive, compassionate, and sustained" infusion of public resources (along with better jobs and training in the private economy) has been understood for a quarter of a century. The moderate and bipartisan commission had no qualms about calling for "one million new jobs in the public sector" in order to stimulate an upward spiral in the beleaguered cities. Others, too, warned that without a commitment to public investment on a new scale, we could expect worsening inner-city disintegration. And they pointed specifically to the "enormous potential," as one observer put it, of setting to "work on the needs of the community":

> Our cities are in dire need of rebuilding, especially at the
> core. In most major cities, the great supplies of housing
> built to accommodate the influx of migrants, from rural
> areas and abroad, in the early part of this century are
> long overdue for rehabilitation or replacement. Our public
> facilities are in similar need of repair. Center-city hospitals,

schools, and colleges are notorious for the deterioration of their physical plants. Our cities' beaches are polluted and their parklands eroded, the parks and playgrounds inadequate to the minimum demands of their people. In the coming years, these needs will multiply almost beyond measure. If we begin now to repair the decay of the past and meet the needs of the future, we can create hundreds of thousands of jobs directly, and indirectly, millions more.

The description could fit any major American city in the 1990s, but the words were written by then-Senator Robert Kennedy in 1967. The root of the spreading social tragedy of the cities today is that we did *not* go on to "meet the needs of the future" by investing in urban communities when their needs were less overwhelming. Instead, blinded by the ideologies of the past (and crippled by our fiscal commitment to the Vietnam War), we took a fateful wrong turn. As a result, we approach the twenty-first century lagging farther and farther behind the rest of the industrial world—hobbled by a resistance to using public investment for public purposes which our more successful competitors have long since abandoned. That resistance has not only brought us the most dreadful urban conditions in the developed world, but is increasingly undermining our ability to keep up in economic terms. Choosing the strategy of inclusion involves much more than compassion for the unfortunate: it now carries our best hope of survival as a First World economy.

I I

How will we pay for it? Writing in the more expansive and hopeful 1960s, Isidor Chein was able to brush aside the question with some impatience. Any society, he wrote, that "sets numerical values to the lives and essential dignities of human beings is, at least, sick, if not positively moribund." Not even the most "callous budget-balancer or meeter of payrolls," he continued, "dares abandon human beings to their misery in undissimulated dollars-and-cents terms." He spoke of the "sense of vitality that comes with the tightening of belts to make available greater resources in the service of dedicated purpose," and reminded his readers that social resources to meet urgent needs "do not come in fixed quantities, but in proportion to the intensity of the will that employs them."

The last insight is no less true today, though we have regressed a long way from the more generous spirit of Chein's era. Financing a strategy of inclusion is a political and moral issue, not simply an economic one. What seem on the surface to be arguments over where we will find the money turn out on closer inspection to be arguments about whether we should spend it at all. In the 1990s, when the federal government has found more than $100 billion over two and a half years to *begin* bailing out the savings-and-loan industry, without popular vote or assent, no one can seriously doubt that we possess the resources to launch a comprehensive strategy to extend social and economic citizenship to all Americans—if we truly wish to. The real issue is how to raise and spend those resources in ways that best contribute to economic health and that fit a larger sense of what we want our society to look like in the nineties and into the next century. Consistent with those aims, there are three key sources of funds for a new kind of "war" on the roots of drug abuse:

CONSERVING HUMAN RESOURCES

One of the most significant, but least discussed, sources of funds in the long term is the savings we will achieve through the strategy of inclusion itself. There is a clear analogy here with our approach to *natural* resources. We now understand that the single most important source of energy for a growing economy is not oil, coal, or nuclear power; it is the energy savings gained through conservation and improved efficiency, which allow us to achieve the same measure of economic activity with less input of resources. In the same way, what we save by *not* having to spend to contain the destructive consequences of mass social exclusion and deprivation means that many features of a strategy of inclusion literally pay for themselves. In some cases, we have detailed and precise estimates of the magnitude of those savings. For each young person who goes through the Job Corps we *gain* $5,000. For every 10,000 infants we keep *out* of intensive postnatal care we save $20 million a *day*. Every 100,000 young people kept out of prison saves us $2.5 billion annually in operating costs alone. If we add in the economic benefits of a better-trained, healthier workforce, the savings become enormous.

What we generally ignore in conventional discussions of social spending is the fundamental truth that inequality is expensive. The waste of productive potential and rampant social pathology that invariably go with it are among the most costly items on any budget, and they have now mounted to the point where state and local governments can no longer bear the burden. As we've seen, the result is a vicious cycle; reactive spending to repair damage we could have prevented makes it impossible to find resources for preventive programs. And thus we spiral endlessly downwards. Reversing that cycle is therefore not only socially progressive but economically urgent.

The same logic holds for other kinds of savings from the creative use of public investment. We could pay for every preventive public-health measure I've suggested by moving from a cumbersome and irrationally complex system of private health-care financing to a publicly controlled, single-payer health-care system like those in Canada and many European countries. Precise estimates vary, but few doubt that the savings would be enormous. Steffie Woolhandler and David Himmelstein of the Harvard Medical School estimate that had the administration of health care in the United States been as efficient as Canada's in 1987, we would have saved between $69 billion and $83 billion—a sum that could guarantee care for the more than 30 million uninsured Americans and simultaneously underwrite the cost of a dramatically expanded system of preventive public-health care for America's stricken cities and rural areas. An even larger estimate comes from a recent study funded by the Robert Wood Johnson Foundation, which calculates that adopting a Canadian-style system would save $241 billion annually, even after spending $14 billion to insure those now not covered—about half the savings coming from reduced administrative costs alone.

Similar savings are achievable through spending on infrastructure. Research by the economist David Aschauer suggests that investment in public works may generate up to three times as much overall economic stimulation as equivalent amounts put into private hands. Other estimates are less spectacular, but across most of the political spectrum there is little disagreement that well-targeted investment in infrastructure—especially in maintenance of existing public facilities—pays back far more than it costs up front. And it holds the promise of generating even greater returns by helping to restore the United States to economic competitiveness. While we allow our public capital to wither, countries without our crippling aversion to public investment are now moving farther and farther ahead of us: The Japanese have embarked on $60 billion worth of public-works projects in the early 1990s; the French have committed $100 billion to the development of high-speed rail systems; the Germans plan to spend even more to rebuild and modernize the industrial base of the former East Germany. Our failure to commit comparable resources to critical public investment is accelerating our precipitous decline into a second-rank economic power. The resources we generate by spending now to bring our infrastructure up to the level common in many other industrial nations are such that, as Heilbroner has written, the investments "could be thought of as costing nothing."

A TWENTY-FIRST-CENTURY TAX SYSTEM

But most of those savings are realized only in the long term, and a shift to a strategy of inclusion will require considerable initial spending. One source is the military budget, to which we'll return. The other is to bring our tax policy closer to those of most European countries. We now tax far less than most other developed nations. Our overall tax revenue was about 30 percent of gross domestic product in 1990—the lowest percentage among all nations of the Organization for Economic Cooperation and Development, including such semideveloped countries as Turkey, Portugal, and Greece. German taxes, *before* their massive program of public investment in the former East Germany, were 38 percent of GDP. These amounts may seem blandly technical in the abstract, but they translate into staggering differences in our ability to invest for public purposes. "At current levels of economic activity," Felix Rohatyn writes, raising our taxes to match the *old* West German level would generate an astonishing $400 billion a year. Only one-twentieth of that amount would be needed to more than triple our current investment in federal employment and training programs. Indeed, with *each* percentage point that we brought our tax revenues closer to Germany's, as a proportion of GDP, we would raise more than $50 billion a year, a sum considerably greater than *all* existing federal spending on education, training, employment, and social services combined. And German taxes are in the *middle* of the European range. The Scandinavian countries, France, Holland, and Austria tax much higher. Their relatively higher tax burdens have apparently not hurt their ability to compete in the international economic arena.

But we should not raise taxes without simultaneously *shifting* the tax burden as well—to offset the extraordinary upward redistribution of income of the past twelve years. Nearly 75 percent of the nation's entire gain in personal income between 1977 and 1989 went to the wealthiest 5 percent of the population—and 60 percent of it went to the top 1 percent alone. A substantial part of that shift reflects unprecedented tax give-aways to the wealthy. Tax cuts for the upper 1 percent of the income scale since 1978 cost the Treasury, in one estimate, over $160 billion annually in lost revenues.

Restoring the tax system to the level of progressivity of the late 1970s, before the full unleashing of the strategy of in-equality, would generate close to $1 trillion from the wealthiest 10 percent of the population alone by the start of the new century. Simply creating a 38 percent upper tax bracket for the highest income earners (who now pay no more than 28 percent) would, according to Jeff Faux of the Economic Policy Institute, produce roughly $60 billion over three years.

All such estimates are necessarily rough ones, but few dis-agree on the general magnitudes of public resources we would free up simply by restoring the hardly egalitarian tax structure we enjoyed prior to the rapacious 1980s. And doing so would not only raise enough resources to begin to underwrite a strategy of inclusion; it would also send the less tangible, but essential, cultural message that as a society we value things other than the accumulation of private wealth and the con-spicuous display of consumer goods.

It is crucial that new revenues raised through higher taxes be *specifically* directed toward productive investment in human resources—not simply dissipated in paying for the routine costs of government, or for purely reactive social programs. That may call for creating a special fund dedicated explicitly to public social investment. Few Americans, realistically, will sup-port higher taxes unless it can be demonstrated that the money is spent in ways that bring tangible and positive results for the quality of life and the character of our cities. What we do now is politically, as well as economically, untenable; we ask citizens to shell out considerable sums to support measures that are destined to fail—and that are guaranteed, since they do not address the causes of the social ills to which they respond, to require continual infusions of new money. Most Americans are put off by that kind of spending, and they are right; it is that kind of unproductive use of public money that has given public spending of any kind a bad name. Opinion polls consistently show that large majorities favor spending that results in more productive and more competent citizens; but they do not like "handouts," and they do not like waste. Those who pay taxes have a right to expect better, and those who spend them have an obligation to show that the money will be well and productively spent.

SEIZING THE PEACE DIVIDEND

The third source of funds for a strategy of inclusion is the military budget. There is no question that the "peace dividend" from the end of superpower hostilities between the United States and the former Soviet Union is potentially enormous. The question is whether we will use it in productive ways or squander it.

It was the perceived fiscal needs of the Vietnam War that derailed our budding attempts to confront the roots of the urban crisis in the 1960s, and the often exaggerated Soviet threat that kept us off track thereafter. With the end of the Cold War, the last justification for neglect of public investment in urban America has evaporated. Between 50 and 70 percent of our total military budget over the last decade has gone specifically for defense against Soviet and Warsaw Pact forces —a sum of between $150 and $210 billion a year. A 1991 study by William Kaufman and John Steinbrunner estimates that even relatively modest reductions in those weapons now devoted to defending us against that rapidly dwindling threat could save up to $620 billion through the 1990s (other measures, such as cooperative security agreements that would shift greater economic responsibility for global defense onto countries like Japan and Germany, would add to the total). Those sums are almost too large to comprehend, but breaking them into smaller pieces illustrates the potential. At this writing, for example, the current administration proposes adding five additional B-2 long-range bombers to the fifteen now authorized. The planes have no purpose other than to defend against a military power capable of launching massive bombing attacks on the United States. With the breakup of the Soviet Union, it takes considerable imagination to come up with a rationale for five more of them. The $3.6 billion that will be paid for the five *additional* bombers in fiscal year 1993 is about twice as much as we spend on all training programs for disadvantaged youth and adults under the Job Training Partnership Act.

Without a shift of military resources to pressing civilian needs, there is a very real danger that peace could *accelerate* America's economic and social deterioration. Defense spending has been our most important source of public employment and job training since the 1950s. It has been especially critical to the livelihoods and advancement of minority workers. It is widely agreed that even the defense cuts now envisioned by the current administration could throw close to 1 million military personnel and civilian employees of the Defense Department out of work, along with another 800,000 workers in private defense-related industries. The latter employed nearly 1.8 million Americans in the mid-1980s, and accounted for close to one in ten manufacturing jobs.

Most research suggests that transferring skills and resources from defense-related industries to civilian projects would result in a net *increase* in the number of jobs in the U.S. economy, because the more labor-intensive civilian public economy generates more jobs per dollar of investment. The Michigan-based Employment Research Associates estimates that by shifting about one-third of our 1990 military spending to civilian needs, we would lose 1.7 million military-related jobs, but gain 2.2 million civilian ones, with the biggest gains in construction, state and local government, and service employment. But those gains will be realized *only* if we move deliberately, and quickly, to put the savings from military reductions to work on civilian *public* needs. If we do not, the outbreak of peace will mean dumping close to 2 million service personnel and defense workers from relatively highly skilled and well-paying jobs into a declining labor market in a generally weak economy. That would be a tragic waste of skills; and it would further exacerbate the social crisis in America's cities.

Fortunately, most Americans recognize the opportunity—and they are willing to make the most of it. In a New York *Times* poll in 1990, more than three out of five respondents said that if the United States were able to "save a lot of money on defense in the next few years," it should be used to "fight problems like drugs and homelessness." Only one in five wanted to use the savings to reduce the deficit, and just one in ten to lower taxes. Two years later, a Los Angeles *Times* poll similarly found that only about one in five respondents wanted to spend the peace dividend to finance a tax cut. In general, close to four in five Americans want to see more spending on domestic public needs like health care and infrastructure, and over two-thirds want to pay for them in part through higher taxes on the wealthy.

As this suggests, moving to address the causes of drug abuse through public investment in social reconstruction is far from Utopian. Given the chance, most Americans would support a strategy of inclusion—especially once they understood that most of its elements are already in place in countries that are in many ways like us, but that lack not only our drug problem but also our chronically volatile cities, our unsafe streets, and our vast expanses of urban and rural poverty. What is truly Utopian is to imagine that there is some shortcut to the end of the drug crisis, or that we can reverse the deepening disaster of the cities by stubbornly clinging to a philosophy of "business as usual." Getting serious about drugs will require a boldness and unfettered social imagination that is never abundant and that has been conspicuously absent in the past decade of denial and cynicism. The dramatic changes in the world balance of power now make boldness a real option: lack of money is simply no longer a valid excuse. What holds us back from doing what we should have done a generation ago, more than anything else, is a kind of corrosive inertia—the knee-jerk rejection of public solutions to public problems, the vain hope that somehow "market forces" or piecemeal tinkering will bail out the cities, the resistance to a positive role for government in creating a sustaining and inclusive society for all. Nearly thirty years ago, Kenneth Clark wrote that the persistence of the dire social conditions of the urban ghetto reflected what he called a "primitive hostility to the creative use of human intelligence." A generation later, that hostility is still very much with us. But if we are ever to deal with the drug problem, much less begin to bring enduring peace, hope, and dignity to our stricken cities, we must put that crippling mentality behind us, once and for all.

A chance this good may not come again. We must not let it pass by; it is the best hope we have had in a generation to finally take up the long-postponed challenge to relieve the human misery that lies at the heart of our continuing drug crisis. We have, after all, been trying the alternatives for forty years. We have tried moral exhortation. We have tried neglect. We have tried punishment. We have even, more grudgingly, tried treatment. We have tried everything but improving lives.

Appendix

A Short Guide to the Hard Drugs

Considerable mythology and misinformation surround our public discussion of illicit drugs. This appendix is meant as a short review of what we know about the effects, methods of use, and long-term consequences of several of the most commonly abused of them. I do not include "soft" drugs like marijuana and LSD, but do include inhalants—which, while they are legal substances, are widely abused, often with unusually troubling consequences. The reader should be aware that our knowledge about the long-term consequences of drug use is often tentative; some of what we know, for example, is derived from animal studies, and may not always be directly applicable to humans. In addition, it is difficult to separate out the specific effects over time of any *single* drug of abuse from those of others the user may be taking simultaneously—including alcohol—and from those that result from other aspects of the abuser's lifestyle.

Cocaine is one of the "stimulant" drugs—a category that also includes the amphetamines—and is widely considered the most potent among them. It acts on the central nervous system in ways that increase pleasure and create a sense of well-being, confidence, and sometimes euphoria. Physically, cocaine dilates the pupils, increases heart rate and blood pressure, and raises body temperature. The intensity and pace of these effects depends on the route of administration as well as the dose level. The most common form—"powder" cocaine, or cocaine hydrochloride—is taken intranasally (snorted) and, less often, injected intravenously. Injection greatly speeds the body's absorption of cocaine, and is accordingly the route of choice for those wishing a more powerful and rapid jolt of the drug. Intranasally, cocaine's first effects appear within three to five minutes, and peak effects in fifteen to twenty minutes; peak effects are reached within only five minutes after injection. Cocaine's effects tend to be quite short-lived: with IV use the effects typically wear off after thirty to forty minutes, somewhat longer for intranasal use. The short duration of what are extremely powerful effects helps account for the tendency of heavy cocaine users toward "binges" of repeated use.

Frequent cocaine use produces a number of distinct effects, both physical and psychological, and even occasional use can pose medical risks—notably cardiovascular problems, including heart attacks and strokes. Cocaine's effect on the cardiovascular system is complex and not entirely understood, but one clear problem is the drug's tendency to increase heart rate and blood flow while simultaneously constricting blood vessels, thus increasing the risk of blood vessel damage and stroke. Whether heavy or prolonged cocaine use leads to any long-range neurological consequences is not entirely clear; the research results are mixed. Heavy use of cocaine does clearly produce a definite "abstinence syndrome" when users stop taking the drug. The cocaine "high" is typically followed by a "crash," characterized by agitation, depression, fatigue, and anxiety. According to some researchers, the crash is followed by a withdrawal phase that may last up to several days, characterized by listlessness and what is often described as a state of "pleasurelessness" or "anhedonia" that generates powerful cravings for cocaine.

In recent years, cocaine has reemerged from relative obscurity to become one of the most widely abused drugs in the United States. In 1991, according to the NIDA Household Survey, close to 12 percent of Americans—almost 24 million —had used the drug in their lifetime, 1.9 million in the past month; the latter figure especially is generally regarded as a considerable underestimate. In 1990, a gram of cocaine sold, depending on purity and location, for about $90 to $120 in most cities.

Crack is a smokable form of cocaine, created by mixing cocaine hydrochloride, which resists heat and does not convert readily into smoke, with baking soda and water and heating them. The result is a waxy "rock" that may make a cracking sound when it is smoked in a pipe (often called a "base pipe")— which, according to some observers, is the source of the name. (Crack is also called, among other things, "rocks" or "hubba.") For many users, crack has two advantages over powder cocaine. Most importantly, smoking provides a faster and more powerful effect: inhaled cocaine apparently can reach the brain in about eight seconds, and its effects reach their peak within a few minutes. In the short run, too, crack is quite inexpensive; in the early 1990s, small rocks were available in New York for as little as $3, and even lower street prices have been reported. But because crack's effects are even more short-lived than those of powder cocaine, as well as more intense, the urge toward repeated use is particularly powerful and the cumulative cost can mount very quickly. At the same time, street research makes clear that crack is not *necessarily* the all-consuming drug often pictured in the media; many use it sparingly or drop it altogether after a few tries.

Though crack is a product of the 1980s, and hit the streets with full force only in the middle of that decade, it resembles "freebase" cocaine, which has been with us considerably longer. "Freebasing" is another way of rendering cocaine hydrochloride smokable by removing the hydrochloride, in this case through a dangerous chemical process involving highly flammable ether. Crack is produced through a far simpler, less dangerous, and less costly process, which helps account for its appeal.

In addition to sharing the health risks of cocaine generally, crack also introduces others specifically related to smoking, notably the danger of lung damage; some researchers have described a specific syndrome they call "crack lung." Unlike powder cocaine, too, crack smoking presents the risk of passive inhalation of fumes by others, including children.

In 1991, the Household Survey estimated that just under 2

percent of Americans, or almost 3.9 million people, had ever used crack, including slightly under half a million who had used it in the past month. Given the biases in this survey away from the poorest, most marginal populations, these figures are surely considerably underestimated.

Heroin is the most significant of the "opiate" drugs—that is, drugs derived ultimately from the opium poppy (or synthetic varieties that are chemically similar); others include codeine and hydromorphone (Dilaudid). Opiates are also often called "narcotics," which can be confusing because the latter term is also sometimes used, incorrectly, to describe all illegal hard drugs, including cocaine. The opiates were originally used primarily as pain relievers, and that remains their most important legal use. Opium and its derivatives came into wide use in a variety of medicinal preparations in the nineteenth century, which resulted in a substantial addiction problem. Heroin was synthesized from morphine—itself a derivative of opium—in the late nineteenth century, and was originally believed to be as useful at killing pain as morphine but without the same potential for addiction. It flourished in inner-city America after World War II, and has surged and receded several times since. Today heroin is once again on the rise.

Heroin may be smoked, snorted, or injected—either subcutaneously ("skin popping") or intravenously. Initially, heroin is often experienced unpleasantly, frequently causing nausea; once mastered, it produces a strong sense of euphoria and content and a pronounced dependence, or tolerance. As with other drugs, heroin's effects depend on purity and route of administration; intravenous use produces the most pronounced impact and greatest dependence. Heroin smoking ("chasing the dragon"), more common in Britain than in the United States, is said to be on the rise in some American cities in response to the risks of illness—especially AIDS—that result from IV use. IV heroin use typically produces euphoric effects within two to five minutes after injection, lasting up to thirty minutes or more—often followed by a longer period of drowsiness and lethargy. Extensive heroin use over time produces a well-defined "withdrawal" response when the drug is discontinued; addicts suffer from abdominal cramps, diarrhea, runny nose, sweating, chills, and often nausea—though the strength of these effects is sometimes exaggerated, especially where the purity of the drug is low.

A variety of medical problems, ranging from hepatitis to heart infections, have traditionally been associated with IV heroin use, largely because of the frequent use of unsterile equipment and needle sharing among users. There is also a very real danger of overdose; death most often results primarily from respiratory failure. Some research, too, suggests that heroin may depress the immune system, making users especially vulnerable to a wide range of infections, including AIDS.

Illegal heroin appears in several different forms and comes from several different sources, including Southeast Asia, Southwest Asia, and Mexico. Southeast Asian heroin tends to be white, fine, and expensive; other varieties vary in cost and color, depending on purity and the kind and levels of contaminants it contains. Mexican heroin is often brown, and a variant called "black tar" heroin—a crudely processed product with the look and consistency of tar—became increasingly common in some cities during the 1980s. The purity of street heroin varies greatly, from as little as 1 or 2 percent to much higher levels (in Chicago in 1989, for example, average purity was about 13 percent), which increases the danger of overdose. High-quality white heroin in Chicago cost roughly $275 to $350 per gram in 1990; black tar heroin in San Diego cost considerably less, about $175 per gram. Heroin is often sold on the street in "bags" of various sizes, the smallest typically being a "dime bag," or $10 worth. Roughly 2.9 million Americans, according to the 1991 Household Survey, have ever used heroin; 700,000 in the past month. These figures understate the actual totals, since heroin use, especially heavy use, is known to be concentrated in parts of the population largely missed by the survey.

Methamphetamine is another stimulant, with effects that in many ways resemble those of cocaine. It is closely related to other members of the amphetamine family—some of which, like Dexedrine and Benzedrine, were in common use for years in the United States, mainly to relieve fatigue. Unlike heroin or cocaine, the amphetamines are entirely synthetic—they are not produced from plants that require any particular terrain or climate, and therefore can be produced anywhere the relevant chemicals can be assembled—a fact with great import for strategies to control illegal drugs by "interdicting" them at the borders. Indeed, methamphetamine is easily synthesized from fairly accessible chemicals, and can literally be produced in a bathroom or basement (novices often learn the precise formulas while in prison). There are thousands of illicit methamphetamine "laboratories" in the United States, mainly (but by no means exclusively) in the West and Southwest, where the drug is endemic: there were 775 reported methamphetamine lab seizures during 1987 alone.

Methamphetamine was widely and deliberately used as a stimulant by the Japanese in World War II to increase stamina among military personnel and war-plant workers; the widespread availability of the drug subsequently fed a major stimulant epidemic in Japan after the war. Methamphetamine remains a major part of the (relatively small) drug picture in Japan, as also in Sweden. The drug attained some notoriety, especially in the San Francisco Bay Area, during the late 1960s, when the "speed freak" became a fixture of the street drug scene.

Methamphetamine (also called "speed," "crank," "crystal," or "crystal meth") typically comes as either a whitish powder or as larger "crystals," and it may be snorted, injected, smoked, or heated on foil and inhaled. (A variety known as "ice," much in the news in the late 1980s, is a highly pure crystal meth-amphetamine, often smoked in a glass pipe.) As with cocaine, smoking and injection produce the fastest and most potent effects; indeed, methamphetamine's capacity to produce a rapid "rush" via smoking or IV use has given it in some quarters the reputation as a "white people's crack." The effects, however, are much longer-lasting than those of cocaine (usually several hours), and the longer duration is seen as a significant plus by serious users. As with cocaine, the overall effect is to increase the sense of well-being and capacity, to enhance a sense of self-esteem, to reduce the need for sleep, and (in the short term) to improve motor performance. "When I slammed [injected] the stuff," according to one respondent in a NIDA-sponsored study, "I would clean the house until it was clean, then I'd mess it up again just to clean it again."

Long-term or heavy use involves several well-established risks. Heavy users often fall into a cycle of several-day "binges" followed by an especially hard "crash" characterized by severe depression, irritability, anxiety, and insomnia. At the extreme, some researchers have described an "amphetamine psychosis" among heavy users which resembles paranoid schizophrenia, complete with auditory and visual hallucinations. Like cocaine, methamphetamine tends to speed up the heart and increase body temperature, and has been associated with cardiovascular problems and deaths from stroke, and, in some research, with long-term neurological damage. IV methamphetamine use, moreover, like all IV drug use, greatly increases the risks of AIDS and a variety of other needle-borne diseases. In 1990, a gram of methamphetamine cost $60 to $80 in San Diego, one of the centers of "crank" use in the United States. A "quarter" or quarter gram, enough for roughly four doses for a moderate user, cost about $25.

Phencyclidine (PCP) (sometimes called, among other things, "angel dust" or "killer weed") is another wholly synthetic drug, once used as an animal tranquilizer, which made its first street appearance in the 1960s. Like methamphetamine, it is mainly produced in clandestine laboratories, often with uneven quality and uncertain contaminants. PCP is an unusual drug with multiple and sometimes contradictory effects, and has a reputation, generally deserved, for potentially causing severe health problems and bizarre or violent behavior. It comes in several forms, ranging from capsules to powder and liquid; it is sometimes sprinkled on marijuana cigarettes (in California, called "Sherms") and smoked. Many users report a pleasant sense of numbness and detachment and/or feelings of power and a sense of great strength and unlimited capacity. PCP can also produce paranoia, intense anger and hostility, depression and a sense of impending doom; it is more closely linked to violence than any other illegal drug, though some researchers believe the links are often exaggerated, especially by the mass media. PCP can clearly produce mental states that closely resemble schizophrenia. Subjects in one recent study of PCP-abusing women reported that "I would fight anyone who touched me" and "My head would tell me things that were not true or were not there. It seems someone was always after me." Though the evidence is somewhat conflicting, PCP is widely feared to have adverse long-term neurological consequences, especially with heavy use.

Given phencyclidine's troubling and often unpredictable effects, it is somewhat astonishing that over 7 million Americans, according to the NIDA Household Survey, have used the drug in their lifetime—about 3.6 percent of the population. Phencyclidine reached something close to epidemic proportions in several American cities, including Washington, D.C., and St. Louis, in the 1980s, just before the flood of crack; in most areas, crack appears to have displaced PCP as the street drug of choice among its regular users. But it remains very much a reality in many inner cities and its potential for widespread abuse remains high—perhaps especially if crack's availability were to diminish.

Inhalants encompass a wide variety of substances, including volatile solvents (such as glue, gasoline, and paint thinner); aerosols (like spray paint or hair spray); anesthetics (including nitrous oxide and ether); and amyl and butyl nitrite ("poppers," used medically to relieve the pain of angina in heart patients and widely used recreationally in the belief that they enhance sexual pleasure). The solvents are the most troublesome part of the problem, and they are cheap and widely accessible: glue was once described by Edward Preble and his coworkers as the "10-cent hallucinogen." They can produce a sense of disorientation and light-headedness, sometimes with visual distortions, which may be felt as pleasurable. One study describes frequent inhalant abusers this way: "Their thought processes are slow, attention span is short, and short- and long-term memory functions are impaired." The solvents in particular are among the drugs with the clearest adverse long-term effects on neurological capacity and mental functioning.

Serious abuse of inhalants is primarily an affliction of the very young and poor: special concern has long been raised over high levels of inhalant abuse among Native American, Hispanic, and "poor white" youth, both rural and urban. In one study in a Hispanic community in the Southwest, four out of five inhalant abusers had started before their fourteenth birthday. Inhalants are an underappreciated part of the drug picture, and their abuse, according to the conventional measures, is both widespread and increasing: the 1991 Household Survey estimated that 11 million Americans had used inhalants in their lifetimes, including 1.2 million during the past month—again probably a significant underestimate of the true numbers of frequent users.

Straddling the territory between licit and illicit use are the sedative drugs, most notably the *barbiturates*, so called because they are derived from barbituric acid. The barbiturates are widely prescribed, indeed overprescribed, as sedatives (and as anticonvulsants); significant numbers of medical emergencies and deaths result from the abuse of prescription barbiturates each year. A few of them—including secobarbitol (Seconal, or "reds" in street language) and pentobarbitol (Nembutal, or "yellows")—are widely abused on the "street," often in combination with other drugs. Heavy doses lead to impaired judgment, confusion, loss of coordination, and slurred speech; at the extreme, to low blood pressure, reduced respiration, coma, and death. Barbiturates are highly addictive, with tolerance developing rapidly, leading to one of the most powerful (and potentially dangerous) withdrawal syndromes of any drug of abuse. They are particularly dangerous when used in combination with alcohol.

Sources: Yuet W. Cheung, Patricia G. Erickson, and Tammy C. Landau, "Experience of Crack Use: Findings from a Community-Based Sample in Toronto," *Journal of Drug Issues*, Vol. 21, No. 1, 1991; Raquel A. Crider and Beatrice A. Rouse, eds., *Epidemiology of Inhalant Abuse: An Update*, Rockville, MD, NIDA, 1988; U.S. Department of Justice, Drug Enforcement Administration, *Drugs of Abuse*, Washington, DC, Government Printing Office, 1989; James N. Hall, Richard S. Uchman, and Roman Dominguez, *Trends and Patterns of Methamphetamine Abuse in the United States*, Rockville, MD, NIDA, 1988; Statement of Jerome Jaffe, Select Committee on Narcotics Abuse and Control, U.S. House of Representatives, Hearing, *The Reemergence of Methamphetamine*, October 24, 1989; Marissa Miller and Nicholas Kozel, *Methamphetamine Abuse: Epidemiologic Issues and Implications*, Rockville, MD, NIDA, 1990; NIDA, Community Epidemiology Work Group, *Proceedings, June 1991*; NIDA, *Drug Abuse and Drug Abuse Research*, Rockville, MD, 1991; NIDA, *National Household Survey on Drug Abuse: Population Estimates 1991*, Rockville, MD, 1991; NIDA, *Problems of Drug Dependence*,

1990; Washington, DC, 1991; Reginald G. Smart, "Crack Cocaine Use: A Review of Prevalence and Adverse Effects," *American Journal of Drug and Alcohol Abuse*, Vol. 17, No. 1, 1991; John W. Spencer and John J. Boren, eds., *Residual Effects of Abused Drugs on Behavior*, Rockville, MD, NIDA, 1990.

Notes

Introduction

4 "Fault lines of our society": The phrase is from Mary Catherine Bateson and Richard Goldsby, *Thinking AIDS*, Reading, MA, Addison-Wesley, 1988, p. 2, where it is used to characterize the worldwide AIDS epidemic.

5 "Easy temptation": U.S. Office of National Drug Control Policy, *National Drug Control Strategy*, Washington, DC, Government Printing Office, 1989, p. 8.

Chapter 1: The American Nightmare

10–11 Smart study: Reginald Smart and Glenn Murray, "Narcotic Drug Abuse in 152 Countries: Social and Economic Conditions as Predictors," *International Journal of the Addictions*, Vol. 20, No. 5, 1985. Note that the data in this study predate both the crack epidemic and Singapore's recent development.

11 "Richer and more liberal": Mark Moore, quoted in Alan L. Otten, "Crisis in U.S. Spawns Theories But No Facts," *The Wall Street Journal*, September 6, 1989.

11 Drug abuse in "source" countries: See, for example, F. Raul Jeri, "Some Recent Facts About Drug Abuse in Peru," in National Institute on Drug Abuse (hereafter cited as NIDA), Community Epidemiology Work Group (hereafter cited as CEWG), *Proceedings, June 1990*, Washington, DC, 1990.

11 British observer: Susanne MacGregor, "Could Britain Inherit the American Nightmare?" *British Journal of Addiction*, Vol. 85, 1990, p. 863.
   Moreover, the advanced industrial country that may come closest, for heroin, is Australia, which also comes closest to matching our rates of poverty. On heroin in Australia, see Michael Gossop and Marcus Grant, "A Six-Country Survey of the Content and Structure of Heroin Treatment Programmes Using Methadone," *British Journal of Addiction*, Vol. 86, No. 9, September 1991, p. 1153.

11–12 European drug problems: See generally Richard Hartnoll et al., "A Multi-city Study of Drug Misuse in Europe," *Bulletin on Narcotics*, Vol. XLI, Nos. 1 and 2, 1989; Karl-Heinz Reuband, "Drug Abuse Trends in West Germany," in CEWG, *Proceedings, December 1989*; Anna Kokkevi, "Illicit Drug Abuse Among Adolescents in Western European Countries," in ibid. For a revealing analysis of Holland's (very limited) problem with what they call *gekookte coke*, or "cooked cocaine"—a form of crack—see Jean-Paul C. Grund et al., "Changing Cocaine Smoking Rituals in the Dutch Heroin Addict Population," *British Journal of Addiction*, Vol. 86, 1991, pp. 439–48.

11–12   English cocaine addicts: In 1989, only 530 cocaine users were reported, or "notified," to authorities by British medical practitioners. The figure certainly underestimates the actual extent of cocaine use, but gives a useful benchmark. Cited in Robert Power, "Patterns of Drug Use and Some Recent Research Developments in Britain," in CEWG, *Proceedings, June 1990*, p. II–87.

12   Drug-related deaths: British figure from Power, "Patterns of Drug Use," p. II–88; Dutch figure from W. Nabitz and T. Ouwehand, "Drug Abuse and Health Service in the Netherlands", in CEWG, *Procedings, December 1989*, p. III–33; methamphetamine-related deaths from NIDA, *Overview of Selected Drug Abuse Indicators*, Washington, DC, 1990, p. 15; Cocaine in Los Angeles, CEWG, *Proceedings, June 1990, Executive Summary*, Exhibit 1. France figure from François-Rodolphe Ingold, Sylvie Ingold, and Mohamed Toussirt, "Trends of Drug Use in France, 1985–1990," CEWG, *Proceedings, June 1991*, p. 353; Boston figure, Michael B. Hoffman, Milly Krakow, and JoAnn Kwass, "Drug Use Trends in Greater Boston and Massachusetts," CEWG, *Proceedings, June 1991*, p. 56.

12   European student surveys: Kokkevi, p. III–55; U.S. comparisons from NIDA, *Drug Use Among American High School Seniors, College Students, and Adults, 1975–1990*, Washington, DC, 1991, Table 10. The American students used hallucinogens at a rate six times that of French students, eight times that of Dutch students, and thirteen times that of Swedish students. Adolescents' use of illegal stimulants ranged from about a fourth of the U.S. rate (in parts of Belgium) to one thirty-third (in seven towns surveyed in Sweden). Similarly, a recent Norwegian survey shows that lifetime prevalence of cocaine use among Oslo adolescents was about 1.5 percent in 1989—versus 10 percent among American high school seniors: Olav Irgens-Jensen, "Changes in the Use of Drugs Among Norwegian Youth Year by Year from 1968 to 1989," *British Journal of Addiction*, Vol. 86, 1991, p. 1450. And a survey of Greek high school students found a lifetime prevalence of cocaine use of 1.6 percent—in a year when the rate for American high school seniors was 16 percent. Anna Kokkevi and Costas Stefanis, "The Epidemiology of Licit and Illicit Substance Use Among High School Students in Greece," *American Journal of Public Health*, Vol. 81, No. 1, January 1991, p. 51.

12   Drug-related killings: Figures are for 1988. England and Wales figure from United Nations, *Demographic Yearbook, 1990*, New York, 1992, p. 469. Washington figure from CEWG, *Proceedings, June 1991*, p. 331; and Federal Bureau of Investigation, *Uniform Crime Report, 1988*, Washington, DC, Government Printing Office, 1989, p. 79. Scandinavia figures (for Denmark, Norway, and Sweden) from Nordic Medico-Statistical Committee, *Health Statistics in the Nordic Countries, 1988*, Copenhagen, NOMESCO, 1990, pp. 54–55. In 1988,

61 percent, or 225, of Washington's 369 homicides were classed as drug-related, as compared with a total of 208 homicides in Denmark, Norway, and Sweden combined.

12–13 AIDS figures: Overall U.S. cases from U.S. Public Health Service, *Morbidity and Mortality Weekly Report*, January 17, 1992, pp. 28–29; Swedish figures from Swedish Ministry of Justice, *National Report on the Drug Abuse Situation in Sweden*, May 1991, p. 3; Dutch figure from Harry J. A. van Haastrecht, Johanna A. R. van den Hoek, Christiane Bardoux, Anne Leentvaar-Kuypers, and Roel A. Coutinho, "The Course of the HIV Epidemic Among Intravenous Drug Users in Amsterdam, the Netherlands," *American Journal of Public Health*, Vol. 81, 1991, p. 59. Figures for the U.S. on pediatric AIDS cases are from the National Centers for Disease Control, as reported in New York *Times*, April 4, 1991; Newark figure from New York *Times*, February 6, 1989. Comparative data from U.S. Bureau of the Census, *Current Population Reports*, Series P–95, No. 80, *Children's Well-Being: An International Comparison*, Washington, DC, 1990, p. 39.

14–15 Arrests: National trends from *Statistical Abstract of the United States, 1991*, p. 184. California arrests from State of California, Blue Ribbon Commission on Inmate Population Management, *Final Report*, Sacramento, CA, 1990, p. 73 (hereafter cited as Blue Ribbon Commission).

15 "High-level trafficking": In 1987, drug possession cases amounted to 22 percent of all felony court cases in Washington, 23 percent in Miami, and 29 percent in New Orleans: John A. Goerdt and John A. Martin, "The Impact of Drug Cases on Case Processing in Urban Trial Courts," *State Court Journal*, Fall 1989, p. 6. Some possession cases, to be sure, involve large quantities and substantial traffickers; but more involve low-level users and addicted street dealers. In general, whether the official charge is possession or sale, the drug war has swept up an extraordinary number of those street users and small-time dealers. In New York, for example, roughly 8,500 of the more than 20,000 drug offenders in the state's prisons are sentenced for the lowest-level felony categories; many are hapless privates in the street drug army given mandatory prison sentences under the state's Second Felony Offender law. (Robert Gangi, Correctional Association of New York, personal communication.) And the proportion of "small fry" is certainly greater in local jails.

15–16 Federal court backlog: New York *Times*, May 28, 1991. Sentence lengths: U.S. National Institute of Justice, *Searching for Answers*, Washington, DC, 1990, pp. 11–12. Ghetto twenty-two-year-old: Henry Weinstein and Charisse Jones, "Busted for Life," San Francisco *Chronicle*, March 25, 1990; LSD case: Dannie M. Martin, "Hard Time for Heavy Paper," San Francisco *Chronicle*, February 9, 1992.

16 Prison population growth: Michigan figure from testimony of Robert Brown, Director, Michigan Department of Corrections, in U.S. Congress, Senate,

Committee on Governmental Affairs, Hearing: *Criminal Justice in Crisis*, March 19, 1990, p. 160. California trends from Blue Ribbon Commission, p. 69; New York figure from New York State Coalition on Criminal Justice, *Update*, Albany, NY, February 1990, p. 5.

16 Florida possession figure: From Michael Isikoff, "Florida's Crackdown on Crime Is Setting Criminals Free," Washington *Post* Weekly Edition, January 14–20, 1991, p. 31. Parole revocations in California: Blue Ribbon Commission, p. 71.

17 Prison spending and overcrowding: $18 billion figure from Isikoff, p. 31; Michigan figure and quote: Brown testimony, p. 63.

17–18 Florida case: Isikoff, "Florida's Crackdown"; James Austin, *The Consequences of Escalating the Use of Imprisonment: The Case Study of Florida*, San Francisco, National Council on Crime and Delinquency, p. 7; David W. Rasmussen et al., *An Economic Analysis of Drug Crime and the Criminal Justice System*, Tallahassee, FL, Joint Legislative Management Committee, 1990, as cited in *Criminal Justice Abstracts*, December 1991, pp. 670–71.

18–19 California budget impacts: See, for example, "State's Budget Deficit Swells to $14.4 Billion," Los Angeles *Times*, May 18, 1991; "County Unveils Budget Proposal," Los Angeles *Times*, May 18, 1991; "L.A. Hears More Grim Fiscal News," Los Angeles *Times*, February 5, 1992; "Probation Cuts Mean Thousands Would Be Unsupervised," Oakland *Tribune*, March 13, 1992.

19 Prisonization: Sentencing Project, *Young Black Men and the Criminal Justice System*, Washington, DC, 1990; New York State Coalition for Criminal Justice and Correctional Association of New York, *Imprisoned Generation*, New York, 1991; Center on Juvenile and Criminal Justice, *Young African-American Men and the Criminal Justice System in California*, San Francisco, 1991; Nevada figure cited in Las Vegas *Review-Journal*, February 11, 1991; National Center on Institutions and Alternatives, *Hobbling a Generation: Young African-American Males in DC's Criminal Justice System*, Washington, DC, 1992. Housing figures calculated from *Statistical Abstract of the United States*, 1990, p. 353.

20 1967 estimates; President's Commission on Law Enforcement and the Administration of Justice, Task Force Report, *Narcotics and Drug Abuse*, Washington, D.C., Government Printing Office, 1967, pp. 2–8.

20–21 Bush quote: Cited in Robert Morgenthau, "Bush's Lip Service on Drugs," New York *Times*, March 9, 1989.

21 "Normalization" of crack: Cf. Joseph B. Treaster, "Inside a Crack House; How Drug Use Is Changing," New York *Times*, April 6, 1990.

22 High-school trends: From NIDA, *Drug Use Among American High School Seniors, College Students, and Young Adults, 1975–1990*, Table 12.

22–23 Household survey: Data from NIDA, *National Household Survey of Drug Abuse, Highlights, 1990,* pp. 66, 71; and NIDA *National Household Survey of Drug Abuse, Population Estimates, 1991,* p. 31. The surveys estimated a total of about 1,900,000 "past month" cocaine users in 1991, versus 1,600,000 in 1990.

23 DUF data: National Institute of Justice, *Drug Use Forecasting: July to September 1989,* Washington, D.C., U.S. Department of Justice, 1989, p. 4. Put another way, the DUF estimated that there were as many frequent cocaine users in the arrested population alone (in 61 cities) as the household survey had estimated for the entire U.S. population.

23 Juvenile results: Richard Dembo, Linda Williams, Eric D. Wish, and James Schmeidler, *Urine Testing of Detained Juveniles to Identify High-Risk Youth,* Washington, DC, National Institute of Justice, 1990, p. 3.

24 Atlanta study: Sally E. McNagny and Ruth M. Parker, "High Prevalence of Recent Cocaine Use and the Unreliability of Patient Self-Report in an Inner-City Walk-in Clinic," *Journal of the American Medical Association,* Vol. 267, No. 8, February 26, 1992.

24 Conventional households: The household survey's target is the "civilian noninstitutionalized population," which excludes most people living in institutions (like prisons or residential drug treatment facilities) and those without a place to live at all. It does include civilians living on military bases, in college dormitories, and some in homeless shelters—but not the transient homeless or others "on the street." See NIDA, *Population Estimates 1991,* p. 1, for a review of the survey methodology.

   The significance of these exclusions is also driven home in a recent study of drug offenders confined at New York City's Rikers Island prison, which revealed that only *13 percent* of the male addicts lived in their own home prior to their arrest. Forty percent were homeless, another 10 percent lived in transient hotels, and 33 percent in someone else's home. Stephen Magura, Andrew Rosenblum, and Herman Joseph, "AIDS Risk Among Intravenous Drug-Using Offenders," *Crime and Delinquency,* Vol. 37, No. 1, January 1991, p. 90.

24 "Mainstream Americans": National Institute of Justice, *Searching for Answers,* p. 16.

25 Transient drug use: New York study, cited in CEWG, *Proceedings, December 1990,* p. II–144. Miami homeless: New York *Times,* December 21, 1991. Runaway teens: Stuart W. Fors and Dean G. Rojek, "A Comparison of Drug Involvement Between Runaways and School Youths," *Journal of Drug Education,* Vol. 21, No. 1, 1991. A recent Canadian study shows similar gaping disparities between the drug use of "street" youth and that of the young people tapped in the conventional surveys. Compared with Toronto adolescents in school, street youth in that city were seven times as likely to have used cocaine in the past year, 24 times as likely to have used speed, and 41

times as likely to have ever injected a drug in their lifetime. Reginald G. Smart and Edward M. Adlaf, "Substance Use and Problems Among Toronto Street Youth," *British Journal of Addiction*, Vol. 86, 1991, p. 1006.

25 Miami delinquents: James Inciardi and Anne Pottieger, "Kids, Crack, and Crime," *Journal of Drug Issues*, Vol. 21, No. 2, 1991, pp. 258–59.

26 Chavez survey: Ernest L. Chavez and Randall C. Swaim, "An Epidemiological Comparison of Mexican-American and White Non-Hispanic 8th and 12th Grade Students' Substance Use," *American Journal of Public Health*, Vol. 82, No. 3, March 1992.

27 1985–89 trends: From NIDA, *Overview of Selected Drug Abuse Indicators*, pp. 12, 7. Methamphetamine deaths, though on a smaller scale, showed a similar trend; they tripled nationally and increased sevenfold in San Diego, eightfold in Los Angeles. Ibid., p. 15.

28 1985–90 trends: Calculated from NIDA, *Annual Medical Examiner Data, 1990*, Washington, DC, 1991, and *Data from the Drug Abuse Warning Network (DAWN) 1985*, Washington, DC, 1986. There were some changes in the DAWN methodology between the two years; for a discussion, and a general overview of the sources and limits of the data, see the 1990 volume, pp. 1–4.

28–29 1991 resurgence: Ronald Ostrow, "Cocaine Use on Rise, U.S. Survey Finds," Los Angeles *Times*, December 19, 1991. The administration's drug "czar," former Florida governor Bob Martinez, responded that he did not believe the rise in emergency episodes "indicates a resurgence of illicit drug use so much as the consequences of long-term heavy drug use. Users who began their involvement with drugs several years ago—at the peak of cocaine use —are now getting into trouble." New York rises: Joseph B. Treaster, "Drug Use Is Growing, Study Says," New York *Times*, July 9, 1992.

29 Persistence: Washington and New York reports from CEWG, *Proceedings, June 1991*, pp. 216–17, 325.

31 Virginia quote: New York *Times*, March 23, 1991.

31–32 Race and the drug war: 1989 arrest figure from *USA Today*, December 20, 1990; jail inmates from U.S. Bureau of Justice Statistics, *Drugs and Jail Inmates*, 1989, Washington, DC, 1991, p. 1; New York prison admissions: New York State Coalition for Criminal Justice, *Update*, February 1990, p. 6; quote in *Update*, May 1989, p. 2. California patterns: BCS *Profile*, p. 68. Youth detentions: U.S. Department of Justice, Office of Juvenile Justice and Delinquency Prevention, *Growth in Minority Detentions Attributed to Drug Law Violators*, Washington, DC, 1990.

32 Response to crack in New York: Steven Belenko, Jeffrey Fagan, and Ko-Lin Chin, "Criminal Justice Responses to Crack," *Journal of Research in Crime and Delinquency*, Vol. 28, No. 1, February 1991.

32 Marijuana arrest patterns: National trends from *Statistical Abstract of the United States, 1990*, p. 178; California trends from BCS *Profile*, p. 9.

32–33 Changing perceptions and marijuana: For an analysis based on the survey data, see Jerald G. Bachman, Lloyd D. Johnston, Patrick M. O'Malley, and Ronald H. Humphrey, "Explaining the Recent Decline in Marijuana Use," *Journal of Health and Social Behavior*, Vol. 29, March 1988.

34 "We don't know": Cf. James Q. Wilson and John J. DiIulio, "Crackdown: Treating the Symptoms of the Drug Problem," *New Republic*, July 10, 1989, p. 25: "We do not know why some people try cocaine and then drop it, others try it and abuse it, and still others do not try it at all."

Chapter 2: Roots of the Drug Crisis

36–37 Postwar figures: Morris Ploscowe, "Some Basic Problems in Drug Addiction and Suggestions for Research," in American Bar Association and American Medical Association, Joint Committee on Narcotic Drugs, *Drug Addiction: Crime or Disease*, Bloomington, Indiana University Press, 1961, pp. 28–31.

37–46 Chein study: The following pages are drawn from Isidor Chein, D. L. Gerard, R. S. Lee, and Eva Rosenfeld, *The Road to H: Narcotics, Delinquency, and Social Policy*, New York, Basic Books, 1964 (hereafter cited as *Road to H*); and Isidor Chein, "Narcotics Use Among Juveniles" (hereafter cited as "Narcotics Use"), in John A. O'Donnell and John C. Ball, eds., *Narcotic Addiction*, New York, Harper & Row, 1966, pp. 123–41.

38 "Packets of heroin": *Road to H*, p. 41.

38 "Strike evenly": *Road to H*, p. 37. Chein and his coworkers did believe that many addicts suffered from quite severe psychological problems: "Although psychiatric diagnoses are apt to vary, a particular set of symptoms seems to be common to most juvenile addicts. They are not able to enter prolonged, close, friendly relations with either peers or adults; they have difficulties in assuming a masculine role; they are frequently overcome by a sense of futility, expectation of failure, and general depression; they are easily frustrated and made anxious; and they find both frustration and anxiety intolerable." *Road to H*, p. 14. Unlike many earlier psychological commentators, however, these researchers situated the addict's individual problems squarely within the larger "pathology" of the community as a whole.

39 "Epidemic areas": *Road to H*, p. 55.

40 "Families of addicts": *Road to H*, p. 123.

40 "Not simply to the material deprivations": *Road to H*, p. 127.

41 "A more comfortable place": *Road to H*, p. 133.

41 "Contribution to a sense of mutuality": *Road to H*, p. 125.

41 "Sense of human solidarity": "Narcotics Use," p. 138. Interestingly, the NYU researchers found that belonging to a youth gang might also help to create something like the sense of "solidarity" that could discourage drug use. "In the popular mind, the delinquent gang is a source of pressure for incontinent use of drugs. This is far from true. Experimentation with drugs may be a part of the delinquent culture, but habituation is not. Group workers in our gang study reported many instances where gang members tried to influence, and exerted strong pressure on, using members to cut down or discontinue the use of heroin." *Road to H*, p. 172.

41 "A common theme": *Road to H*, p. 92.

41 "Prevailing atmosphere": "Narcotics Use," p. 138.

42 "Follow the fad": *Road to H*, p. 128.

42 "Surplus of vulnerability": *Road to H*, pp. 73–74.

43 "Segments of communities," "quick and royal route": "Narcotics Use," pp. 137, 140.

44 "Contagious disease": *Road to H*, p. 328.

44 "Simple fact of the matter": *Road to H*, p. 385.

45 "Most general objectives," "price of moral indignation": *Road to H*, pp. 385–86. The point about linking moral indignation and civic responsibility was central to the NYU researchers' view. They repeatedly argued that society had no right to deny addicts their pleasures—even though the pleasures were "inferior" ones—if it was not simultaneously willing to address the causes of that form of "adaptation": "Taking away this inferior mode of adaptation on the high-sounding excuse that it is good for the person while doing nothing to help him find and remove the obstacles to a superior form of adaptation is the sheerest hypocrisy and a refined form of cruelty." *Road to H*, p. 366.

46 "Human misery": *Road to H*, p. 381.

46–51 Chicago study: The following pages are drawn from Harold Finestone, "Cats, Kicks, and Color," *Social Problems*, Vol. 5, No. 1, July 1957 (hereafter cited as "Cats"); and Harold Finestone, "Narcotics and Criminality," in O'Donnell and Ball, *Narcotic Addiction*, pp. 141–64. The Chicago Area Project was a well-known, innovative program with many useful lessons for the present. For descriptions, see Steven Schlossman and Michael Sedlak, *The Chicago Area Project Revisited*, Santa Monica, the Rand Corporation, 1983; Harold Finestone, "The Chicago Area Project in Theory and Practice," in Irving Spergel, ed., *Community Organization: Studies in Constraint*, Beverly Hills, Sage Publications, 1972.

46 "Highest concentrations": "Narcotics and Criminality," p. 145. "Frenetic search": Ploscowe, "Some Basic Problems," p. 61.

47 "Pinpointed with great accuracy: "Cats," p. 3.

47 "Pitiful figure": "Cats," pp. 8, 3.

49 "Emergence of the self-conception": "Cats," p. 9.

49 "Exclusion from the serious concerns": "Cats," p. 9.

50 "Tradition of accommodation": "Cats," pp. 6–7.

51 "Largely a pose": "Cats," p. 10.

51 "Total social milieu": "Narcotics and Criminality," pp. 163–64.

52–56 Cloward and Ohlin study: Richard A. Cloward and Lloyd Ohlin, *Delinquency and Opportunity: A Theory of Delinquent Gangs*, New York, Free Press, 1959.

55 "Social setting": Ibid., p. 211.

55 "Deprived of both": Ibid., p. 172.

55 "Slum neighborhoods": Ibid., p. 211.

56–59 Harlem study: The following is drawn from Harlem Youth Opportunities, Inc., *Youth in the Ghetto: A Study of the Consequences of Powerlessness and a Blueprint for Change*, New York, 1964 (hereafter cited as Haryou): and Kenneth B. Clark, *Dark Ghetto: Dilemmas of Social Power*, New York, Harper & Row, 1965.

56 "Massive deterioration": Haryou, p. xi.

56 "Habitual narcotics use": figures from Haryou, p. 144.

56–57 "Roots of the multiple pathology": *Dark Ghetto*, p. 106.

57 "Occupational roots": Haryou, p. 250.

57–58 Interviews: *Dark Ghetto*, pp. 94–95; dealer, Haryou, pp. 16–17.

58 "Strategy of Despair": *Dark Ghetto*, p. 220. Clark did not explicitly link drug use to the "strategy of despair," but the connection is implicit; "to abandon hope, to withdraw, in the presence of oppression is to adjust to and accept the condition." Ibid.

58 Harlem minister: *Dark Ghetto*, p. 91.

59 Labor estimates: Haryou, p. 259.

60–63 Preble and Casey study: Edward Preble and John J. Casey, Jr., "Taking Care of Business: The Heroin User's Life on the Street," *International Journal of the Addictions*, Vol. 4, No. 1, March 1969.

61 "Actively engaged," "fast, purposeful stride": Ibid., p. 2.

61 Heroin user as businessman: Ibid., p. 21. Preble and Casey also described another aspect of this phenomenon: the addict actually contributed in several ways to the economic life of low-income communities. Given their lack of legitimate opportunities, addicts frequently stole to support their habits. But they usually did their stealing outside their own neighborhood—"not out of community loyalty but because the opportunities are better in the wealthier neighborhoods"—and then brought the goods back to the neighborhood "for sale at high discounts"—mainly to "ordinary, legitimate members of the community": "Housewives will wait on the stoop for specialists in stealing meat (known as cattle rustlers) to come by, so that they can get a ham or roast at a 60% discount. Owners of small grocery stores buy cartons of cigarettes stolen from the neighorhood supermarket. The owner of an automobile places an order with a heroin user for tires, and the next day he has the tires, with the wheels . . . This results, to some extent, in a redistribution of real income from the richer to the poorer neighborhoods." Ibid., p. 19. That redistributive aspect of endemic drug use helps explain why it is by no means universally or wholeheartedly condemned in the communities in which it most thrives.

62 "Real hustling dope fiend": Ibid., p. 20.

62 "Life in the slums": Ibid., p. 22.

63 "Hell of a game": Ibid.

64 Sutter study: The following is drawn from Alan G. Sutter, "The World of the Righteous Dope Fiend," *Issues in Criminology*, Vol. 2, Fall 1966; and "Worlds of Drug Use on the Street Scene," in Donald Cressey and David Ward, eds., *Delinquency, Crime, and Social Process*, New York, Harper & Row, 1969 (hereafter cited as *Worlds*).

64 "Romantic pull": *Worlds*, p. 816.

64 "Polished works": Ibid.

64–65 Feldman study: Harvey W. Feldman, "Ideological Supports to Becoming and Remaining a Heroin Addict," *Journal of Health and Social Behavior*, Vol. 9, No. 2, June 1968.

65 "Stand-up cat": Ibid., p. 133.

65 "Buckle to the strength of heroin": Ibid., p. 135.

66 Klein and Phillips study: Julius Klein and Derek L. Phillips, "From Hard to Soft Drugs: Temporal and Substantive Changes in Drug Usage Among Gangs in a Working-Class Community," *Journal of Health and Social Behavior*, Vol. 9, No. 2, June 1968.

66 "Comparatively more stable": Ibid., p. 145.

68–71 Finestone view on assimilation: "Cats," pp. 12–13: ". . . it may be that the unique problems of Negro migrants to our metropolitan areas will lead to a few or several sacrificed generations in the course of the tortuous process of urbanization . . . [but] insofar as the social type of the cat represents a reaction to a feeling of exclusion from access to the means toward the goals of our society, all measures such as improved education which put these means within his grasp will hasten the extinction of this social type. Just as the 'hoodlum' and 'gangster' types tend to disappear as the various more recently arrived white ethnic groups tend to move up in the status scale of the community, so it can confidently be expected that the cat as a social type will tend to disappear as such opportunities become more prevalent among the colored population."

71 "Ultimate solution": Preble and Casey, "Taking Care of Business," p. 23.

72 "New faith": Haryou, pp. 571–72.

72 "Principal aspiration": Haryou, p. 567.

Chapter 3: Lessons Ignored

78 Heroin in household survey: In 1991, for example, the survey estimated that 1.4 percent of the total population over age twelve had ever used heroin. It should be noted that the resulting absolute figure is not small; it adds up to nearly 2.9 million people. NIDA, *Population Estimates 1991*, p. 104.

78 Robins study: Lee N. Robins and George E. Murphy, "Drug Use in a Normal Population of Young Negro Men," *American Journal of Public Health*, Vol. 57, No. 9, September 1967, p. 1594.

78 Brunswick study: Ann F. Brunswick, Cheryl R. Merzel, and Peter A. Messeri, "Drug Use Initiation Among Urban Black Youth," *Youth and Society*, Vol. 17, No. 2, December 1985, pp. 201, 212.

78–79 Lukoff study: Irving Lukoff, "Consequences of Use: Heroin and Other Narcotics," in Joan Dunne Rittenhouse, ed., *The Epidemiology of Heroin and Other Narcotics*, Washington, DC, NIDA, 1977, pp. 202, 213.

79–80 Perez study: Robert Perez, Amado Padilla, Alex Ramirez, Robert Ramirez, and Manuel Rodriguez, "Correlates and Changes over Time in Drug and Alcohol Use Within a Barrio Population," *American Journal of Community Psychology*, Vol. 8, No. 6, 1980, p. 633.

80 Puerto Ricans: Ronald Glick, "Survival, Income, and Status: Drug Dealing in the Chicago Puerto Rican Community," in Ronald Glick and Joan Moore, eds., *Drugs in Hispanic Communities*, New Brunswick: Rutgers University Press, 1990; Joseph P. Fitzpatrick, "Drugs and Puerto Ricans in New York City," in ibid.; quote from p. 116.

81 Crack in Washington: NIDA, *National Household Survey of Drug Abuse, 1990, Main Findings*, p. 144.

81 Bowser study: Benjamin P. Bowser, Mindy Thompson Fullilove, and Robert E. Fullilove, "African-American Youth and AIDS High-Risk Behavior: The Social Context and Barriers to Prevention," *Youth and Society*, Vol. 22, No. 1, September 1990; quote from p. 57.

81 Medical data: Heroin and cocaine deaths from NIDA, DAWN *Annual Medical Examiner Data, 1990*, p. 24. Hispanic AIDS deaths: Bruce Lambert, "AIDS Travels New York–Puerto Rico Air Bridge," New York *Times*, June 15, 1990. Black women and AIDS: L. Remez, "AIDS-Related Mortality Increased Almost Fourfold Among U.S. Women Aged 15–44," *Family Planning Perspectives*, Vol. 22, No. 6, November–December 1990, pp. 276–77. Children and AIDS: CEWG, *Proceedings, December 1990*, p. 29.

82 Lukoff findings: Paula Holzman Kleinman and Irving Faber Lukoff, "Ethnic Differences in Factors Related to Drug Use," *Journal of Health and Social Behavior*, Vol. 19, June 1978, pp. 194–95.

82 O'Donnell findings: cited in Bruce Johnson, "The Race, Class, and Irreversibility Hypotheses: Myths and Research About Heroin," in Rittenhouse, *Epidemiology*, p. 53.

82 White ethnic youth: John A. Carlisi, "Unique Aspects of White Ethnic Drug Use," in George M. Beschner and Alfred S. Friedman, eds., *Youth Drug Abuse: Problems, Issues, and Treatment*, Lexington, MA, Lexington Books, 1979, pp. 522, 525. See also the description of the social context of inhalant abuse among the poor white in Terence M. McSherry, "Program Experiences with the Solvent Abuser in Philadelphia," in Raquel A. Crider and Beatrice A. Rouse, *Epidemiology of Inhalant Abuse: An Update*, Washington, DC, NIDA, 1988, Table 3.

82 White dropouts: Ernest Chavez, Ruth Edwards, and E. R. Oetting, "Mexican American and White American School Dropouts' Drug Use, Health Status, and Involvement in Violence," *Public Health Reports*, Vol. 104, No. 6, November–December 1989, p. 598.

83 Miami delinquents: Fernando Sorianno and Mario De La Rosa, "Cocaine Use and Criminal Activities Among Hispanic Juvenile Delinquents in Florida," in Glick and Moore, *Drug Use in Hispanic Communities*, pp. 66–67. "Regular" use was defined as more than three times a week.

A recent study of pregnant adolescents in Prince Georges County, Maryland, shows a similar racial pattern. Among the mostly low-income young women in the study, whites were considerably more likely than blacks to be classified as at "high risk" of drug abuse during pregnancy, or as current users of illicit drugs while pregnant. Though the majority of pregnant teens in this clinic sample were black, the majority of those at highest risk of drug abuse were white; about two out of five pregnant white teens were either using illicit drugs during pregnancy or had stopped only on learning they were pregnant, or were living with (or close friends with) a known drug abuser. Paul R. Marques and A. James McKnight, "Drug Abuse Risk Among Pregnant Adolescents Attending Public Health Clinics," *American Journal of Drug and Alcohol Abuse*, Vol. 17, No. 4, Winter 1991.

83 Seattle deaths: CEWG, *Proceedings, June 1990*, p. I-246.

83 Methamphetamine deaths: In the second quarter of 1991, one in five men and one in four women arrested in San Diego tested positive for methamphetamine; National Institute of Justice, *Drug Use Forecasting, Second Quarter, 1991*, Washington, DC, 1991, pp. 3–4. "Thirty-two year-old white male": David N. Bailey and Richard G. Shaw, "Cocaine- and Methamphetamine-Related Deaths in San Diego County (1987): Homicides and Accidental Overdoses," *Journal of Forensic Sciences*, Vol. 34, No. 2, 1989. NIDA study: NIDA, *Trends and Patterns of Methamphetamine Abuse in the United States*, Washington, DC 1988, p. 3.

83 Holland patterns: Govert F. van de Wijngaart, "Heroin Use in the Netherlands," *American Journal of Drug and Alcohol Abuse*, Vol. 14, No. 1, Spring 1988, p. 157; see also Grund et al., "Changing Cocaine Smoking Rituals," p. 444; Nabitz and Ouwehand, "Drug Abuse and Health Service in the Netherlands," p. III–32–33.

84 Pearson study: Geoffrey Pearson, *The New Heroin Users*, Oxford and New York, Basil Blackwell, 1987, and Geoffrey Pearson, Mark Gilman, and Shirley McIver, *Young People and Heroin Use in the North of England*, London, Department of Social Work, Middlesex Polytechnic, 1985, Appendix 1.

84 Wirral research: Howard Parker, Keith Bakx, and Russell Newcombe, *Living with Heroin: The Impact of a Drugs "Epidemic" on an English Community*, Milton Keynes, Open University Press, 1988, pp. 16, 18, 67.

85 Glasgow data: Research by Sally Haw, cited in Institute for the Study of Drug Dependence, *Surveys and Statistics on Drugtaking in Britain*, London, 1986, p. 3.

85 Nottingham study: John Giggs, Philip Bean, David Whynes, and Christine Wilkinson, "Class A Drug Users: Prevalence and Characteristics in Greater Nottingham, *British Journal of Addiction*, Vol. 84, 1989, pp. 1473–77. See also John Wilkinson et al., "Problematic Drug Use and Social Deprivation," *Public Health*, Vol. 101, 1987, pp. 165–68.

85 Unemployment in household survey: *NIDA Household Survey, 1990, Main Findings*, pp. 59, 65, 69.

86 DUF data: National Institute of Justice, *1988 Drug Use Forecasting Annual Report*, Washington, DC, March 1990, pp. 22–23.

86 Ohio data: Harvey A. Siegel, "Intravenous Drug Abuse and the HIV Epidemic in Two Midwestern Cities: A Preliminary Report," *Journal of Drug Issues*, Vol. 20, No. 2, 1990, pp. 283–84. Harlem figures: Bruce D. Johnson et al., *Taking Care of Business: The Economics of Crime by Heroin Abusers*, Lexington, MA, D. C. Heath, 1985, p. 182.

86 Wirral data: Parker et al., *Living with Heroin*, p. 77.

87 Detroit crack users: Cited in *Criminal Justice in Crisis*, p. 506.

87 Bush official: Cited in New York *Times*, December 20, 1991.

87–88 Plant research: David F. Peck and Martin A. Plant, "Unemployment and Illegal Drug Use: Concordant Evidence from a Prospective Study and National Trends," *British Medical Journal*, Volume 293, October 11, 1986, pp. 929–31.

88 Parker evidence: Parker et al., *Living with Heroin*, p. 77.

88–89 DeFleur Study: Lois B. DeFleur, John C. Ball, and Richard W. Snarr, "The Long-Term Social Correlates of Opiate Addiction," *Social Problems*, Vol. 17, No. 2, 1969, pp. 225–33.

89–90 Vaillant study: George Vaillant, "What Can Long-Term Follow-up Teach Us About Relapse and Prevention of Relapse in Addiction?" *British Journal of Addiction*, Vol. 83, 1988, pp. 1151–52; see also "A Twelve-Year Follow-up of New York Narcotic Addicts, IV: Some Characteristics and Determinants of Abstinence," *American Journal of Psychiatry*, Vol. 123, No. 5, November 1966.

90 Miami figures: Inciardi and Pottieger, "Kids, Crack, and Crime," p. 260; Sorianno and De La Rosa, "Hispanic Delinquents," p. 62.

91 Pearson quote: *New Heroin Users*, pp. 50–51.

91 Neighborhood effects: See, for example, Jonathan Crane, "The Epidemic Theory of Ghettoes and Neighborhood Effects on Dropping Out and Teenage Childbearing," *American Journal of Sociology*, Vol. 96, No. 5, March 1991, pp. 1226–59.

91–92 Families at risk of drug abuse: See, for example, William J. McCarthy and M. Douglas Anglin, "Narcotics Addicts: Effect of Family and Parental Risk Factors on Timing of Emancipation, Drug Use Onset, Pre-addiction Incarcerations and Educational Achievement," *Journal of Drug Issues*, Vol. 20, No. 1, 1990; Denise Kandel and Ora Simcha-Fagan, "Risk Factors for Delinquency and Illicit Drug Use from Adolescence to Young Adulthood," *Journal of Drug Issues*, Vol. 16, 1986; Irving Maltzman and Avraham Schweiger, "Individual and Family Characteristics of Middle-Class Adolescents Hospitalized for Alcohol and Other Drug Abuse," *British Journal of Addiction*, Vol. 86, 1991; Ora Simcha-Fagan, Joanne C. Gersten, and Thomas S. Langner, "Early Precursors and Concurrent Correlates of Patterns of Illicit Drug Use in Adolescence," *Journal of Drug Issues*, Vol. 16, No. 1, 1986; Judith R. Vicary and Jacqueline V. Lerner, "Parental Attributes and Adolescent Drug Use," *Journal of Adolescence*, Vol. 9, 1986; Robert D. Schweitzer and Patricia A. Lawton, "Drug Abusers' Perceptions of Their Parents," *British Journal of Addiction*, Vol. 84, 1989.

92 Child-abuse link: Richard Dembo et al., "Physical Abuse, Sexual Victimization, and Illicit Drug Use: Replicaton of a Structural Analysis Among a New Sample of High-Risk Youths," *Violence and Victims*, Vol. 4, 1989, pp. 121–35. Canadian study: Cyril Greenland, *Preventing CAN Deaths: An International Study of Deaths Due to Child Abuse and Neglect*, London, Tavistock, 1987. On the link between poor employment and child abuse, see generally Richard J. Gelles and Murray A. Straus, *Intimate Violence*, New York, Simon and Schuster, 1988, Chapter 4, where the "prototypical abusive parent" is described as "unemployed or employed part-time," most likely in "a manual labor job": "Economic adversity and worries about money pervade the typical violent home" (p. 85).

93 Page study: J. Bryan Page, "Streetside Drug Use Among Cuban Drug Users in Miami," in Glick and Moore, *Drug Use in Hispanic Communities*, pp. 169–81.

93–94 Fourteen-year-old: From Elliott Currie, *Dope and Trouble: Portraits of Delinquent Youth*, New York, Pantheon, 1992, pp. 77–78.

94 Latchkey children: Cited in Anne C. Roark, "Drug Use Seen Higher Among Latchkey Youth," Los Angeles *Times*, September 6, 1989.

95–96 Sullivan study: Mercer A. Sullivan, *Getting Paid: Youth Crime and Work in the Inner City*, Ithaca, Cornell University Press, 1989, pp. 203–26.

97 San Francisco study: Bowser et al., "African-American Youth," pp. 59–63.

97–98 Hamid research: Ansley Hamid, "The Political Economy of Crack-Related Violence," *Contemporary Drug Problems*, Spring 1990, p. 67.

98 Sixteen-year-old: In Currie, *Dope and Trouble*, p. 260.

99 Desmond and Maddux study: David P. Desmond and James F. Maddux, "Mexican-American Heroin Addicts," *American Journal of Drug and Alcohol Abuse*, Vol. 10, No. 3, 1984, p. 339. Perez study: Perez et al., p. 632.

100 Brooklyn study: Kleinman and Lukoff, "Ethnic Differences," pp. 194–97.

100–2 Puerto Rican youth: Carmen Noemi Velez and Jane A. Ungemack, "Drug Use Among Puerto Rican Youth: An Exploration of Generational Status Differences," *Social Science and Medicine*, Vol. 29, No. 6, 1989, pp. 779–87.
    The pattern of increasing drug use with longer time away from the culture of origin is not just an American phenomenon. Dutch research, for example, shows that young Surinamese and Moroccan migrants to the Netherlands cities typically begin using heroin or cocaine several years *after* they immigrate. Charles D. Kaplan, Dirk Korf, Paul van Gelder, and Jella Sijtsma, "The

Netherlands: Floating Drug-Using Populations in Europe," in CEWG *Proceedings, June 1990*, p. II–124.

102 Fitzpatrick research: "Drugs and Puerto Ricans in New York," pp. 110, 113. Glick research: "Survival, Income, and Status," pp. 82–86. As Glick notes, the same breakdown of long-standing communal and family networks is now occurring on the island itself as a result of the impact of the international economy. Cf. Hamid, "Political Economy of Crack-Related Violence," for a discussion of a similar process in Trinidad.

104 "Complex human meanings": A classic statement of this view is Howard S. Becker, "Becoming a Marijuana User," *American Journal of Sociology*, Vol. 59, November 1953, pp. 235–42.

105–6 Bullington study: Bruce Bullington, *Heroin Use in the Barrio*, Lexington, MA, Lexington Books, 1977, pp. 105–9.

106 Glick research: "Survival, Income, and Status," pp. 80–85.

107 Page study: "Streetside Cocaine Use," pp. 181, 186.

107–8 Seventeen-year-old: Currie, *Dope and Trouble*, p. 236.

108–9 London studies: Lee O'Bryan, "Young People and Drugs," in Susanne MacGregor, ed., *Drugs and British Society*, London, Routledge, 1989, pp. 66, 71, 75; Angela Burr, "An Inner-City Community Response to Heroin-Use," in ibid., pp. 85–86, 95.

109 Pearson research: Pearson et al., *Young People and Drugs in the North of England*, p. 26.

109 Howard Parker and his colleagues, similarly, sum up their findings on youthful heroin use this way: "We should not ignore the attractions of the deviant lifestyles in which users have become immersed. Being a 'smackhead' has potential attractions for all youth, but particularly for the unemployed surplus youth to be found in Wirral's recession-hit urban areas. For them the commitment to conventional lifestyle is strained or made tenuous by their lowly socioeconomic position and the fact that coping strategies of an illegal nature are . . . condoned in their neighborhood, particularly in the absence of legal ones." *Living with Heroin*, p. 110.

109–10 Women and heroin: Marsha Rosenbaum and Sheigla Murphy, "Women and Addiction: Process, Treatment, and Outcome," in Elizabeth Lambert, ed., *The Collection and Interpretation of Data from Hidden Populations*, Washington, DC, NIDA, 1990, pp. 121–22; see also Marsha Rosenbaum, *Women on Heroin*, New Brunswick, Rutgers University Press, 1981.

110 "Some are in it for the money": A sixteen-year-old female crack dealer, quoted in Currie, *Dope and Trouble*, pp. 40–41.

110–11 Inciardi study: Inciardi and Pottieger, "Kids, Crack, and Crime," p. 269. Taylor study: Carl Taylor, *Dangerous Society*, East Lansing, Michigan State University Press, 1989, p. 53.

111 Hamid quotes: "Political Economy of Crack-Related Violence," pp. 67–68. Bourgois quotes: Philippe Bourgois, "In Search of Horatio Alger: Culture and Ideology in the Crack Economy," *Contemporary Drug Problems*, Winter 1989, pp. 629, 639.

113 "Chronic hassles": Norweeta Milburn and Ann D'Ercole, "Homeless Women: Moving Toward a Comprehensive Model," *American Psychologist*, Vol. 46, No. 11, November 1991, p. 1163. "Palliative coping": Ibid., p. 1167.

113 Marsh and Shevell quote: Jeanne C. Marsh and Steven K. Shevell, "Males' and Females' Perceived Reasons for Their Use of Heroin," *Social Service Review*, March 1983, p. 88.

113 Preble quote: Edward Preble, "Social and Cultural Factors Related to Narcotic Use Among Puerto Ricans in New York City," *International Journal of the Addictions*, Vol. 1, No. 1, January 1966, p. 40.

114 Drugs and depression: See, for example, Kazuo Yamaguchi and Denise B. Kandel, "Patterns of Drug Use from Adolescence to Young Adulthood: III. Predictors of Progression," *American Journal of Public Health*, Vol. 74, No. 7, July 1984, p. 679. Yamaguchi and Kandel also note that youthful marijuana users suffering from depression were more likely to move up to harder drugs than those who were not depressed; moreover, revealingly, drugs seemed to *work* for them: "The depression seemed to abate over a six-month interval with continued use of these illicit drugs, suggesting that illicit drugs served a self-medicating function for some youths."

114 Toronto youth: Smart and Adlaf, "Substance Use and Problems Among Toronto Street Youth," pp. 1006–9.

114 Marsh and Shevell findings: "Males' and Females' Perceived Reasons for Their Use of Heroin," p. 83.

114–15 Moore findings: Joan Moore, "Mexican-American Women Addicts: The Influence of Family Background," in Glick and Moore, *Drugs in Hispanic Communities*, p. 138. Jorquez quote: Jaime Jorquez, "Heroin Use in the Barrio: Solving the Problem of Relapse or Keeping the Tecato Gusano Asleep," *American Journal of Drug and Alcohol Abuse*, Vol. 10, No. 1, 1984, p. 70.

115 Massachusetts study: Margaret L. Griffin et al., "A Comparison of Male and Female Cocaine Abusers," *Archives of General Psychiatry*, Vol. 46, 1989, as cited in *NIDA Notes*, Winter 1989–90, p. 15.

115–16 Pearson quotes: *New Heroin Users*, pp. 31–35. I've slightly rearranged the quotes for continuity.

116–17 Vaillant findings: "Long-Term Follow-up," p. 1150.

117 Parker quote: *Living with Heroin*, p. 49. Burr study: "An Inner-City Community Response to Heroin," p. 83.

117–18 Pearson quote: *New Heroin Users*, p. 181.

118 Vaillant quote: "Long-Term Follow-up," pp. 1152, 1154–55. The importance of caring for others as a support for abstaining from drugs is vividly expressed by one of Jaime Jorquez's interviewees: "I'd keep saying to myself, 'As long as I hang in there, good things will start happening' . . . So I hung in there. I stop and think about my baby, and I look at him . . . and I stop thinking about dope." "Heroin Use in the Barrio," p. 70.

118 Faupel and Klockars study: Charles E. Faupel and Carl B. Klockars, "Drugs-Crime Connections: Elaborations from the Life Histories of Hard-Core Heroin Addicts," *Social Problems*, Vol. 34, No. 1, February 1987, pp. 60–61. British quote: Pearson, *New Heroin Users*, pp. 48–49.

119 Bowser quote: "African American Youth," pp. 59–60.

120 Fitzpatrick quote: "Puerto Ricans and Drugs," pp. 122, 124.

120–21 Pearson study: *New Heroin Users*, pp. 38, 183.

121 Jorquez quote: "Heroin Use in the Barrio," p. 72.

121–22 Women addicts: Rosenbaum and Murphy, "Women and Addiction," pp. 122–23. Cf. Glick. "Status, Income, and Survival," pp. 81, 86.

122 Chein quote: Isidor Chein, "The Status of Sociological and Social Psychological Knowledge Concerning Narcotics," in Robert B. Livingston, ed., *Narcotic Drug Addiction Problems*, Bethesda, MD, U.S. Public Health Service [1959?], p. 156.

123 Perplexed commentator: Nathan Glazer, "The Lessons of New York City," *The Public Interest*, No. 104, Summer 1991, p. 46.

124–25 Kasarda research: John Kasarda, "Urban Industrial Transition and the Underclass," *Annals of the American Academy of Political and Social Science*, No. 501, January 1989, pp. 26–47.

126 Chicago neighborhoods: William Julius Wilson, Robert Aponte, Joleen Kirschenman, and Loic J. D. Wacquant, "The Ghetto Underclass and the Changing Structure of Urban Poverty." In Fred R. Harris and Roger W. Wilkins, eds., *Quiet Riots: Race and Poverty in the United States*, New York, Pantheon, 1988, p. 139.

126 Suburban gains: Kasarda, "Urban Industrial Transition," p. 29. Atlanta findings: Gary Orfield and Carole Ashkinaze, *The Closing Door: Conservative Policy and Black Opportunity*, Chicago, University of Chicago Press, 1991, pp. 54, 64. Cars in Chicago: Kasarda, "Urban Industrial Transition," p. 40. Schneider and Phelan study: Mark Schneider and Thomas Phelan, "Blacks

and Jobs: Never the Twain Shall Meet?" *Urban Affairs Quarterly*, Vol. 26, No. 2, December 1990, p. 309.

126–27 Puerto Ricans: Marta Tienda, "Puerto Ricans and the Underclass Debate," *Annals of the American Academy of Political and Social Science*, No. 501, January 1989, pp. 105–19.

127–28 Senate study: U.S. Congress, Senate Budget Committee, *Wages of American Workers in the 1980s*, Washington, DC, Government Printing Office, 1988, cited in Elliott Currie, "Heavy with Human Tears: Free Market Policy, Inequality, and Social Provision in the United States," in Ian Taylor, ed., *The Social Effects of Free Market Policies*, London, Harvester/Wheatsheaf, 1990, pp. 305–6.

128–29 Tilly study: Chris Tilly, "Reasons for the Continuing Growth of Part-Time Employment," *Monthly Labor Review*, March 1991, pp. 11–14.

129–30 Minimum-wage comparisons: Calculated from data in Robert Sheak and David Dabelko, "Conservative Welfare Reform Proposals and the Reality of Subemployment," *Journal of Sociology and Social Welfare*, Vol. 17, No. 1, March 1991, p. 59. Figures on "underemployed": Ibid., p. 56.

130–32 Lichter study: Daniel S. Lichter, "Racial Differences in Underemployment in American Cities," *American Journal of Sociology*, Vol. 93, No. 4, January 1988, pp. 771–92.

132 Danziger findings: Sheldon Danziger and Gregory Acs, "Educational Attainment, Industrial Structure, and Male Earnings, 1973–1987," as cited in U.S. Congress, Committee on Ways and Means, *Overview of Entitlement Programs*, Washington, DC, Government Printing Office, 1991, p. 561.

133 Luxemburg Income Study: See Timothy M. Smeeding and Barbara Boyle Torrey, "Poor Children in Rich Countries," in Jerome H. Skolnick and Elliott Currie, eds., *Crisis in American Institutions*, 8th ed., New York: HarperCollins, 1991, pp. 131–35.

134 Benefit cuts: Data from Currie, "Heavy with Human Tears," p. 305.

135 Families with children: Data from Howard V. Hayghe, "Children in Two-Worker Families and Real Family Income," *Monthly Labor Review*, December 1989, p. 51. Rising child-care expenses added to the burden. Thus, for single mothers with two chidren and child-care expenses, overall disposable income fell by a *third* from 1972 to 1984. Committee on Ways and Means, *Overview of Entitlement Programs*, p. 1081.

135 125 percent of poverty level: *Statistical Abstract of the United States, 1990*, p. 459.

135 Hispanic urban poverty: Anne M. Santiago and Margaret G. Wilder, "Residential Segregation and the Links to Minority Poverty: The Case of Latinos

in the United States," *Social Problems*, Vol. 18, No. 4, November 1991, p. 499.

135 Minority income deficit: U.S. Bureau of the Census, Current Population Reports, Series P–60, No. 168; *Money Income and Poverty Status in the United States, 1989*, Washington, DC, Government Printing Office, 1991, p. 77.

135–36 Census study: Mark Littman, "Poverty in the 1980s: Are the Poor Getting Poorer?" *Monthly Labor Review*, June 1989, pp. 12–17.

137 Wilson findings: Wilson et al., "Ghetto Underclass," p. 126. Hispanic concentration: Santiago and Wilder, "Residential Segregation," p. 501.

137–38 "Stably active": Tienda, "Puerto Ricans and the Underclass Debate," pp. 112–13. Hispanic labor force participation: see, for example, Santiago and Wilder, "Residential Segregation," p. 508. Overall rise in full-time but poor workers: Sheak and Dabelko, "Conservative Welfare Reform Proposals," p. 56. Rural-urban comparisons: Scott Barancik, *Rural Disadvantage*, Washington, DC, Center on Budget and Policy Priorities," 1990, pp. 8–9.

138 Families over $50,000: Census, *Money Income and Poverty Status in the United States, 1989*, pp. 35–36.

138 Ways and Means Committee figures: Cited in New York *Times*, March 25, 1990.

138–39 Relative income: U.S. Bureau of the Census, Current Population Reports, Series P–60, No. 177; *Trends in Relative Income: 1964 to 1989*, Washington, DC, Government Printing Office, 1991, pp. 2–6.

139–40 Orfield quote: Orfield and Ashkinaze, *The Closing Door*, p. 233.

140 "Slashed more deeply": National Low Income Housing Coalition, *Low Income Housing Policy Statement*, Washington, DC, 1987. Percentage figure: Maria Foscarinis, "The Politics of Homelessness: A Call to Action," *American Psychologist*, Vol. 46, No. 11, November 1991, p. 1233. For a helpful discussion of the complexity of trends in housing assistance in the 1980s, see Committee on Ways and Means, *Overview of Entitlement Programs*, pp. 1438–47.

140 Rental unit figure: Joint Center for Housing Studies, *The State of the Nation's Housing, 1988*, Cambridge, MA, 1989, p. 6.

140 Average housing benefits: According to Census data, the average value of "noncash" housing benefits for poor families fell, in real dollars, by 37 percent from 1979 to 1986, and by 14 percent for single persons. Littman, "Are the Poor Getting Poorer?" p. 16.

140 Median rent burden: Joint Center for Housing Studies, *State of America's Housing*, p. 14. Atlanta data: Orfield and Ashkinaze, *The Closing Door*, p. 218. Kerner discussion: *Report* of the National Advisory Commission on Civil Disorders, Washington, DC, Government Printing Office, p. 475.

141 Waiting lists: Cited in Foscarinis, "Politics of Homelessness," p. 1233.

141–42 Wallace study: Rodrick Wallace and Deborah Wallace, "Origins of Public Health Collapse in New York City," *Bulletin of the New York Academy of Medicine*, Vol. 66, No. 5, September–October 1990, pp. 391–426.

142–43 Taylor findings: *Dangerous Society*, p. 130.

143 Consumption aspirations: See Eileen M. Crimmons, Richard A. Easterlin, and Yasuhiko Saito, "Preference Changes Among American Youth: Family, Work, and Goods Aspirations, 1976–86," *Population and Development Review*, Vol. 17, No. 1, March 1991, pp. 122–27. The proportion of high-school seniors responding that "having lots of money" was "quite" or "extremely" important, for example, rose from 46 percent in 1976 to 63 percent a decade later; the proportion feeling similarly about having "at least two cars" rose from 14 to 29 percent.

144 Taylor quotes: *Dangerous Society*, pp. 59–60.

Chapter 4: Rethinking Criminal Justice

149 "Third Way": I have borrowed this phrase from two separate sources: Eduard van Thin, mayor of Amsterdam, quoted in Rone Tempest, "Drugs: Dutch Gain with a Tolerant Tack," Los Angeles *Times*, September 2, 1989; and Susanne MacGregor, "Could Britain Inherit the American Nightmare?" p. 869.

150–51 Deterrence and incapacitation: For a more extended discussion of these mechanisms as applied to the problem of street crime, see Elliott Currie, *Confronting Crime: An American Challenge*, New York, Pantheon, 1985, Chapter 3.

151 Estimates of hard-drug users: NIDA, *National Household Survey of Drug Abuse, Population Estimates, 1991*, pp. 31, 37, 43, 49, 104.

152–53 Johnson findings: *Taking Care of Business*, pp. 185–86.

153 Drugs in prison: Andrew H. Malcolm, "Explosive Drug Use Creating New Underworld in Prisons," New York *Times*, December 30, 1989.

154 Bennett quote: New York *Times*, July 20, 1989.

154 Brown study: Barry S. Brown, Susan K. Gauvey, Marilyn B. Meyers, and Steven D. Stark, "In Their Own Words: Addicts' Reasons for Initiating and Withdrawing from Heroin," *International Journal of the Addictions*, Vol. 6, No. 4, December 1971, pp. 639–42. Federal survey findings: D. Dwayne Simpson, George W. Joe, Wayne E. K. Lehman, and S. B. Sells, "Addiction Careers: Etiology, Treatment, and 12-Year Follow-up Outcomes," *Journal of Drug Issues*, Vol. 16, No. 1, 1986, p. 117.

155 Detroit gang members: Taylor, *Dangerous Society*, p. 135. Naturally, due allowance must be made for youthful bravado and exaggeration in interpreting these assertions. But the sheer fact that young dealers adopt this as their public attitude is revealing.

155 Brown quote: "In Their Own Words," p. 639.

156 Ford Report: *Dealing with Drug Abuse: A Report to the Ford Foundation*, New York, Praeger, 1972, p. 27. Ball research: J. C. Ball, J. W. Shaffer, and D. N. Nurco, "The Day-to-Day Criminality of Heroin Addicts in Baltimore," *Drug and Alcohol Dependence*, Vol. 12, 1983, pp. 119–42. California addicts: Elizabeth Piper Deschenes, M. Douglas Anglin, and George Speckart, "Narcotics Addiction: Related Criminal Careers, Social and Economic Costs," *Journal of Drug Issues*, Vol. 21, No. 2, 1991, p. 405. Harlem addicts: Johnson et al., *Taking Care of Business*, p. 171. Recent review: Harry K. Wexler, Douglas S. Lipton, and Bruce D. Johnson, *A Criminal Justice System Strategy for Treating Cocaine/Heroin Abusing Offenders in Custody*, Washington, DC, National Institute of Justice, 1988, p. 5.

157 Miami crack dealers: Inciardi and Pottieger, "Kids, Crack, and Crime," pp. 266–67.

157 Harlem research: Johnson et al., *Taking Care of Business*, pp. 170–72.

157 "Winners": Marcia R. Chaiken and Bruce D. Johnson, *Characteristics of Different Types of Drug-Involved Offenders*, Washington, DC, National Institute of Justice, 1988, p. 19.

158 Fagan study: Jeffrey Fagan, "Do Criminal Sanctions Deter Drug Offenders?" in Doris L. MacKenzie and Craig Uchida, eds., *Drugs and the Criminal Justice System: Evaluating Public Policy Initiatives*, Beverly Hills, Sage Publications, 1992; quote from p. 25.

159 "Predatory drug-involved offenders": Chaiken and Johnson, *Characteristics*, pp. 18–19.

160 Sixteen-year-old: Currie, *Dope and Trouble*, p. 39. Miami dealers: Inciardi and Pottieger, "Kids, Crack, and Crime," p. 269; Youth Authority inmates: Joan Petersilia, "When Probation Becomes More Dreaded Than Prison," *Federal Probation*, March 1990, p. 24.

160–61 Taylor quotes: *Dangerous Society*, pp. 51–52.

161 "Shutting them off from participation": This effect has been described in studies of hard-drug users for years. Bruce Bullington, for example, discussing the effect of prison on the "hope-to-die dope fiend," notes: "The local addict expression, 'in the spoon by noon,' aptly describes this person's behavior once returned to the streets after a prison term. Bitterness engendered by the prison experience often makes this type of addict completely intractable, and in all likelihood he will be unable to spend more than a few

months on the streets at any one time. . . . In most cases, this type of addict has been removed from society for such extensive time periods that he finds himself unable to function acceptably in the community for any lengthy periods of time." *Heroin Use in the Barrio*, pp. 107–8.

161 "Youth tries to pay": New York *Times*, March 27, 1992.

162 Skolnick research: Jerome H. Skolnick, Rick Blumenthal, Theodore Correl, Elizabeth Navarro, and Roger Rabb, *The Social Structure of Street Drug Dealing*, Sacramento, CA, California Bureau of Criminal Statistics, 1989, p. 13.

163 Prison as an improvement: Something similar was pointed out by Edward Preble and John Casey as far back as the 1960s: "Respite from the arduous life they lead comes to heroin users when they go to jail. . . . In the present study, it was found that 43% of the subjects were in some type of incarceration at any given period of time. In jail they rest, get on a healthy diet, have their medical and dental needs cared for, and engage in relaxed socialization . . ." "Taking Care of Business," p. 20.

163 Family connection: Data from U.S. Bureau of Justice Statistics, cited in Petersilia, "When Probation Becomes More Dreaded Than Prison," p. 24.

163 "To get a place to stay": Magura et al., "AIDS Risk Among Intravenous Drug Offenders," p. 91.

164 Free-market advocates: The noted conservative economist Milton Friedman, for example, proposes to distribute all drugs "the way aspirin is distributed," with the single exception of a ban on advertising; quoted in *Financial World*, October 3, 1989, p. 34. The rejection of drug regulation by "free-market" conservatives goes back a long way. In the 1940s, Ludwig von Mises, one of the fathers of the free-market wing of contemporary conservative economics, wrote that though it was commonly assumed that "only doctrinaires could be so dogmatic as to object to the government's regulation of the drug traffic," matters were not so simple, for once government was allowed to regulate narcotics it would inevitably come to regulate the whole of life; "once the principle is admitted that it is the duty of government to protect the individual against his own foolishness, no serious objections can be advanced against further encroachments . . . Why not prevent him from reading bad books and seeing bad plays, from looking at bad paintings and statues and from hearing bad music?" *Human Action: A Treatise on Economics*, New Haven, Yale University Press, 1949, pp. 728–29.

164–65 British system: a useful discussion of the development of British policy is Trevor Bennett, "The British Experience with Heroin Regulation," *Law and Contemporary Problems*, Vol. 51, No. 1, Winter 1988, pp. 299–314.

165–66 Dutch policy: for a general overview, see E. L. Engelsman, "Dutch Policy on the Management of Drug-Related Problems," *British Journal of Addiction*, Vol. 84, 1989, pp. 211–18; Govert van de Wijngaart, "A Social History of Drug

Use in the Netherlands: Policy Outcomes and Implications," *Journal of Drug Issues*, Vol. 18, No. 3, 1988, pp. 481–95; for a revealing analysis of street police practice with regard to drugs in Holland, see Hans T. Verbraeck, "The German Bridge: A Street Hookers' Strip in the Amsterdam Red Light District," in Lambert, *The Collection and Interpretation of Data from Hidden Populations*, pp. 146–55. German court: An appeals court in the city of Lübeck ruled in early 1992 that "laws against possession of marijuana and hashish are unconstitutional"; New York *Times*, March 3, 1992.

166 Zurich policy: Burton Bollag, "To the Swiss and Dutch, Tolerance Is Anti-Drug," New York *Times*, December 1, 1989.

166 "Warriors" versus free-market advocates: Cf. Susanne MacGregor, "American Nightmare," p. 869; "The American debate is posed largely between free-marketeers and conservatives."

166–67 Philosophical principles: For recent general discussions of the issue, see, among others, Ethan Nadelman, "The Case for Legalization," *The Public Interest*, No. 92, Summer 1988, pp. 3–31; Doug Bandow, "Dealing with Legalization," *The American Prospect*, No. 8, Winter 1992, pp. 82–91, for the positive side. For critiques from several different vantage points: James B. Jacobs, "Imagining Legalization," *The Public Interest*, No. 101, Fall 1990, pp. 28–41; John M. Kaplan, "Taking Drugs Seriously," *The Public Interest*, No. 92, Summer 1988, pp. 32–50; James Q. Wilson, "Against the Legalization of Drugs," *Commentary*, February 1990, pp. 21–28. Some of my own discussion in the following pages first saw the light in "The Limits of Legalization," *The American Prospect*, No. 8, Winter 1992.

167 Recent advocate: Bandow, "Dealing with Legalization," p. 89. "Primary and secondary effects": I am borrowing the terms from Engelsman, "Dutch Policy," p. 214.

168 "The bulk of murders and property crimes": Bandow, "Dealing with legalization," p. 84.

169 British study: Philip T. Bean and Christine K. Wilkinson, "Drug Taking, Crime, and the Illicit Supply System," *British Journal of Addiction*, Vol. 83, 1988, p. 533.

169 Ball and Anglin research: Cited in Bernard A. Gropper, *Probing the Links Between Drugs and Crime*, Washington, DC, National Institute of Justice, 1985, p. 3. See also M. Douglas Anglin and George Speckart, "Narcotics Use and Crime: A Multisample, Multimethod Analysis," *Criminology*, Vol. 26, No. 2, 1988, pp. 197–233.

It should be noted, too, that these links between levels of drug use and levels of crime are correlations which do not necessarily imply a causal relationship—or indicate its direction. For example, the fact that drug use rises in harness with rising property crime may simply mean that addicts who commit many crimes have more money to buy drugs. On this point, see the useful discussion in Richard Hammersly, Alasdair Forsyth, Valerie Morrison, and John B. Davies, "The Relation Between Crime and Opioid Use," *British Journal of Addiction*, Vol. 84, 1989, pp. 1033–34.

169–70 Vaillant finding: "Long-Term Follow-up," p. 1150. Federal survey: Christopher A. Innes, *Drug Use and Crime*, Washington, DC, U.S. Bureau of Justice Statistics, 1988, p. 1.

170 Faupel and Klockars findings: "Drugs/Crime Connections," p. 56.

170–71 Nurco study: David N. Nurco, Thomas F. Hanlon, Mitchell B. Balter, Timothy W. Kinlock, and Evelyn Slaght, "A Classification of Narcotic Addicts Based on Type, Amount, and Severity of Crime," *Journal of Drug Issues*, Vol. 21, No. 2, 1991, pp. 429–48. Interestingly, the "uninvolved" tended to have started drug use at a later age—about twenty-five on average—suggesting again that involvement in crime may have more to do with the lifestyle of early drug users than with drug use per se.

171–72 Johnson et al. research: Bruce D. Johnson, Eric D. Wish, James Schmeidler, and David Huizinga, "Concentration of Delinquent Offending: Serious Drug Involvement and High Delinquency Rates," *Journal of Drug Issues*, Vol. 21, No. 2, 1991, p. 220.

172 Elliott and Huizinga quote: Cited in John K. Watters, Craig Reinarman, and Jeffrey Fagan, "Causality, Context, and Contingency: Relationships Between Drug Abuse and Delinquency," *Contemporary Drug Issues*, Fall 1985, p. 359.

172–73 Finestone quote: "Narcotics and Criminality," pp. 150–51.

173 Goldstein study: Paul J. Goldstein, Patricia A. Belluci, Barry J. Spunt, and Thomas Miller, "Volume of Cocaine Use and Violence: A Comparison Between Men and Women," *Journal of Drug Issues*, Vol. 21, No. 2, 1991. An earlier discussion of the three forms of drug-related violence may be found in Paul Goldstein, "The Drugs/Violence Nexus: A Tripartite Conceptual Framework," *Journal of Drug Issues*, Vol. 15, No. 4, 1985, pp. 493–506.

173 "Systemic" homicides: Paul J. Goldstein, Henry H. Brownstein, Patrick J. Ryan, and Patricia Belluci, "Crack and Homicide in New York City, 1988: A Conceptually Based Event Analysis," *Contemporary Drug Problems*, Winter 1989, pp. 651–85. The researchers attribute the high proportion of "systemic" homicides to the "powerful weaponry" carried by serious drug traffickers, which tends to make systemic violence more lethal than the routine violence committed by users; p. 684.

174–75 "Zeros": Taylor, *Dangerous Society*, pp. 56–57.

176 Oakland gang: Lance Williams, "Bloodshed in Oakland Traced to 3-year Feud," San Francisco *Examiner*," February 9, 1992.

176–77 Scottish drug users: Hammersly et al., "Relationship Between Crime and Opioid Use," pp. 1038–41; Richard Hammersly, Alasdair Forsyth, and Tara Lavelle, "The Criminality of New Drug Users in Glasgow," *British Journal of Addiction*, Vol. 85, 1990, pp. 1584–92.

177 London prescribing studies: See Graham Jarvis and Howard Parker, "Can Medical Treatment Reduce Crime Amongst Young Heroin Users?" *Home Office Research Bulletin*, No. 28, London, 1990, p. 29; T. Bennett and R. Wright, "The Impact of Prescribing on the Crimes of Opioid Users," *British Journal of Addiction*, Vol. 81, 1986, pp. 265–73. Bennett and Wright did find, however, that the amount of crime diminished when addicts were receiving prescribed opiates.

178 Burr study: A. Burr, "A British View of Prescribing Pharmaceutical Heroin to Opiate Addicts: A Critique of the 'Heroin Solution' with Special Reference to the Piccadilly and Kensington Market Street Scenes in London," *International Journal of the Addictions*, Vol. 21, No. 1, 1986, pp. 90–93.

178–79 Bean and Wilkinson quote: "Drug Taking, Crime, and the Illicit Supply System," p. 538.

180 Swedish example: On drugs and drug policy in Sweden, see, for example, Swedish National Council for Crime Prevention, *Current Swedish Legislation on Narcotics and Psychotropic Substances*, Stockholm, 1990; Swedish Ministry of Justice, *National Report on the Drug Abuse Situation in Sweden*, Stockholm, 1991; Arthur Gould, "Cleaning the People's Home: Recent Developments in Sweden's Addiction Policy," *British Journal of Addiction*, Vol. 84, 1989, pp. 731–41.

181 "Egregious mistakes": I have argued this point more extensively in "Drugs and Crime: Reclaiming a Liberal Issue," in John F. Sears, ed., *Franklin D. Roosevelt and the Future of Liberalism*, Westport, CT, Meckler, 1991, pp. 71–88.

182 Myth of dire consequences: Probably the best-known critique of the view that drug use necessarily results in uncontrollable addiction is Norman Zinberg, *Drug, Set and Setting: The Basis for Controlled Intoxicant Use*, New Haven, Yale University Press, 1984.

182 Ravensholt estimates: R. T. Ravensholt, "Addiction Mortality in the United States: Tobacco, Alcohol, and Other Substances," *Population and Development Review*, Vol. 10. No. 4, December 1984, pp. 714–16.

182–83 Harlem hospital figures: David Bateman, "Infant Morbidity in Harlem: A Status Report," *Journal of Health Care for the Poor and Underserved*, Vol. 2, No. 1, Summer 1991, p. 42. Ten percent of inner-city women: Lynn T. Singer, Rachel Garber, and Robert Kliegman, "Neurobehavioral Sequelae of Fetal Cocaine Exposure," *Journal of Pediatrics*, Vol. 119, No. 4, October 1991, p. 667. Bronx pregnancies: Wendy Chavkin, Cynthia R. Driver, and Pat Forman,

"The Crisis in New York City's Perinatal Services," *New York State Journal of Medicine*, December 1989, p. 660. Overall estimates of babies "exposed to cocaine": Cited in Singer et al., "Neurobehavioral Sequelae," p. 667. Recent review: Quote from Singer et al., "Neurobehavioral Sequelae," p. 668. See also Mark Mirochnick, Jerrold Meyer, Jean Cole, Tim Herren, and Barry Zuckerman, "Circulating Catecholamine Concentrations in Cocaine-Exposed Neonates: A Pilot Study," *Pediatrics*, Vol. 88, No. 3, September 1991; and, most recently, Michael J. Corwin, Barry M. Lester, Carol Sepkoski, Sarah McLaughlin, Herbert Kayne, and Howard L. Golub, "Effects of In Utero Cocaine Exposure on Newborn Acoustical Cry Characteristics," *Pediatrics*, Vol. 89, No. 6, June 1992, pp. 1199–1203. For a general overview, see U.S. General Accounting Office, *Drug-Exposed Infants: A Generation at Risk*, Washington, DC, Government Printing Office, 1990.

183–84 Harlem babies: Bateman, "Infant Morbidity," p. 43. New York low birth weight: Chavkin et al., "Crisis in New York City's Perinatal Service," p. 660.

184 Moore finding: Joan Moore, "Mexican-American Women," p. 148. PCP findings: Laura Wachsman, Sally Schuetz, Linda S. Chan, and Willis A. Wingert, "What Happens to Babies Exposed to Phencyclidine (PCP) In Utero?" *American Journal of Drug and Alcohol Abuse*, Vol. 15, No. 1, 1989, pp. 31–32. PCP use generally declined in most cities with the advent of crack, so the 12 percent figure would probably not be replicated in the early 1990s.

184 HIV and syphilis in newborns: Bateman, "Infant Morbidity," pp. 44–45.

184 "Best evidence": Singer et al., "Neurobehavioral Sequelae," pp. 669–70.

185 Chasnoff findings: Ira J. Chasnoff, Dan R. Griffith, Catherine Freier, and James Murray, "Cocaine/Polydrug Use in Pregnancy: Two-Year Follow-up," *Pediatrics*, Vol. 89, No. 2, February 1992. See also the commentary on this study by Barry Zuckerman and Deborah A. Frank, " 'Crack Kids': Not Broken," in ibid., pp. 337–39.

185–86 Zuckerman research: Barry Zuckerman et al., "Effects of Maternal Marijuana and Cocaine Use on Fetal Growth," *New England Journal of Medicine*, No. 320, March 1989, pp. 762–68. "More recent studies": Quotes from Singer et al., "Neurobehavioral Sequelae," p. 669. This article is a useful, balanced review of the issue.

186 Bateman quote: "Infant Morbidity," p. 43. Passive cocaine exposure: Ibid., p. 43. Child-abuse trends: See Dean Baquet, "New York City Neglect Hearings Upheld in Newborn Cocaine Cases," New York *Times*, May 30, 1990; J. C. Barden, "Foster Care System Reeling, Despite Law Meant to Help," New York *Times*, September 21, 1990; Nancy Lewis, "Child Neglect, Abuse Up 60% in D.C.," Washington *Post*, May 20, 1992; Bateman, "Infant Morbidity," p. 43.

187 Other primary costs: On the health effects of adolescent drug abuse, see, for example, Ann F. Brunswick and Peter Messeri, "Drugs, Lifestyle, and Health," *American Journal of Public Health*, Vol. 76, No. 1, January 1986, pp. 552–57, which found that inhalant, methadone, and heroin use in adolescence (for women) were associated with a decline in young urban blacks' health in early adulthood; Michael D. Newcomb and P. M. Bentler, "The Impact of Late Adolescent Substance Use on Young Adult Health Status and Utilization of Health Services," *Social Science and Medicine*, Vol. 24, No. 1, 1987, pp. 71–82, which found that "hard drug use was associated with increased emergency physician visits during adolescence and increased perceived trouble with health as young adults."

187 Community demoralization: Compare the discussion fifteen years ago by Irving Lukoff, in "Consequences of Use: Heroin and Other Narcotics," pp. 205–6: " . . . when we see such large segments of particular populations involved either directly, or through family and friends, with heroin use, then the apparently libertarian approach to heroin use becomes less tenable . . . the dimensions of the problem force a reassessment, one that focusses not on individuals alone . . . but on the impact this has on the communities where heroin use is endemic. A large proportion of heroin users generally become involved at relatively youthful ages—late teens and early twenties, years during which the rest of their age-mates are finishing school, exploring the world of work, entering the military, getting married—all the activities which are essential for the assumption of adult roles. This truncation of significant socialization processes can only occasionally be recapitulated at a later age . . . Significant segments of the population are literally removed from the creative work of the community. And the communities involved are those that are in the weakest positions with respect to carrying out successful efforts on their own behalf . . . energies that could be spent on community development are, instead, diverted into social control mechanisms, drug treatment programs, and dealing with the consequences of large congeries of addicted persons, crime, and the attendant social disorganization." These comments were made well before the crack and cocaine explosion dramatically multiplied the numbers addicted to hard drugs in those communities.

187–88 Alcohol consumption and availability: For a useful review of these issues, see Mary Jane Ashley and James G. Rankin, "A Public Health Approach to the Prevention of Alcohol-Related Problems," *Annual Review of Public Health*, Vol. 9, 1988, pp. 247–54.

188 Harlem blacks: Colin McCord and Howard Freeman, "Excess Mortality in Harlem," *New England Journal of Medicine*, No. 322, 1990, pp. 173–77. Deaths from drug abuse also figure disproportionately in overall death rates for Hispanics, especially Puerto Ricans; cf. Donna Shai and Lewis Aptekar, "Factors in Mortality by Drug Dependence Among Puerto Ricans in New

York City," *American Journal of Drug and Alcohol Abuse*, Vol. 16, Nos. 1 and 2, 1990, pp. 97–107.

188 OECD tobacco study: Murray Laugeson and Chris Mends, "Tobacco Advertising Restrictions, Price, Income, and Tobacco Consumption in OECD Countries, 1960–86," *British Journal of Addiction*, Vol. 86, No. 10, October 1991, p. 1352. For the impact of alcohol advertising, see the discussion in Ashley and Rankin, "A Public Health Approach," pp. 260–62. For both alcohol and tobacco, these studies suggest that price has a more significant effect than advertising on consumption. Since price would be expected to fall with legalization of hard-drug sales, that has troubling implications for the free-market approach.

191–92 Dutch penalties: Engelsman, "Dutch Policy," p. 213. Swedish sentences: *National Report on the Drug Situation in Sweden*, p. 3, and generally Swedish National Council for Crime Prevention, *Current Swedish Legislation*. Study of Swedish policy: Michael Finkelstein, "Drug Abuse Reduction Schemes: A Comparison Between Sweden and the United States," *Brooklyn Journal of International Law*, Vol. 14, No. 3, 1988, p. 671. Swedish drug use trends: *National Report*, p. 1.

192–93 Delaware study: John Doble, Stephen Immerwahr, and Amy Richardson, *Punishing Criminals: The People of Delaware Consider the Options*, New York, Public Agenda Foundation, 1991, p. 35.

193–94 Dutch policy: From Engelsman, "Dutch Policy," esp. pp. 212–17.

194 Proportion in contact with helping agencies: Ibid., p. 217.

195 California possession figures: Blue Ribbon Commission, p. 69.

195 DC survey: Cited in CEWG, *Proceedings, December 1990*, pp. 322–23. This has been a consistent finding since at least the mid-1980s. In 1986, an ABC/Washington *Post* poll found that roughly 85 percent of respondents agreed that "the best place for most drug users is in a treatment program and not jail"—while just 4 percent agreed that "all drugs should be made legal." Cited in U.S. Bureau of Justice Statistics, *Sourcebook of Criminal Justice Statistics, 1987*, p. 194. Similarly, only 4 percent of respondents to a 1990 Gallup poll said that arresting users "deserved the most money and effort" in the fight against drugs. Cited in *Sourcebook of Criminal Justice Statistics, 1990*, p. 235.

The idea of separating the response to users from that toward serious traffickers is, of course, not a new one in the United States. The position I've taken here is quite similar, for example, to the one adopted by the Ford Foundation-sponsored Drug Abuse Survey Project in the early 1970s: "We believe that the individual and social harm caused by imposing criminal sanctions on drug users far outstrips the benefits of this approach . . . as a first step in bringing the problem back into perspective, criminal penalties for possession of illegal drugs for personal use only should be abandoned in many jurisdictions. If this were done, drug users—but not drug traffickers

—could then be handled on a public health and social welfare basis . . . We have seen no evidence that eliminating the criminal penalties for possession of illegal drugs for personal use would materially impede the effectiveness of law enforcement efforts against trafficking or remove an incentive for drug users to seek treatment or have other unfortunate consequences . . . Eliminating criminal penalties for possession for personal use would neither legalize a particular drug nor permit its use. Law enforcement efforts would, and in our opinion should, continue, but they would be directed at illegal distribution . . . Finally, law enforcement could continue to act as an intake unit for treatment programs for those drug abusers accused of minor trafficking or other crimes. Where the drug taking results in dangerous antisocial acts, it is not unjust to require the offender to undergo treatment as a condition of liberty or even to offer it to him within the confines of the institution. But law enforcement's main focus would be directed at illegal drug wholesalers. In this endeavor, it would have the wholehearted backing of vast numbers of Americans, young and old alike." *Dealing with Drug Abuse*, pp. 36–37.

195 "Trickle up": Franklin Zimring and Gordon Hawkins, *The Search for Rational Drug Control*, Cambridge, Cambridge University Press, 1992, pp. 109–10.

196 "Social disaster": *National Drug Control Strategy*, 1990, p. 5. Dutch drug use trends: Engelsman, "Dutch Policy," p. 212.

197 Prison drug figure: Marcia R. Chaiken, *Prison Programs for Drug-Involved Offenders*, National Institute of Justice, October 1989, p. 1. California figures: Center on Juvenile and Criminal Justice, *Parole Violators in California: A Waste of Money, a Waste of Time*, San Francisco, 1991, p. 7. Commission quote: Blue Ribbon Commission, p. 72.

198 "Drug-related area": Center on Juvenile and Criminal Justice, *Parole Violators*, pp. 2, 7. "Limited options": Blue Ribbon Commission, pp. 74–75.

199 Vaillant findings: "Long-Term Follow-up," pp. 1153–54.

199–200 Declining resources: Blue Ribbon Commission, p. 111. Compare the conclusion in a recent report from a national organization of state court administrators: "Prisons are overcrowded, probation is underfunded, adequate alternatives to incarceration do not exist, and treatment programs are largely unavailable. Judges often see the same people appear in court over and over again." Robert D. Lipscher, "The Judicial Reponse to the Drug Crisis," *State Court Journal*, Fall 1989, p. 15.

200–1 Evaluations of prison treatment: See generally National Task Force on Correctional Substance Abuse Strategies, *Intervening with Substance-Abusing Offenders: A Framework for Action*, Washington, DC, National Institute of Corrections, 1991, pp. 28–50; Harry K. Wexler, John Blackmore, and Douglas S. Lipton, "Project Reform: Developing a Drug Abuse Treatment Strategy for Corrections," *Journal of Drug Issues*," Vol. 21, No. 2, 1991, pp.

469–90. "Survival needs": Ibid., p. 485. For an analysis of one attempt to institute effective treatment in a city jail setting, see Karen A. Klocke, "Drug-Related Crime and Addicted Offenders: A Proposed Response," *Notre Dame Journal of Law, Ethics, and Public Policy*, Vol. 5, No. 3, 1991, on programs in New York's Rikers Island prison.

201 Passages program: National Task Force, *Intervening with Substance-Abusing Offenders*, pp. 119–21. See also Jim Murphy, Nancy Johnson, and Wanda Edwards, *Addicted Mothers, Imprisonment and Alternatives*, New York, New York State Coalition for Criminal Justice, 1992.

201 GAO findings: Cited in *Criminal Justice Newsletter*, Vol. 22, No. 21, November 1, 1991, pp. 2–3.

202–3 Boot camps: See generally Merry Morash and Lila Rucker, "A Critical Look at the Idea of Boot Camp as a Correctional Reform," *Crime and Delinquency*, Vol. 36, No. 2, April 1990, pp. 204–22; Doris Mackenzie, "Boot Camp Prisons: Components, Evaluations, and Empirical Issues," *Federal Probation*, September 1990: U.S. National Institute of Justice, *NIJ Reports*, No. 222, November–December 1990, pp. 2–8; Dale Sechrest, "Prison 'Boot Camps' Do Not Measure Up," *Federal Probation*, September 1989, pp. 15–20.

203 California boot camps: National Council on Crime and Delinquency, "California Governor Signs Legislation Creating "Bootcamp" for Juveniles at the California Youth Authority," News Release, San Francisco, March 5, 1992.

205 Crackdown studies: See generally the review by Lawrence W. Sherman, "Police Crackdowns: Initial and Residual Deterrence," in Michael Tonry and Norval Morris, eds., *Criminal Justice Review Annual*, 1990, Chicago, University of Chicago Press, 1990, pp. 18–25.

206–7 Skolnick research: Jerome H. Skolnick, *Policing Drugs: The Cultural Transformation of a Victimless Crime*, Jurisprudence and Social Policy Program, University of California, Berkeley, 1986, pp. 47–49.

207 Sherman quote: "Police Crackdowns," p. 25.

208 Albuquerque mini station: Described in U.S. Office of National Drug Control Policy, *Fighting Back*, Washington, DC, December 1989. New Haven police: Sentencing Project, *Report* from the Sentencing Project, Washington, DC, Summer 1991, p. 2.

208 British study: Trevor Bennett, "The Effectiveness of a Police-Initiated Fear-Reducing Strategy," *British Journal of Criminology*, Vol. 31, No. 1, Winter 1991.

209 New York experience: George James, "In Every Category, Crime Statistics Declined Last Year in New York City," New York *Times*, March 25, 1992.

210 Bronx program: Milton S. Eisenhower Foundation, *Youth Investment and Community Reconstruction: Street Lessons on Drugs and Crime for the Nineties*, Washington, DC, 1990, p. 39.

211 Moore and Kleiman quote: Mark Moore and Mark Kleiman, *The Police and Drugs*, Washington, DC, National Institute of Justice, 1989, p. 5.

Chapter 5: Redefining Treatment

215 "Disease concept": Norman S. Miller and Mark S. Gold, "The Disease and Adaptive Models of Addiction: A Re-evaluation," *Journal of Drug Issues*, Vol. 20, No. 1, 1990, pp. 31–32.

216 "Relapsing disorder": Congress of the United States, Office of Technology Assessment (OTA), *The Effectiveness of Drug Abuse Treatment: Implications for Controlling AIDS/HIV Infection*, Washington, DC, 1990, p. 1 (hereafter cited as *Effectiveness of Treatment*).

218 Early studies: See Lee Robins, "Addict Careers," in Robert L. DuPont et al., *Handbook on Drug Abuse*, Washington, DC, NIDA, 1979; and Ploscowe, "Some Basic Problems," pp. 88–91. Ploscowe cites the finding that only 2 of 30 young addicts in Chein's NYU study treated at New York's Riverside Hospital were abstinent one year after discharge; 22 of the 30 were reinstitutionalized in a jail or hospital (p. 91).

218 Ford conclusion: *Dealing with Drug Abuse*, p. 21.

218 Federal surveys: The best concise analysis of the uses and limits of these surveys is the OTA's *Effectiveness of Treatment*, Chapter 4, from which most of the following data are drawn.

219 Clinic closings: William H. McGlothlin and Douglas M. Anglin, "Shutting Off Methadone: Costs and Benefits," *Archives of General Psychiatry*, Vol. 38, 1981, pp. 885–92.

219–20 Ball study: John C. Ball, W. Robert Lange, C. Patrick Myers, and Samuel R. Friedman, "Reducing the Risk of AIDS Through Methadone Maintenance Treatment," *Journal of Health and Social Behavior*, Vol. 29, September 1988, p. 218.

220 TOPS data: OTA, *Effectiveness of Treatment*, p. 85.

221 Vaillant quote: "Long-Term Follow-up," p. 1147.

221–22 Smart quote: Reginald D. Smart, "Comments on Sells' Paper," in Rittenhouse, *Epidemiology of Heroin and Other Narcotics*, pp. 180–81.

222 Kleinman study: Paula Holzman Kleinman, Irving F. Lukoff, and Barabara Lynn Kail, "The Magic Fix: A Critical Analysis of Methadone Maintenance Treatment," *Social Problems*, Vol. 25, No. 2, December 1977, p. 212.

222-23 Dropouts: Ball et al., "Reducing the Risk of AIDS," p. 221; TOPS findings on TCs: OTA, *Effectiveness of Treatment*, pp. 81, 83.

Treatment dropout rates are also high in other countries. Thus from 40 to 70 percent of clients in German programs, according to a recent review, drop out within six months. Rolf Wille, "Drug Addiction in the Federal Republic of Germany: Problems and Responses," *British Journal of Addiction*, Vol. 82, 1987, p. 853.

223 Smart quote: "Comments on Sells' Paper," p. 179.

223-24 Ball finding: "Reducing the Risk of AIDS," p. 221.

224 Long Island program: William Feigelman, Merton M. Hyman, Kenneth Amann, and Beverly Feigelman, "Correlates of Persistent Drug Use Among Former Youth Multiple Drug Abuse Patients," *Journal of Psychoactive Drugs*, Vol. 22, No. 1, January–March 1990, p. 64.

224-25 ACI: Charles Winick, "Retention and Outcome at ACI, a Unique Therapeutic Community," *International Journal of the Addictions*, Vol. 25, No. 1, 1990, pp. 1-25.

225 Recent review: M. Douglas Anglin and Yih-Ing Hser, "Treatment of Drug Abuse," in Michael Tonry and James Q. Wilson, *Crime and Justice: Annual Review*, 1990, as cited in OTA, *Effectiveness of Treatment*, pp. 88–89.

225 Mexican-American data: Cited in Joseph E. Trimble, Amado M. Padilla, and Catherine S. Bell, eds., *Drug Abuse Among Ethnic Minorities*, Washington, DC, NIDA, 1987, p. 27. Chicanos and methadone: Yih-Ing Hser, M. Douglas Anglin, and Chih-Ping Chou, "Evaluation of Drug Abuse Treatment: A Repeated Measures Design Assessing Methadone Maintenance," *Evaluation Review*, Vol. 12, No. 5, October 1988, p. 568. See also Mary W. Booth, Felipe G. Castro, and M. Douglas Anglin, "What Do We Know About Hispanic Substance Abuse? A Review of the Literature," in Glick and Moore, *Drugs in Hispanic Communities*, pp. 21–44.

226 Maddux and Desmond quote: "Mexican-American Heroin Addicts," pp. 333-34. The researchers provide this dreary breakdown of the status of a group of Mexican-American addicts followed up to age fifty: 10 percent still using opiates daily; 14 percent on methadone; 15 percent abusing alcohol; 15 percent institutionalized; 19 percent dead (mainly from homicide, overdose, liver disease, and accidents); 8 percent unknown; 19 percent "abstinent, not alcoholic" (p. 334).

227 Ford estimate: *Dealing with Drug Abuse*, p. 22. Houston study: Mark L. Williams, "Intergenerational Differences in IV Drug Use Behaviors: Implications for HIV Prevention," *International Journal of the Addictions*, Vol. 26, No. 4, 1991, p. 461. New York sample: Jeffrey Fagan and Ko-Lin Chin, "Social Processes of Initiation into Crack," *Journal of Drug Issues*, Vol. 21, No. 2, 1991, p. 320. IV women: Theodore Hammett, Dana Hunt, Michael Gross,

William Rhodes, and Saira Moini, "Stemming the Spread of HIV Among IV Drug Users, Their Sexual Partners, and Children: Issues and Opportunities for Criminal Justice Agencies," *Crime and Delinquency*, Vol. 37, No. 1, January 1991, p. 107; jail inmates: U.S. Bureau of Justice Statistics, *Drugs and Jail Inmates 1989*, Washington, DC, 1991, p. 11.

227 55 percent: Williams, "Intergenerational Differences," p. 463. Johnson findings: *Taking Care of Business*, pp. 161–62.

228 GAO study: U.S. General Accounting Office, *Methadone Maintenance: Some Treatment Programs Are Not Effective*, Washington, DC, 1990, p. 30. New York survey: New York *Times*, December 5, 1991. The GAO study found that as of June 1989 there were 900 people on waiting lists for methadone treatment in New York, and cited a telephone survey finding 600 available methadone treatment "slots" in August of that year (p. 31).

228–29 Treatment capacity figures: NIDA, *Highlights from the 1989 National Drug and Alcohol Treatment Unit Survey (NDATUS)*, Washington, DC, 1990, p. 3. The figures include programs offering only drug abuse treatment and those providing both drug and alcohol treatment. Again, public programs in especially hard-hit cities are generally fuller; public clinics in New York City, according to one estimate, were operating at 97 percent of capacity in 1990. CEWG *Proceedings, June 1991*, p. 215.

229 Waiting list figure: From a 1989 survey by the National Association of State Alcohol and Drug Abuse Directors, cited in OTA, *Effectiveness of Treatment*, p. 57. The survey apparently does not cover all treatment "units" and therefore somewhat underestimates the backlog; but it also includes both "alcohol and other drug treatment," thus biasing the figure in the other direction.

229 Johnson quote: *Taking Care of Business*, p. 166. Among addicts receiving methadone while in Rikers Island prison in New York, 93 percent reported that they "intended to enroll in a methadone program when released, but only 50 percent actually did, and only 20 percent remained in treatment five months after release. Magura et al., "AIDS Risk Among Intravenous Drug-Using Offenders," p. 95.

230 "Most rejected treatment": Patrick Biernacki, "Recovery from Opiate Addiction Without Treatment: A Summary," in Lambert, *The Collection and Interpretation of Data from Hidden Populations*, p. 115. Cf. Fitzpatrick, "Drugs and Puerto Rican Communities," p. 117: "Most of the heavy drug users and addicts in this study . . . have never been in programs of any kind, and they do not want to be."

230 Parker quote: *Living with Heroin*, p. 67. Pearson quote: *New Heroin Users*, p. 161. For related British research on the utilization of treatment, see Margaret Sheehan, Edna Oppenheimer, and Colin Taylor, "Who Comes for Treatment:

Drug Misusers at Three London Agencies," *British Journal of Addiction*, Vol. 83, 1988, pp. 311–20.

232 Winick study: Charles Winick, "Maturing Out of Narcotic Addiction," *Bulletin on Narcotics*, January–March 1962, pp. 1–7.

233 Robins findings: Robins and Murphy, "Drug Use in a Normal Population of Negro Men," p. 1595.

233–34 Waldorf study: Dan Waldorf, "Life Without Heroin: Some Social Adjustments During Long-Term Periods of Voluntary Abstention," *Social Problems*, Vol. 18, No. 2, Fall 1970; quote from p. 232.

234–35 Vietnam addicts: Lee N. Robins, Darlene H. Davis, and David N. Nurco, "How Permanent Was Vietnam Drug Addiction?" *American Journal of Public Health*, Supplement, Vol. 64, December 1974, pp. 38–43.

235 "Recent review": Robb Stall and Patrick Biernacki, "Spontaneous Remission from the Problematic Use of Substances: An Inductive Model Derived from a Comparative Analysis of the Alcohol, Opiate, Tobacco, and Food/Obesity Literatures," *International Journal of the Addictions*, Vol. 21, No. 1, 1986, pp. 1–23. For a recent affirmation of the finding with respect to smoking, see "Kicking the Habit Without Help," New York *Times*, May 29, 1990; reporting on a University of Wisconsin study finding that twice as many people who try to quit smoking on their own succeed as those who enroll in formal antismoking programs.

236–37 Brunswick findings: Ann F. Brunswick and Peter A. Messeri, "Pathways to Heroin Abstinence: A Longitudinal Study of Urban Black Youth," *Advances in Alcohol and Substance Abuse*, Vol. 5, No. 3, Spring 1986, pp. 125–30.

237–38 Ray study: Marsh B. Ray, "The Cycle of Abstinence and Relapse Among Heroin Addicts," *Social Problems*, Vol. 9, 1961, pp. 132–40.

238 Waldorf findings: "Life Without Heroin," pp. 232–34.

239 Biernacki quote: "Recovery from Opiate Addiction," p. 117.

239 Stall and Biernacki: "Spontaneous Remission," p. 18.

239–40 Vaillant findings: "Long-Term Follow-up," pp. 1149–54. Given the drastic budget cuts and rising caseloads in many parole agencies, it is unlikely that conventional parole works as well in this respect in many jurisdictions today. On the state of parole in one state, see Anthony J. Costello, *The Revolving Door: A Study of Parole Violators in California's Failing System of Corrections*, Honors Thesis, Department of Sociology, University of California, Berkeley, 1992.

241 Vaillant in sixties: George Vaillant, "A Twelve-Year Follow-up of New York Narcotic Addicts, IV: Some Characteristics and Determinants of Abstinence," *American Journal of Psychiatry*, Vol. 123, 1966, p. 573.

241–42 Dutch specialist: Govert van de Wijngaart, "What Lessons from the Dutch Experience Can Be Applied?" *British Journal of Addiction*, Vol. 84, 1989, p. 991.

242 Ball on counseling: John C. Ball and Eric Corty, "Basic Issues Pertaining to the Effectiveness of Methadone Maintenance Treatment," in Carl Leukefeld and Frank M. Tims, *Compulsory Treatment of Drug Abuse: Research and Clinical Practice*, Washington, DC, NIDA, 1988, pp. 812–83. GAO finding: *Methadone Maintenance*, p. 23. In general, the GAO found: "Programs are lax in providing vocational and educational services." The GAO also found that even the frequency of counseling was minimal: "In many programs, counselors spent no more than half an hour twice a month per patient." The caseload per counselor ranged as high as 96 to 1 (p. 25).

242 "Figures may exaggerate": Having once worked in a methadone treatment program where my job, among other things, was to write the reports to state and federal authorities describing our level and frequency of services, the tendency of programs to exaggerate these efforts is one with which I am intimately familiar.

243 Proportion still using: Cited in *NIDA Notes*, Spring–Summer 1989, p. 15.
   The finding on staff turnover is especially important since salaries tend to be low and retention of staff uncertain: the GAO found that half of the counselors in the twenty-four programs studied had been employed for less than a year (*Methadone Maintenance*, p. 24).

243 Standards: On this issue generally, see McAuliffe, "Health Care Policy Issues," pp. 372–74.

243 Engelsman quote: "Dutch Drug Policy," p. 215.

244 "User-friendly," "low-threshold": Cf. Engelsman, "Dutch Drug Policy," p. 216; Parker et al., *Living with Heroin*, p. 142.

245 Ball on services: "Basic Issues," pp. 183–84.

245–46 Compelled to enter treatment: See generally Leukefeld and Tims, *Compulsory Treatment*; but see the caveats in Ball and Corty's paper in the same volume.

246 Mexican-Americans: Desmond and Maddux, "Mexican-American Heroin Users," pp. 335, 340. Hispanic interviewer: Cited in Desmond and Maddux, p. 337. See also the discussion in Booth et al., "What Do We Know About Hispanic Substance Abuse?" and Mario De La Rosa, J. H. Khalsa, and Beatrice M. Rouse, "Hispanics and Illicit Drug Use: A Review of Recent Findings," *International Journal of the Addictions*, Vol. 26, No. 6, 1990, p. 678.

246–47 Treatment and the poor: For a sensitive discussion of this issue with respect to white lower-class solvent abusers, see McSherry, "Solvent Abuser in Philadelphia," p. 116: "Most chronic abusers are unable to read and write at a literate level. They have difficulty negotiating transportation networks, buying food, and handling many basic life-management tasks . . . Initial engagement strategies need to appeal to such basic needs as warmth, food, and human contact."

247 NIDA study: Robert Booth, Stephen Koester, J. T. Brewster, Wayne W. Weibel, and Richard B. Fritz, "Intravenous Drug Users and AIDS: Risk Behaviors," *American Journal of Drug and Alcohol Abuse*, Vol. 17, No. 3, 1991, pp. 337–53. Fullilove findings: Robert E. Fullilove, Mindy Thompson Fullilove, Benjamin A. Bowser, and Shirley A. Gross, "Risk of Sexually Transmitted Disease Among Black Adolescent Crack Users in Oakland and San Francisco, Calif.," *Journal of the American Medical Association*, Vol. 263, No. 6, February 9, 1990, pp. 851–55. For a general review of the issue, see OTA, *Effectiveness of Treatment*, Chapter 2.

247–48 "Urgent attention": A good overall discussion of these strategies is Don Nutbeam, Virginia Blakey, and Richard Pates, "The Prevention of HIV Infection from Injecting Drug Use: A Review of Health Promotion Approaches," *Social Science and Medicine*, Vol. 33, No. 9, 1991, pp. 977–83.

248 Amsterdam needle exchanges: J. A. R. van den Hoek, H. J. A. van Haastrecht, and R. A. Coutinho, "Risk Reduction Among Intravenous Drug Users in Amsterdam Under the Influence of AIDS," *American Journal of Public Health*, Vol. 79, No. 10, October 1989; van den Hoek et al., "Course of the HIV Epidemic Among Intravenous Drug Users in Amsterdam"; Australia: Jael Wolk, Alex Wodak, James J. Guinan, Petra Macaskill, and Judy M. Simpson, "The Effect of a Needle and Syringe Exchange on a Methadone Maintenance Unit," *British Journal of Addiction*, Vol. 85, 1990.

249 "Change their ways": A good general discussion is Samuel R. Friedman, Don C. Des Jarlais, and Claire E. Sterk, "AIDS and the Social Relations of Intravenous Drug Users," *Milbank Quarterly*, Vol. 68, Supplement 1, 1990, pp. 85–110. See also, in addition to the studies cited below, Joseph Guydish, George Clark, Delia Garcia, Moher Downing, Patricia Case, and James L. Sorenson, "Evaluating Needle Exchange: Do Distributed Needles Come Back?" *American Journal of Public Health*, Vol. 81, 1991, pp. 617–19.

249–50 Baltimore study: David Vlahov, James C. Anthony, David Celentano, Liza Solomon, and Nurul Chowdury, "Trends of HIV-1 Risk Reduction Among Initiates into Intravenous Drug Use," 1982–1987," *American Journal of Drug and Alcohol Abuse*, Vol. 17, No. 1, 1991, pp. 39–48.

250 Portland study: Beverly Sibthorpe, David Fleming, Helen Tesselaar, and Jeanne Gould, "Needle Use and Sexual Practices: Differences in Perception of Personal Risk of HIV Among Intravenous Drug Users," *Journal of Drug Issues*, Vol. 21, No. 4, 1991, pp. 699–712.

250 Condom study: Diane K. Lewis, John K. Watters, and Patricia Case, "The Prevalence of High-Risk Sexual Behavior in Male Intravenous Drug Users with Steady Female Partners," *American Journal of Public Health*, Vol. 80, 1990,

pp. 465–66. On the difficulty of altering high-risk sexual behavior, see also Friedman et al., "AIDS and the Social Relations of Intravenous Drug Users"; Fen Rhodes et al., "Risk Behaviors and Perceptions of AIDS Among Street Injection Drug Users," *Journal of Drug Education*, Vol. 20, No. 4, 1990, pp. 271–88; Robert F. Schilling, Nabila El-Bassel, Louisa Gilbert, and Steven P. Schinke, "Correlates of Drug Use, Sexual Behavior, and Attitudes Toward Safer Sex Among African-American and Hispanic Women in Methadone Maintenance," *Journal of Drug Issues*, Vol. 21, No. 4, 1991, pp. 685–98.

252 Hawkins quote: J. David Hawkins and Richard F. Catalano, "Aftercare in Drug Abuse Treatment," *International Journal of the Addictions*, Vol. 20, Nos. 6 and 7, 1985, p. 939.

252 GAO finding: *Methadone Maintenance*, p. 27. McAuliffe study: William E. McAuliffe, "A Randomized Controlled Trial of Recovery Training and Self-Help for Opioid Addicts in New England and Hong Kong," *Journal of Psychoactive Drugs*, Vol. 22, No. 2, April–June 1990, pp. 197–209.

253 Hawkins and Catalano quote: "Aftercare in Drug Abuse Treatment," p. 926.

253 Van de Wijngaart quote: "Social History of Drug Use in the Netherlands," p. 491.

254–56 Wildcat: Lucy N. Friedman, *The Wildcat Experiment: An Early Test of Supported Work in Drug Abuse Rehabilitation*, Washington, DC, NIDA, 1978. "Critical vehicle": Ibid., p. 125.

256–57 MDRC findings: Manpower Demonstration Research Corporation, *Summary and Findings of the National Supported Work Demonstration*, New York, Ballinger, 1980, Chapter 9.

257 BTI: See Cynthia B. Hanson, "Binding Together Addicts' Lives," *Christian Science Monitor*, July 30, 1990.

259–60 "Sporadically engaged": For an early discussion of these issues, see Michael J. Polich et al., *Strategies for Controlling Adolescent Substance Abuse*, Santa Monica, Rand Corporation, 1984. TOPS finding: R. L. Hubbard, E. R. Cavanaugh, S. G. Craddock, and J. V. Rachal, "Characteristics, Behaviors, and Outcomes for Youth in the TOPS," in Alfred S. Friedman and George M. Beschner, *Treatment Services for Adolescent Substance Abusers*, Washington, DC, NIDA, 1985, p. 57.

260 "Feel that they are helped": Cited in George Beschner and Alfred S. Friedman, "Treatment of Adolescent Drug Abusers," *International Journal of the Addictions*, Vol. 20, Nos. 6 and 7, 1985, p. 984.

260 Feldman quote: Harvey W. Feldman, Jerry Mandel, and Allen Fields, "In the Neighborhood: A Strategy for Delivering Early Intervention Services to Young Drug Users in Their Natural Environments," in Friedman and Beschner, *Treatment Services*, p. 121.

260 Dembo quote: Richard Dembo, James Schmeidler, William Burgos, and Robert Taylor, "Environmental Setting and Early Drug Involvement Among Inner-City Junior High School Youths," *International Journal of the Addictions*, Vol. 20, No. 8, 1985, p. 1251.

261 "Most important factor": Richard F. Catalano, Elizabeth A. Wells, Jeffrey M. Jenson, and J. David Hawkins, "Aftercare Services for Drug-Using Institutionalized Delinquents," *Social Service Review*, December 1989, p. 566.

261 Brunswick finding: Ann F. Brunswick, "Black Youths and Drug Abuse Behavior," in George Beschner and Alfred S. Friedman, eds., *Youth Drug Abuse*, Washington, DC, NIDA, 1979, p. 475. TOPS figure: Hubbard et al., "Characteristics, Behaviors, and Outcomes," p. 60.

261 Dembo findings: Richard Dembo, James Schmeidler, Robert Taylor, David Agresti, and William Burgos, "Preferred Resources for Help with a Drug Problem Among Youths Living in Different Inner City Neighborhood Settings," *Advances in Alcohol and Substance Abuse*, Vol. 2, No. 4, Spring 1983, p. 69. Bowser quote: "Crack and AIDS: An Ethnographic Impression," *Journal of the National Medical Association*, Vol. 81, No. 5, April 1989, p. 540. Miami youth: Inciardi and Pottieger, "Kids, Crack, and Crime," p. 269.

261–62 TOPS finding: Hubbard et al., "Characteristics, Behaviors, and Outcomes," p. 51.

263 Sweden quote: Swedish Ministry of Health and Social Affairs, *The Swedish Way*, Stockholm, 1987, p. 1.

263 "Not encouraging": British research came to similar conclusions. For a concise review, see Parker et al., *Living with Heroin*, pp. 114–16. "It is now widely recognized," they write, "that school-based education programmes which have tried to deter young people from taking illegal drugs have generally been ineffective, and sometimes counterproductive" (p. 114).

264 Tobler review: Nancy S. Tobler, "Meta-analysis of 143 Adolescent Drug Prevention Programs," *Journal of Drug Issues*, Vol. 16, No. 4, 1986, pp. 537–67. More recent review: Robert L. Bangert-Drowns, "The Effects of School-Based Substance Abuse Education: A Meta-analysis," *Journal of Drug Education*, Vol. 18, No. 3, 1988, p. 260.

264 Project Alert: Phyllis L. Ellickson and Robert M. Bell, "Drug Prevention in Junior High: A Multi-site Longitudinal Test," *Science*, Vol. 247, March 16, 1990, pp. 1299–1305.

264–65 MPP: U.S. Department of Health and Human Services, *HHS News*, June 1, 1990, p. 3; Mary Ann Pentz, Elizabeth A. Trebow, William B. Hansen, David P. MacKinnon, James H. Dwyer, C. Anderson Johnson, Brian R. Flay, Stacey Daniels, and Calvin Cormack, "Effects of Program Implementation on Adolescent Drug Use Behavior," *Evaluation Review*, Vol. 14, No. 3, June 1990, pp. 264–89. Two important caveats should be kept in mind: first, the findings are based on self-reports of drug use; second, the lower rates for program youth do not represent *declines* in their drug use, but slower *rises* in early adolescence as compared with the controls.

267–68 DYC: Milton S. Eisenhower Foundation, *Youth Investment and Community Reconstruction: Street Lessons on Crime and Drugs for the Nineties*, Washington, DC, 1990, pp. 30–34. Youth Investment Corporation: Ibid., pp. 66–72.

270 Hagan study: Cited in Loretta P. Finnegan, Teresa Hagan, and Karol A. Kaltenbach, "Scientific Foundation of Clinical Practice: Opiate Use in Pregnant Women," *Bulletin of the New York Academy of Medicine*, Vol. 67, No. 3, May–June 1991, p. 224.

270 Women and illegal work: Cited in Rebecca Moise, Beth G. Reed, and Virginia Ryan, "Issues in the Treatment of Heroin-Addicted Women: A Comparison of Men and Women Entering Two Types of Drug Abuse Programs," *International Journal of the Addictions*, Vol. 17, No. 1, 1982, p. 134. More recently, Jeffrey Fagan has described women's subordination within the street crack culture as a reflection of "their secondary status in both the formal and underground economies . . . Women are both excluded from and, given the frequent victimization of sellers, may choose not to participate in, the drug selling . . . The sexual exploitation of women in this context is, sadly, not surprising." Jeffrey Fagan, "Drug Selling and Licit Income in Distressed Neighborhoods: The Economic Lives of Street-Level Drug Users and Dealers," in A. Harrell and G. Peterson, eds., *Drugs, Crime, and Urban Opportunity*, Washington, DC, Urban Institute, forthcoming.

270 Housing issues: Finnegan et al., "Scientific Foundation," p. 228.

271 "Virtual absence of ties": Moise et al., "Issues in the Treatment of Heroin-Addicted Women," p. 133.

271 Race and class: See, for example, Thomas R. Kosten, Bruce J. Rounsaville, and Herbert D. Kleber, "Ethnic and Gender Differences Among Opiate Addicts," *International Journal of the Addictions*, Vol. 20, No. 8, 1985, pp. 1143–62.

271 67 programs: Rebecca Johnson and Vince Bielski, "Recovering for Two," *San Francisco Bay Guardian*, May 9, 1990.

271 Rosenbaum finding: Rosenbaum and Murphy, "Women and Addiction," p. 120.

272 Mothers on methadone: Kathleen B. Fiks, Helen L. Johnson, and Tove S. Rosen, "Methadone-Maintained Mothers: 3-year Follow-up of Parental Functioning," *International Journal of the Addictions*, Vol. 20, No. 5, 1985, p. 659.

272 Kail finding: Barbara Lyn Kail and Irving F. Lukoff, "The Black Female Addict's Career Options: A Typology and Theory," *American Journal of Drug and Alcohol Abuse*, Vol. 10, No. 1, 1984, p. 44.

273 Moise quote: "Issues in the Treatment of Heroin-Addicted Women," p. 134. Stereotypes: Cf. Jeanne C. Marsh and Nancy A. Miller, "Female Clients in Substance Abuse Treatment," *International Journal of the Addictions*, Vol. 20, Nos. 6 and 7, 1985, p. 1005. "Hope of economic improvement": Finnegan et al., "Scientific Foundation," p. 226.

273 New York State finding: Murphy et al, *Addicted Mothers, Imprisonment, and Alternatives*, p. 33.

274 "Most of the women": Ibid, pp. 9, 31.

274–75 Detroit program: Marcia D. Anderson, "Personalized Nursing: An Effective Intervention Model for Use with Drug-Dependent Women in an Emergency Room," in Rebecca S. Ashery, ed., *Progress in the Development of Cost-Effective Treatment for Drug Abusers*, Washington, DC, NIDA, 1985, pp. 67–82.

275 Chavkin quote: Chavkin et al., "Crisis in New York City's Perinatal Services," p. 661.

275–76 GAO finding: U.S. General Accounting Office, *Drug-Exposed Infants: A Generation at Risk*, Washington, DC, 1990, p. 37. Fifty-four of 78 treatment programs surveyed in New York denied treatment to pregnant women. Ibid., p. 36. Babies at home: Ibid., p. 39. San Francisco findings: Johnson and Bielski, "Recovery for Two," p. 23. Similar, though perhaps less severe, problems have emerged in Britain. Cf. Parker et al., *Living with Heroin*, pp. 138–39.

276 Harlem figure: Bateman, "Infant Morbidity in Harlem," p. 45. 50 percent figure: Finnegan et al., "Scientific Foundation," p. 229. GAO finding: *Drug-Exposed Infants*, p. 38.

277 Chavkin quote: Wendy Chavkin, "Drug Addiction and Pregnancy: Policy Crossroads," *American Journal of Public Health*, Vol. 80, No. 4, April 1990, p. 486.

277–78 Family Center: Finnegan et al., "Scientific Foundation," pp. 228–31.

Chapter 6: Reconstructing Communities

282 Kennedy quote: Robert F. Kennedy, *To Seek a Newer World*, New York, Bantam Books, 1968, p. 36.

286–87 Workforce Commission findings: From Statement of Ira Magaziner, Chair, Commission on the Skills of the American Workforce, in U.S. Senate, Committee on Labor and Human Resources, Hearing: *Meeting the Challenges of a New Workforce*, Washington, DC, July 19, 1990, pp. 54–69.

288–90 Lerman and Pouncy study: Robert I. Lerman and Hillard Pouncy, "The Compelling Case for Youth Apprenticeships," *The Public Interest*, No. 101, Fall 1990, pp. 62–77.

290–91 Minimum-wage effects: Cf. most recently Alison J. Wellington, "Effects of the Minimum Wage on the Employment Status of Youths," *Journal of Human Resources*, Vol. 26, No. 1, 1990, which finds "no discernible effect on measured unemployment" of teenagers from a 10 percent increase in the minimum wage (p. 27).

291 "Solidaristic" policy: see Gosta Rehn, "Swedish Active Labor Market Policy: Retrospect and Prospect," *Industrial Relations*, Vol. 24, Winter 1985; Robert Kuttner, *The Economic Illusion*, Boston, Houghton Mifflin, 1984, pp. 149–55. "Binding wage floors": Gary Loveman and Chris Tilly, "Good Jobs or Bad Jobs? Evaluating the American Job Creation Experience," *International Labour Review*, Vol. 127, No. 5, 1988, p. 607.

292 Atlanta finding: Orfield and Ashkinaze, *The Closing Door*, p. 177. Training fund: Coalition for Democratic Values, *A New Program for a High-Wage, High-Productivity Economy*, Silver Spring, MD, 1992, p. 3; David Crawford, Prepared Statement, in Committee on Labor and Human Resources, *Meeting the Challenges of a New Workforce*, pp. 51–52.

292 "Recent estimate": Ronald B. Mincy, "Raising the Minimum Wage: Effects on Family Poverty," *Monthly Labor Review*, July 1990, pp. 18–24.

293 "Internalizing costs": Coalition for Democratic Values, *A New Program*, p. 4.

293 OECD data: From A. Reutersward, "A Flexible Labour Market in the 1990s," *OECD Observer*, Vol. 104, 1990, as reprinted in *International Journal of Health Services*, Vol. 21, No. 1, 1990, p. 192.

295 CETA program: Nancy E. Rose, "From the WPA to Workfare," *Journal of Progressive Human Services*, Vol. 1, No. 2, 1990, p. 25. Federal employment spending: *Budget of the United States Government, 1992*, Washington, DC, Government Printing Office, 1992, Part 7, pp. 42–43.

295–96 "Wrong 5 percent": Crawford, Prepared Statement, p. 50. GAO finding: Cited in New York *Times*, August 20, 1991. JTPA in Atlanta: Orfield and Ashkinaze, *The Closing Door*, pp. 202–3, 217.

296–97 Rockefeller study: Jason DeParle, "Skills-Training Policy Opening Doors to Jobs," New York *Times*, October 25, 1990.

297–98 Job Corps data: Jane Gross, "A Remnant of the War on Poverty, the Job Corps Is a Quiet Success," New York *Times*, February 17, 1992; U.S. Congressional Budget Office, *How Federal Spending for Infrastructure and Other Public Investments Affects the Economy*, Washington DC, 1991, pp. 64–68. In 1989, 74 percent of Job Corps enrollees had "positive terminations" from the program—meaning that they were either employed or engaged in further training or schooling (Ways and Means Committee, *Overview of Entitlement Programs*, p. 1455).

For a helpful general discussion of the characteristics of effective youth employment programs, see Ronald L. Taylor, "Improving the Status of Black Youth: Some Lessons from Recent National Experiments," *Youth and Society*, Vol. 22, No. 1, September 1990, pp. 85–107.

300–1 NYA: Lewis L. Lorwin, *Youth Work Programs: Problems and Policies*, Washington, DC, American Council on Education, 1941, pp. 66–69. "A civilized plane:" Dorothy Canfield Fisher, *Our Young Folks*, New York, Harcourt, Brace, 1943, p. 132.

301–2 Kolata quote: Gina Kolata, "Despite Its Promise of Riches, the Crack Trade Seldom Pays," New York *Times*, November 26, 1989. Detroit gang: Thomas Mieczkowski, "Geeking Up and Throwing Down: Heroin Street Life in Detroit," *Criminology*, Vol. 24, No. 4, 1986, pp. 645–64. I've calculated the earnings from figures on p. 653.

Similar findings appear in a number of other studies. A Rand Corporation analysis in Washington, DC, found that adult dealers earned an annual average of $24,000 (in the late 1980s); meanwhile, during each year they were dealing, they faced a 1.4 percent chance of dying, a 7 percent chance of serious injury, and a 22 percent chance of going to jail. Cited in Greater Washington Research Center, *Money from Crime*, Washington, DC, 1990, p. 3. Ansley Hamid describes the crack trade as "a story of widespread demand, instant riches, rapid impoverishment and sudden death": "Political Economy of Crack-Related Violence," p. 57. Cf. Terry Williams, *The Cocaine Kids*, New York, Addison-Wesley, 1989.

305 Falling federal funding: Douglas Martin, "As the City's Poor Grow Sicker, Their Health Clinics Grow Poorer," New York *Times*, March 6, 1991.

305 "Developing countries": Katherine Kaye, "Health Problems Associated with Urban Poverty: A Narrowing Gap Between the Third and First Worlds," *New York State Journal of Medicine*, Vol. 89, No. 12, December 1989, p. 649.

306 Bateman quote: "Infant Morbidity in Harlem," p. 47.

306–7 DC clinics: Washington *Post*, December 7, 1991.

307–8 Aral and Holmes analysis: Sevgai O. Aral and King K. Holmes, "Sexually Transmitted Diseases in the AIDS Era," *Scientific American*, Vol. 264, No. 2, February 1991, pp. 62–69.

307 Mayors' survey: Jayne Garrison, "Cities Face Wave of AIDS Cases," San Francisco *Examiner*, June 14, 1991.

308 Hispanic health care: Eli Ginzberg, "Access to Health Care for Hispanics," *Journal of the American Medical Association*, Vol. 265, No. 2, January 9, 1991, p. 239.

308 Hospital wait survey: Philip J. Hilts, "Public Hospital Wait for Bed Can Be Days, U.S. Study Says," New York *Times*, January 30, 1991. California figures:

Claire Spiegel and Irene Wielawski, "Care Rationed at Crowded County-USC," Los Angeles *Times*, December 16, 1991.

309 New York perinatal care: Chavkin et al., "Crisis in New York City's Perinatal Services," pp. 658–62.

309–10 Washington clinic: Janny Scott, "Trying to Save the Babies," Los Angeles *Times*, December 24, 1990.

310 Other needs: Felicia R. Lee, "Needless Breast Cancer Toll Cited Among New York Poor," New York *Times*, October 31, 1990; Philip J. Hilts, "Modest Spending to Combat Lead Poison Is Planned," New York *Times*, February 21, 1991.

311–12 Family leaves: Data from Sheila B. Kamerman, "Child Care Policies and Programs: An International Overview," *Journal of Social Issues*, Vol. 47, No. 2, 1991, pp. 186–90; "Paid Maternity Leave: Most Nations Follow International Guidelines," *World Monitor*, December 1991, p. 10; Patricia Garrett, Deeann Wenk, and Sally Lubeck, "Working Around Childbirth: Comparative and Empirical Perspectives on Parental-Leave Policy," *Child Welfare*, Vol. 69, No. 5, September–October 1990, pp. 401–13.

312 Zigler quote: Edward F. Zigler, "Addressing the Nation's Child Care Crisis: The School of the Twenty-first Century," *American Journal of Orthopsychiatry*,Vol. 59, No. 4, October 1989, p. 484.

312 "Heavily subsidized": Kamerman, "Child Care Policies," p. 182.

312–13 Recent report: National Research Council, *Who Cares for America's Children*, Washington, DC, 1990, cited in San Jose *Mercury News*, March 15, 1990.

313 Data on child-care workers: Zigler, "Child Care Crisis," pp. 485–88. French practice: Hillary Rodham Clinton, "In France, Day Care Is Every Child's Right," New York *Times*, April 7, 1990.

313 Department of Labor study: Peter Cattan, "Child Care Problems; An Obstacle to Work," *Monthly Labor Review*, Octoer 1991, pp. 3–9. Cf. David J. Maume, Jr., "Child Care Expenditures and Women's Employment Turnover," *Social Forces*, Vol. 70, No. 2, December 1991, pp. 495–508.

314 "Major review": Sheila B. Kamerman and Alfred J. Kahn, "Social Services for Children, Youth, and Families in the United States," *Children and Youth Services Review*, Vol. 12, Nos. 1–2, 1990, pp. 7–15.

314–15 PEIP: David Olds et al., "Improving the Life Course Development of Socially Disadvantaged Mothers: A Randomized Trial of Nurse Home Visitation," *American Journal of Public Health*, Vol. 78, 1988, pp. 1436–45; Lisbeth B. Schorr, *Within Our Reach: Breaking the Cycle of Disadvantage*, New York, Doubleday, 1989, pp. 169–75.

315 Forthright report: U.S. Advisory Board on Child Abuse and Neglect, *Child Abuse and Neglect: Critical First Steps in Response to a National Emergency*, Washington, DC, Government Printing Office, 1990, p. 81. The Advisory Board points out that home visitation programs "are universal in many developed countries," and that "what used to be an extensive network throughout the United States of supportive public health nurses who would see most newborns and their mothers for health supervision has disappeared."

315–16 Center for Family Life: Kamerman and Kahn, "Social Services for Children, Youth, and Families," pp. 135–38. On the concept of family support programs generally: Ibid., pp. 133–35; Robert Halpern, "Poverty and Early Childhood Parenting: Toward a Framework for Intervention," *American Journal of Orthopsychiatry*, Vol. 60, No. 1, January 1990, pp. 14–16.

316–17 Head Start: For a useful discussion of current issues and funding needs in the program, see Judith A. Chafel, "Funding Head Start: What Are the Issues?" *American Journal of Orthopsychiatry*, Vol. 62, No. 1, January 1992, pp. 9–21.

317 Housing units: Cited in Charles Kiesler, "Homelessness and Public Policy Priorities," *American Psychologist*, November 1991, p. 1246.

317 Innovative programs: For a useful discussion of programs addressing the special needs of homeless substance abusers, see Dennis McCarty, Milton Argeriou, Robert B. Huebner, and Barbara Lubran, "Alcoholism, Drug Abuse, and the Homeless," *American Psychologist*, November 1991, p. 1139–48.

318 Canadian policy: Peter Dreier and J. David Hulchanski, "Affordable Housing: Lessons from Canada," *The American Prospect*, No. 1, Spring 1990, pp. 119–25.

318 "As a beginning": Cf. Barry Zigas, *A Program to End America's Low Income Housing Crisis*, Washington, DC, National Low Income Housing Coalition, 1991.

319 House committee estimates: U.S. Congress, House Committee on Banking, Finance, and Urban Affairs, *Summary of HR 4073, Emergency Community Development Act of 1992*, Washington, DC, 1992.

319–20 Weatherization: Michael Renner, *Jobs in a Sustainable Economy*, Washington, DC, Worldwatch Institute, 1991, pp. 26–27. This study usefully suggests a variety of other ways of linking job creation with environmental needs.

320 Heilbroner quotes: Robert Heilbroner, "Seize the Day," in Skolnick and Currie, eds., *Crisis in American Institutions*, pp. 608–10.

320 New York bridges: Calvin Sims, "New York Report Lists Dozens of Weak Bridges," New York *Times*, February 27, 1991.

320 CBO estimates: Heilbroner, "Seize the Day," p. 609.

321 Railroad spending: Congressional Budget Office, *Federal Spending on Infra-structure*, p. 14.

322–23 Kerner quotes: *Report* of the National Advisory Commission on Civil Disorders, Washington, DC, Government Printing Office, pp. 420–21, 467–76.

323 Kennedy quote: *To Seek a Newer World*, p. 38.

323–24 Chein quotes: *Road to H*, p. 324–25.

325 Health care savings: Steffie Woolhandler and David U. Himmelstein, "The Deteriorating Administrative Efficiency of the U.S. Health Care System," *New England Journal of Medicine*, Vol. 324, No. 18, May 2, 1991; Milt Freudenheim, "Potential Savings of National Care," New York *Times*, November 12, 1991.

326 Aschauer estimate: Congressional Budget Office, *Federal Spending on Infra-structure*, p. 24.

326 Foreign public investments: Felix Rohatyn, "The New Domestic Order?" *New York Review of Books*, November 21, 1991, p. 8. Germany, for example, plans to spend $30 billion to modernize the former East German telephone system alone; see Ferdinand Protzman, "German Overhaul Is Led by Phones," New York *Times*, March 11, 1992.

326 Heilbroner quote: "Seize the Day," p. 610.

327 Tax comparisons: From *The Economist*, September 21, 1991, p. 123. Rohatyn quote: "The New Domestic Order?" p. 7.

327 Income gains: Sylvia Nasar, "The 1980s: A Very Good Time for the Very Rich," New York *Times*, March 5, 1992. $160 billion estimate: Robert S. McIntyre, "Are the Democrats Really So Stupid?" New York *Times*, May 14, 1990.

328 $1 trillion estimate: Cited in Tom Wicker, "A Time for Action," New York *Times*, May 29, 1991. 38 percent bracket: Jeff Faux, "Fight Now, Pay Now," New York *Times*, February 19, 1991.

328–29 Special fund: Others have made similar suggestions. See, for example, John Kenneth Galbraith, "Let's Borrow More Money," New York *Times*, May 16, 1991, which proposes, among other things, a "latter-day Reconstruction Finance Corporation" devoted specifically to public investment, especially in infrastructure.

329–30 Kaufman study: William W. Kaufman and John D. Steinbrunner, *The Post-Cold War Defense Program*, as cited in Leonard Silk, "Getting the Benefit of Military Cuts," New York *Times*, September 20, 1991.

330 Bombers and JTPA: In fiscal year 1991 federal outlays for training the disadvantaged under JTPA came to $1.67 billion—about a third the level

spent on job training for the poor in 1980. Ways and Means Committee, *Overview of Entitlement Programs*, p. 1454.

330 Employment effect of defense cuts: Peter Richards, "Of Arms and the Man: Possible Employment Consequences of Disarmament," *International Labour Review*, Vol. 130, No. 3, 1991, pp. 279–87; "The Pentagon Goes on the Defensive," *The Economist*, September 28, 1991, pp. 25–27.

Fifty-three percent of workers in the job categories hardest hit by budget cuts in Los Angeles County's aerospace industry are minority (Los Angeles *Times*, March 17, 1992). More than 31,000 aerospace jobs were lost during 1991 alone in the county.

330 Employment Research Associates: Cited in Richards, "Of Arms and the Man," pp. 286–87.

331 Opinion polls: Los Angeles *Times*, February 14, 1992. A more recent New York *Times* poll found only 11 percent of Republicans (and 7 percent of Democrats and Independents) wanting to use military spending reductions to cut taxes; New York *Times*, January 22, 1992. Opinion on domestic needs: *Time* magazine/CNN poll, January 2, 1992, cited in Barbara Rudolph, "A Quick Fix Is Not Enough," *Time*, January 13, 1992, p. 39.

332 Clark quote: *Dark Ghetto*, p. 212.

Index

ABOUT THE AUTHOR

ELLIOTT CURRIE is the author of *Dope and Trouble: Portraits of Delinquent Youth* and *Confronting Crime,* an award-winning work hailed as "original and incisive, offering the only realistic hope in years" (Tom Wicker, *The New York Times*). Co-author of the classic text *Crisis in American Institutions,* Currie has taught sociology and criminology at Yale University and the University of California at Berkeley. He has been a consultant to a wide range of organizations, including the National Advisory Council on Economic Opportunity and the National Council on Crime and Delinquency, and currently serves as vice-chairperson of the Board of Directors of the Milton S. Eisenhower Foundation. Currie presently teaches in the legal-studies program at the University of California at Berkeley.